BEYOND THE POWER MYSTIQUE

BEYOND THE POWER MYSTIQUE

*Power as Intersubjective
Accomplishment*

Robert Prus

State University of New York Press

Published by
State University of New York Press, Albany

© *1999 State University of New York*

All rights reserved

Printed in the United States of America

For information, address State University of New York Press
State University Plaza, Albany, New York 12246

Production by Dana Foote
Marketing by Patrick Durocher

Library of Congress Cataloging-in-Publication Data
Prus, Robert C.
Beyond the power mystique : power as intersubjective
accomplishment / Robert Prus.
p.   cm.
Includes bibliographical references (p.   ) and indexes.
ISBN 0–7914–4069–9 (hc : alk. paper)
ISBN 0–7914–4070–2 (pb : alk. paper)
1. Power (Social sciences)   2. Symbolic interactionism.   I. Title.
HM136 .P924 1999
303.3—dc21   98–43622
                                                         CIP

10 9 8 7 6 5 4 3 2 1

The author acknowledges permission from the following publishers to reprint selected portions of the works listed below:
Herbert Blumer. 1966. "Sociological Implications of the Thought of George Herbert Mead." *American Journal of Sociology* 71: 535–548. Copyright © 1966 by the University of Chicago. Extracts reprinted by permission of the University of Chicago Press.
Herbert Blumer. 1969. *Symbolic Interactionism.* Englewood Cliffs, N.J.: Prentice-Hall. Copyright © 1969 by Prentice-Hall, Inc. Extracts reprinted by permission of Prentice-Hall, Inc.

*This volume is dedicated to those who are interested in
the study of human lived experience . . .*   redundant?

*And in memory of Aristotle, who emphasized the
importance of developing theories of essences that are
grounded in examinations and comparisons of the
instances in which the essences find expression.*

Contents

Foreword by Marvin Scott   *xi*

Preface   *xiii*

PART I
INTRODUCTION

1 *Power and Human Interchange*   *3*

Toward an Interactionist Conceptualization of Power   *6*

The World of Human Lived Experience   *7*

Power as Intersubjective Accomplishment   *9*

Overviewing the Chapters   *10*

PART II
THE POWER MOTIF

2 *Structuralist Variants in the Literature*   *17*

Rational Order Structuralism   *20*
*Max Weber • Emile Durkheim • Talcott Parsons •
Robert Merton • Anthony Giddens • Synthetic
Order Theorists • The Stratificationists • The
Exchange (and Equity) Theorists*

Power Motifs within the Marxist Nexus   *29*
*Acknowledging Fundamentalist Orientations •
Postmodernist Ventures • Cultural Studies •
Marxist-Feminism • Pluralist Offshoots (Mills,
Dahrendorf, Lukes, and Clegg) • Robert Michels
and Columbia Socialism • Is There a Way Out?*

Conceptual Limitations *52*

3 *Tactical Themes in the Social Sciences* *65*

The Compliance and Influence Literature in Psychology *65*

Collectivist Approaches *68*
Georg Simmel • Robert Park • Herbert Blumer •
Neil Smelser • Orrin Klapp • John McCarthy and
Mayer Zald • Bert Klandermans and John Lofland •
Carl Couch and Clark McPhail • Ralph Turner
and Associates

Interest Group Dynamics and Political Arenas *77*

Mass Communication Themes *78*

Community Studies *82*

Conceptual Limitations *84*

4 *Enduring Tactical Themes* *89*

Acknowledging Early Greek (and Roman) Roots *90*

Providing Political Advice: Machiavelli and De Callières *105*

Other Purveyors of Advice *108*

In Context *110*

PART III
POWER AS INTERSUBJECTIVE ACCOMPLISHMENT

5 *Attending to Human Interchange* *123*

The Interactionist Paradigm *124*
Orientational Premises • Common Misconceptions •
Subcultural Mosaics and Intersubjective Realities •
The Ethnographic Quest for Intersubjectivity •
Generic Dimensions of Association

Interactionist Materials on Power 145

Envisioning Power in Interactionist Terms 152
Power as Definitional • Power as Processual •
Associated Problematics

In Perspective 159

6 *Engaging in Tactical Enterprise* 167

Assuming Tactical Orientations 171

Enhancing Practices 172
Formulating Plans and Making Preparations •
Attending to Target Circumstances • Shaping
Images of Reality (and Invoking Deception) •
Cultivating Relationships

Focusing Procedures 184
Indicating Lines of Action • Promoting Target
Interests

Neutralizing and Debasing Strategies 186

Leveraging Tactics 188
Establishing Consensus • Usurping Agency • Using
Inducements and Other Treatments • Bargaining
with Targets • Appealing to Existing Relationships
and Community Affiliations

Autonomizing Endeavors 198

Exercising Persistence and Experiencing Openness 199
Exercising Persistence • Experiencing Tactical Openness

7 *Extending the Theater of Operations* 209

Working with Third-Party Agents 210
Consulting with Third Parties • Obtaining
Representatives (Agents) • Making Third-Party
Referrals • Pursuing Adjudication

Developing Collective Ventures   *214*
Establishing Associations • Objectifying
Associations • Encountering Outsiders

Generating (and Enforcing) Policy   *218*

Pursuing Positional Control   *221*

Promoting Totalizing Associations   *225*

Using the Media   *228*

Developing Political Agendas   *231*
Implementing Governmental Forums • Invoking
Military Operations • Establishing Control Agencies

In Context   *241*

8 *Experiencing Target Roles*   *251*
    (with Lorraine Prus)

Assuming Target Roles   *251*
Defining Self as Subject to Influence •
Acknowledging the Receptive Self • Experiencing the
Vulnerable Self • Developing a Restrained Self •
Deploying the Elusive Self

Invoking the Tactician Self   *256*
Initiating Activity toward [Tacticians] • Resisting
Tacticians • Claiming Target Status

Assuming Competitive Stances   *259*

Participating in Collective Events   *261*

In Perspective   *265*

9 *Engaging the Power Motif*   *271*

References   *279*
Index of Names   *317*
Index of Terms   *324*

Foreword

The concept of power has assumed such prominence in sociological theorizing over the past decade that today we might appropriately describe the discipline of sociology as being caught in the grip of a "power mystique."

The "power mystique" is an emergent paradigm derived from a variety of overlapping, family-resembling sources, such as Foucaultian poststructuralism, Irigarian feminism, and Seidmanic queer theory. In each case one may hear the voice of a marginalized other calling for empowerment.

From the point of view of the researcher in the field, however, all this is both too distant and too unidimensional to catch the realities of power as lived experience.

Robert Prus, one of the spectacular ethnographers that Canada so magically produces, is engaged in a twofold task in this work. First, to deconstruct the power mystique the pragmatic way—by demonstrating how we can exhaustively study the lived experience of power through the sensitizing categories associated with the quadrumvirante of Simmel, Mead, Blumer, and Goffman; second, to introduce students to the range of theories of power and guide them for its study in any social milieu.

In both tasks, Prus has wondrously succeeded. The power mystique is dissolved when placed in the context of understanding human relations more generally. Though he succeeded in letting the fly out of the bottle, Prus's concluding position is not new (being stated by early pragmatists like Dewey and Bentley), namely, that the study of power is the study of human relations and community life. And so the end of all our searchings is to enable us for the first time to see what we know.

For the student of sociology there is a bonanza awaiting. Prus will specify how a pragmatic paradigm may be employed to study the range of power from micro to macro, embracing interpersonal encounters to collective movements. In the process of doing this, he provides useful summaries of the major positions, micro and macro, as they relate to issues of power.

Prus's erudition and clarity will bring joy even to the most critical reader.

Marvin B. Scott
New York City

Preface

Writing a book about power seems a bit like jumping into a bottomless pit. There are a lot of things around you, but there is also this overwhelming sense of emptiness. There are things to be encountered and grasped at along the way, but for the most part they are so mixed and ungrounded. To be sure, one finds lots of tactical advice, as well as a great deal of moral and ethical direction. Likewise, one encounters a great many quests for equalization, liberation, recognition, realization, and legitimation, as well as concerns about regulation and control. There is, it seems, an endless stream of talk, much of which is extremely sincere and thoughtful. But there is very little material that more directly examines power as a realm of human enterprise.

As I moved more deeply into this topic, I also became aware that without conceptual coordinates of some sort, one is apt to become entirely overwhelmed. To a large extent, I have been working with a reference point, the criterion that, to be viable, any source has to contribute not just to our understanding of human relations but also to our ability to study power as it is enacted in the here and now of human group life. I mention this specifically, because although I have been endeavoring to maintain this focus for some time, I have also been turfing and reworking much of my own writing in light of this same criterion. My objective is not just to provide a different vision of power from those I have encountered in mainstream social science but, more fundamentally, to enable people who are interested in the human condition to engage the study of [power] in more direct, participant-informed manners. I don't know if there is much basis for optimism, given the tendencies of a great many scholars to avoid sustained study of the processes by which the people out there come to terms with one another, but I hope, in some way, that I can contribute to that venture. If we can't give some concerted attention to the necessity of studying human community life in the making, then we are apt to enlarge the bottomless pit or black hole of the human sciences by producing endless, even if often quite eloquent and intriguing, discourses about power.

author's note, September 27, 1997

Several years ago, I began to consider the possibility of developing an interactionist statement on power. I wasn't at all certain what this would look like, but I had become attentive to the claims of some sociologists (especially the marxists, but also the functionalists) that symbolic interaction couldn't handle the issue of power or other macro-processes in society. Although neither the functionalist nor marxist versions of power were very compelling, I had to admit that the interactionists hadn't said much about power in any sustained or systematic fashion. More recently, this arena has become further dramatized by those who identify themselves as "postmodernists" (or post-structuralists) and/or as in "cultural studies." They, too, claim exceptional insight into the power question.

There is, it seems, a certain intrigue with "power" in academia, both within sociology and across the social sciences more generally. Still, despite their claims and intentions, these "experts" haven't been explaining power as much as they have been contributing to, and perpetuating, "the power mystique."

In contrast, my basic starting point was very simple. If power is a human essence, then power should revolve around the things that people do; that is, how people engage one another in the course of ongoing community life.

Doubtless, there are others who might better have represented the interactionist tradition with respect to power, but they have not engaged this project very directly. Perhaps, this volume will serve as a useful starting point. For my part, though, I have endeavored to build rather directly on the writings of Herbert Blumer (1969) who, in turn, locates his own enterprise in the works of George Herbert Mead and the pragmatist tradition. The approach taken here, then, is very much situated in the Chicago-school or Blumerian tradition of symbolic interaction. Blending the pragmatist orientation with ethnographic inquiry, Blumer is centrally concerned about studying human group life in the making, about attending to the processes by which human group life takes place. The empirical social world, for Blumer, is the world of human lived experience; it is constituted of the realms of activity (enterprise and interaction) whereby people do things.

Rather broadly stated, the interactionist agenda is primarily concerned with learning about the ways in which community life is accomplished by living, thinking, acting and interacting beings. Those in this tradition also take the viewpoint that, to understand the human condition, it is necessary that one achieve intimate familiarity with one's subject matter; to examine, in sustained, participant-informed detail, the (enacted) social essences of the human group.

At first, this project seemed relatively straightforward. Although many people had said that symbolic interaction couldn't handle power, I saw this not as an impossible task, but rather one that required some reorientation. What is this [power] thing? How should it be conceptualized as a human experience? How do people engage [power]? These were the sorts of concerns that first occupied my attention.

Along the way, too, I began to read more statements on power. I

wanted to see more precisely what others had to say about this phenomenon. Reviewing the existent literature became an extremely challenging
task in itself. Not only had a great many people written about power, but this
theme ran (explicitly and implicitly) through the writings of a great many,
highly prolific scholars. It was becoming quite apparent that I would be
disagreeing with, if not more directly challenging, many of the most re-
nowned scholars of all time, as well as those contemporaries who have built
their own careers around these works.

It also was rather unclear just how one might best deal with this massive body of conceptually diffuse materials, both for my own comprehension
and for any presentational purposes. I was grateful to encounter some other
authors who had undertaken related projects. I would learn from them. My
own review of the literature is far from exhaustive, but I tried to address the
major themes (and players) in the literature. Hopefully, this paper trail will
benefit others embarking on related projects.

Since an assortment of "power theorists" are addressed in some detail
within this volume, I would like to speak more generally at this point. One
prevailing idea that runs through the literature is that power is the key to
understanding community life. Somewhat relatedly, is the notion that, to
understand power, you have to look at the "big picture," to consider structure, institutions, industrialization, class, race, conflict, nation states, politics, and other things of that sort (amen!).[1] Power is most often viewed as a
structural element, if not also a macro-level force. Power is generally depicted as "something out there," an objective and often pervasive, if not
sinister, fact of community life. While denoting some omnipresent, elusive,
almost mystical, phenomenon, power (it seems) can still be discussed intel-
ligibly, if not rationally, by referencing the appropriate (structural) images
and thinkers.

In trying to come to terms with the power motif, I examined a great
many sources. In all cases, though, I was looking for something that could
be used to study the ways that people "accomplish" this power thing. No
doubt, there will be those who think that I have been too critical of those
promoting various structuralist (e.g., functionalist, marxist, postmodernist[sic]) viewpoints or that I should have engaged in more intensive study of
particular sources so that I might appreciate the real essentials or intricacies
of those theories. While many theories offer interesting and instructive
insights, I think that we are much better advised to concentrate on the
question of how people actually engage one another in power relations.

Readers might also observe that, in contrast to many who talk about
power, I set out a relatively clear criterion for assessing the works that one
might encounter. As noted elsewhere, it is a severe criterion, one that raises
rather fundamental questions about the relevance of much "social theory"
for human lived experience. The ensuing criticisms do not reflect on peo-

ple's analytical abilities or their sincerity in general, but rather focus on analysts' senses of direction and their apparent lack of concern about studying human group life in the making.

Among other things, the literature took me back to the Greek classics. For someone who hadn't had any background in this literature, this turned out to be a somewhat overwhelming and, yet most rewarding, experience. It also created some procedural dilemmas, particularly since I encountered (and began to realize the potential of) this material relatively late in the project. Should I delve more deeply into this literature (yes), and should I consider replacing some other things I had written with materials I had come across in this literature (yes). I decided on the latter, not because my familiarity with the classics is very good, but because some of the things I encountered in the classics are so good.

The writings of Plato, Aristotle, Isocrates, and others, provide social scientists with some valuable cross-cultural reference points but, much more importantly still, these scholars were grappling with concepts and issues that parallel contemporary considerations in the sociology of knowledge or the social construction of reality (Berger and Luckmann, 1966). As well, although the connectedness of early Greek (and Roman) scholarship with contemporary social thought has become rather obscured over the millennia, these root statements have a rather enduring currency in considerations of power.

Obviously, the stance (pragmatist, interactionist, constructionist) adopted in this volume is not "new" and, indeed, I trace aspects of these notions back to the early Greeks (chapter 4). But the emphasis on *power as a (humanly) formulated, enacted or accomplished essence* has vital implications for what passes as "social theory." Quite directly, a pragmatist/ethnographic orientation to the power phenomenon calls for an extended recasting or reconceptualization of both the sociological and the broader social science enterprise.

It is essential that social theory respect the intersubjective and activity-based essences of the human condition; that social theory directly acknowledge the abilities of people to engage in minded enterprise, to interact, to coordinate, to cooperate, to resist, to compete, and so forth. Whether I have succeeded in fostering the linkage of social theory and human activity in the present volume or not, social theory should be developed in ways that encourage research into community life in the making and, in turn, theory should be open to more informed reformulations that reflect ethnographic encounters with "the people out there."

Those more familiar with my work will recognize an enduring and profound indebtedness to both those who have toiled in ethnographic research and those who have articulated the conceptual foundations of the intersubjectivist (especially the interactionist, constructionist, ethno-methodological) tradition. I can only hope that I have represented these materials adequately because this book is much more genuinely a product of these earlier efforts than anything I've done on my own.

There are, no doubt, others to whom I am indebted in developing this manuscript, but I would at least like to express my appreciation to the following people for their thoughts and suggestions along the way: Patti Adler, Peter Adler, Shiela Ager, Cheryl Albas, Daniel Albas, David Altheide, Lonnie Athens, Michael Atkinson, Hans Bakker, Robert Benford, Joel Best, Scott Brandon, Kathy Charmaz, Tina Chester, Jim Curtis, Donna Darden, Lorne Dawson, Scott Grills, Bob Farmer, Peter Hall, Scott Harris, Richard Helmes-Hayes, Robert Hiscott, David Hughes, John Johnson, David Karp, Daniel Kubat, Ronald Lambert, John Lofland, Stan Lyman, Clark McPhail, Danny Miller, Gale Miller, Richard G. Mitchell Jr., Tom Morrione, Adie Nelson, Joseph Novak, Frank Nutch, Clint Sanders, Stan Saxton, Bill Shaffir, Charlie Smith, Jennifer Smith, David Snow, Dee Southard, Robert Stebbins, Chuck Tucker, Ed Vaz, Keith Warriner, and Audrey Wipper.

I would especially like to thank Marvin Scott for the vibrant interest he has taken in this project and for writing the scenic foreword for this volume. The foreword is a brief, but tantalizing sample of "vintage Scott." But even more, though, I am grateful to Marvin for his discerning, stimulating, and entertaining conversations about power as a social essence.

Zina Lawrence, acquisitions editor at SUNY Press, deserves some special consideration, not just for her attentiveness to this project throughout its development, but also for her insights, congeniality, and enthusiasm. I also very much appreciate Dana Foote's (production editor) efficient and affable assistance in putting this manuscript in a more publishable state. More generally, I would like to thank the SUNY staff for their assistance in all stages of this project. It is a pleasure to work with such a fine publishing house.

My wife, Lorraine, continues to amaze me with her thoughtfulness, helpfulness, and charming disposition. I am truly grateful for the interest that she has taken in my work generally and the great many contributions that she has made to the present manuscript. While any shortcomings of the volume are entirely attributable to me, I am pleased to coauthor chapter 8 with Lorraine. In this way, her contributions to this volume might be a little more adequately acknowledged.

Notes

1. *Amen*—from the Greek (may it be so). I couldn't resist this (bit of humor). Virtually everyone who has ever taken an introductory sociology or political science course has been encouraged to think this way.

PART I

INTRODUCTION

1 Power and Human Interchange

SOCRATES: . . .I'm sure you've heard the song people sing at parties which offers a list of human advantages: 'The very best thing is health, second good looks, and third'—according to whoever made up the song—'honest wealth.' . . .

GORGIAS: Yes, I have. But why are you bringing it up?

SOCRATES: Well, suppose a doctor, a trainer, and a businessman—who are the people responsible for the qualities the song-writer commended—were standing right there next to you. . . .

'But Gorgias here doesn't agree,' we'd point out. 'He claims that his area of expertise is responsible for something which is more beneficial than anything yours can produce.' . . .

So, Gorgias, please add their imagined request to mine, and tell us what this thing is which is the greatest blessing people can have, according to you, and which you can procure for them.

GORGIAS: When I say there's nothing better, Socrates, that is no more than the truth. It is responsible for personal freedom and enables an individual to gain political power in his community.

SOCRATES: Yes, but what is it?

GORGIAS: I'm talking about the ability to use the spoken word to persuade—to persuade the jurors in the courts, the members of the Council, the citizens attending to Assembly . . . in short, to win over any and every form of public meeting of the citizen body. Armed with this ability, in fact, the doctor would be your slave, the trainers would be yours to command, and that businessman would turn out to be making money not for himself, but for someone else—for you with your ability to speak and to persuade the masses.

—Plato, Gorgias, *451d–452e [Waterfield, trans.]*

Few terms in the social sciences have engendered as much mystique (fascination, curiosity, fear) as "power." In addition to the great many casual references to power (e.g., having power, positions of control, being influential, and empowering) that one finds in the social sciences, a considerable amount of published work has been developed around topics such as power, control, domination, influence, and the like. As will be indicated, however, most of this literature (and the premises on which this material has been developed) is fundamentally flawed with respect to the manners in which power is conceptualized, studied, and analyzed. Expressed rather directly, the problem is that most analysts have failed to attend to the ways in which people experience (or engage) the power phenomenon on the "here and now" basis in which human group life takes place.

The statement on power developed here is not only attentive to the actualities of ongoing human interchange, but it also invokes a methodological position (ethnographic inquiry) that would enable scholars to study aspects of the power process in more situated, participant-informed fashions.

Envisioning power as denoting instances of meaningful interchange that involve varying arrays of individuals, groups, and interactive alignments, this volume focuses on (a) people's attempts (as tacticians) to shape the situations (and experiences) of others in more direct manners, (b) tacticians' efforts to extend their capacities for influence by involving additional parties in their dealings with (target) others, and (c) the ways that people (as targets) define and make adjustments to the instances of influence they experience. The material presented here, thus, considers people's definitions of, and routings into, situations of [power],* as well as the dilemmas they face, the strategies they assume, and the limitations they encounter as they enter into interchanges with others on both more individualized and collectively coordinated bases and in both long-term and more situated instances.

Rather than reduce power to factors, structures, resources, and the like, power is envisioned as a dynamic, socially constructed essence. Consequently, attention is given to the ways in which people attempt to define and shape (and resist) the directions that human group life assumes. It is hoped that this statement may help to demystify power as a sociological concept not only by attending to this phenomenon as a problematic, reflective, negotiated, feature of ongoing community life, but also by indicating the ways in which scholars methodologically may examine the actual instances of influence that people experience.

Following a disucssion of the "power motif" in the literature in chapters 2, 3, and 4, the subsequent chapters represent an application of the symbolic interactionist approach associated most centrally with George Herbert Mead (1934) and Herbert Blumer (1969) to the matter of power. The interactionist tradition has often been described as "micro-sociological,"

---

*Readers might note that I have bracketed [terms] in some instances (e.g., [power], [the world], [objects]) to draw attention to the particularly problematic nature of the phenomenon referenced by the term or concept under consideration.

atheoretical, and unable to deal with power (see chapter 5). In what follows, however, I intend to show that symbolic interactionism not only represents a theoretically coherent means of transcending "micro-macro" realms of human association, but that it is eminently suited, theoretically and methodologically, for the study of the "power phenomenon" across the range of human association. This volume, thus, is intended not only to establish the conceptual parameters of an interactionist approach to the study of power but also to outline a research agenda that would enable scholars to methodologically engage every instance of power that people might experience.

The material presented in this volume has been developed with one central guiding theme—our conceptualization (theoretical and methodological) of power must attend to the *actualities* of human experience, to the viewpoints, activities, and interactions of the *people* about whom we, as social scientists, purport to speak. The emphasis is on power, not as an objective condition or a subjective experience, but as a matter of *intersubjective accomplishment*.

This means focusing on people's experiences with power in a comprehensive, definitional, action-oriented sense, and attending to the ways in which people manage interchanges with others in practice. The objective, thus, is to develop a transsituational or transcontextual conceptualization of power that would lend itself to empirical investigation (and theoretical reformulation) through sustained ethnographic inquiry of people's experiences with [power] in the various here and now situations in which they find themselves. Working with this central mission of comprehending human lived experience, there is no attempt to suggest remedies or prescriptions for human practices pertaining to aspects of power, however bothersome or troublesome some may find particular human behaviors (orientations, activities, traditions or organizational practices) in this or that regard.

Likewise, there is no attempt to propose a synthesis of the various theoretical viewpoints that people have developed in discussing power (and related phenomena). Some worthwhile insights into the power phenomenon have been (and will continue to be) generated in a great many sources, but the literature introduced here is subjected to one primary criterion— does it attend to power as a matter of intersubjective accomplishment; *does the approach* (theoretical viewpoint, conceptual scheme, methodology) *under consideration enable us to envision and study the ways in which human interchange is worked out in the ongoing instances of the here and now in which community life takes place?* This emphasis represents the primary anchorage or reference point in dealing with what otherwise is a massive, complex, and highly diffuse literature. However, as indicated in chapters 2 and 3, this becomes a rather severe reference point for assessing existing work in the social sciences.

Those more characteristically assuming "pluralist" or "eclectic" orientations, as well as those presuming particular (structuralist, moralist-advocacy) viewpoints, may be troubled by this tact, but the emphasis is on "respecting the world of human lived experience" (Blumer, 1969; Strauss, 1993; Prus, 1996b, 1997b). This means developing theory that is methodologically grounded in (and informed by) people's experiences with [the world] rather than embarking on high-level (grand) theorizing or pursuing agendas intended to change or control the nature or direction of community life.

Toward an Interactionist Conceptualization of Power

Although it is unfortunate in certain respects that the interactionists have not attended to power in more sustained and explicit manners, this same "inattentiveness" to power has been most beneficial for the development of a more genuine social science. On the one hand, this means that the interactionist literature is more difficult to characterize in [power] themes. On the other hand, and in a much more important sense, though, it has meant that the interactionists could approach the study of the human condition without being encumbered by the sorts of power agendas or motifs that have overshadowed and distorted the analytical renderings of a great many scholars.

While providing a conceptual frame and a methodological orientation for pursuing the study of power in interactionist terms, I clearly do *not* intend to refocus the interactionist agenda by suggesting that considerations of power be placed at the center of interactionist concerns. Rather, this volume represents a necessary corrective to those social scientists who, in the quest for an analysis of "power," have failed to locate considerations of power within the more fundamental features of human lived experience. Unless more directly challenged, these scholars may divert the social science community even further from its central mission of comprehending the human condition.

The interactionist emphasis on the ways in which people engage [the world] about them has some vital implications for the ways in which social scientists approach [power]. First, the interactionist emphasis on examining the ways in which people do things focuses attention on the situated or "here and now" instances of human enterprise that constitute human group life in the making. Because they examine the ways in which people engage the world in accomplishing particular sets of activities, the interactionists have developed an exceptionally extensive, viable, and grounded awareness (and literature) of human enterprise of a wide diversity of life-worlds. Nothing comparable exists, as a basis for developing theory (and research) on human interchange, in any other realm or tradition of the social sciences.[1]

Although the interactionist approach only recently has been explicitly cast in terms of multiple social worlds (Strauss, 1978a, 1982, 1984, 1993) or a "subcultural mosaic" (Prus, 1997b), the interactionist community has long been attentive to the notions of a pluralistic, subculturally constituted society. Notions of these sorts may be traced back to Wilhelm Dilthey (1833–1911) and Georg Simmel (1858–1918), but they also have been the perpetual by-products of virtually every instance of research conducted within the Chicago (interactionist/ethnographic) tradition.

On the surface, a mosaics or multiple-life world orientation seems relatively innocuous or mundane. Its potential, however, vis-à-vis the [power] phenomenon is rather consequential. Instead of subscribing to overarching rationalities or grand images of power that might somehow encompass broader societies, it becomes apparent that any society is made up of a plurality of human life-worlds and considerations of the power phenomenon (and human relations more generally) should be approached in manners that centrally acknowledge these multiple life-worlds.

Third, while pursuing the pragmatist agenda of attending to the ways in which people accomplish activity in practice, the interactionists have also been long concerned with the task of developing concepts that would enable researchers to make comparisons across the multiple life-worlds that they encounter. Thus, although power represents a situated, definitional element from an interactionist viewpoint, the conceptual understandings of [power] developed from an interactionist perspective are not limited to political arenas or overt instances of confrontation or control, for instance. They are relevant to *any* life-world setting in which the participants invoke images of power, influence, control, resistance, and the like. The material that follows is critical of much of the social science enterprise revolving around considerations of power. At the same time, however, this volume is intended to make the *study* of power much more accessible to those in the social sciences by grounding a research agenda in the multiple life-worlds in which human group life is accomplished.

The World of Human Lived Experience

Let me begin by identifying the empirical social world in the case of human beings. This world is the actual group life of human beings. It consists of what they experience and do, individually and collectively, as they engage in their respective forms of living; it covers the large complexes of interlaced activities that grow up as the actions of some spread out to affect the actions of others; and it embodies the large variety of relationships between the participants. . . . The empirical world, in short, is the world of everyday experience. . . . Ongoing group life, whether in the past or the present, whether in the case of this or that people, whether in one or another geographical area, is the empirical social world of the social and psychological sciences.

—*Blumer, 1969:35*

In adopting an interactionist position (see chapter 5 for more detail), we begin with the observation that *all* human behavior is to be understood within the context of ongoing community life. As Mead (1934) and Blumer (1969) emphasize, society consists of people with selves in interaction, but people *only* develop selves through linguistic (or symbolic) interchange with those who have predated their presence within the human community. As well, because people "do things," it is essential that social scientists develop a more explicit appreciation of all of the *activities* entailed in both the human struggle for existence and any other pursuits in which people may meaningfully engage.

In contrast to those who might study other objects (i.e., as in the physical sciences), the interactionists argue for a social science that theoretically *and* methodologically *respects the human essence.* Thus, at a most fundamental level, the interactionists observe that people have capacities to (1) use language (symbols) to communicate with others regarding [the world] around them; (2) assign differing meanings to [objects];[2] (3) take themselves and others into account in acting toward the world; (4) deliberately invoke specific behaviors in engaging the world; (5) influence and resist one another; (6) develop selective affiliations or associations with other people; and (7) attend to notions of emergence, sequence or temporality. In other words, this requires that scholars of the human condition recognize the (1) intersubjective, (2) multiperspectival, (3) reflective, (4) action-oriented, (5) negotiable, (6) relational, and (7) processual dimensions of human community life.[3]

Because acknowledgements or assumptions of this sort differentiate humans from other objects of study, the interactionists (Blumer, 1928; 1969) have been long concerned about developing a methodology that respects the *social* essences of the human group. While acknowledging the importance of (a) observation as an information gathering procedure, the interactionists have centrally employed (b) extended open-ended interviews with those whose life-worlds are being studied and (c) sustained participant-observation in those settings as the primary methods for *achieving intersubjectivity* with those whose life-world experiences they seek to establish familiarity.

Observations of people's activities may provide researchers with preliminary images of other people's life-worlds, enable researchers to develop some issues for subsequent inquiry, and serve as a basis for assessing information attained in other ways. However, if researchers are to develop *intimate familiarity* (Blumer, 1969) with the life-worlds of others, then it is necessary to achieve an "insiderness" with these other people. This is *attainable only when* others linguistically share their experiences (viewpoints, meanings, activities) with researchers.

As much as possible, then, the interactionists attempt to achieve comprehensive levels of intersubjectivity by immersing themselves (ethnographically) in the life-worlds of "the other." Ethnographers often assume member or participant roles as a means of more completely accessing others (and their experiences) in the setting, but even more consequential is the matter of engaging the participants in sustained interchange. In these ways, the interactionists attempt to uncover people's experiences with the world in as complete and thorough manners as possible. As Blumer (1928) observes these practices are far from perfect and people studying the human condition are unable to achieve the rigor or precision associated with much research in the physical sciences. Still, there is no other way that researchers may serve as effective (intersubjective) conduits between those whose life-worlds are being studied and those wishing to learn about the life-worlds of other people:

> (T)he empirical social world consists of ongoing group life and one has to get close to this life to know what is going on in it. If one is going to respect the social world, one's problems, guiding conceptions, data, schemes of relationship, and ideas of interpretation have to be faithful to that empirical world. This is especially true in the case of human group life because of the persistent tendency of human beings in their collective life to build up separate worlds, marked by an operating milieu of different life situations and by the possession of different beliefs and conceptions for handling these situations. (Blumer, 1969:38)

Power as Intersubjective Accomplishment

Locating power more directly within an interactionist framework, this volume not only permeates much of the mystique shrouding "power," but also provides a conceptual scheme and methodological approach for examining instances of control (influence and resistance) within the interchanges characterizing ongoing community life.

Viewing power as a matter of intersubjective accomplishment, the material presented here examines power as a *collectively enacted* phenomenon. Addressing the full range of association (e.g., communication, cooperation, conflict, competition, compromise, celebration) occurring in small group settings to large-scale (e.g., media, government, military) theaters of operation, this volume provides a conceptually viable means of synthesizing so-called "macro" and "micro" realms of power.

Rather than assuming that power is an omnipresent phenomena, this volume examines the ways in which notions of power, control, influence, and the like *are brought into existence* in human association and the sorts of roles and relationships that people (as both tacticians and targets) develop with respect to this phenomenon as they go about their day-to-day activities in a world in which reality is not theirs alone to determine. The two following passages (extracted from chapter 5) centrally address this notion.

Power represents a phenomenon the existence of which . . . *is always contingent on instances of human definition and enterprise for its essence.* . . . Power implies an intent and a capacity on the part of a person or group to influence, control, dominate, persuade, manipulate, or otherwise affect the behaviors, experiences, or situations of some target. As a quality imputed to a situation by some audience, *power is brought into existence only when someone defines the situation in power or influence (and resistance) terms of some sort.*

This means that *the essential starting point for any analysis of power hinges on the definitions that people make,* however tentatively, of specific situations in reference to matters of influence, control, domination, and the like. In the absence of definitions implying power dimensions, the situations in question may be viewed in many other ways, such as play, fun, fascinating, work, frustrating, confusing, boring, instructive, educational, challenging, cooperative, helpful, and so forth.

Because of its attentiveness to people's situated experiences (definitions, activities, interchanges), interactionism provides a particularly viable means of approaching the *study* of power (as it is manifested within the human community). Not only is the interactionist viewpoint more amenable to considerations of the ways in which [power] is brought into existence, implemented, experienced, sustained, objectified, resisted, dissipated, and reconstituted in actual practice than are other approaches in the social sciences, but interactionism (by means of ethnographic inquiry) also provides the essential methodology for examining power as an element of human lived experience. Like other aspects of human group life, power is an *intersubjective* phenomenon. If social scientists are to respect the intersubjective essence of the human condition, then our notions of power must reflect the social (linguistic, interpretive, active, interactive) foundations of the human community.

Overviewing the Chapters

To further set the stage for the reader, brief descriptions of the contents of the subsequent chapters are presented.

Part 2: The Power Motif

Chapters 2 (*Structuralist Variants in the Literature*) and 3 (*Tactical Themes in the Social Sciences*) provide a historical and contemporary overview of the ways in which social scientists have approached power as an element of community life. To this end, the writings of a number of foundational social theorists (e.g., Weber, Durkheim, and Marx) are given attention as are some more contemporary authors and researchers whose works reflect these earlier sources and related themes. In addition to outlining the baseline positions of these scholars as these pertain to power, consideration is given to the question of whether these sources approach power as denoting instances of intersubjective accomplishment.

Chapter 4, *Enduring Tactical Themes*, locates concerns with human interchange (and power relations) within a yet broader historical and substantive framework. Although often overlooked in more contemporary discussions of social thought (and power), the writings of the early Greek (and Roman) scholars are much more instructive for comprehending human power relations and contemporary social thought than seems commonly supposed. The writings of a series of tactical (and practical) advisors, from Isocrates and Aristotle to Machiavelli onward, are considered here. Suggesting a great many insights and avenues of inquiry for those interested in community life, this material constitutes a valuable backdrop for comprehending human interchange.

Part 3: Power as Intersubjective Accomplishment

The chapters in Part 3 have been developed mindfully of the literature (academic and tactical) considered in chapters 2–4. However, rather than representing a sustained synthesis of this literature, the emphasis is on developing a means of examining power as an enacted phenomenon. This implies establishing a conceptual frame, outlining a methodological orientation, and specifying a set of arenas for studying human interchange as instances of group life in the making.

It is hoped that these materials may enable the community of social scientists to examine human relations in process terms, from the viewpoints of the participants, in all of its manifestations, and in comparative fashions. It is most unlikely that our understandings of human relations will ever be complete, but if the legacy that we pass on to subsequent generations of scholars is to be more adequate, then we have an obligation to do more than talk (and moralize) about power; we need to examine [power] in the instances of the here and now in which human group life is constituted.

Chapter 5 (*Attending to Human Interchange*) introduces the interactionist tradition and lays the conceptual groundwork for a theory of power that is interpretive, activity-based, and interactive in its essence. Following a consideration of the interactionist paradigm and interactionist materials that deal more directly with power, attention is given to the definitional, processual, and engaging features of human relations.

Chapters 6–8 focus on people's experiences as tacticians and targets in a variety of arenas. These range from dyadic and triadic encounters to all levels and manners of extended associations. Building on the existing ethnographic literature, this material suggests a series of research sites in which matters of influence and resistance may be empirically (i.e., ethnographically) pursued and conceptually synthesized.

Chapter 6 (*Engaging in Tactical Enterprise*) deals with the more fundamental forms of influence work that people may deploy across interactional settings. Thus, consideration is given to the ways that people may endeavor to influence others by invoking (assortments of) enhancing practices, focusing procedures, neutralizing (and debasing) strategies, and leveraging tactics. While addressing dyadic relations in rather central manners, this material is relevant to all levels (and complexities of association).

Chapter 7 (*Extending the Theater of Operations*) examines the ways in which tacticians may endeavor to involve others in their dealings with targets. The tactical considerations outlined in chapter 6 are extended consequentially (into more "macro" realms) by focusing on matters such as working with third parties, developing collective ventures, using the media, and pursuing political agendas (governmental forums, military operations, and control agencies).

Chapter 8 (*Experiencing Target Roles*) both reflects and qualifies the preceding discussions of tactician roles. Beyond (a) the identification of a variety of roles that people may assume as targets, explicit recognition is given to (b) targets' capacities for tactical resistance (and active engagement) in both more solitary and collective manners, and (c) people's involvements as targets and tacticians in competitive arenas and (other) collective events. Recognizing the interchangeability of standpoints of targets and tacticians, the material found in chapter 8 is essential for comprehending influence work as intersubjective accomplishment.

Serving as a concluding statement, chapter 9 (*Engaging the Power Motif*) addresses the broader agenda of attending to human group life as it is accomplished in practice and the particular importance of approaching the study of power through sustained ethnographic inquiry.

As they examine this volume, some readers may feel that the viewpoints of various classical social theorists have been shuttled aside in favor of a relatively new orientation (symbolic interaction) to the realm of social theory. While rather specifically focused on the *power* phenomenon, the present statement resonates with aspects of the writings of a great many "social theorists," from Plato, Aristotle, and the sophists who preceded them to Machiavelli, Hobbes, and Rosseau, to Marx, Weber, and Durkheim, to Parsons, Homans, and Foucault, as well as Dilthey, Simmel, and Dewey, for instance. Albeit working with a wide variety of assumptions and intentions, all of these scholars have struggled with the matter of people's relations with one another within the context of community life. Likewise, there may be considerable merit in indicating more explicitly how one can find aspects of interactionist thought in the works of these and other scholars whose work generally is seen to fall in other traditions. Still, the statement provided here is not intended as a textbook on social theory, nor is it synthetical or eclectic in its emphasis.

The ideas of a great many classic and contemporary social theorists are intriguing and speak to a variety of consequential features of group life. Likewise, one may well appreciate the creative, sophisticated, or complex (often geniuslike) conceptualizations of community life that these scholars have articulated. However, because their ideas are compelling in many respects and their analyses so multifaceted, it is necessary to maintain a steadfast focus on our primary objective, namely the task of examining power as an *enacted* phenomenon within human lived experience.

This requires that we concentrate on the baseline assumptions (and parameters) of the works of various theorists who have addressed the matter of power. Otherwise, it is easy to become distracted by the many fascinating arrays of moralities, rationalities, conceptual schemes, methodological stances, and agendas that these same authors may have pursued in one or another of their writings.

Although particular statements embedded within their larger works suggest that most of these social theorists acknowledge aspects of people's more immediate life-world circumstances (and experiences), these scholars' searches for solutions to the "problems of the time" and their quests for overarching rationalities or master schemes seem to have diverted them from attending, on a more explicit and sustained basis, to community life *in the making*. Quite directly, most of the social theorists who have addressed the power phenomenon have failed to envision human group life as centrally constituted by thinking, acting, interacting beings who engage [the world] on a perpetual here and now basis.

Notes

1. Although this volume is centrally defined from an interactionist perspective, many will recognize substantial affinities of the present project with the phenomenological sociology of Alfred Schutz (1962, 1964), which, rather notably, has been pursued by Peter Berger and Thomas Luckmann (1966) as "the social construction of reality" and Harold Garfinkel (1967) under the rubric of "ethnomethodology." Albeit with somewhat different emphases, these scholars all focus on the ways in which people make sense of the world or manage encounters with "reality."

Like many in the interactionist community, I have very much benefited from the work that Schutz, Berger and Luckmann, Garfinkel, and others in this interpretivist tradition have done. Not only have they helped clarify the philosophical underpinnings of the interpretive processes that characterize human group life, but some of those (mostly ethnomethodologists) working in this tradition have attempted to come to terms with the practical accomplishment of everyday life by directly studying the things that people do on a more situated basis. In these regards, then, the present project may also be seen as an extension of the broader phenomenological, social constructionist, or ethnomethodological enterprise.

While many phenomenological sociologists (and ethnomethodologists) seem only marginally acquainted with the works of Mead, Blumer, and the Chicago ethnographic research tradition of symbolic interaction, there are many affinities within the two traditions. Valuable review statements on ethnomethodology can be found in Meehan and Wood (1975), Zimmerman (1978), Leiter (1980), and Coulon (1995). Readers may observe that the present volume is very much concerned with the ways in which people make sense of the world on a situated (and enduring) basis, but places proportionately greater (and more consistent) emphasis on the ways in which people *engage* one another within the context of ongoing community life.

Those more familiar with "ethnomethods" may also note that the present work is sharply at variance from much "conversational analysis" (that which resembles content analysis, presumes underlying linguistic structures, or is conducted from transcripts interpreted largely without the aid of direct interchange with the speakers). This genre violates the basic intersubjectivist essences of Schutzian phenomenology. However, there is much mutuality with other strands of ethnomethodology (especially those scholars who focus on the "doing of activity from member perspectives").

2. It should be acknowledged that people may not only define and act toward [things] in a great many ways but they also vary greatly in the [object distinctions] with which they work. This is not to deny the existence of "things," but rather to point to the socially (intersubjectively identified, defined, and objectified) and situationally enacted essences of [objects]. Approached thusly, an object *is any item, thing, distinction, concept, behavior, or image to which people may refer (i.e., become aware of, attend to, point to, acknowledge, consider, discuss, or otherwise act toward) [Prus, 1996b:30]*. For further elaboration on [objects] and the human condition, see Prus (1997b).

3. Mead (1934), Blumer (1969), Strauss (1993), and Prus (1996b, 1997b) provide more extended discussions of these and related theoretical and methodological matters.

PART II

THE POWER MOTIF

—

2 Structuralist Variants in the Literature

It does not seem extreme to say that those brilliant social philosophers who have developed the sociology of conflict might have found adequate material for their discussions without having left their own classrooms. Nearly all the classic concepts apply to life in the school room, war, feuds, litigation, conflict of ideals, victory, conciliation, compromise, conversion, accommodation, and assimilation.

—*Waller, 1932:351*

While not engaging the rather diverse literature that deals with power in extended detail,[1] it is important to briefly discuss the central themes that these productions entail to better situate an interactionist analysis of power within the social sciences more generally. To this end, I will reference the scholars whose works have been most foundational with respect to contemporary discussions of power, comment on some of the more notable contemporary statements in the literature, and indicate some of the major limitations of this material with respect to analysts approaching power as a matter of human lived experience.

Denoting concerns with influence and control, autonomy and resistance, domination and independence, matters pertaining to power are evident across the range of recorded history.[2] These statements (see the histories of the Greeks, Hebrews, and Chinese, for instance) are filled with accounts of clashes of interests and of individualized and coordinated attempts at influence and resistance.[3,4] Although the ensuing interchanges may have had consequential effects on countless generations of people as well as the life-worlds of those more immediately caught up therein, surprisingly little consideration has been given to the *study* of power as a generic, enacted feature of human association.

This is not to deny (a) the emergence of various "folk wisdoms" about human affairs in all manners of contexts; (b) the achievement of wide manners of collective arrangements for promoting, averting, and reconciling disputes; (c) the development of a vast assortment of tactics, procedures, and technologies for engaging others in more direct ways; (d) the long-standing practice of documenting major confrontations and dynasties; or (e) the related considerations of moral guidelines, political forums, and associational practices.

Since concerns with people's abilities to shape the lives of others represent enduring focal points, the available literature on power is rather vast. It is also sprawling and sketchy, characterized by seemingly endless agendas and conceptual twists. Often (diversely) moralistic and prescriptive in emphasis, this material represents a challenging, somewhat bewildering set of statements. Further, while some discussions of power are highly abstract, others are heavily embedded in depictions of warfare, politics, education, work, religion, the media, morality, and the like. Still, the more explicit *study* of ongoing human interchange (i.e., human relations as intersubjective accomplishment) is quite another matter.

Concerns with [power relations] can readily be located in the writings of the early Greeks or Hellenes (c. 500 B.C.) who were attentive to wide varieties of engagements with other peoples as well as an assortment of domestic affairs. However, while some Hellenistic notions of structuralism seem to have persisted over the millennia, much of the impact of early Greek (and Roman) scholarship (particularly as this pertains to considerations of power) has become highly diffused, if not largely obscured, in its presence.

Thus, despite the numerous sources on which they could have drawn, many contemporary theorists of power in sociology and political science seem to have derived fundamental inspiration from Thomas Hobbes's (1588–1679) sovereign order (as a means of rationally managing human passions) thesis; Karl Marx's (1818–1883) notions of economic determinism, ideological exploitation, and collective upheaval; Emile Durkheim's (1858–1917) emphasis on system maintenance (tendencies toward value consensus, social regulation, social integration); and Max Weber's (1864–1920) conceptualization of power, authority, and rational-economic organizational routines.

Comparatively less sustained attention has been given to Niccoló Machiavelli's (1469–1527) portrayal of power as an instance of the "strategic" maintenance of control,[5] Robert Michels's (1876–1936) "iron law of oligarchy," Georg Simmel's (1858–1918) notions of "forms" of association (and domination), and Wilfredo Pareto's (1848–1923) "circulation of elites" thesis.

With the exception of Machiavelli and Simmel, who more explicitly attend to human agency and the mutuality of influence, the theorists referenced to this point very much assume that "structures" of sorts act on people to produce certain kinds of outcomes (particular types of societies, or [usually vaguely articulated] instances of conforming or disruptive behaviors). Although differing in emphasis with respect to notions of social change, cooperation, and conflict, the predominant emphasis for these foundational figures is on structuralist conceptualizations of power or control.[6]

Power becomes centrally defined by virtue of the positions that people occupy with respect to another. Envisioning power as embedded in the organizational arrangements in which people find themselves,[7] virtually all of these authors (and those who have subsequently built on their works) see control as inhering in structures, resources, rules, norms, and values.

Another theme pursued by some theorists of power revolves around matters of control through psychological manipulation. These notions seem rooted in the experimental works of Wilhelm Wundt (1832–1920) and J. S. Mill (1806–1873), and the conditioning theory of B. F. Skinner (1904–1990),[8] but have taken some other twists as well. Although much more precise in their specification of both "factors" and "outcomes" than the other sources just cited, those working in this tradition also assume a heavy structuralist viewpoint, with power (again) contingent on those in position to manipulate the outcomes that others experience.

Of the foundational figures on which contemporary theorists of power have drawn, Friedrich Nietzsche (1844–1900) is the most incongruent with those referenced to this point. Although largely neglected by those in the social sciences for decades, Nietzsche's (totalizing and debilitating) cynicisms of human endeavor and (the rather discordant) "will to power" (and self-realization) have been resurrected by those promoting poststructuralist/postmodernist orientations. Even here, however, there is a notable (albeit conceptually dissonant) emphasis on structural determinism with respect to notions of power.

Without achieving closure on the many viewpoints on power that have been developed over time in the social sciences, it is instructive to acknowledge some more contemporary endeavors along these lines as well as notions of power that have been more enduring in their presence. For convenience of presentation, these are located under nine broad headings:[9] (1) rational order structuralism; (2) power motifs within the marxist nexus; (3) the (psychological) compliance and influence literature; (4) collectivist approaches; (5) interest group dynamics; (6) mass communication themes; (7) community studies; (8) purveyors of tactical advice; and (9) symbolic interaction.

Although the conceptual flow has been organized around (a) varying modes of thought, (b) successive lines of influence among authors discussing power, and (c) historical sequencing, respectively, this strategy has only been sustainable within certain parameters of theory development. Not only, for instance, is allegedly new theory often founded on earlier ideas, but it may also compete (on a contemporary basis) with earlier versions of that (basic) theory. Likewise, some of those developing statements on power have combined rather different (i.e., mixed, discordant) lines of thought into their own analyses, making it more difficult to maintain consistent conceptual categories as well as follow particular lines of conceptual development on a more sustained basis.

This discussion of the literature has been divided into four chapters for presentational purposes. The remainder of chapter 2 deals with rational order structuralism and a variety of ventures that may be assumed by the marxist nexus. Chapter 3 attends to the compliance literature, collectivist approaches, interest group dynamics, the mass media, and community studies. The authors introduced in chapter 3 tend to invoke a greater tactical emphases in their approaches overall, but many of these scholars are conceptually welded to variants of the structural analyses introduced in chapter 2. Focusing on purveyors of tactical advice, chapter 4 attends both to relatively neglected historical and directive materials on power. Assuming a pragmatist (experiential, enacted) orientation to the study of power, symbolic interactionism represents the conceptual core of the present project and is discussed separately in chapter 5. Rather than embark on a highly detailed consideration of this broader literature, the more immediate concern in chapters 2–5 is one of establishing some baseline parameters against which to locate the subsequent formulation of power as intersubjective accomplishment.

Rational Order Structuralism

Reflecting the inputs of scholars such as Thomas Hobbes (1588–1679), David Hume (1711–1776), and Adam Ferguson (1723–1816), a great deal of the social science literature (as Clegg [1989] observes) emphasizes the more mechanistic, causal, structural, legislated, rational features of human interchange. Whereas these earlier "order theorists" were concerned with establishing rules and constraints that would foster social order among members of communities, they were to be followed by others in the social sciences who tended to concentrate on structures, variables, and resources.

Working within a general positivist (structuralist, causal, quantitative) tradition (inspired by Auguste Comte, Emile Durkheim, Max Weber, Wilhelm Wundt, and J. S. Mill), many scholars in sociology, psychology, and political science have developed approaches that rest centrally on attempts to specify, operationalize, and determine the direction of power relations. For scholars of this ilk, power is seen to inhere in the (structuralist) circumstances in which people are located.

Although their texts will be only briefly discussed here, a number of order themes pertinent to a consideration of power appear in the works of

Weber, Durkheim, Parsons, Merton, Giddens, and some others assuming a synthetic orientation. These will be followed by considerations of scholars whose works may be encompassed by stratification issues and exchange theory. Some other sources might have been introduced here, but as a set these works cover a considerable range of what might be encompassed by "rational order" structuralism.

Max Weber

Of the rational order theorists, Max Weber's (1864–1920) works have maintained an exceptional degree of currency among contemporary scholars grappling with the concept of power. While often reformulated in minor ways, Weber's (1968:53) definition of power—"the probability that one actor in a social relationship will be in a position to carry out his own will despite resistance, regardless of the basis on which this probability rests"— has been accepted by a great many scholars in the field.[10] Likewise, Weber's relatively detailed conceptualizations of organizational domination and authority (rational-legal, traditional, and charismatic) continue to shape many current images of power in society.

A great definer, compiler, and categorizer, who employed comparative systemic analysis in developing his more abstract, formalized conceptualizations of group life, Max Weber is frequently cited as the quintessential expert in discussions of power and authority with respect to organizational or structural positions. However, his analysis does not lend itself to the sustained inquiry that might be anticipated on the surface.

Weber (1968) indicates that domination (particularly emphasizing domination revolving around [a] constellations of interests and [b] domination by authority) may assume a number of forms, but he does not attend substantially to the ways in which people actually work out matters of interest or authority in practice. Weber makes fleeting references to wide ranges of situations in which domination may be problematic and similarly acknowledges the transitional aspects of domination, but in developing typifications of various organizational routines he disregards the human interchange that domination entails.

Instead of focusing on the processes by which human arrangements are implemented, Weber (a) presents readers with elaborate (structural) typologies of human arrangements; (b) attempts to establish the normative practices associated with these typologies by invoking ideal representations; (c) discusses the dependencies of particular arrangements on other developments in certain societies; and (d) asks about the impact of particular modes of normative organization on the broader society. By proclaiming these themes as the proper domains for sociological enterprise and directing people's attention accordingly (into what may be envisioned as a labyrinth of typologies, normative structures, and broad, multifaceted specu-lations), Weber diverts attention away from the actualities of human experi-ence and enterprise.

In the case of bureaucracy, for instance, Weber (1968:956–1005) deals with the matters of: characterizing modern bureaucracy; the formal position of the official; monetary considerations of bureaucracy; the quantification of administrative tasks; the impact of changes on administrative tasks; the technical superiority of bureaucracy; the concentration of lines of authority; the leveling of social differences; the perpetuation of bureaucracy; the inde-terminate economic consequences of bureaucracy; the political impact of bureaucracy; the development of centers of expertise; and the interconnec-tions of bureaucracy and education. While Weber has successfully capti-vated the imaginations of many scholars with extended discussions of bu-reaucracy and other organizational matters, those who follow Weber's line of instruction tend to remove themselves from considerations of the ways in which the affairs of office (in bureaucratic or any other contexts) are actu-ally accomplished.

Weber's discussion of charisma has a more explicit processual em-phasis than does his work on bureaucracy and most of his other statements on domination. Thus, Weber addresses the genesis of charisma, the selec-tion of leaders and successors, and the transmission of charisma. Even here, however, Weber primarily discusses charisma as an "ideal type" rather than focusing on the ways in which charisma is achieved or accomplished in practice.[11] Drawing on various historical and ethnological accounts as well as his own knowledge of contemporary scenes, Weber provides some in-structive insights into the influence process. Still, even here, by dwell-ing on charisma as something unique unto itself, Weber encourages an approach that is only partially mindful of influence work as interactive accomplishment.

As well, Weber provides no indication of the desirability of pursu-ing an analysis that is informed by sustained, communicative contact with those invoking, supporting, witnessing, objectifying, transmitting, or contesting instances of "charisma."[12] Instead, Weber largely disre-gards or minimizes the interpretive practices of the social actors in the setting(s).[13] Minimal concern is given to the matter of examining partici-pants' (working or invoked) viewpoints on "rationality" or "tradition."[14] Indeed, had Weber endeavored to assess his ideal type constructs with respect to instances of human enterprise in the making, he would likely have become quickly aware of the shortcomings of his typifications for comprehending the human condition. This is not to deny the richness of Weber's insights or the expansive nature of his conceptual horizons, but rather to observe that Weber's work on power obscures a more fundamental emphasis on process (and the ongoing [minded] production of human activity).

Emile Durkheim

Emile Durkheim (1858–1917) is seldom referenced as a theorist of power, but (given his impact on the discipline of sociology) it may be instructive to comment briefly on his work as it pertains to the present project. While Durkheim (*Division of Labor, Moral Education*) focuses on authority (primarily the functions thereof) rather than power in developing his analysis of community life, authority (as Nesbit [1966] observes) represents a central theme in Durkheim's conception of social order.

Durkheim's notions of authority are qualified somewhat by his (1933) distinction between mechanical and organic solidarity. But in all modes of community life, from the most homogeneous to the most technologically developed, Durkheim's notions of authority can be seen as established expressions of the value orientations of the collectivity at hand. For Durkheim, authority (and the ensuing social order [and resulting personal organization]) is contingent on both the regulatory arrangements in effect in particular settings and people's senses of integration within those community contexts.

On a more contemporary (organic) plane, Durkheim's work suggests that all associations (state, institutions, collectivities, guilds) in the community imply particular instances of collectively legitimated realms of normative control. The claim, as well, is that particular associations tend to be more effective in imposing authority over their members when the discipline (social regulation) that they invoke is more consistent with the precepts of the association at hand and when members experience greater senses of affinity (social integration) with those particular associations. On a more organic or organizationally complex level, also, Durkheim can be seen to struggle with notions of individual freedom relative to the control(s) of the state and (multiple) other group traditions that may be seen to impact on particular people.

Durkheim stops short of proposing an extended, pluralistic model of social order (contradictions, confusions, conflicts). Likewise, and no less importantly, he fails to consider the ways in which people implement (e.g., establish, define, attend to, or resist) particular lines of authority associated with the state or other groups within the community. One might contend that Durkheim works with an implicit theory of pluralistic, enacted power, but had he been more attentive to the processes (and problematics) of human interchange as these occurred in practice, Durkheim well may have rejected the (structuralist) foundations that undergird his theory of social order.

Talcott Parsons

Talcott Parsons's (1963) statement on power attempts to synthesize aspects of Weber's and Durkheim's work with a symbolic-communicative orientation to the essence of power. Paralleling influence (as power) to the use of money (as a limited but interchangeable resource), Parsons introduces notions of intentionality, definitions of situations, and differing relationships of actors amidst matters of conflict, cooperation, institutional accommodation, and normative expectations. As the discussion unfolds, however, Parsons's expressed concerns with meanings, language, and intentionality are left quickly behind as he attempts to establish a normatively arranged system of rational-economic influences.[15] Reverting to his structuralist roots, Parsons gives little attention to ongoing enterprise and interactive adjustments that denote power in process.[16]

Robert Merton

Like Parsons, Robert Merton (1957) also derives considerable inspiration from Weber and Durkheim. Although not addressing power in an explicit manner, Merton is concerned with matters of legitimation, authority, bureaucracy, organizational arrangements, role-sets, reference groups, and modes of interpersonal influence (cosmopolitans and locals) as these structure (and regulate) people's behaviors within community contexts.

Merton's depictions of human associations are more multifaceted than Durkheim, more social psychologically oriented than Weber, and more empirically oriented than Parsons. Still, by maintaining an emphasis on structures, manifest and latent functions, and typifications (organizational configurations, group properties, stylistic orientations, and personal characteristics), Merton also overlooks the ways in which people actively engage one another in the various arenas of society. Likewise, although stressing the importance of developing "theories of the middle range," the research that Merton has in mind focuses primarily on structures and other variables (e.g., group properties, normative traditions, class position).

Like Weber, Merton espouses a relativist position (e.g., the Thomas theorem) at times, and occasionally Merton uses quotations from actual people (e.g., cosmopolitans and locals) to illustrate his points, but he makes no reference to the necessity of attending to the manners in which people accomplish their activities in practice. Focusing on role relationships, Merton's work may be seen as more closely linked to a processual analysis of influence work than is that of Weber, Durkheim, or Parsons, but, like these others, Merton stops short of pushing theory (and methods) to the level of (the actualities and problematics of) ongoing human endeavor.

Anthony Giddens

Pursuing a somewhat different agenda, Anthony Giddens's (1976:110–113; 1984:283) commentaries on power are more explicit than those of Durkheim and Merton, but Giddens's work is considerably more limited than that of Weber or Parsons. Still, Giddens's material is noteworthy as a consequence of his attempt to incorporate power into a theory of "structuration." Interestingly, while Giddens's depiction of structuration is significantly more hermeneutical and processual in its thrust than are the theoretical emphases of these other scholars,[17] Giddens notions of power remain quite structuralist in emphasis.

Acknowledging human agency (as also at times do Weber, Parsons, and Merton), Giddens (1976:110–113) posits that "power is a feature of every human interaction" and that one can "talk of power being 'stored up' for future occasions of use." Giddens makes some general references to the reflective implementation of power within structured contexts, but his material appears to be concerned more with the distribution of power within society than with the ways in which people (as individuals and/or groups) actually influence each other on a more situated basis.[18]

Synthetic Order Theorists

The term "synthetic order theorists" refers to a set of scholars who (like Giddens) have explicitly endeavored to incorporate notions of conflict, process, and human agency into overarching structuralist/systems considerations of power relations. The works of French and Raven (1959), Wrong (1979), Burns and Flam (1987), and Pfeffer (1981, 1992, 1997) are representative here.

Envisioning power relations in terms of actor (systemic) interdependencies, John French and Bertram Raven (1959) identify five forms or bases of social power: reward, coercive, legitimate, referent, and expert. While attending to the differential circumstances of (various) agents of influence (relative to their targets) along these lines, French and Raven posit that power relations are importantly moderated by *targets' perceptions* of (and notions of dependency on) the agents in question.

Despite its promise for integrating some more singularistic theories of power by more explicitly acknowledging the centrality of target attributions (definitions) for influence contexts, French and Raven's (1959) typology of power relations does little to indicate either the ways that people engage one another in more direct, experiential manners or how one might more effectively study these interchanges.

Noting that his interest in power was piqued by the exchanges between Talcott Parsons and C. Wright Mills (discussed later), wherein power was depicted as social resource (Parsons) versus an instrument of control and oppression (Mills), Dennis Wrong (1979) also proposes a more comprehensive typology of power relations than that assumed by most order theorists.

Viewing power as "the capacity of some persons to produce intended and foreseen effects on others," Wrong distinguishes control efforts signified by (a) force, (b) covert manipulation, (c) interpersonal persuasion, and (d) authority. As well, Wrong more explicitly recognizes the centrality of coordinated enterprise for larger scale power relations than do Parsons or Mills, for instance.

However, instead of asking how people directly engage one another (as individuals or groups) in instances of power relations, how people actually coordinate their activities with others, or how researchers might examine the ways in which people develop interchanges in practice, Wrong turns toward the questions of "why" people try to use power in their dealings with others and "what sort of institutional base" enables them to do so.

In his updated (1988) preface to the (1979) volume, Wrong recasts his analysis somewhat by referencing the writings of Anthony Giddens and Michel Foucault (discussed later). Thus, Wrong acknowledges an affinity with Giddens's contention that power is something *mobilized* by people (as opposed to an existing set of resources) and recognizes with Foucault the importance of envisioning power relations across a *multiplicity* of power sites. Wrong also links his (revised) position to that of Eliot Friedson (1986) who, assuming an interactionist viewpoint, contends that power exists only through the human agents who engage others in the course of implementing particular tasks and perspectives. Unfortunately, Wrong does not elaborate theoretically on these matters, nor does he provide any indication of how the study of power relations might be pursued mindful of these considerations.

Although less explicitly focused on power, Tom Burns and Helena Flam's (1987) *The Shaping of Social Organizations* represents another attempt to extend the structuralist paradigm in related terms. Consistent with an order emphasis, Burns and Flam posit that organizational life centrally revolves around a system of rules. At the same time, though (and in a manner somewhat akin to Giddens), Burns and Flam directly incorporate notions of process, conflict, and human agency into their model. Thus, they insist that people be seen as the producers, conveyers, and implementers of rules, as well as sources of discrepancy, conflict, and change. Further, Burns and Flam acknowledge both overarching systems of rules across the broader community and other, more localized or more particularistic, systems of rules that may be invoked (either interrelatedly with, or independently of, any larger rule system) in the multiple spheres of community life.

Still, Burns and Flam's emphasis on human agency and collective interchange dissipates in their ensuing analysis. Like Weber who acknowledges *verstehen* but generally fails to incorporate interpretive understanding into his subsequent analyses of community routines, Burns and Flam are unable to achieve an enduring synthesis of human agency and structuralist imagery. Burns and Flam encourage a conceptualization of organizational life that is notably problematic, pluralist, and processual; a viewpoint that is attentive to a fuller range of human enterprise, including conflict, cooperation, and compromise. However, given their more fundamental concerns with structuralist models and factors, Burns and Flam end up focusing on organizations as the products and producers of various environmental / systems variables. Somewhat by default, then, they disengage from the task of examining the *enacted* features of human activity (and interchange) in the "here and now" spheres of endeavor that constitute organizational life in the making.

Because his writings on power and organizations span two decades, Jeffrey Pfeffer (1981, 1992, 1997) provides an instructive base for examining structuralist/order perspectives on power relations. Whereas Pfeffer's (1997) *New Directions for Organization Theory* overviews the field (especially as practiced in business and management schools), his (1981) *Power in Organizations* attempts to establish the conceptual parameters of a structural approach to organizational practices.

Working in more conventional sociological terms, Pfeffer (1981) locates power within the division of labor or the hierarchical task-specialization of organizations. Relatedly, Pfeffer is attentive to matters of centralization, legitimation, bureaucracy, rules, rational decision-making, efficiency, and productivity. Likewise, he is concerned with causality, factors, measurements, and the prediction and control of organizational behavior. At the same time, though, Pfeffer finds that a more conventionalist structuralist approach cannot deal with the human enterprise that characterizes organizational practice. Thus, he also explicitly recognizes differing actor skills, enterprise, variable tactical alignments, and human (symbolic) interchange. Because Pfeffer (1981) wants to acknowledge actual organizational practices, his volume is suggestive in many respects. Still, the underlying structuralist assumptions and (quantitative) methodology to which he is committed do not enable researchers to study organizational life in the making. Representing a more discursive, popularized version of his 1981 text, Pfeffer's (1992) *Managing With Power* does little to clarify or resolve these issues.

More consequentially, Pfeffer's (1997) statement indicates that despite a continued proliferation of programs, paradigms, debates, and publications, those working in the broader management tradition have been unable to bridge the gap between social theory and human action in organizational settings. And, to this point, they show little promise of doing so. It has become increasingly apparent that structuralist approaches are inadequate for comprehending (and studying) the processes by which human interchange takes place, but the alternatives (humanistic, marxist, postmodernist, narrative) with which people in the organizations/management field have been working lack both a conceptual base and a methodological capacity for examining the human production of organizational life.

The Stratificationists

Although they have taken somewhat different tacts than the theorists just discussed, one might acknowledge another set of structuralists who envision their work as central to power relations in society. While seldom defining themselves as "power theorists," per se, sociologists involved in stratification, mobility, or inequality research often talk about power (and related structural inequities). Working within the broader structuralist paradigm, these scholars commonly invoke variants (and mixes) of Weberian, Durkheimian, and Marxist (discussed later) analyses to account for differences in people's present situations (e.g., income, education, occupations, living standards, mortality rates) by virtue of their (typically class defined) positions in society.

Comparing various measurements of people's successes (and well-being) with indicators of their "positions in the social structure" (on community, national, or international levels), the stratificationists spend a great deal of time conjecturing about power and its embeddedness in various structures in society. Ironically, while the data with which these researchers work displays an almost complete disregard of people's day-to-day activities and experiences, this [highly speculative] literature on power has become a consequential theme in the sociological theater.[19]

The Exchange (and Equity) Theorists

On another, but somewhat related (rational order) front, a number of sociologists and social psychologists have been involved in the study of power relations through the development of "exchange theory" (and its offshoot, "equity theory"). Deriving some impetus from Skinnerian (conditioning) psychology and general notions of economic rationality,[20] these theorists (e.g., Homans, 1958, 1961; Emerson, 1962, 1976; Blau, 1964; Coleman, 1990) have developed variants of power theories that revolve around people's abilities to affect the outcomes that others experience.[21]

Following Homans and Blau, both of whom attempted to establish the elementary forms of association (particularly as this pertains to the pursuit of desired objects or other attractions) and acknowledge some processual dimensions of interchange,[22] those working in the field may be seen as pursuing a broader rationalist agenda. More directly, they attempt to explain organizational routines by virtue of the "accounting" tendencies that people (are presumed to) invoke as they calculate resources, costs, rewards, investments, and alternatives in ways that are mindful of their interests, obstacles, and positions in the social structure.[23]

Power Motifs within the Marxist Nexus

A Marxism without some concept of determination is in effect worthless. A Marxism with many of the concepts of determination it now has is quite radically disabled.

—Williams, 1977:83

Although they also assume structuralist orientations, a set of approaches represented as marxist analysis, critical theory, cultural studies, marxist-feminist analysis, and postmodernist analysis, amongst others,[24] address the matter of power relations in the community. These and other derivatives of marxist analysis, here referenced collectively as the (marxist) nexus or matrix, are somewhat distinct from the others, but all *nexus notions of power* are located within (and obscured by their embeddedness within) variants of the oppression thesis.

Power relations represent but one aspect of marxist analysis. However, it is in the realms of power, conflict, and the like that those in the matrix claim their greatest relevance to the social sciences. Albeit pursued within an increasingly wide variety of contexts, amidst a continually broadened set of "pertinent issues" and ever shifting sets of fronts and guises, the scenarios of power and oppression that characterize the variants of the marxist nexus are rather stereotypic in thrust.

Marxist oppression theses are most centrally developed around the notions of materialist determinism and exploitation. Often buttressed by claims of scholarly (if not scientific vs. religious) humanism,[25] the (identified) conflict is located in (structurally based) power imbalances that are alleged to foster and perpetuate (in material and ideological terms) situations defined as intolerable by those in the nexus.

Power becomes envisioned in terms of structural arrangements of inequality. In classic marxism, power and inequity are most centrally located in property relations, but other emphases (e.g., gender, race, media) may be deemed more pivotal (than property relations) by those working within the broader matrix. Still, structurally defined power relations are taken to represent the focal point not only of the problem(s) at hand, but of the human condition more generally. Human relations, thus, are portrayed centrally in conflictual, binary terms with those cast into victim roles envisioned as exploited by the (more powerful) villains.

The hope for the future lies in the vision of a new moral order, one in which power imbalances are radically altered through broad structural upheaval and the villains (now objectified by marxist analysis) are dispensed with in a totalizing manner. This vision is to be achieved through collective resistance.

Those caught up in the marxist matrix assume wide assortments of postures on the appropriate forms of collective resistance. These range from the violent ("blood, guts, and death"), universalistic revolution associated with Marx and Engels, to more genteel, situated policy changes (cultural studies, marxist-feminism), to notions of cynical despair (some postmodernist themes), to the vaguely expressed hopes that socialism will provide for all according to "their needs."

Because those involved in the nexus have invoked a variety of theoretical positions and moral agendas, and focused on a relatively wide range of substantive topics over the years (on mixed, sequential, concurrent, and revisionist bases; sometimes in explicit opposition to one another), this statement begins with a consideration of more fundamentalist marxist ventures. This is followed by separate discussions of postmodernism, cultural studies, marxist-feminism, some more isolated marxist-inspired authors who address the concept of power, and Robert Michels and Columbia socialism. This may allow us to address some of the complexities and strains in this literature.

Acknowledging Fundamentalist Orientations

Although Karl Marx (1818–1883) is often envisioned as epitomizing, if not initiating, the socialist revolutionary effort, many of the ideas associated with Karl Marx (and Friedrich Engels) were fairly well articulated by his predecessors, most notably, perhaps, Claude Henri, comte de Saint-Simon (1760–1825).[26] As Kolakowski (1978, vol. 1:220–221) observes, notions of the historical evolution of socialism, the materialist foundations of oppression, the pressures of technological advance and competition in capitalist society, and the necessity of working class upheaval are evident in works of earlier writers; as also are the objectives of utopian socialism (e.g., abolition of the private ownership of production, planned economics catering to people's needs, the development of individual capacities, and socialism as a boon to humanity).[27] What may distinguish Marx's writings more directly, are (a) his emphasis on alienation as a product of capitalist economy, (b) his insistence on the necessity of a massive, violent upheaval, and (c) his concerns about finding ways to ensure that the workers assume active (collective, intense, and timely) roles in overthrowing their oppressors.

Subscribing to variants of structuralist determinism and the ideology of oppression, those assuming more fundamentalist marxist positions assert that power or control is (objectively) embedded in the relations that develop over time between people with respect to the ownership of property and the control of labor. Contending that the ruling ideas of society are those of the ruling class (defined by property ownership), and that the ideology of the ruling class has so permeated the consciousness of the working class that these people are unable to differentiate their interests from those of the ruling class (resulting in a state of self-perpetuating "ideological reproduction"),[28] the fundamentalists have spent much time and effort encouraging violent, collective upheaval as a means of "empowering the masses."[29,30]

Marx's class analysis has been the site of considerable debate (see Kolakowski, 1978, vol. 2), as has his related thesis of the evolutionary progression of various social orders. Still, there is considerable consensus among those in the nexus that (a) workers (frequently now depicted as "people generally") are exploited by capitalist interests, (b) ideological repression is so pervasive that workers are unaware of the gravity of their own circumstances (i.e., false consciousness), and (c) the central mission is to provoke upheaval en route to a communist state.

While marxist writers have continually sought out new ways to define (and redefine) situations in ways that one may envision the ruling class to have maintained ideological domination (see Clegg, 1989: especially 158–166), these authors have not been particularly attentive to the ongoing dynamics of human interchange. Some versions of (fundamentalist) marxism are more interpretivist in emphasis, but even those producing these materials continue to subscribe to (and promote) the basic doctrine of a ruling class conspiracy (and the underlying images of sovereignty of control and the false consciousness that this implies).

Although power (and conflict) is a major theme in their analysis, marxist theorists have provided surprisingly little insight into power as a social, enacted essence. Despite a long-standing insistence by Marx and Engels that socialist analyses be rigorously grounded in empirical research,[31] very little overall attention (initially or subsequently) has been directed toward a scholarly examination of the ways in which people influence one another in actual practice.[32] Instead, the vast effort has been focused on the mobilization of people in pursuit of a communist state.[33] Much time has been spent vilifying "capitalist systems" (and variants thereof) and encouraging discontent and insurgency, but minimal sustained consideration has been given to influence and resistance as matters that merit careful methodological inquiry and theoretical focus.[34]

From the viewpoint of traditional Marxism, each sector of the community is seen either as an obstacle to be destroyed or a resource to be used to further the cause of global communism.[35] Every group is to be realigned (ideally cognitively, but deceptively or forcibly as necessary) so that it might be used to attain the larger control mission. As "moral entrepreneurs" (Becker, 1963), the marxists have assumed engaging, tactical orientations toward the human community (see Frankel, 1983), but their work better denotes instances of persistent political opportunism than concerted, scholarly analyses of influence work. Marxist endeavors in academia and elsewhere may be seen as ventures in the quest for social control, but exceedingly few of these authors systematically have used their own forums as research sites (i.e., marxists as ethnographers or participant-observer researchers) to better comprehend power as human accomplishment.[36] Their concerns with political agendas greatly overshadow a respect for the ethnographic other.

Marxism has been subject to long-standing critiques from within by revisionists of various sorts (see Lenin's [1970] defense of Marx; also Kolakowski, 1978, vol. 2) and there have been numerous efforts on the part of academics to generate versions of marxist thought that are less tied to Marx's and Engels's views of class and historical materialism, their related notions of evolution, their insistence on global communism, and their visions of a massive, violent revolution.

Challenges to fundamentalist marxist notions have become even more evident over the past few decades. Reflecting concerns, variously, about (a) fostering other agendas (e.g., feminism, race, age, sexual preferences), (b) "sanitizing" the revolutionary platform associated with a violent, warlike proletarian mission for more polite or "politically correct" audiences, (c) incorporating aspects of marxist thought into postmodernist/poststructuralist ventures, (d) coming to terms with the (1990s) collapse of the soviet-communist state, and (e) maintaining (nexus) authors' own personal "genteel" situations and life-styles, much recent nexus discourse has lost a great deal of fundamental marxism. Still, those in the nexus are sympathetic to the general cause of establishing communist principles (and states).

At present, the marxist community (and literature) seems in a state of heightened disarray. Many seem to long for "the good old days," and some continue to insist on the correctness of fundamental Marxism (Callinicos, 1989), but Aronson's (1995) preface in *After Marxism* is particularly telling. Acknowledging that marxism had been seen as in a state of crises for some time, Aronson nevertheless observes that "the end of Marxism" came as a profound shock to many on the left.

Representing a deep, disabling, and seemingly enduring contradiction of the bedrock foundations of the ideological viewpoints and expectations that had vitalized marxist agendas, the mission of transforming humanity into a massive socialist state appears to have reached an abrupt, disheartening end. In response to the question of "where to go from here" Aronson asks what one might salvage of the values implied in the older, apparently defunct, marxist vision and agenda.

The topics in Aronson's book are similarly revealing. Consider, for instance, "Marxism without Marxism," "Emancipating Modernity," "We Should Be Talking About Right and Wrong," and "Sources of Hope."

Thus, some (e.g., Mayer, 1994) continue to reformulate marxist agendas in yet other manners, and some have adopted modified agendas as cultural critics of capitalist regimes (Williams, 1977; Grossberg et al., 1992; Hall, 1980, 1992). For many others (as Agger [1992] notes), the transition to postmodernism represents an appealing alternative. Their attractions to postmodernism are multifaceted, but apart from those who argue for a fundamental Marxist distinctiveness (e.g., Callinicos, 1989), the highly amorphous postmodernist/poststructuralist umbrella rather simultaneously provides advocates with a means of both depriviliging other viewpoints and (yet) another intellectual or scholarly facade for promoting marxist inspired agendas.

Postmodernist Ventures

> *At the heart of postmodernist thought is an extreme or complete skepticism of, or disbelief in, the authenticity of human knowledge and practice. Accordingly, all claims of expertise and science are invalidated or at least are considered no more viable than any other "stories, narratives, fictions, myths or accounts." Partially shaped by the Nietzschean tenet that "Language is the first and great lie," all versions of reality are considered instances of self-perpetuating myths. At best, the postmodernists contend, humans may convince themselves to think that they know something, when in actuality, all that is known is but another version of a myth, another linguistic or textual reality which has no truth value beyond itself.*
>
> *—Dawson and Prus, 1995:107*

As noted elsewhere (Dawson and Prus, 1993b), those embarked on postmodernist ventures display some affinities with the interactionist position developed here. Rather centrally, one may observe tendencies on the part of those assuming postmodernist postures to acknowledge multiple, linguistically (textually) mediated realities (as opposed to singularistic, objectivist viewpoints or meta-narratives), as well as human capacities for reflectivity and negotiated social productions. However, postmodernist denials of the authenticity of all knowledge claims and (relatedly) the primacy given to "the text" over activity (and the fundamental human struggle for existence) takes postmodernist ventures into realms of (debilitating) cynical relativism and subjective idealism that are at sharp variance from the interactionist emphasis on the pragmatics of human accomplishment or the study of community life in the making (Dawson and Prus, 1993a, 1993b, 1995; Prus and Dawson, 1996).[37]

Characterized by conceptual ambiguities, obscurities, and contradictions in formulation and the assumption of wide varieties of "poetic licence" in expression, postmodernism defies succinct conceptual definition. However, one dominant practice invoked by those defining themselves as postmodernists has been to disavow the integrity of all modernist (i.e., non-postmodernist) practices (ideas, knowledge, activities, productions). This they do by *claiming* that all human knowledge claims have no value or validity beyond themselves.

Despite the totalizing (and self-contradictory) relativism that this position implies, those adopting postmodernist stances go on to emphasize the [truth] value or integrity of their own positions, as somehow more informed, more enabling than anything that has preceded them. Depriveleging other viewpoints, thusly, the postmodernists subsequently embark on expressions of any sort that they deem appropriate (i.e., denying any accountability to those "locked into" modernist images of knowledge). Working under this pretext, those adopting postmodernist mantles have engaged in extended criticism of any realms of knowledge and practice that they find disenchanting. Presuming privileged insight, they propose remedies to the conditions they find troubling in some respect.

The conceptual problems and dilemmas inherent in postmodernist positions are massive, but the practitioners seem undaunted by such matters. Critics typically are dismissed as (hopelessly) tied to modernist trappings and the quest for new forms of postmodernist expression (denigrating, shocking, entertaining, moralizing, missionizing) is given primacy.

Although the more unique and compelling themes associated with postmodernism centrally revolve around Neitzchian cynicism, these writings are extensively fused with the conceptual schemes developed by Marx, Heidegger, Freud, and Wittgenstein, amongst others. Indeed, it should be noted that the major progenitors of postmodernism (i.e., Michel Foucault, Jacques Derrida, Jean Baudrillard, and Jean-Francois Lyotard) all were long-standing marxists. They may have become disillusioned with the grandiose determinism associated with marxist structuralism and (related) communist utopias, but their writings continue to resonate with the Frankfurt school of marxism (see the subsequent discussion of cultural studies).

The progenitors of postmodernism may have redefined their approach(es) in some cynicizing and multifaceted respects, but they retain variants of the structuralist oppression thesis. Further, a great many subsequent applications of postmodernist/poststructuralist analysis are centrally informed by marxist moralities, both in their definitions of problematic conditions and in the remedies they propose to deal with these.

Somewhat ironically, and in contrast to the baseline cynicism (and frequent poetic playfulness) that pervades postmodernist thought, the matter of *power* represents one realm in which at least some of the major proponents of postmodernism (e.g., Foucault, 1979; Lyotard, 1984) wish to be taken very seriously (i.e., make strikingly evident *claims* of authenticity). Given the rapidly expansive but conceptually elusive literature encompassed by postmodernism (poststructuralism), the immediate discussion focuses on Michel Foucault (1979). Foucault seems to have provided the most definitive (widely acknowledged) material on power within this genre of discourse.

One of the central figures in the postmodernist/poststructuralist movement, Foucault has attracted a great deal of attention with his notion of "disciplinary power." Rejecting notions of Marxist sovereignty (dominant ideology and false consciousness) at a general level, Foucault argues for an image of society that reflects multiple sites of discourse (disciplinary practices or sites of power).[38]

In purporting to dispense with objectivism (and privileged standards) of all sorts, Foucault envisions society to be constituted by an assortment of power sites or arenas that, while operative at particular places and time, are seen to permeate people's essential existences. For Foucault, all of these (institutionalized) frames of reference are disenchanting as a consequence of the repression and coercion they imply (both explicitly and implicitly from Foucault's viewpoint). None of these arenas or cognitive frameworks are to be privileged or authenticated over others. Viewed in this manner, all disciplines are arbitrary and textually defined; in that sense, mythical. Still, all of these constructions are seen as oppressive, to wreak (seemingly genuine) havoc on the human condition. The various "texts" or cultural themes (and practices) implied in each context may be resisted, challenged, and replaced over time. However, any "new texts" also dictate (in substituted realms and manners only) the nature of people's routines and experiences.

For Foucault, these multiple, seemingly dispersed arenas of disciplinary influence do not represent sources of freedom with which, or denote the foundations on which, people may pursue their interests (amidst diversities of opportunities, obstacles and accomplishments). Instead, Foucault contends, each site of power (with its own discourse and practices) threatens to deprive all of those situated within of their freedoms. There are no havens, only ever shifting configurations of power sites and within each, only variations in the sorts of repressions to which human bodies and minds are subjected. While Foucault notes that participants may value certain disciplinary themes, his emphasis is largely on the disenchanting and degrading experiences of power to which people may be subjected in these particular arenas. Power emerges as a force seemingly administered by people, but yet (organizationally) estranged from human purveyors who, themselves, are hopelessly bound in realms of discourse-mediated reality.

Foucault appears to have avoided the marxist trap of a sovereign power center, but only by arguing for the existence of a multiplicity of (relatively sovereign) power centers. While allegedly breaking away from marxist notions of centralized and pervasive ideological domination, Foucault's work still maintains a strong element of structural determinism, for each of these sites represent microcosms of ideological repression.[39]

It should be noted that Foucault provides little indication of how these power sites emerge, become established, persist, are experienced, challenged, adjusted to, or replaced. Notably, too, despite his extended criticisms of power sites, Foucault provides no feasible methodology for defining, examining, or detailing the processes he discusses. One of his favored strategies is that of selecting some (typically disturbing or enticing) setting and subjecting it to a historical deconstruction, in which he points out (makes claims to) the unavoidably sinister, surreptitious underpinnings of the themes he deems operative in that setting. Like many authors, Foucault's work contains various insights into the human condition, but he subjects idiographic instances to rather sweeping historical (and quasi-marxist notions of repression) generalizations as he *speculates* about the developments and operations of these "power sites."

Although Foucault claims that all conceptual productions (and reproductions) are mythical, arbitrary, and merely represent the means of consolidating particular power sites, and he simultaneously denies that he is invoking privileged frames in conducting his analysis, Foucault nevertheless appears very serious about objectifying his critiques of the (multiple) power centers that he envisions as dominating the human condition.

The disciplines, traditions, or realms of discourse to which Foucault refers are seen to cut unevenly across various aspects of people's lives. Still, Foucault is more concerned about depicting [the structures] underlying their origins and emphasizing the dehumanizing implications of the linguistic or textual frames that emerge within these organizational contexts than attending to either the essence of human lived experience or the enterprise entailed in promoting, sustaining, challenging and replacing these disciplines or traditions.

The present analysis has more affinity with the pluralist position on power taken by Foucault (1979) than the fundamentalist marxists. However, in contrast to Foucault who emphasizes, dramatizes, and objectifies what he claims to be the sinister, constraining, dehumanizing, alienating aspects of the entire array of "power sites," the approach taken in the present volume emphasizes the necessity of attending to the multiple and potentially shifting viewpoints of the people actually involved in particular associations (and subcultural mosaics—Prus, 1997b). This means acknowledging the full range of definitions (e.g., restricting, obstructing, humanizing, enabling, uplifting) that people may attribute to particular associations, discourses, practices, actions, interactions, and disciplines and organizations of all sorts.

Further, in contrast to the subjective idealism (and structural representations) associated with postmodernism, *the present analysis very much rests on activity* (and the human struggle for existence) as a central feature for appreciating the human condition. The recognition of intersubjective human agency (meaningful activity) presupposes a privileging of viewpoints. In acting toward the world, people *inevitably* privilege, prioritize, or make claims (as even does Foucault). These presumptions may be revised or rejected along the way (as people encounter the resistances associated with [humanly experienced] obdurate reality),[40] but they enable people to "do things." Thus, in direct contrast to postmodernist [cynicism, moralism, and playfulness], it is observed that *people privilege claims (and frames of reference) as an essential matter of the practical accomplishment of human life* (see Dawson and Prus, 1993a, 1993b, 1995; Prus, 1996b; Prus and Dawson, 1996):

> *Postmodernism . . . might achieve viability in a world where no "knowledge" would be privileged over any other "knowledge" because it is never tested or used to accomplish anything. However, in a world of action or human enterprise, we can speak of intentionality, application, accomplishment, and assessment. In each of these instances, by being invoked, tested, used to perform certain tasks, and being evaluated with respect to other forms of knowing, particular forms of knowing do acquire privilege. People may later decide that they were mistaken in taking this or that tact or they may have experienced doubts along the way, but in order to "do something," people have to privilege certain forms of knowing over others. This human use of knowledge straightforwardly violates . . . "the postmodernist sensibility." (Dawson and Prus, 1993b:199)*

> *Even language, which moderates action, exists only, and takes its form, shape or essence, through action. Language is, thus, an ongoing manifestation of human agency and interchange. The preponderant emphasis that postmodernists place on language and metaphors serves to disembody humans from their selves, their actions (and interactions), and the products of their "blood, sweat, and tears." Without these elements, without activity, without the ongoing struggle implied in human lived experience, however, language is nothing more than an empty shell. (Dawson and Prus, 1993a:169)*

While the postmodernists purport to reject all notions of modernity (i.e., all nonpostmodernist knowledge claims), even those statements (Foucault, 1979; Lyotard, 1984) that address aspects of power in presumably sincere manners offer little that is sufficiently coherent conceptually or methodologically viable to sustain the direct examination of human experiences with power (or any other feature of the human group life). The postmodernists may draw attention to aspects of human experience through dramatic (albeit often misconstrued) representations, but they have contributed little that is new or instructive to an appreciation of power as *intersubjective accomplishment*.

Cultural Studies

Associated most directly with the Birmingham Centre for Cultural Studies, *cultural studies* has developed somewhat concurrently with postmodernist thought and the two have become interfused over the years. Still, it is appropriate that the discussion of postmodernism precede a consideration of cultural studies. Not only have those working within the cultural studies tradition attended more extensively to the progenitors of postmodernism than vice versa, but those in cultural studies have tended to engage the social sciences in generally more responsible (i.e., more scholarly, less cynical, less playful) manners. As with those caught up in the marxist nexus more broadly, those in cultural studies are embedded in a series of conceptual and methodological contradictions, but have been somewhat more explicitly attending (e.g., Williams, 1977; Johnson, 1991; Hall, 1992) to these matters.

Like postmodernism, cultural studies defies straightforward definition (see Hall, 1980, 1992; Grossberg, 1986; Johnson, 1991; McRobbie, 1992; and Nelson et al., 1992). In many ways, cultural studies is also reminiscent of the "critical theory" approach associated with the Frankfurt school in that cultural studies was informed by those working in this earlier (marxist) tradition.[41] Both sets of practitioners maintain claims of a more humanist, artistic, communications, cultural emphasis that extends the boundaries often associated with more traditional (property relations) marxist analysis. At the same time, though, those in cultural studies have tended to downplay the more traditional marxist emphasis on false consciousness and (until more recently) had largely divested themselves of psychoanalysis (which justified [and obscured] notions of false consciousness within the Frankfurt camp).

Since cultural studies is very much identified with the writings of Stuart Hall,[42] it is instructive to be mindful of what Grossberg (1986: 63) identifies as Hall's three major agendas: (1) to pursue a theory of ideology that is attentive to people's communicative practices, (2) to describe contemporary practices of cultural and political struggles, and (3) to foster a "marxism without guarantees." Those in cultural studies have attended to wide ranges of topics that in one or other ways may be seen as culture-related, but Hall's agendas run through the core of most works conducted within this genre.

In their introduction to an edited collection on cultural studies, Nelson et al. (1992) attempt to add some clarity to this rather nebulous arena of scholarship. Thus, they observe that cultural studies is intended as a transdisciplinary, if not also a counter-disciplinary approach. They liken cultural studies to anthropology in certain respects, but emphasize both the contemporary scene and the interpretive and evaluative features of the methodologies that its practitioners employ. As well, they argue that while traditional humanism focuses on high culture, those in cultural studies attend to all cultural practices and to their relationships with social and historical structures. Notably, too, they more pointedly contend that its adherents:

> *see cultural studies not simply as a chronicle of cultural change but as an intervention in it, and see themselves not simply as scholars providing an account but as politically engaged participants . . . [C]ultural studies has regularly theorized in response to particular social, historical, and material conditions. (Nelson et al., 1992:5–6)*

While (a) taking issue with some features of fundamental marxism, particularly those revolving around matters of (more singularistic) class-based conflict, false consciousness, ideological vagueness, and utopian socialism (e.g., see Hall, 1992; McRobbie, 1992), (b) acknowledging more constructionist, multileveled and multicontextual notions of conflict, and (c) professing concern about pursuing more empirically grounded research, those in cultural studies have continued to foster versions of the oppression thesis and pursue visions of new moral orders that approximate socialist states.

For those in cultural studies, *power* has become an even more diffuse phenomenon than implied in either more traditional marxism or postmodernism (à la Foucault or Lyotard, for example). While more or less continually reaffirming loyalties to the "New Left" and infusing their analyses with moral imperatives, those in cultural studies have somewhat simultaneously been working with two rather incompatible notions of power (and culture).

As Hall (1980) observes, considerable (conceptual) tension has existed in cultural studies between a base superstructural (deterministic) metaphor and a concern about examining culture as something in the making. While expanding their emphasis beyond what they define as the narrow, excessively deterministic imagery of traditional marxism, those in cultural studies, nevertheless, have continued to define power (relations) very much in binary, conflictual terms, albeit now relative to a (potentially expanding) series of structural dimensions (class, race, gender, sexual orientation). Contrasted (and conflated) with this structural/deterministic orientation is the other cultural studies' viewpoint, namely that culture consists of a multiplicity of ongoing, situated realms of (political) struggle.

Given the mixed (and shifting) images of power and culture with which they work, those in the cultural studies community have become caught in a set of paradoxes that revolve around (a) moral prescriptions (and reform) versus social science agendas,[43] and (b) structuralist versus interpretivist assumptions regarding analysis of the human community.

The somewhat related matter of (c) epistemology is treated even more chaotically within the cultural studies framework. Virtually no articulated rationales (or standards) exist for assessing data or drawing linkages between theory, methods, and data. While continuing to pass themselves off as "critical" scholars, it seems that any sort of study or statement represented as sympathetic to the general orientation of socialism will be tolerated, if not readily "welcomed into the fold."

Notions of methodological discipline (and competence) regarding versions of either quantitative or qualitative research appear almost entirely beside the point. One may observe occasioned insistence in this literature, following the (vague) encouragements of Marx and Engels and Gramsci (whose historical emphasis was once very fashionable in cultural studies) to study community life on a more sustained basis. Good intentions aside, though, not much viable research along these lines has been done.

No less lamentable is the pronounced tendency of "researchers" in the matrix to rely so heavily on ideologically informed "content analysis" of human productions instead of examining the ways in which people see themselves as engaging the world. Like those in the nexus more generally, those in cultural studies rather freely impose meanings on those purportedly being studied instead of making the effort to learn about the life-worlds of these others through sustained (attentive-to-the-other) interchange.

In an attempt to broaden their horizons on power, oppression, and reform (and perhaps simultaneously establish supporters and alliances with kindred spirits in the nexus), those in cultural studies also have incorporated feminist and postmodernist ventures into their intellectual package. Although much academic feminism is also rooted in marxist images of structuralist oppression, the integration of feminism within cultural studies has resulted in some repackaging of the cultural studies project.

As Hall (1992:282–283) observes, those in cultural studies began to (a) more explicitly envision power in personal, experiential terms, (b) attend more directly to issues of gender and sexuality in reference to power, (c) assume a renewed emphasis on subjective experiences, and (d) incorporate psychoanalysis into their overall theoretical program.[44] Because of its marxist affinities, much feminism may be seen as reaffirming the general direction of the cultural studies agenda, but its synthesis contributes to an increasing diffusion of images of power within the cultural studies camp and adds yet other theoretical (including psychoanalysis) and methodological ambiguities to an already highly problematic set of academic practices.

Hall (1992:283) also contends that encounters with semiotics and

(French) structuralism and poststructuralism/postmodernism have resulted in a greater attentiveness on the part of those in cultural studies to matters of language, textual representation, metaphors, and multiple sites of power. As with those in the nexus more generally, postmodernism has certain allures for many of those in cultural studies.

The totalizing relativism (and debilitating cynicism) associated with postmodernism, as represented in the works of Foucault and Derrida, for instance, provides those in cultural studies with a handy device for discrediting (undesired) aspects of "modernity." While *asserting* that all knowledge (and scientific) claims are relativistic fabrications that have no validity beyond their own textuality and that none (therefore) have any greater integrity than any others, those endorsing postmodernism subsequently (in a shell-game fashion) tout their own claims and agendas as equal, if not superior (à la postmodernist "authorities"), to all other (modernist) realms of thought and practice.

When contrasted with those more directly assuming postmodernist (pervasively cynical) orientations, many of those in cultural studies may be seen to engage in more sincere academic discourse. Still, those promoting the cultural studies framework have continued to let matters of epistemological coherence and methodological substance recede to the background. They routinely subordinate academic objectives to the task of achieving whatever variants (shifting with the fads and fashions of the times) of a marxist agenda that they might wish to impose on the situation(s) at hand. Accordingly, scholars may also be wary of those who encourage syntheses along these lines.

Thus, for instance, Norman Denzin's *Symbolic Interaction and Cultural Studies* (1992) represents an attempt to *"recast this framework [symbolic interaction] into a critical cultural studies framework" (154).* Although one could take issue with both Denzin's renderings of symbolic interaction (see Mead 1934; Blumer, 1969) and Denzin's (trendy, postmodernist) notions of ethnographic research,[45] Denzin errs most fundamentally in his attempt to *subordinate* the intersubjective essences of the human condition to the structuralist ideology of cultural studies.

In his apparent enthusiasm for a synthesis, Denzin uncritically adopts the frames of the marxist nexus (marxist, critical theory, postmodernist, feminist, cultural studies). Not only does Denzin prioritize class, race, and gender (i.e., treat these as objective arrangements that *structure* human relations) over human interchange, but he also assumes the practice of establishing closure on the theoretical and methodological dimensions of the social sciences whenever it might facilitate nexus agendas: *"it is not sufficient, as Marx argued so many times, to just understand the world; the key is to change it"* (Denzin, 1992:167). Depreciating or conveniently relinquishing the task of pursuing an intersubjectively informed social science in the promotion of nexus structuralisms and agendas, Denzin's proposed synthesis is flawed at a baseline level.

Marxist–Feminism

> *Feminism is a movement, and a set of beliefs, that problematize gender inequality. Feminists believe that women have been subordinated through men's greater power, variously expressed in different arenas. They value women's lives and concerns, and work to improve women's status.*
>
> —*DeVault, 1996:31*

> B: *Why do I feel that marxist-feminists are marxists who simply want to add women into their theories? . . .*
> A: *. . . I particularly object to marxist-feminists . . . because they think they've found the truth and they particularly want you to accept this. And so you spend all your time arguing in their terms . . .*
>
> —*Stanley and Wise, 1993:17*

Like others adopting a mixture of scholarly and advocacy perspectives, it is difficult to achieve clear or consistent images of the ways in which feminist social scientists approach the study of the human condition on either theoretical or methodological levels. Some, such as Fee (1983), suggest that it may be useful to characterize feminist scholars as liberal, radical, or marxist, while others, such as Stanley and Wise (1993), observe that there is very little consistency regarding "feminist theory."

Although feminism encompasses a much broader terrain then that implied by the term, *marxist-feminism,* this realm of activity has come to represent an important extension of the marxist legacy in academia. Because they invoke variants of the oppression thesis in ways that parallel or build more directly on traditional marxism, critical theory, postmodernist, and cultural studies approaches, many feminists fall within the marxist nexus, and their writings are subject to limitations and criticisms that parallel those in the nexus more generally.

Despite a great deal of concerted enterprise on the part of feminist scholars, matters of theory, concepts, research methods, and substantive inquiry remain in nebulous, if not contradictory, states. Far from achieving clarity or coherence, those defining themselves as feminists have assumed (and been debating) an increasingly broadened set of viewpoints. Thus, other than alleging that feminists (somehow) deal with matters of (purported) relevance to those of a female gender, it is difficult to achieve an operational definition that encompasses the great diversity of theoretical and methodological stances that feminists engage. Indeed, even this definition may be inadequate, for there are those (feminists) who posit that only by attending to community life in more direct, open, and encompassing fashions may one hope to understand the experiences of those within who are considered female. For those acknowledging that *people* are to be understood in terms of the totality of their experiences (activities, identities, relationships, and so forth) within the community, the oppression thesis is rendered problematic (if not obstructionist) in the quest for a more comprehensive appreciation of human lived experience.[46]

Methodologically, the issues are no less clouded. Reinharz (1992), Stanley and Wise (1993), Olesen (1994), and DeVault (1996) observe that there is virtually no consensus on what constitutes a feminist research methodology. Likewise, some feminist attempts to mimic postmodernist "methods" have only obscured the matter of focused (and responsible) scholarship. Indeed, a common tendency seems one of justifying (and accepting) any methodology used to foster the feminist agenda in some respect.[47]

While the centralizing perspective is that women represent a neglected and often deprivileged, if not oppressed, category of people in community life, the realms, extent, and foundations in which this is alleged to occur varies quite extensively (Stanley and Wise, 1993; Simon, 1995).

Likewise, considerable divergency of thought revolves around the concept of gender (and what it means to be "female" or "male") and in what ways notions of gender might be qualified or emphasized relative to other variables, structures, circumstances, or processes. This takes both those working more squarely within the feminist tradition and those attempting to understand these positions into what might be termed the "gender problematic."

On the surface, many feminists appear to subscribe to a "constructionist" (Berger and Luckmann, 1966) or "interactionist" (Mead, 1934) approach to gender.[48] For instance, Julia Wood (1994) explicitly acknowledges an interactionist viewpoint in her depiction of "gendered lives." People may be classified as male or female based on biological attributes but *much more fundamentally* they become "masculine" or "feminine" through association with others.

Denoting more generalized features of community interchange, the meanings and behaviors associated with gender are expected to vary relative to the culturally entrenched practices of people's role partners, both on a cross-cultural basis and over timeframes within. For Wood, then, gender denotes a product (and process) of the socially objectified milieus in which people find themselves, wherein people's social designations suggest subsequent lines of involvement and activity.

Still, because she maintains an overarching structuralist perspective,[49] Wood encounters difficulty sustaining a focus on community life as intersubjective accomplishment. Like a great many feminist scholars, Wood's treatment of gender represents a marshalling of issues and research that focus (and objectify) gender on contemporary and cross-cultural planes. Wood displays considerable sensitivity to the human condition more generally, but much of her analysis is developed, presented, and projected in binary (female/male) terms. Thus, it is difficult to miss the underlying conflict that she associates with, or builds into, the (relatively homogenized, essentially oppositional) female/male categories with which she works.

For Wood and many feminists, the prevailing images of gender are both pervasive and threatening (if not projected as highly sinister in some cases).[50] Because it is seen to define and promote genderized oppression, culture is seen as the problem in an enduring, fundamental sense. Most, if not all, prevailing modes of communication and action within community life are seen to contribute to ideologically gendered images (and oppressive relations) and therefore in need of extensive and enduring revision.

Consistent with the oppression thesis more generally, it has become relatively commonplace to dramatize evils associated with gender differentiation. Some feminists (e.g., Stanley and Wise, 1993; Sommers, 1994, 1995) explicitly have objected to the tendencies of other feminists to "hallucinate" gender crimes and to foster gender relations that reflect paranoic qualities. However, the emphasis on oppression (and exploitation) and the ensuing casting of categories of people into victim and villain roles has been widely employed to promote (e.g., foster recruitment, generate solidarity, encourage sacrifices) variants of the feminist movement. The resulting images of fear and distrust have also been used to encourage distancing on the part of newcomers (to academia) from nonfeminist traditions of thought and to generate images of, and focus attention on, safe, relevant, intellectual (feminist) havens. As Stanley and Wise (1993) note, practices of these sorts may well have enabled some feminists to promote their own careers (e.g., speakers, authors, academics, publishers, activists) in ways that otherwise may not have been possible.

Given her emphasis (and academic background), Dorothy Smith's (1990) statement, *The Conceptual Practices of Power,* suggests some noteworthy affinities with the present project. Fashioning what she terms an "insider's feminist materialism," Smith implements a version of structural oppression wherein she draws on marxist metaphors to build on and foster feminist consciousness. Smith also derives some inspiration from Marx's notions of ideological reasoning, as this might be applied to historical and social process considerations of organizations and relationships more generally. Still, Smith finds Marx shortsighted with respect to the study of women's lived experience. It is here that she turns to an ethnomethodological (Garfinkel, 1967) emphasis on the situated accomplishment of activity.

Acknowledging some ethnomethodological insights, Smith also takes issue with the postmodernist position on power formulated by Foucault and Derrida. Thus, Smith (1990:80) observes that power "is always a mobilization of people's connected activities." Still, despite the extensive potential of the ethnomethodological enterprise (see Garfinkel, 1967; Mehan and Wood, 1975; Zimmerman, 1978; Leiter, 1980; Coulon, 1995) into which Smith taps, her analysis and methodology is confused by her (marxist) oppression thesis and an insistence on singularly (uniquely) focusing on female experiences.

Given the wide (and increasing) dissensus of the theoretical, methodological, and advocacy positions among those identifying themselves as feminists, both inside and outside of academia (see Stanley and Wise, 1993; Benhabib, et al., 1995; Simon, 1995), it may be instructive at a more rudimentary level to indicate some affinities and disjunctures between variants of feminism and the position adopted here vis-à-vis the study of *power*.

As in the assessments of other approaches to the study of power, the primary criterion applied here is whether these conceptions enable researchers to examine the ways in which human interchange is accomplished in practice. Given the extended array of feminist positions on these matters, readers are best able to judge the proximity of the conceptual and methodological position of symbolic interaction with the particular authors with whom they may be familiar.

First, we are in full agreement with those scholars (feminists and others) who envision the self as a linguistic, intersubjectively informed, and reflective process that (a) is derived through interchange with others in the community and (b) achieves its fundamental existence in people's experiences with the world.[51] The position taken here is attentive to the multiple life-worlds that constitute the subcultural mosaic of community life and emphasizes the necessity of examining all human activity as situated accomplishment. Thus, in contrast to those who presume overarching cultural structures or rationalities, the emphasis is on the great many social arenas in which human experience assumes its most compelling (i.e., enacted) dimensions. This attentiveness to emphasis on the reflective, enacted, processual, and multifaceted nature of human interchange contrasts markedly with those who homogenize or polarize human relations at binary structural or categorical levels.

As well, whereas most feminists insist on the importance of attending (often exclusively) to women's viewpoints and experiences (see Stanley and Wise [1993] for a review), the position developed here insists on the importance of attending to *everyone's* viewpoints and experiences in highly detailed, participant-informed manners. This means representing the diversity and the similarities of viewpoints, practices, and interchanges across the range of those (people) engaged in any particular life-worlds, and attending to any changes or adjustments that these people make as they interact with others in the setting.

While some feminist-inspired research (e.g., Harrison and Laliberté,

1994; Wolf, 1994; McMahon, 1995; Whittier, 1995) is more consistent with the agenda of examining human experiences more directly (as instances of intersubjective accomplishment), those who adopt positions that are more structuralist (e.g., marxist, functionalist, factors-oriented, postmodernist) in emphasis, are subject to criticisms similar to those noted in considerations of those (underlying base) approaches (also see Stanley and Wise, 1993).

In contrast to those (marxist-feminists *and* others) who promote the viewpoints of particular groups or categories of people, the position taken here is notably nonpartisan. Likewise, it is concerned neither with fostering nor suppressing notions of justice, fair play, equality, independence, control, and the like. The objective, more modestly, but steadfastly, is one of achieving a greater comprehension of the human condition in *all* of its forms and variants of experience (and expression).

On a further, methodological, note, the viewpoint taken here acknowledges that members of categories (or typifications) who study members of the same categories may be advantaged as ethnographers in certain respects, but rejects the argument that only those who may be assigned to particular categories of people may adequately study others assigned to those categories. Without overlooking the advantages that sometimes accrue to researchers who may be envisioned as (particularized) categorical insiders,[52] much more central matters of ethnographic inquiry revolve around (a) the rapport and trust that particular researchers are able to achieve (beyond particularized category membership) with those in the setting, (b) researcher attentiveness, openness, and receptivity to *all* of the viewpoints and practices of the others, and (c) researcher concerns about representing the ethnographic other to the reader in the most direct, open, intersubjectively informed and balanced manners.[53]

The emphasis is on examining the experiences (viewpoints, practices, relationships) of any and all participants in the human community in careful, extended detail. This is not to deny or minimize the importance of any categories of people (that might be developed within community life) for people's interactions with one another. However, social scientists should be extremely careful not to prestucture their analyses by invoking typologies of people or their circumstances; to presume that people who might be assigned to one or other categories (as those typed as female, rich, elderly, or deviant, for instance) are homogeneous in the ways in which they interpret and engage the world. Likewise, it is essential that broader categories of people not be confused with those who are actively engaged in particular subcultural life-worlds or those embarking on various realms and instances of collective behavior. This is not to deny the great many category-related (feminist and other) associations that may exist for longer and shorter periods of time in the course of history or the importance of studying these as instances and realms of meaningful human interchange in the here and now.

To the contrary, if we are to develop a genuine intersubjective social science, it is deemed essential to attend to the views of all of those who engage the particular life-worlds (including feminist subcultures) that constitute community life and to carefully examine the ways that people involved in any realm of activity deal with all aspects of their circumstances (and relate to others in the community more generally). This should not only enable scholars to understand when and how people may define and experience things along gender, religious, age, or other categorical lines, but also to comprehend other aspects of people's involvements in community life in manners that are unencumbered by either presumptions of overarching structures, rationalities, or more singularized (vs. mosaical) notions of culture.[54]

Pluralist Offshoots (Mills, Dahrendorf, Lukes, and Clegg)

Although also inspired by marxist notions of conflict and domination, some other theorists have developed statements on power that largely fall outside the nexus variants discussed to this point. Noteworthy here are the works of C. Wright Mills, Ralph Dahrendorf, Stephen Lukes, and Stuart Clegg. Their popularity among social scientists appears to have receded somewhat relative to that currently associated with the proponents of postmodernism, cultural studies, and marxist-feminism, but these scholars continue to be envisioned as significant neomarxist theorists.

Attending to marxist images of domination in capitalist society, C. Wright Mills (1956) outlines what he envisions as the power elite in American society. In contrast to most marxists, Mills more explicitly discusses the interactive webs of people involved in top levels of political, corporate, and military spheres. Still, he does so in rather speculative terms. While making numerous interesting observations about these people's life-worlds and the ways the other strata in (American) society are subjected to the policies that those in the power elite establish, Mills's argument is sweepingly presumptive (and conspiratorial in emphasis).[55] He provides little in the way of sustained conceptual analysis that pertains to the ways in which people influence others in more precise, enacted terms.

Also envisioning conflict (and order) in more pluralist terms, Ralph Dahrendorf's (1959) tact is quite different from that of Mills. Like Mills, Dahrendorf envisions conflict in society as reflecting sets of interests (and a plurality of interest groups) that extend beyond property relations. However, Dahrendorf is more attentive to the uneven overlaps of people's interests (group affiliations) within community contexts.

When people belong to more distinct (i.e., nonoverlapping) sets of interest groups, Dahrendorf posits that conflict between people who are situated in these more exclusive constellations of interest groups within communities is apt to intensify. Likewise, he contends that when members of particular interest groups include people who have memberships in (other) groups that might otherwise be oppositional in thrust, these over-lapping affiliations will serve to moderate relations between members of the potentially oppositional interest groups included therein. In the first instance, multiple memberships within more distinct sectors of the community are thought to polarize people's viewpoints because they define more realms of interest disparity. In the second instance, the overlapping memberships may serve to diffuse potentially hostile relations (between oppositional interest groups) because the people involved have shared or sympathetic interests in other areas.

While still positing that class-related interests are central to configurations of these sorts, Dahrendorf introduces a theoretical context that recognizes notions of social change and stability that go beyond more prototypical (marxist) class conflict. In this way, Dahrendorf more explicitly draws attention to matters of routinization and authority, diversity of perspectives, multiple realms and forms of association, variable tendencies toward conflict, concerns with conflict resolution, and negotiated accommodations.

Although focused primarily on capitalist societies, Dahrendorf's analysis assumes a more generic quality, suggesting that notions of these sorts characterize all societies. Working with images of communities as consisting of a plurality of interest groups, Dahrendorf (1959: see especially 236–240) propositionalizes the conditions (e.g., intensity and violence of confrontations, radicalness of structural change) of class conflict. Pitched at a high level of abstraction, however, Dahrendorf provides minimal insight into the ways in which people collectively embark upon and experience missions of change and confrontation. Neither does he offer any methodology by which one might study the ways in which people engage one another in confrontational or accommodative exchanges.

Stephen Lukes (1974) also strives for a theory of power unencumbered by revolutionary agendas. In contrast to Mills and Dahrendorf, though, Lukes's work retains a more explicit commitment to structuralist control (and the dominant ideology thesis). Lukes envisions his major contribution to the field to be a three-dimensional theory of power. Here, Lukes argues not only for attending to (a) people's actual decision-making practices and the outcomes of these (which he terms one-dimensional power) and (b) people's non-decision-making practices, which may affect their experiences (two-dimensional power), but also (c) latent (systemic) conflict and the inference that people may not know their real interests (three-dimensional) even when they seem in position to act mindfully of their own interests. However, even Lukes is troubled by this third (latent or false consciousness) dimension. Thus, he openly concludes with an acknowledgement of the problematics of defining people's actual interests with respect to this third dimension of power. His initial commitment to a "radical" (Marx-Gramsci) vision of society encourages him to argue for notions of hegemony or the unconscious domination of people's thoughts and interests by virtue of their positions in the social structure, but Lukes does so only half-heartedly in the end.

Stuart Clegg (1989) may be seen as both extending and critiquing Lukes's statement by incorporating aspects of the thought of Machiavelli (see chapter 4) and Foucault into a theory of power. Clegg begins by acknowledging the enterprising, tactical features of Machiavelli's work as foundational to notions of power as an enacted phenomenon, but Clegg seems particularly inspired by Foucault's (1979) portrayal of multiple power sites (discussed earlier). Thus, Clegg takes issue with Lukes and other marxists who endorse a (singular) hegemonic or dominant ideology thesis.

Although Clegg does not subscribe to either the more cynical or more playful features of postmodernism, he is attentive to power as a multilocational essence. His solution is to encourage scholars to envision the study of power by reference to "circuits of power." These, he alleges, are most centrally connoted by the state, organization, and the market. Unfortunately, Clegg concludes on a rather nebulous note. He wants to draw attention to the desirability of viewing power in dialectic terms, denoting "irremediable entrapment within webs of meaning together with our organizational capacity to transform these" (Clegg, 1989:239–240). In the end, however, he offers little more than vaguely focused discourse.

Like Mills, Dahrendorf, and Lukes, Clegg strives for a more pluralistic notion of conflict (and power relations). At the same time, though, his analysis is of limited value to those interested in studying power an an enacted aspect of community life. As with these other authors, Clegg's work is suggestive in certain respects but it remains conceptually underdeveloped, empirically uninformed, and offers little in the way of methodological direction.

Robert Michels and Columbia Socialism

In *Political Parties* (1915), Robert Michels introduces the "iron law of oligarchy" to draw attention to the tendency on the part of those who have attained positions of power to concentrate and expand their realms of influence over others (while simultaneously restricting the opportunities of outsiders to share in the process).

Although Michels had been an active supporter of the socialist cause, his work represents a noteworthy (i.e., sobering) critique of the [utopian democracy] often associated with the marxist agenda of world (and regional) communism. Even proletariat-based bureaucracies, Michels contends, will become no more than oligarchical entities (effectively only replacing one set of elites with another) whenever they may succeed in over-throwing existing (capitalist or other) governments. Like Machiavelli (chapter 4), Michels alerts social scientists to the enterprising nature of control endeavors, but (still attending to marxist imagery) Michels focuses on the (structural) factors enabling elites to protect, maintain, and extend, their positions in bureaucratic settings.

Emphasizing "the factors associated with domination," Michels is vague about the ways that people actually consolidate their positions in practice. Still, his insightful treatment of the matters of centralizing and selectively shaping forms of domination in the public domain has inspired efforts on the part of others to pursue related themes (especially the contingencies and limitations of Michels's iron law of oligarchy) as these pertain to the democratic process in both larger and more specific contexts.

Michels could not have anticipated it when he developed this study, but his work (sharply critical as it is of socialist visions of social order) represented an avenue along which marxism would be incorporated more directly into mainstream American sociology. Michels's critique has very much receded into the background, but marxist sociology achieved considerable legitimation through its sponsorship by a group of scholars (associated with Columbia University) who used Michels's statement as an important stepping stone into mainstream sociology.

The works of Lipset et al. (1956), Lipset (1960), and Selznick (1966) represent noteworthy attempts to explore and extend Michels's iron law of oligarchy. Interestingly, as with Michels (1915), both Lipset and Selznick (see Lipset, 1996) had been extensively involved in promoting variants of the marxist agenda prior to their encounters with the iron law of oligarchy. Reflecting subsequent (graduate school) Columbia influences (especially Robert Merton and Paul Lazarsfeld), both Lipset and Selznick also display a structural-functionalist, quantitative orientation to the study of the centralization of power. Thus, while their analyses of the typographical union (Lipset et al. 1956) and the Tennessee Valley Association (Selznick, 1966) reflect case studies of sorts, they are heavily factors-driven and fail to achieve an attentiveness to constructed social process that sustained (intersubjective) ethnographic inquiry would have provided. Nevertheless, engaging central features of Michels's work, these studies were envisioned by many as consequential, if not exemplary, for empirically bridging notions of conflict and consensus in sociological thought.

Addressing these and related issues, Lipset's (1996) autobiographical account (especially when combined with Coser, 1976) is useful in helping to account for the broader assimilation of marxist, functionalist, and positivist emphases in contemporary mainstream sociology (and by inference, prevailing notions of power, therein). These themes intersect in the works of several scholars. Thus, beyond Talcott Parsons, Robert Merton, and Paul

Lazarsfeld, who were so pivotal in fostering an overarching functionalist, quantitative tone within the discipline, one might acknowledge some other people who significantly promoted one or more of these three emphases to the relative exclusion of other approaches to the study of community life. While one set of scholars such as Robert Bellah, James Coleman, Lewis Coser, Kingsley Davis, Wilbert Moore, Neil Smelser, and Robin Williams are more notably functionalist and positivist in orientation, others such as Daniel Bell, Nathan Glazer, Seymour Martin Lipset, Peter Rossi, and Philip Selznick are more distinctively marxist and positivist in their emphases.

Like Michels, these Columbia-trained socialist-sociologists were much more attentive to the importance of conceptual clarification and quantitative investigation than are most others in the nexus. However, while skeptical of marxist oppression theses and emphasizing focused scholarship over revolutionary thrusts in their sociological endeavors, the works of the Columbia group appear to have been consequential for fostering and legitimating versions of marxist thought in the social sciences more generally.

As with the *pluralist* offshoots more generally, the more scholarly (skeptical, empirical, theoretical) emphasis associated with the Columbia school seems to have receded into the background. Although frequently referenced, it is very much overshadowed by versions of nexus thought that have championed the oppression thesis and the pursuit of new moral orders.

Is There a Way Out?

As an explanatory 'system' it [Marxism] is dead, nor does it offer any 'method' that can be effectively used to interpret modern life, to foresee the future, or cultivate utopian projections. Contemporary Marxist literature, although plentiful in quantity, has a depressing air of sterility and helplessness, in so far as it is not purely historical.

—Kolakowski, 1978, V3: 529[56]

In his haste to promote a socialist moral order, Marx may have been prepared to presume that he understood the human condition. However, the rather inescapable conclusion is that the matter of understanding the human condition is not only far from being achieved but, effectively, has been substantially *hindered* by those who constitute the marxist nexus.

Although many of those caught up in the marxist nexus are capable scholars who seem sincere in their quest to develop an intersubjectivist social science, their other (and often more primary) objective of forging a new moral (socialist) order has resulted in a series of conceptual contradictions and methodological confusions that serve to frustrate, nullify, and obstruct, in major ways, the capacities of these scholars to pursue the task of developing a genuine, intersubjectively informed, social science.

Collectively, nexus scholars have spent so much time debating, extolling, explaining, qualifying, defending, repackaging, and "marketing," marxist frameworks of one or another sort that most have shown little regard or taken little time to examine the ways in which people *engage* one another within the here and now instances that constitute community life.

This is not to deny the potential utility of some of the insights and concepts that scholars working within the marxist nexus have developed over the years. However, none of the positions subsumed by those in the nexus is able to provide an adequate basis for developing a social science that is genuinely attentive to the social construction (i.e., intersubjective accomplishment) of human lived experience.

[handwritten: set up not to really discuss but rather to repudiate]

Conceptual Limitations

Before moving to chapter 3, it may be instructive to review the central thrusts and limitations of the preceding material relative to the parameters of the present volume.

First, we see that both the classical and contemporary authors considered in this chapter generally have been inattentive to power as it is *accomplished by people,* both in their daily routines and the more exceptional circumstances they may encounter. While concerned with power as an element of the human condition, most of these scholars have disregarded the ways in which *the people* who participate in the social worlds under consideration actually define, experience, and engage power (and related situations). Instead, these authors have not only *presumed* to know how people do things, but also "what motivates them."

Despite the generally explicit recognition of some diversity of viewpoints among people in society by all of these authors, most have presumed overarching rationalities that could somehow encompass all forms of human engagement.[57] Virtually all of the social theorists referenced here would agree that the "structures" that they discuss have been developed through human association. However, in their attempts to formulate general principles of social life, almost all have relegated human enterprise to such a low priority that they effectively treat organizational structures as if they have a "mind of their own." People very much become envisioned as pawns (with minor flexibilities) in the organizational structures of the societies in which they are embedded.

Likewise, although working with an assortment of assumptions and agendas, both the foundational theorists of power and most of those who have followed them rather extensively ignore *the intersubjective essence of the human condition.* There is very little appreciation of the socially constructed, linguistically mediated worlds that people actively engage on a day-to-day basis. Little consideration is given to the symbolic, interpreted, interactive life-worlds in which human beings operate.[58]

Rather centrally, the vast majority of theorists considered here *neglect (meaningful) human enterprise and interchange,* the ways in which community life is worked out *by people* on a "here and now" basis, across situations. Overall, there is a remarkable tendency on the part of power theorists to disregard the fundamental human enterprise entailed in building up, recruiting, sustaining, accepting, resisting, changing, and reformulating (all associational [and organizational]) routines.

There is also a pronounced *tendency to assume a power motif.* For many social theorists, power is seen as an omnipresent phenomenon, as inhering and enduring in the social structures that they (theorists) have objectified. Once these analysts envision situations in (structuralist) power terms, limited concern is given to the matter of ascertaining participant viewpoints or the idea that humans may have other concerns or interpretations than those revolving around "power."

Much theory about power has also been *developed at a "grand level"* and even that intended as "empirical" is so largely "factor" driven so that *"real people" are given little opportunity to "talk back to the theorist,"*[59] to tell the scholar about the life-worlds and situations that they experience. Despite the considerable effort that has gone into developing their statements on power, most of the theorists discussed here also *invoke undue closure in depicting the human condition.* Working with an assortment of agendas revolving around ideology and morality, prediction, control, rehabilitation and general enlightenment, or discontent and revolution, these scholars have attempted to *formulate theory about power* rather than to build notions of power by carefully attending to the ways in which people do things.

Somewhat relatedly there also is a *pronounced inattentiveness to the multiple realms of activity that constitute people's lives* on a day-to-day basis. In part, this disregard of what might be termed "the subcultural mosaic" (Prus, 1997b) reflects the earlier mentioned tendencies to ignore human intersubjectivity, enterprise, and accomplishment. At a foundational level, it means that most theorists of power have failed to recognize that it is *people* who become involved in, and work their ways through, a great many (differing) arenas of influence and resistance as *they accomplish community life.*[60]

Notes

1. For some other reviews of the literature on power, see Blau (1964), Nesbit (1966), Rose (1967), Lukes (1974), Wrong (1979), Ng (1980), Tedeschi and Rosenfeld (1980), Berger (1985), Seibold et al. (1985), Clegg (1989), and the edited collection that Olsen and Marger (1993) have assem-

bled. Readers may also find Martindale (1981) useful in providing background information and source references to many of the theorists cited here. Readers are cautioned, however, that the literature on power does not lend itself to neatly codified treatments. Ng (1980) provides the most comprehensive summary of this literature that I have been able to locate, but Berger (1985) and Seibold et al. (1985) offer two valuable statements on the treatment of power and influence in the fields of communications and (psychological) social psychology.

2. Focusing largely on "powerful" states, predominant governing arrangements in various nations, and major intergroup confrontations, Mann (1986, 1993) has undertaken the (exceedingly challenging) task of providing a historical overview of power. Encompassing such an enormously broad frame, Mann's (structuralist) analysis of power is inevitably vague, fragmented, and uneven. Whitmeyer (1997) is somewhat less critical, but also insists that Mann's conceptualization of social power requires a more concerted focus on the people whose behaviors are affected.

3. Attending to the history of social thought, Bogardus (1960) and Becker and Barnes (1978) provide an instructive starting point.

4. Drawing more on pictographs, hieroglyphics, and other indications of human encounters on the part of prehistoric peoples, the archaeological literature provides yet further (but more speculative) evidence of expressions of diversity and conflict.

5. While Machiavelli's (see chapter 4) work is often cited in discussions of power, most social theorists rather quickly dispense with his work by implying that it is "manipulative" in essence and endorses an elitist form of power that they find contemptible. Clegg (1989), who sets the tone for his volume by contrasting Hobbes's and Machiavelli's positions on power, represents an interesting exception. As indicated later, aspects of Machiavellian thought have been incorporated, albeit somewhat implicitly, in research in the (interrelated and predominantly experimentalist) realms of communications and social psychology (Berger, 1985; Seibold et al., 1985).

6. Readers familiar with the works of Plato and Aristotle (see chapter 4), for instance, will recognize that subsequent scholarly concerns with moral orders and the pursuit of organizational structures with which to achieve viable social orders represent resurrected (or reinvented) rather than novel issues. Also see Popper (1957), Gouldner (1965), and Becker and Barnes (1978).

7. Although Durkheim deals with power more implicitly than does Weber or Marx, Durkheim remains centrally committed to images of control via the collective conscience and the regulatory and integrative mechanisms established to maintain social order.

8. For a succinct but insightful discussion of power in Skinnerian behaviorism, see Ng (1980:143–149).

9. Not only is there some conceptual overlap among these categories, but most of the authors cited here address themes that extend beyond the categories into which they have been placed.

10. It is worth noting that Weber (1968:52) recognized the amorphous nature of power as thusly defined and expresses a preference for the term, *domination,* by which he means "the probability that a command with a specific intent will be obeyed by a given group of persons." It is not apparent, however, that his formulation of domination as a concept is much more effective in explaining the ways in which (influence) is achieved in actual practice.

11. This limitation is obscured (and confounded) by some other conceptual problems. For instance, although noting that charismatic leadership typically develops around crises situations that some group of people experience and entails extraordinary solutions to pressing problems, Weber insists on maintaining a religious base in developing his material. Likewise, he wishes to dispense with matters of rationality and tradition for "purer" charismatic episodes, even though (as he indicates) this seems questionable in many, if not most, instances.

12. While Weber is often credited with having introduced the concept of charisma to social theory, it may be worth noting that some of the early Greeks, such as Aristotle (*Rhetoric* and *De Rhetorica Ad Alexandrum*), and Isocrates (*To Demonicus* and *To Nicocles*) are much more attentive to the social constructed (imaged, presented, contested, and sustained) features of charisma (and character more generally) than is Weber.

13. For a more extended statement on the limitations of Weber's *verstehen* sociology, see Prus (1996b:40–45).

14. Readers interested in rationality as a human consideration are referred to Schutz (1943) and Dawson (1988). Because it examines the ways in which people "make sense" of their situations, much ethnography grapples with the matter of "achieving rationality in practice."

15. See Prus (1989a, 1989b, especially 1989b) for an empirically (ethnographically) grounded statement that serves as a critique of the rational-economic model as applied to people's practices in the marketplace.

16. Rogers (1974) also attempts to arrive at a systemic formulation of power. Although explicitly distinguishing "instrumental resources" (things used to reward, punish or persuade) from "infra-resources" (contingencies affecting the implementation or invocation of instrumental resources) and emphasizing a dyadic or relational viewpoint on power, Rogers's work does not move appreciably beyond Parsons.

17. For a more detailed consideration of Giddens's notions of structuration as these pertain to the interpretive tradition more generally, see Prus (1996b:91–94).

18. I do not intend to be harsh with Giddens (1976, 1984), who deals

with power somewhat in passing in an otherwise instructive conceptual scheme, and one that resonates in many respects with Blumerian interactionism. However, some further reconceptualization of Giddens's notions of power is essential for developing a more coherent theory of structuration. Like most people writing about power, Giddens lacks an ethnographic base on which to appreciate and depict power as interactive accomplishment. As a consequence, Giddens is not adequately attentive to either (a) the definitional nature of power or (b) the extent to which power is realized or accomplished through interaction (albeit often uneven and occasionally unilaterally) among the parties in the situation.

19. Readers may refer to Hollingshead (1949), Porter (1965), Duncan et al. (1972) for some illustrative monographs that deal with stratification [and power], or to Boyle (1989), Rossides (1990), and Grimes (1991) for some reviews of this literature. However, the mainstream sociological literature is replete with this sort of material (e.g., see most issues of the *American Journal of Sociology* or the *American Sociological Review* over the past fifty years). For an instructive interactionist appraisal of this literature, see Strauss (1971).

20. Those interested in early notions of "exchange (and equity) theory," albeit cast within a framework of justice, may wish to examine Aristotle's *Nicomachean Ethics* (especially Book V).

21. Ng (1980:173–185) presents a compact, but instructive, review of exchange theory. Lawler (1992), Skvoretz and Willer (1993), and Whitmeyer (1994) provide more recent updates of some of this literature, as well as fairly prototypic instances of the experimental research that has been generated around these notions.

22. Both Homans (1958) and Blau (1964) indicate a clear indebtedness to Georg Simmel (discussed later) with respect to notions of gaming and people's capacities to assume roles as agents in pursuing their interests. As well, both seem intent in pursuing a processual, reflective, interactive vision of exchange. However, this concern is notably overshadowed by their quest to establish rational-economic parameters of exchange. To date, exchange (and equity) theorists have not built theory that is (intersubjectively) attentive to the actual viewpoints and experiences of people involved in developing interchanges with others.

23. Although his work seems atheoretical in certain respects, one may also locate Hubert Blalock's (1989) volume on power in an exchange/ resource mobilization format. Epitomizing a structuralist, "factors" approach to the study of power, Blalock outlines massive sets of variables (most especially resources and ideological positions) that he associates with power, group mobilization, and conflict. While people are seen to have objectives, ideological viewpoints, and resources, Blalock's notions of "social

processes" very much refer to arrows in flow charts that connect particular sets of variables.

24. Because those within the nexus seem fond of relabeling (and repackaging) marxist agendas (as one or other variants fall into disfavor), it is impossible to establish a definitive listing of the approaches that might be encompassed within the marxist matrix.

25. Although Marx and Engels claimed that their approach (in contrast to "religion") is scientifically informed and focused, they were quick to establish closure on the scientific enterprise whenever it was convenient to do so. Many others in the nexus also claim (explicitly and implicitly) scientific, if not academic, status as a means of privileging themselves over religious spokespeople and others. Still, some within the broader matrix (most notably the "critical theorists" and the postmodernists) have deprivileged science to such an extent that they would seem to deny (other) marxists of any scientific or knowledge-based superiority over other viewpoints.

26. Readers are referred to Kolakowski (1978, vol. 1) for an extended consideration of the pre-Marxist roots of socialism (i.e., socialism as a more enduring social movement).

27. Popper (1957) and Gouldner (1965) suggest that a number of limitations associated with Marx might be located in Plato's *The Republic.* Likewise, some of the failings associated with Plato's (idealistic) state can be identified in the works of his student Aristotle (*Politics,* BII) who, overall, is much more attentive to the actualities of human affairs.

28. For a fuller statement on "ideological reproduction" or "class hegemony" as this pertains to the analysis of power, see Clegg (1989).

29. More sustained overviews of earlier socialist/communist/marxist (and related) agendas, are available in the multivolume works of Cole (1959) and (especially) Kolakowski (1978).

30. Carver (1983) provides a very thoughtful analysis of the Marx-Engels relationship as well as insightful portrayals of their individual (highly interrelated) and coauthored works. Kolakowski (1978, vol. 1) presents a valuable review of the writings of Marx and Engels.

31. As Carver (1983: especially 71–76) observes in reference to Marx and Engels: . . . *the authors announced a programme for studying 'the actual life-process and activity of the individuals of each epoch'. The methodology was to be empirical (no 'empty phrases'), though abstractions derived from observation would play a role in arranging material and indicating sequence. . . . (Carver, 1983:71)*

This research motif was a significant theme in both Marx and Engels's earlier (1845–46, then unpublished) *The German Ideology* and Marx's (1859) preface to *A Contribution to the Critique of Political Economy.* As has been the case since, however, this intention has been vastly disregarded relative to the concern with promoting "the destiny of the communist manifesto."

32. This is not to imply that the marxists have not attempted to devise various agendas and strategies for promoting local, regional, and world communism, but to observe that their mission is not one of developing a social science around the topic of influence work. Rather, their efforts in these areas may be paralleled in many respects to those of people promoting business ventures, religions, political parties, or military agendas.

33. Marx and Engels appear to have given rather limited consideration to the sorts of human relations that would exist after the purging of the capitalism. However, those who associate a life of autonomy and self-determination with the Marx-Engels scheme seem quite mistaken. To the contrary, as Nesbit (1966) observes, Engels (and Marx did not challenge him on this) envisions the kind of continuing authority bound up in the disciplines of technology and the large-scale factory:

> *All these workers, men, women, and children, are obliged to begin and finish their work at the hours fixed by the authority of the steam, which care nothing for individual autonomy. . . . [T]he will of the single individual will always have to subordinate itself, which means that questions are settled in an authoritarian way. The automatic machinery of a big factory is much more despotic than the small capitalists who employ workers ever have been. . . . If man, by dint of his knowledge and inventive genius, has subdued the forces of nature, the latter avenge themselves upon him by subjecting him, in so far as he employs them, to a veritable despotism, independent of all social organization. Wanting to abolish authority in large-scale industry is tantamount to wanting to abolish industry itself, to destroy the power loom in order to return to the spinning wheel. (Nesbit, 1966: 140)*

34. The work of Robert Michels (1962 [1915]) represents a notable exception as does some of the dialogue that this volume and the related works that it stimulated in (the then communist state of) Poland (see Lipset in Michels, 1962:21).

35. Although Marx and Engels (e.g., see Avineri, 1969; Carver, 1983) spoke clearly of the mission of global communism and were quite critical of those they saw embarking on premature or petty side agendas, many marxists have pursued variants of local or situated agendas that would be difficult to reconcile with the vision that Marx and Engels projected.

36. It would seem highly productive to embark on an ethnographic study of "marxism as a social movement (or sets thereof)" attending to the strategic definitions and tactical adjustments that members of this overlapping set of subcultures have developed, both in their dealings with one another and in their dealings with outsiders.

37. For some other interactionist critiques of the postmodernist/poststructuralist approach to the social sciences, see Best (1995), Charmaz

(1995), Sanders (1995), Maines (1996a, 1996b), Dunn (1997), and Lyman (1997).

38. As Clegg (1989) observes, Foucault rejects both Hobbesian and Marxist notions of sovereign control, the idea that someone or some group can control the thoughts and interests of the community at large. The image promoted is one of power taking shape in the multiple and diverse associations and discourses that develop around certain kinds of situations.

39. Jean-Francois Lyotard (1984), another disaffected marxist, also argues against the tendency to invoke grand narratives in the human quest for knowledge (and scientific endeavor). In a manner somewhat paralleling Foucault, Lyotard encourages a recognition of pluralistic, localized power sites each characterized by ongoing concerns (and struggles) with legitimating themselves through realms of (reciprocally reinforcing) discourse. Still, while attending to the legitimation process in general terms (Lyotard, 1984: especially 47), he seems more intent on promoting a version of science (and knowledge) characterized by the search for discrepancies than outlining the processes by which knowledge (and the power implied therein) is accomplished by people in this and that (local) setting.

40. For an elaboration of the obdurate reality (Blumer, 1969) experienced by human beings, see Prus and Dawson (1996).

41. Lukács, Korsch, Horkheimer, Adorno, and Marcuse are among the better known contributors to the (neomarxist) Frankfurt school whose beginning may be situated in the 1920s. Readers interested in this tradition may find it instructive to refer to the historian Leszek Kolakowski (1978, vol. 3) for a detailed discussion of critical theory and related marxist developments in the twentieth century. Those familiar with "critical theory" (which also incorporates aspects of the thought of Nietzsche and Freud) will find much here that resonates with, and clearly predates, the purportedly "new" (French) postmodernism.

42. Noting that "cultural studies" has developed somewhat haphazardly, Hall (1992) cites his 1974 paper on "Marx's notes on Method . . ." as the statement that may have provided the central kernel for this variant (of the marxist nexus). It should be observed, though, that Hall's work was centrally buttressed by Williams's (1977) *Marxism and Literature*. Here, Williams engages two themes, organized roughly around the two parts of this book. The first theme is a sophisticated "philosophical dance" with marxism, whereby Williams tries to maintain the integrity of fundamental marxism by extensive qualification of marxist concepts and a diffusion of Marx and Engels's views of revolutionary upheaval. The second theme is intended to foster an appreciation of culture through an examination of linguistic and artistic expression of all manners (i.e., literature in a very broad sense). Although Williams highlights a number of issues to which scholars interested in literature might attend, his analyses of authors, forms,

genres, and mediums are highly rudimentary. Methodologically (and epistemologically), Williams's portrayal of both cultural theory (employing sophisticated marxist analysis) and literary theory (comparatively nebulous) is of limited utility. Nevertheless, Williams's work, along with Hall's "personification" of cultural studies seems to have provided much of the preliminary impetus for this realm of endeavor.

43. Although the fusion of moralistic agendas and the social science enterprise has plagued all of those working in the marxist nexus, the Frankfurt (critical theory) school and (especially) the postmodernists have been the most vocal in attempting to disprivilege the (entire) scientific enterprise in attempts to justify their own positions.

44. The Freudian "bogey-man" has haunted marxism for some time, most notably through the Frankfurt (Critical Theory) school, but has seen a resurgence in the writings of some feminists and postmodernists.

45. For a more detailed critique of Denzin's attempt to do "postmodernist ethnography," see Dawson and Prus (1993a, 1993b) and Prus (1996b).

46. For variants on these themes, see Stanley and Wise (1993) and Simon (1995).

47. Ehrlich (1976), for example, who argues that one may distinguish between "good" and "bad" research, insists that the most vital criterion for good feminist research is that it encourage political change in profeminist directions. This position is not shared by all feminists (e.g., Stanley and Wise, 1993; Simon, 1995), but the tendency to tolerate (if not encourage) work that is supportive of the agenda of political change, as within the nexus more generally, is widespread among marxist-feminists.

48. It might be noted that a somewhat parallel position, pointing to the linguistic, relativistic, socially constructed nature of [gender-sex roles] was articulated some decades ago by the symbolic interactionist Manford Kuhn in a critique of the Kinsey studies on sexuality:

> *Sex acts, sexual objects, sexual partners (human or otherwise) like all other objects toward which human beings behave are* social objects; *that is, they have meanings because meanings are assigned to them by the groups of which human beings are members . . . there is nothing in the physiology of man which gives any dependable clue as to what patterns of activity will be followed toward them. The meanings of these social objects are mediated by means of language just as in the case of all other social objects . . . it is even most likely that differences between male and female sexual activity in our own society are attributable to the* social *sex role differentiation rather than to anatomical or physiological differences between the sexes. (M. Kuhn, 1954:123)*

49. A predominant tendency on the part of those adopting structuralist viewpoints is to use gender (m/f) as a causal or explanatory factor (i.e., independent variable) in accounting for certain behaviors or other outcomes (dependent variables). In many cases, gender is treated as the primary explanatory concept.

50. Some other feminists are much less subtle in their viewpoints on gender and their proposals for social action than is Wood. Marilyn French (1992), for instance, takes the viewpoint that men have in all places and all times waged a *war* against women. Alleging that every known society (historical and cross-cultural) only represents another (expressive) variant of men's war against women, the problem for French (and those who share her mindset) is not one of culture as much as the implied biological determinism that is presumed to permeate (and structure) every single realm of male-female (cultural) relations. She openly encourages women to "fight back on every front" to the serious, sustained, sinister war that she portrays in her writings.

51. As Stanley and Wise (1993) observe, a great deal of feminist theory is structuralist/positivist in its emphasis. Thus, despite commonplace claims that particular versions of feminist theory are hermeneutically informed, only in a relatively small proportion of cases are these notions sustained at more fundamental (intersubjectivist) levels.

52. It should also be appreciated that while insider-outsider status may be envisioned along singular lines (such as one's biological sex-typing or other categorical memberships), the people "out there" typically define others (researchers included) in a *plurality* of ways, of which some category (presumed central or beneficial to the researcher) may or may not be seen as especially important to those encountering the researcher.

Indeed, parallel category memberships sometimes represent obstacles to particular lines of association (and disclosure). Certain advantages may accrue to researchers in the field who are viewed as (a) outsiders in some regard or (b) unencumbered by particular category or group loyalties, moralities, or agendas. This includes researcher interchanges with people who are intensively (and ideologically) caught up in the particular life-worlds under study.

Much more important than the issue of whether one shares various categorical memberships with those one encounters is whether researchers achieve an openness with the other that is conducive to a sustained appreciation of the life-world (experiences and activities) of the other.

53. For a further elaboration of processes and problematics of doing ethnographic research, see Becker (1970), Lofland and Lofland (1995), and Prus (1997b).

54. A more extended consideration of subcultural mosaics and inter-

subjective realities, along with the many ethnographic research sites that these notions suggest is available in Prus (1997b).

55. Rose (1967) provides a valuable, extended consideration (and critique) of both Floyd Hunter's (1953, 1959) and C. W. Mills's (1956) economic-elite-dominance theses, as these notions might be applied to American society. Whereas Rose addresses the pluralistic nature of political influence in the United States, the emphasis in the present volume is on achieving a conceptualization of power that would lend itself to ethnographic inquiry in any community (or societal) context.

56. Clearly, this commentary on the value of marxist thought as an analytical tool within the social sciences is not intended to deny the use of marxist thought as a political device. As Kolakowski (1978, vol. 3:529–530) observes, *"The effectiveness of Marxism as an instrument of political mobilization is quite another matter. . . . Communists have shown great skill in exploiting this state of mind and channelling aggressive feelings in various directions according to circumstances, using fragments of Marxist language to suit their purpose."*

57. Emphasizing pluralities of disciplinary power sites and local institutional settings, Foucault and Lyotard might also seem to be notable exceptions, but they still maintain a heavy structuralist emphasis with respect to these individualized power sites. The exchange theorists (see Homans [1958] and Blau [1964], for instance), likewise, see their notions as applicable to any variety of social realms, but they remain committed to particular forms of (structuralist) rationality as appropriate for the society at large.

58. Although Foucault and many other postmodernists seem to insist on the centrality of human discourse and reflectivity, they rather simultaneously disregard the essential role of human interaction, intersubjectivity and human activity (meaningful enterprise and emergent interchange) for the human condition (see Dawson and Prus, 1993a, 1993b, 1995; Prus, 1996b; Prus and Dawson, 1996).

59. Denoting living, thinking, interacting beings who actively engage the world on a here and now basis, the notion of "real people" is contrasted with the representations or presumed prototypic people (the psychological and sociological "dopes"—Garfinkel, 1967) who presumably populate the worlds imagined by those fostering structuralist (and postmodernist) analyses.

60. As indicated in "a reformulation of the cultural problematic" (Prus, 1997b), part of the problem of conceptualizing power (and comprehending the human condition more generally) revolves around a rather common tendency to envision culture in more singularistic or homogeneic terms. Some postmodernists (e.g., Foucault, Lyotard) and cultural studies scholars (e.g., Williams, 1977; Hall, 1992) seem attentive to some multi-contextual features of societies, but these authors have very much dis-

regarded both the ways in which people *engage* the particular life-worlds in which they find themselves and the more generic or cross-contextual features of human enterprise (and interchange) that reflect activities of those sorts.

3 Tactical Themes in the Social Sciences

Your political scientist thinks he is going a long way afield and that he is meritoriously portraying "actual" government when he inserts in his work some remarks on the machine, the boss, and the practical virtues and vices of men practicing politics.

—*Bentley, 1908:162*

In a very direct manner, this chapter continues the task of providing a baseline overview of the literature on power. Whereas chapter 2 dealt with (1) rational order structuralism and (2) the marxist nexus, this chapter focuses on (3) the compliance and influence literature in psychology, (4) collectivist approaches, (5) interest group dynamics, (6) mass communication themes, and (7) community studies. The materials introduced in this section evidence a greater overall emphasis on tactical aspects of power relations, but the chapter break was generated more by a concern with presentational matters than consistently sharp conceptual shifts.

Our primary anchorage point remains constant. Like the materials introduced in chapter 2, the works outlined here will be subject to one basic criterion: *does the approach* (theoretical viewpoint, conceptual scheme, methodology) *under consideration enable us to envision and study the ways in which human interchange is worked out in the ongoing instances of the here and now in which community life takes place?*

The Compliance and Influence Literature in Psychology

Despite a profound emphasis on matters of power and control, the theorists considered in chapter 2 have given relatively little attention to the ways in which people (as tacticians) endeavor to "get their own way" (individually or collectively) in dealing with others. Everyone whose work has been discussed to this point seems (at least implicitly) aware of people's capacities to act reflectively, resourcefully, collectively on occasions, and in manners that outstrip their "resources," but the predominant emphasis has been to resort to "structures" of various sorts rather than human enterprise in explaining power.

The idea that "people affect one another," as implied by the terms *compliance* and *influence,* is the feature that most centrally distinguishes social psychology from the field of psychology more generally. Still, embedded within a discipline that is deeply mired in positivist epistemology (i.e., characterized by notions of causation, objectification, quantification, and experimentation), those working in psychological social psychology have been highly structuralist (i.e., invoking organizational factors, environmental stimuli, roles, personality traits, attitudes and values, perceptions) in their emphasis.[1]

Most of this literature, thus, involves a quest for factors or variables intended to enable psychologists to explain, if not also to predict and control, human behavior. As a result, most considerations of power or influence deal with "source (tactician) characteristics," "target characteristics," or "situational determinants or conduciveness" (e.g., Tedeschi and Bonoma, 1972; Berger, 1985; Seibold et al., 1985). What has been missing for the most part in psychological social psychology (rather oddly) is an attentiveness to ongoing human interpretive practices, enterprise, and interaction.

Still, some scholars working in psychological social psychology have attempted to deal with interpersonal tactics on a more explicit basis. Building somewhat on Goffman (1959), Thibault and Kelly (1959), and Homans (1961), Edward Jones's (1964) work on *Ingratiation* is noteworthy here, as is James Tedeschi's (1972) edited volume, *The Social Influence Process.* Some other (quantitative) research on interpersonal tactics has been pursued by Marwell and Schmitt (1967), Wood et al. (1967), Finley and Humphries (1974), Clark and Delia (1976), Falbo and Peplau (1980), Kipnis et al. (1980), Rule et al. (1985), and Howard et al. (1986).

While Jones and Tedeschi also deal with target reactions, most of this literature has concentrated on tactician options. Those working in this genre typically invoke listings of tactician orientations and practices, such as threats, rewards, coercion, ingratiation, blocking, reasoning, withdrawal, bargaining, invoking norms, and forming coalitions. In these respects (and like the exchange theorists discussed in chapter 2), they do address matters of tactician enterprise. However, these scholars have concentrated primarily on studies of the (frequency) distributions of tactics within various subpopulations (e.g., as defined by age, gender, positional relationship) and the factors the researchers think might dispose people to use particular tactics.

This material is suggestive in certain senses, but it does not provide much insight into people's experiences (or activities) as tacticians. Even less consideration is directed toward people's experiences as targets, the interchanges that take place between involved parties, the ways in which activities may be interpreted by the various parties involved, or the adjustments that people make (individually and collectively) to each other as their interchanges unfold. However, despite these limitations, this material stands out in psychology as having been attentive to some tactical features of human interchange.

Although somewhat marginal to the field of psychology, two relatively recent statements on rhetoric are pertinent to the literature on power (and influence). Whereas most contemporary theory dealing with power fails to recognize the classical (Greco-Roman) tradition associated with the study of rhetoric, the Cooper and Nothstine (1992) and Billig (1996) volumes are notable exceptions.

Directly grounding the study of persuasion in Aristotle's *Rhetoric,* Martha Cooper and William Nothstine (1992) attend to concepts such as (in their terms) motivation, credibility and image management, the symbolist perspective, the institutional perspective, persuasive campaigns, social movements, and ideology. While Cooper and Nothstine incorporate some philosophical themes into their analysis and display considerable familiarity with the psychological literature, this volume is remarkably inattentive to the sociological literature that deals directly with many closely related topics. See, for instance, matters of impression management (Goffman, 1959; Klapp, 1964), symbolic interaction (Mead, 1934; Blumer, 1969) and the corpus of ethnographic materials associated with the interactionist tradition, and reality construction theory (Schutz, 1962, 1964; Berger and Luckmann, 1966). The result, somewhat ironically, is a relative disregard of rhetoric as an *enacted* (engaged and experienced) realm of interchange. Even so, this volume importantly takes psychology more directly into the realm of contested meanings as intersubjective accomplishment, or at least suggests a base on which this might be pursued.

Michael Billig (1996) also grounds the psychological study of influence work in the classics (particularly Plato, Aristotle, and Protagoras). Billig's critique of the neglect of rhetoric on the part of psychologists is highly pertinent, as relatedly are the shortcomings that he associates with the experimental method. However, Billig takes his analysis yet further afield by attempting to contemporize his own theorizing with the postmodernist turn. Billig is quite correct in tracing postmodernist subjectivity (and the related notion of multivocal voices) back to some of the early sophists (notably Protagoras [c. 490–420 B.C.]). Still, even though Billig astutely works his way through these literatures (psychological, classical, and postmodernist) and concludes by emphasizing the "dialectic spirit of contradiction," he provides minimal direction (conceptual and methodological tools) for examining the ways in which arguing, thinking, and acting are accomplished in practice.

Collectivist Approaches

The term *collectivist approaches* is used to encompass another set of scholars, many of whom might also be seen to fall under rational order structuralism. What differentiates those discussed here from the latter, though, are more explicit recognitions (variously) of (a) pluralist positions in the quest for community life, (b) tactical enactments (and engagements), and (c) social process. To some extent, the emphasis is a matter of degree, for both sets of authors exhibit considerable diversity. Generally speaking, however, the present set of scholars evidence a greater attentiveness to conflict as a central dimension of community life. On an overall basis, though, they differ quite notably from most of those in the marxist nexus. Thus, the scholars introduced here (a) tend to be more attentive to notions of pluralistic social orders and (b) are intent on developing theory that would enable one to comprehend a broader array of communities rather than using theory to foster socialist/communist agendas.

Included herein are considerations of the writings of Georg Simmel and Robert Park, and some of those attending to their work, as well as those focusing on the field of collective behavior more generally. Readers may also note some affinities of these scholars with those discussed under the rubric of purveyors of tactical advice (in chapter 4). Indeed, some of those whose works are discussed here have derived considerable inspiration from those assuming this latter orientation. At the same time, though, concerns with advice tend to be offset or dominated by attempts to develop more generic or cross-contextual appreciations of the human condition on the part of those whose work is discussed here. These scholars also display some affinities with the community studies scholars discussed later in this chapter. However, while those assuming collectivist approaches tend to be more focused conceptually than are the community studies people, few have ventured out into the community on any sustained ethnographic basis.

Georg Simmel

Envisioning society as constituted by people involved in shifting and diverse "webs of affiliation" and participating in a wide variety of "forms of association," Georg Simmel (1858–1918) lays the groundwork for a broader, thoroughly pluralistic vision of community life.

For Simmel, the community is a setting in which groups and individuals with diverse interests (and capacities) engage one another in cooperative, conflictual, competitive, compromised, and playful manners. Although Simmel never developed a methodology for empirically studying ongoing group life, his emphasis on the forms of association is not only pertinent to power relations, but also represents a profoundly generic, processual approach to the study of community interchange.

In developing his work, Simmel acknowledges human capacities for tactical endeavor, secrecy, deception, coalitions, and process. He also recognizes the interdependencies (and bondedness) of people who engage one another in community life. Thus, for instance, Simmel not only distinguishes (a) domination under a principle from (b) domination under a plurality and (c) domination by an individual, but emphasizes the *fundamental interdependence* of (presumed) leaders and followers in all situations of influence.

Simmel's relevance for the study of human interchange does not stop here. Observing that content provides the inevitable background material of community life, Simmel is very much concerned about developing an abstracted set of social processes (e.g., cooperation, conflict, competition, playfulness, secrecy) that would extend across the entire range of human relations.[2]

Robert Park

One finds a partial extension of Simmel's scholarship in the works of Robert Park (Park, 1972 [1904]; Park and Burgess, 1921). Park (1864–1944) not only introduced the term *collective behavior* to sociology, but also was instrumental in shaping subsequent conceptualizations of collective behavior in the literature. Since Park's views clearly dominated the Park-Burgess formulations of collective behavior, it is worth noting that Park attempted to synthesize fragments of Simmel's work with that of Gustave LeBon, Gabriel Tarde, Wilhelm Windelband, and others (see Park, 1972).

Park and Burgess drew attention to some pluralistic dimensions of social order as well as fundamental features of coordination, conflict, control, and resistance. However, because of the peculiar mix of scholars to which Park attended, both Park and Burgess and those who followed them became ensnared in a series of side issues that confounded (and partially displaced) the processual emphasis associated with Simmel's work. These issues revolve around crowd minds, the irrationality and pathology of the crowd, the differences between groups and crowds, and the like (see Couch, 1968). Those following Park also became absorbed in developing typologies of modes of collective behavior and subtheories to account for these variants, thereby removing themselves somewhat from a more direct emphasis on social process.

Over the past several decades the field of collective behavior has assumed a number of directions, perhaps most notably reflecting: the extension of Park's work by Herbert Blumer (1939); Smelser's (1962) "value-added" theory; the celebrity and identity seekership motifs of Orrin Klapp (1964, 1969); the introduction of "resource mobilization theory" (McCarthy and Zald, 1977); and the development of some more structurally oriented interactionist analyses of collective behavior (reflecting the writings of Carl Couch, Clark McPhail, Ralph Turner, Lewis Killian, and their associates). It is to these authors that we now turn.

Herbert Blumer

The agenda set by Robert Park found its most direct and potent expression in Herbert Blumer's (1939) outline of the field of collective behavior. In pursuing this task, Blumer discusses circular reactions, social unrest, acting and expressive crowds, mass behaviors, publics and such, effectively establishing a new, dynamic field within sociology. Attending to process *in Park's terms,* however, Blumer emphasizes the contagious, spontaneous, irrational, unwitting features of the behavior of crowds and other emergent public gatherings. This, it should be noted, is inconsistent with the more focused symbolic interactionism that Blumer develops by building on Mead's work.[3] Presenting an extended typology of collective behavior, Blumer (1939) fails to acknowledge (in more characteristically Blumerian [1928, 1969, 1971] terms) the ways in which people make sense of, assemble with, and interact with (persuade and resist) one another.

Like those writing before him, Blumer's (1939) writings on collective behavior lack intimate familiarity (i.e., ethnographic intersubjectivity) with those participating in these endeavors. Nevertheless, and however atypical of his other (Meadian influenced) work that Blumer's (1939) outline of collective behavior may have been, this statement became central to the field. In addition to its (essentially nonrevised) reappearances in various editions of both the Park (1939) and Lee (1951, 1955, 1969) editions of *Principles of Sociology,* parts of Blumer's (1939) outline have appeared in many other publications.

In a later statement, on "social problems as collective behavior," Blumer (1971) largely divests himself of Park's influence. Here, Blumer emphasizes the necessity of attending to the *definitional* and *interactional* features of collective behavior. Blumer wrote this statement in clear opposition to those scholars who allege that instances of collective behavior are the products of, or are caused by, particular objective or structural conditions or notions of relative deprivation. Likewise, he points to the variety of perspectives (and rationalities) that people may assume and the meaningfully constructed enterprise (strategic alignments, resistances, adjustments) in which the parties involved may engage.

Depicting a "natural history" of social problems, Blumer delineates five stages or subprocesses: (a) emergence (initial awareness and publicity); (b) legitimation (public and official acknowledgement); (c) attempts to mobilize for action (assess information, suggestions, and probabilities); (d) formation of an official plan; and (e) implementation of the official plan (and the problematics of doing so).

At each point, Blumer observes, the process is negotiable and problematic, with outcomes reflecting potentially wide assortments of interchange and the myriad of knowledge, beliefs, resources, and political maneuverings that various parties (as persons and groups) invoke as they endeavor to (a) promote their interests relative to the issues at hand and (b) resist those taking action that appears to be at variance from their viewpoints.[4]

Throughout his (1971) statement, Blumer emphasizes the necessity of attending to people's (potentially multiple) perspectives, ongoing enterprise, the problematics of internal coordination, the influence work that people may direct toward others (insiders and outsiders), the wide range of resistances that insiders, targets, and outside third parties may invoke, and the ensuing adjustments of various interacting units to one another. It is to issues of these sorts that Blumer encourages social scientists to attend as they examine the ways in which macro-level expressions of community life take shape within interactional contexts. However, as the discussion following indicates, most scholars in collective behavior, like Blumer (1939) via Park, have also become caught up in the broader structural (and typological) legacy.[5]

Neil Smelser

In developing his theory of collective behavior, Neil Smelser (1962) envisions collective behavior occurrences (i.e., "noninstitutionalized behavior," such as panics, riots, crazes, rumor transmission) as social products to be explained by reference to the broader structural and cultural features characterizing the particular periods in which these events take place. While acknowledging Blumer's (1951 [1939]) material in certain respects, Smelser's work is much more attentive in its overall emphasis to Parsonian functionalism.

Attempting to account for instances of collective behavior, thus, Smelser makes reference to (1) structural conduciveness (e.g., broad economic pressures, social change); (2) structural strain (wherein people experience losses or deprivations); (3) growth of generalized beliefs that deal with these issues (and ensuing fears, hostilities, apprehensions); (4) precipitating factors (or events that are interpreted as dramatically epitomizing the fears, losses, and so on, associated with elements 1, 2, and 3); (5) mobilization of participants for action (role of leaders, instigators); and (6) the operation of social control.

Smelser sees these factors as taking shape in terms of a natural history or sequencing of stages, with people's involvements at each point (not determining the next stage as much as) increasing the probability that particular events will follow. He uses the term, *value added* as an economic metaphor to denote the eventual, more complete pattern or product that emerges as one stage contributes to the shaping of the next in a now altered but more definable manner.[6]

In a festschrift tribute to Ralph Turner (who assumes a role-theory orientation toward collective behavior), Smelser (1994) provides a very succinct set of contrasts between his own work on collective behavior and that of the more interactionist (albeit eclectically) oriented Turner (discussed later). First, while locating Turner's roots partially within the Chicago tradition (Everett Hughes, Louis Wirth, and Herbert Blumer), Smelser cites Parsons as his own major mentor and notes his lack of exposure to Meadian social psychology. Second, Smelser observes that where the Turner (and Lewis Killian) approach is more attentive to "interacting persons," his emphasis is on the "factors" associated with the occurrence of certain events. Third, Smelser says that whereas he intends to emphasize the affective (e.g., anxiety, wish fulfilment, anger) features of collective behavior, Turner and Killian stress the cognitive, definitional aspects of people's experiences. Smelser also claims to have striven for a "theory" of collective behavior as opposed to developing a "perspective" (Turner and Killian, 1972) for approaching the phenomenon. Finally, and in contrast to Turner and Killian's emphasis on developmental processes, Smelser states that he wanted to identify the content and structure of collective events as well as the conditions and causes of collective behavior.

Orrin Klapp

Orrin Klapp's (1964, 1969, 1971) writings denote a significant conceptual affinity with the work of Simmel, Park, and Blumer. Focusing on the dynamics of people achieving celebrity status, the Chicago-trained Klapp (1964, 1971) draws attention to the socially constructed nature of "heroes, villains, and fools." He addresses the interpretive, dynamic, adjustive actor-audience interchanges that revolve around presented, acknowledged, contested and adjusted images on the part of those involved. Although relatively neglected, Klapp's work on "social types" offers much conceptual insight vis-à-vis the achievement, maintenance, and loss of celebrity (political and other) status in the community.

In *The Collective Search for Identity*, Klapp (1969) considers people's search for a (meaningful) sense of self through their involvements in collective ventures. Klapp's data (mostly drawn from media accounts) is some distance removed from those participating in the life-worlds of which he writes, but Klapp provides some highly suggestive process-oriented material on people's involvements in fashions, cults, and crusades.[7]

Albeit laying in the shadows for some years, Klapp's (1969) statement also displays an affinity with a more recent interest in "new social movements" and the recognition that people's identities are somehow linked to social movements.[8] While the "newness" aspect of new social movements reflects an analytical shift rather than any especially new forms of human association, an attentiveness to people's senses of self-engagement in social movements is long overdue.[9] Readers may refer to the edited collections of Morris and Mueller (1992) and Larana, Johnston, and Gusfield (1994) for instances of the new social movements literature. This material also evidences a greater appreciation of the preexisting interconnectedness (e.g., relationships, coalitions, existing organizations) of the persons and groups who constitute social movements at given points in time (Johnston et al., 1994:24–28).

John McCarthy and Mayer Zald

Attending more explicitly to the problems that social movement activists have expressed about trying to maintain viable operations, John McCarthy and Mayer Zald (1977) criticize Smelser and others for presuming both (a) that objective sets of conditions predispose people to engage in collective behavior and (b) that people hold generalized sets of beliefs that foster these alignments. Under the rubric of *resource mobilization theory*,[10] McCarthy and Zald argue that any group with access to resources may be in a position to define problems, create discontent, and mobilize others in ways that generate instances of collective behavior (regardless of "objective conditions" or existing belief structures). In addition to acknowledging a wide range of things that participants may use as "resources," McCarthy and Zald also draw attention to the relationship of social movements to the media and other parties in the community, as well as to the interaction between various social movement organizations.[11,12]

On the surface, resource mobilization theory might seem very promising for those attending to the enterprising or activity dimensions of human group life. However, despite an expressed regard for a number of the socially constructed features of collective behavior, those working in this tradition largely presume rational-economic (costs, benefits, expectations) notions of motivation and emphasize the structural conditions affecting the forms, resource flows, and survival of social movement organizations.

These authors have been much more attentive to the theories and circumstances of activists, such as Mao, Lenin, and Alinsky (McCarthy and Zald, 1977), than most other structuralists, and have endeavored to incorporate social process into their theories. Still, attempting to formulate structural theories of process that pertain to organizational longevity and success, almost all resource mobilization theory (and research) has been developed "from a distance" (denoting historical or survey analysis of social trends, media renditions, and content analysis).

Despite the imagery associated with mobilization that these theorists introduce (e.g., matters of arousing discontent, recruiting and coordinating members, encountering and dealing with resistance, and developing coalitions), almost no ethnographic work has been conducted mindful of the ways in which those within social movement organizations actually engage other people within or outside these associations. Resource mobilization theorists have alerted scholars to some of the dynamics of interchange involving social movement organizations, but they have given little consideration to the situated examination of the interpretive, enterprising, interactive features of human relations that undergird all of these matters.[13]

Bert Klandermans and John Lofland

More extended overviews of the social movement organization (SMO) and the related resource mobilization theory (RMT) literature can be found in the works of Bert Klandermans and John Lofland who attempt to develop models of the processes and factors that they deem most central to the study of social movements.[14]

In *The Social Psychology of Protest*, Klandermans (1997) is primarily interested in (a) why people become involved (and sustain involvements) in social movements and (b) the conditions and factors affecting social movements and their successes. Like those promoting RMT more generally, Klandermans's analysis is heavily steeped in motivational/structuralist imagery. Klandermans also argues for the necessity of longitudinal studies (i.e., survey and experimental inquiry) to uncover factors associated with individual participation and SMO continuity. Still, he gives very little consideration to the ways in which participants and others make sense of, and more directly engage in activities pertaining to, SMOs (i.e., as social essences formulated through human enterprise).

Reviewing the broader collective behavior literature, Lofland's (1996) *Social Movement Organizations* is theoretically and methodologically considerably more encompassing than the Klandermans volume. Not only does Lofland outline a series of case-study procedures (and questions) for examining SMOs, but he also provides readers with a series of propositions that are intended both to summarize the literature in this area and to focus research along these lines. Accordingly, Lofland asks what are SMO beliefs, how are SMOs organized, why do people join SMOs, what are SMO strategies, and what are the effects of SMOs. While more attentive to participant viewpoints and activities than is Klandermans, Lofland's volume also assumes an overarching structuralist frame. Thus, matters of reflectivity, agency, and tactical interchange are subjugated to structural conditions, typologies, and factor-related images. Despite its overall sophistication,

Lofland's project reveals the conceptual difficulties that beset attempts to synthesize interpretivist and structuralist approaches to the study of social movements. On another note, Lofland alerts readers to the striking paucity of participant-informed research on people's experiences with social movements more generally and stresses the centrality of ethnographic inquiry for learning about SMOs.

Carl Couch and Clark McPhail

Reflecting approaches to the study of collective behavior that are rooted in Kuhnian (Manford Kuhn) interactionism,[15] Carl Couch and Clark McPhail attempt to outline the most basic or fundamental forms of collective association. Whereas Couch et al. and his students (Couch, 1986a, 1986b, 1987) have relied heavily on the analysis of videotaped materials (particularly laboratory designed negotiations), McPhail and his associates (McPhail and Wohlstein, 1986; McPhail, 1991, 1994, 1997) have concentrated on personal observations of crowd behavior.

Emphasizing observables (versus intersubjective communications with the participants), neither Couch nor McPhail have focused on the ways in which people engage one another in terms that are meaningful to them (participants). At the same time, though, their relative closeness to the phenomenon at hand has enabled them to develop some noteworthy critiques of the broader field of collective behavior (see Couch, 1968, 1989; and McPhail, 1991).

Challenging notions of crowd (and charismatic) generated irrationalities, these scholars have emphasized the importance of researchers attending to the ways in which the people assemble, develop communications, achieve mutual orientations, and coordinate lines of activity. In criticizing their predecessors for imposing singular (and external) rationalities in their considerations of crowd behavior, Couch and McPhail draw attention to the centrality of social process and multiple, emergent notions of rationality (and reality) for the study of collective interchanges.

Ralph Turner and Associates

Another significant set of works on collective behavior can be found in the writings of Ralph Turner (Platt and Gordon, 1994) and his associates (Turner and Killian, 1972; Snow, 1979, 1986; Zurcher and Snow, 1981; Rochford, 1982; Snow, Rochford, Worden, and Benford, 1986; Benford and Zurcher, 1990; Benford and Hunt, 1992; Benford, 1993a, 1993b, 1997).[16]

Focusing more specifically on emergent features of collective behavior, Turner and Killian (1972) developed what was to become a highly consequential textbook on collective behavior. Albeit an uneven analytical mix of structuralist notions of collective behavior and Meadian informed interactionism with the extant literature, this volume has served to sustain interest in the field more generally rather than providing a firm sense of direction for its development.

Reflecting an eclectic interactionism, Turner and his associates have vacillated in their own work between attempts to examine participant viewpoints in more direct (interviews, participant observation) manners and tendencies to presume structuralist factors. However, in contrast to most collective behavior theorists, Turner and his associates have interactively engaged participants in the field. Generally, as well, they have been mindful of people's capacities to act (and engage others) in reflective and tactical (influence and resistance) manners.

Attending to the "framing" (Goffman, 1972) of people's experiences, Snow, Benford, and Hunt consider the ways in which participants make sense of, and orient themselves toward, particular episodes of collective behavior. These scholars have yet to publish more sustained ethnographic accounts of their works, but some of their conceptual work has been absorbed by those promoting both the "new social movements" and "resource mobilization theory" aproaches (see Benford, 1997).

While the collective behavior literature, more generally, has been overlooked in many considerations of power, the scholars working in this area have produced a body of material that indicates, in important ways, how the power phenomenon extends beyond (what often seems) the more obvious or intrusive instances of control, resistance, revolution, and the like. It is essential that social scientists interested in power recognize that people actively influence (and resist) one another in a great many ways. This includes their involvements in rumors,[17] fashions, mobs, protests, scapegoating, panic, recruitment, conversion, subcultural life-worlds, and negotiation endeavors.

Still, many of those working in the field of collective behavior have had difficulty divesting themselves of notions of group minds, group pathology, and a structuralist (vs. processual and interpretivist) emphasis. Additionally, for all of their scholarly productions, very few of those writing in this venue have engaged those of whose activities they speak in any sustained ethnographic inquiry. However, even with these drawbacks, the collective behavior material attests to (a) the multiplistic forms of association that Simmel emphasized and (b) the importance of addressing the power phenomenon in negotiated-process terms. This material also suggests (c) that an (ethnographically grounded) appreciation of collective behavior may provide the key for comprehending the ways in which seemingly macro-level phenomena are achieved as instances of intersubjective accomplishment.

Interest Group Dynamics and Political Arenas

Although cast in quite different terms, another version of a collectivist approach to the study of power can be found in the political science literature. This theme denotes a vision of society as consisting of a series or multiplicity of groups that exist in potential and enacted opposition to one another. Notions of factions and self-serving interest groups have been traced to James Madison's (1788) contributions to *The Federalist Papers,* #10 (Truman, 1951; Ornstein and Elder, 1978),[18] but (still) one of the most sustained theories of political life (and society) as revolving around a multiplicity of interest groups was articulated by Arthur F. Bentley (1908) who, in *The Process of Government,* observes:

> *(W)e shall never find a group interest of society as a whole. We shall always find that the political interests and activities of any given group—and there are no political phenomena except group phenomena—are directed against other activities of men, who appear in other groups, political or other. The phenomena of political life which we study will always divide the society in which they occur, along lines that are very real, though in varying degrees of definiteness. The society itself is nothing other than the complex of groups that compose it.* (Bentley, 1908: 222)

While clearly critical of socialist (and marxist) theory, Bentley's volume is informed somewhat by the writings of Karl Marx and Ludwig Gumplowicz. However, he seems to have derived more central (albeit epistemologically mixed) inspiration from Auguste Comte, Georg Simmel, and John Dewey. Bentley's work seems almost unknown to sociologists who, more generally, have tended to envision Dahrendorf's (1959) statement on interest groups as a groundbreaking advance over marxist notions of class conflict.[19] And, although some political scientists have worked with notions of interest (and lobby) groups since the 1920s, only partially have Bentley's ideas been "discovered" in this discipline (perhaps most notably following Truman's [1951], *The Governmental Process;* also see Odegard, 1967).

Like those in the field of political science more generally, Bentley hoped for a mathematically (Comtean positivism) informed study of politics. More basically yet, though, Bentley emphasized (à la Simmel) the importance of attending to the multiple groups that constitute society in a most fundamental sense. Additionally, reflecting a pragmatist (via Dewey) orientation, Bentley stressed the importance of examining political interchanges (and interest groups) in terms of *activity,* the things that people do to promote (influence and resist) their interests with respect to others. As Bentley envisioned society, these themes were to be centrally acknowledged across the entire realm of government, at every level of political endeavor.

Following Bentley (and particularly Truman),[20] political scientists appear to have become more cognizant of interest groups (formation, maintenance, tactics, interrelationships) at all levels of formal government and some have embarked on case studies of mobilization and confrontation (see Odegard, 1967; Ornstein and Elder, 1978; Walker, 1991). However, in their apparent desire to embrace the (mainstream) positivist agenda, most have disregarded the importance of examining political processes as "activity in the making."[21]

Although Bentley had insisted on the study of activity, he never resolved the positivist/pragmatist contradictions in his work and offered no methodology that would effectively enable scholars to attend to the ways in which people actually engage aspects of the political process. In textbooks and other learned discourse, political scientists continue, rather routinely, to talk about the things that politicians, voters, and other participants do in various political arenas. However, most seem inattentive to the necessity of examining the ways in which people accomplish (political) activity in any here and now sense.

When they have ventured into the field to gather data on people's activities in particular instances, political scientists have tended to imitate journalists (Ornstein and Elder, 1978) rather than ethnographers in a more comprehensive sense. Even Milbrath (1963), whose study of *The Washington Lobbyists* is fairly well developed in an ethnographic sense, seems unaware of the concepts, premises, and (processually comparative) parallel studies in the interactionist literature or the affinities of his study with anthropological fieldwork more generally.

Thus, despite Bentley's (1908) emphasis on both interest group dynamics and the necessity of attending to human activity (group life in the making) in the field, those in political science have not realized the potential of studying politics (or power) as instances of human enterprise and intersubjective accomplishment.

Mass Communication Themes

We walk around with media-generated images of the world, using them to construct meaning about political and social issues. The lens through which we receive these images is not neutral but evinces the power and point of view of the political and economic elites who operate and focus it.

—Gamson et al., 1992:374

Although not as tightly wedded to power considerations as some of the preceding approaches, one encounters considerable discourse regarding power that revolves around the possession and distribution of information. In addition to those who broadly proclaim that "knowledge is power" (or vice versa), we may also acknowledge those who claim that generalized or strategic advantages are associated with particular communication practices (e.g., oratory and other presentational forums,[22] or the deployment of the print and electronic media). As well, there are those who argue that "we are the products of the mass media," presumably including print and electronic (e.g., newspapers, magazines, radio, television, and computerized) communications of all sorts.

In most respects, it is more appropriate to locate power and communication themes within broader theoretical frames rather that positing that communication denotes a distinct viewpoint on power. At the same time, though, one may observe that many of those who have written about power (in their quest to arrive at factors, resources, and other "structural" features of the situation) have extensively disregarded concerns with human images of the world and related interactions (including herein all manners of communication). Thus, despite a great unevenness in both emphasis and orientation, the "communications" literature merits some direct consideration.

Over the past century, much attention has been directed toward matters such as propaganda, mind control, advertising, marketing, and image-making.[23] One of the most general implications is that the availability of existing and emergent forms (and technologies) of mass communication has generated new realms of vulnerability on the part of the citizenry. A related concern is that persons and groups with greater access to the communications process may use these in ways thought to be detrimental to the well-being of other individuals, groups, or the community at large.[24]

It is generally recognized that the media may be deployed in reference to wide ranges of objects (goods, services, concepts, moralities, governments) and may be pitched to any and all of those thought able to comprehend the messages that users might wish to generate. Concerns with power, thus, may be extended to any concept that someone might somehow package and present through the media. Indeed, on a more global basis, the graphic and electronic media have permeated almost every realm of contemporary experience, encompassing, for instance, work, religion, politics, sexuality, consumption, and recreation.

Beyond this, some are more specifically concerned about the media as communicative devices that (variously): promote capitalism at the cost of socialism (Gramsci, 1971); result in centralized control of information on both national and global levels (Bagdikian, 1990); foster (postmodernist) surrealism (Baudrillard, 1983, 1988); generate (undue) fragmentation and confusion (Bennett, 1988); or fail to provide readers with adequate depictions of "the broader social forces" that affect their lives (Gamson et al., 1992).

As a consequence of both (a) a wide variety of control and influence concerns on the part of academics and the citizenry at large and (b) the motivated interests characterizing those involved in encouraging (i.e., selling, producing) the use of the media as a tool for communicating with others, we have also witnessed an extended *media mystique*. The ensuing fears, aspirations, and "hype" about the media have obscured fundamental aspects of the communication process that scholars concerned with the power phenomenon should address in direct, detailed manners.

In many ways, life in contemporary society seems more complex than has been true in the past.[25] This is particularly evident with respect to technological developments and people's opportunities to establish almost instantaneous contact with others around the globe. But before we "huff and puff ourselves into some magical postmodernist era," it is important to observe that the sensation of being the most advanced and sophisticated people in existence is unlikely to be unique unto us in a historical, cross-cultural, or futuristic sense. Thus, for instance, before we discount the significance of earlier (or other seemingly "more primitive") modes of communication, we must be careful, as analysts, to envision the products or technologies of other eras or peoples within the contexts that *they* view and utilize these things rather than adopting the posture of remarkably informed folk "visiting a museum."

Similarly, before we pay homage to the notion that "the Media" represents some uniquely sovereign power, let us recognize that the media (in whatever forms it may exist in any society) most fundamentally denotes a means of communication. Likewise, the media is not one thing, unto itself, but connotes a multi-faceted set of social products and social processes.

In dealing with the media, thus, it is necessary to establish some baseline parameters. The first and most central of these involves a recognition that people as intersubjective, interacting entities have always been dependent on image-mediated realities. These images may be communicated or represented (and shared) in many different ways (e.g., talk, pictures, noise, reenactments, storytelling, dramatizations, gossip) and may vary in sincerity, deception, creativity, fabrication, and the like.

The sharing of images may be highly limited (e.g., two people) or they may be cast more widely through gossip, rumors, assemblies, theaters, graphic displays, or electronic technologies that may involve large segments of the community on a concurrent, sequential, or interactive basis. Further, whether exposed to single or multiple communications and similar or diverse viewpoints on things, people face the task of interpreting (making sense, addressing) the various images of the world to which they may be exposed and incorporating these images of the world into their ongoing experiences (and activities).

In what probably is still the most extensive rendering of mass communications theory available, McQuail (1983:54) identifies nine major theoretical tangents in the literature. These are theories of (a) mass society, especially class and ideological domination, structure and function; (b) effects of media on institutions and society; (c) normative [prescriptive] order; (d) organizations applied to media work; (e) form and substance of media messages; (f) distribution and audience choice and use; (g) audience composition, behavior, and feedback; (h) symbolic interaction and socialization; and (i) media effect. While carefully crafting discussions of these themes, McQuail finds that the field is so conceptually disjointed that a synthesis of this literature is an unrealistic consideration. He concludes, observing, *(M)edia potency has more to do with what those with power fear for, or dream of, than with what the media can or do actually achieve. (McQuail, 1983: 225)*

There are, it seems, almost endless departure points from this literature, and it simply is not possible to provide a sustained assessment of all of these notions in this volume. Given our primary focus, though, we may ask whether this body of literature enables social scientists to develop more viable appreciations and examinations of people's experiences with influence and resistance endeavors as matters of intersubjective accomplishment.

On a general level, there is a pronounced recognition of the media as a tactical resource that people may deploy in attempts to influence others in some manner. After that, however, the literature, as a whole, breaks down. More recently, there has been a notable acknowledgement of audiences as more active participants in the media process in some sectors of this literature (e.g., McQuail, 1983; Fiske, 1987; Gamson et al., 1992). However, as Blumer (1933), Blumer and Hauser (1933), Altheide (1985), and Prus (1993a) observe, there is (still) limited cognizance of recipients (and consumers) of the mass media as interpreting, enterprising, interacting entities who, both individually and collectively, may attend to, analyze, adjust to, and use the media in ways that are quite different from those intended by those producing (or sponsoring) those messages.

Likewise, a few ethnographies aside (e.g., see Altheide, 1974; Tuchman, 1978; Fishman, 1980; Powell, 1985; Ericson et al., 1987, 1989; Prus 1989b), little attention has been given to the study of the ways in which people engage the media as sponsors, marketers, media sales representatives, producers, writers, directors, artists, and so forth. As a result, and despite a great deal of discourse and debate about the media and its implications for all manner of mind control, social scientists have a great deal to learn (and reconsider) at a very fundamental level, about the ways in which people experience (construct, present, encounter) the media.

This criticism of the prevailing orientations to the media is not intended to dismiss scholarly concerns with the mass media, but rather to suggest that these matters should be reconceptualized in ways that enable researchers to examine the mass communication process as it is more directly experienced (and engaged) by all parties involved in its existence as a community essence. Although the citizenry at large may work with whatever sets of images of the media that they might deem appropriate, it is important that social scientists acknowledge more basic features of the human condition (and symbolic interchange) as *anchorage points* in their comprehensions of "the media."

Not only will this require a much greater ethnographic attentiveness to *the activities of all participants* whose lives intersect through particular instances of the media process, but also a recognition that people are more or less continuously *engaged* in a variety of communications (interpersonal and other media) in the course of pursuing various aspects of their lives.

This means (1) focusing on the many ways that people may attempt to use the media, such as generating public awareness of events and dangers, providing instruction, invoking behavioral control, shaping (and negating) public opinion both generally and with respect to specific preferences, fostering group solidarity, and neutralizing and destroying competitors or opponents. This implies (2) attending to those whose work (and recreational pursuits) involves attempts to develop, produce, support, sustain, assess, regulate, and challenge particular media forms, messages, and content themes. This also entails (3) inquiring into how people as recipients (variously as witnesses, targets, seekers, or users) deal with the media phenomenon on an ongoing, here and now basis.

Regardless of the media employed (e.g., direct small group interaction, gossip and rumors, assemblies, theaters, graphics, electronic technology), this implies a much greater appreciation of the *entire* human communication process than is evident in the communications literature. It also stresses the importance of demystifying (in comparative terms) any "new" communication technology or practice.[26]

Community Studies

Those engaged in "community studies" have often been overlooked in considerations of the power phenomenon, but these scholars deserve particular recognition because of their willingness to venture (as researchers) into broad social arenas.[27]

Few of these studies have a strong ethnographic cast, or attend to the ways in which people actually engage one another in more direct or situated manners. Further, most of these accounts of community-life suffer from a relative lack of concepts that would better enable scholars to appreciate human interchanges in more generic terms. Still, these materials provide approximations of some of the complexities (e.g., multiple interpretations, differing interests, and instances of cooperation, conflict, compromise, coalitions, deception) that the power dynamics of human communities entail.

Although community studies appear to have had their popularity peak (at least temporarily), more noteworthy endeavors along these lines include: Warner and Lunt's *The Social Life of a Modern Community* (1941); Whyte's *Street Corner Society* (1943); Hollingshead's *Elmstown's Youth* (1949); Lantz's *People of Coal Town* (1958); Vidich and Bensmen's *Small Town in Mass Society* (1958); Gans's *The Levitowners* (1967); Suttles's *The Social Order of the Slum* (1968); Lucas' *Minetown, Milltown, Railtown* (1971); and Clairmont and Magill's *Africville* (1974).

As a set, these studies appear to have had a variety of sources of origin and are very much characterized by vaguely articulated or mixed theoretical viewpoints. Gans's (1976) statement on urban ethnography may provide some clues to the failure on the part of these scholars to develop sustained, grounded theory about community life. Gans suggests that these researchers (a) have been attending to (and probably were overwhelmed by) the grand theories of urbanization spun out by Durkheim, Weber, Simmel, and others, theories that are considerably more vast than could be empirically examined; and (b) have tended to envision (perhaps protectively) their works as essentially exploratory and descriptive.[28]

Although reflecting an assortment of stratification issues, theories of rural-urban transition, and overarching organizational structures and rationalities,[29] the studies referenced here provide some valuable insights into community life, including people's experiences in politics, work, education, religion, family life, recreation, and the like. Still, the levels of generality with which these materials are presented typically obscure the ways in which people conduct their activities in more direct terms. Because of this, and the multiple (and mixed) frames with which these studies have been developed, it is difficult to compare (and synthesize) the results of any two or more projects.

The problem is not one of venturing into the community of the other. Indeed, this is essential if we are to achieve a viable social science. But instead of developing vague, more encompassing community projects, what is required are more focused considerations of the ways in which people engage one another in the various and particular life-worlds or subcultures that constitute the community. These latter studies, inevitably, would address aspects of broader community life, but would provide more (methodologically and analytically) viable departure points for attending to matters of influence (and resistance) in the day-to-day settings in which community interchange takes place.

Conceptual Limitations

As a set, the materials introduced in chapter 3 fare somewhat better relative to the criterion of envisioning power as intersubjective accomplishment than do those in chapter 2. Still, because many of these works reflect variants of the structuralist dimensions introduced in chapter 2, they are vulnerable to the conceptual problems noted therein.

As a topic, *power* may receive somewhat less explicit attention in chapter 3, but we see a greater concern about acknowledging human relations more generally. Some readers may be critical of what seems a de-emphasis of the central theme in this volume, but this transition is essential if we, as analysts, are to avoid becoming caught up in the power mystique.

The study of power *is* the study of human relations and community life, *not* because power determines human relations and community life, but because one must comprehend human relations (and community life) on a highly sustained basis if one hopes to comprehend power.

What remains strikingly apparent, though, throughout the literature cited in chapters 2 and 3, is a general reluctance on the part of social scientists to directly examine the subject matter of which they purport so knowingly to speak. Proportionately few of those addressing the power phenomenon have been concerned about studying the ways in which people actually engage one another in the course of ongoing community life.

Notes

1. For insider critiques of this structuralist/positivist literature in psychological social psychology, see Harré and Secord (1972), Elms (1975), Koch (1981), Gergen (1982, 1985), Carlson (1984), and Billig (1996). Blumer (1969) and Prus (1996b) provide extended critiques of positivist/structuralist orientations in the social sciences more generally.

2. It was Simmel (see Simmel, 1955; Coser, 1967), too, who discussed "the functions of conflict for social order."

3. Those familiar with Blumer's overall work will recognize that Blumer attends much more to Park (who is comparatively more eclectic, typological) in developing materials on collective behavior, fashion, and race relations than he does to Mead (who focuses more directly on social

process, reflectivity, and intersubjectivity). Somewhat ironically, Couch's (1968) and McPhail's (1991) critiques of the field of collective behavior (and Blumer [1939]) are highly consistent with the sort of (Meadian-informed) critique that Blumer directs toward the social sciences (see Blumer, 1969, 1971) more generally.

4. Working in similar veins, Estes and Edmunds (1981) and Wiseman (1983) make concerted pleas for theory of policy analysis and implementation (vs. interventionist sociology).

5. John Lofland, whose valuable study of the *Doomsday Cult* (1966) is clearly developed in process terms and who (1970, 1976) also has written important pieces on generic social processes, has openly struggled with (and became intertwined in) the tendencies to focus on typologies of collective behavior (1981, 1996). In these latter cases, Lofland's notions of generic forms seem more reminiscent of Weber's "ideal types" than Simmel's social processes. At the same time, though (and at variance from Weber), Lofland sees his typification schema as a device for generating more precise analytical comparisons of studies of directly enacted and intersubjectively informed instances of collective behavior.

6. For two field studies conducted particularly mindfully of Smelser's (1962) model, see Zurcher et al.'s (1971) study of two antipornography campaigns and Wipper's (1977) study of two rural protest movements in Kenya.

7. Although somewhat more mixed conceptually, Hoffer's (1951) *True Believer,* likewise, is highly thought provoking. However, neither Klapp nor Hoffer provide a viable methodology for studying collective behavior "in the making."

8. Johnston, Larana, and Gusfield (1994:3–35) provide an overview of the debates and issues characterizing this literature.

9. Some of these notions are also evident in Gusfield's (1963, 1981) depiction of "symbolic crusades."

10. McCarthy and Zald (1977) and Zald and McCarthy (1979:1–7) cite a number of others as contributing to the foundations of resource mobilization theory. These include Olson (1965), Zald and Asch (1966), Lipsky (1968), Turner (1969), and Tilly et al. (1975). However, McCarthy and Zald have been particularly instrumental in crystallizing (and focusing attention on) this "subtradition" within collective behavior.

11. Readers may recognize some of these notions from Zald and Asch (1966).

12. Making specific reference to the interconnectedness of the "women's" and "peace" movements, Meyer and Whittier (1994) extend these notions somewhat with the term, *social movement spillover.* In addition to commenting on (a) organizational coalitions, they also draw attention to

(b) overlapping social movement communities, (c) shared personnel, and (d) mutual utilization of particular political opportunity structures in the broader community.

13. Lofland is a notable exception in this regard vis-à-vis some of his other work (especially Lofland, 1966), but as he (1996) acknowledges, one finds very few ethnographic depictions of people's involvements in SMOs.

14. For other reviews of resource mobilization theory, see Zurcher and Snow (1981), Klandermans (1984), Snow et al. (1986), Klandermans et al. (1988), Buechler (1993, 1995), Tarrow (1994), and Stoecker (1995).

15. In more general terms, one may contrast those who work in more of an "Iowa school" [Manford Kuhn] tradition with those pursuing Chicago-style symbolic interaction. See Meltzer and Petras (1972) and Prus (1996b) for further elaborations of the Iowa-Chicago orientations to interactionism.

16. Several of the scholars cited here have been centrally influenced by Ralph Turner or his students. For an interesting autobiographical account of his eclectic academic background (and structural-interactionist orientation), see Turner (1994).

17. The work of Shibutani (1966) and Rosnow and Fine (1976) deals with the social transmission of rumors.

18. As Odegard (1967) observes, in introducing a reprint of Bentley's (1908) volume, the notion of government as denoting a series of interest groups in ongoing association was well established in the journalistic literature of the time. These notions, however, had not been articulated in the academic literature prior to Bentley's endeavor.

19. Most sociologist also seem oblivious to Blumer's (1954) statement on power relations and interest groups, as well as his (1960, 1964) critiques of marxist analyses of industrialization.

20. For other materials focusing on interest groups, see the overview provided by Odegard (1967). Revised editions of Key's textbook, *Politics, Parties, and Pressure Groups* (1955) have also fostered a generalized emphasis on (multiple) interest groups. Other works along these lines include Hrebenar and Scott (1982), Caplan (1983), Wolpe (1990), and Maisel (1994).

21. This is not to deny extensive academic discourse on a great many aspects of politics or the development of more particularistic advice on how to win elections (e.g., Shadegg, 1964; Paizis, 1977; Simpson, 1981; and Schwartzman, 1989) and the like; only to distinguish between learned "shop talk," tactical advice, and the more sustained study of the ways in which people actually experience (and enact) these and other aspects of the political process. Thus, while the authors cited here all draw upon their own experiences with political campaigns, the emphasis is on providing tactical advice for organizing (and winning) campaigns rather than providing detailed depictions of the ways that campaigns are experienced (and enacted) by the people involved in particular aspects of their development.

22. Concerns with mass communication are evident (see chapter 4) in the works of the early Greeks (sophists, orators, politicians, entertainers, and rhetoricians).

23. The mass communications (and related) literature is quite massive. Lasswell et al., (1935, 1962, 1969) provide bibliographies of some of this literature, but readers may find the reviews of McQuail (1983), Altheide (1985), Delia (1987), Giles and Wiemann (1987), and Gamson et al. (1992) particularly valuable for overviewing this material. However, anyone looking for conceptual coherence (or even multiple themes readily lending themselves to synthesis) is apt to be disappointed.

24. Presumably, those most concerned about domination through the media are those who envision the media in highly singularizing, totalizing, and potentially corrupting terms. In a broader context, it might be appreciated (see chapter 4) that concerns with misuse of the communication process minimally can be traced back to Socrates, Plato, and Aristotle, whose distrust of the sophists is associated with their use of rhetoric and other communication practices in public forums.

25. And no doubt, we have lost some complexities, if only through inattention, associated with people's life-worlds in other places and times.

26. In a somewhat sensationalized analysis, Nimmo and Combs (1983) attempt to draw attention to the matter of "mediated political realities" emphasizing the uncertainty, multiplicity, and dramatized nature of human mediated-reality(ies). As will become apparent in chapter 5, the notion of image-mediated reality has been central to a pragmatist/interactionist approach to the study of human group life for several decades, as are related concerns with enterprise, symbols, interaction, negotiation, and ongoing accomplishment.

27. While they may also see themselves as involved in community studies, the "stratificationists" (introduced in chapter 2, within rational order structuralism), who primarily rely on demographic data and survey research, have been excluded from this discussion. There is, however, another set of rational order structuralists that are sometimes included within a broader community studies category. I am referring to what has been termed, "network analysis." Attending to abstracted "lines of influence," *network analysis* has developed largely through the (sociometric modeling) depiction of "contacts" (and overlaps) of people on various corporate boards and governing bodies. Power is presumed (rather blindly and speculatively) to flow from people's links and concentrations in directorates, committees, or other decision-making arenas.

Although it would be very worthwhile to examine the ways that people attain, occupy, and enact various positions of prominence in the community, those involved in network analysis have virtually neglected (as a realm of study) the ways in which the people (of whom analysts speak) actually envision their situations, engage their roles, or interact with one another within the context of ongoing community life.

See Hunter (1953) and Troustine and Christensen (1982) for more outgoing (broader) instances of community studies using network analysis. Cook and Whitmeyer (1992) and Mizruchi (1996) provide review statements of network analysis (especially corporate interlocks). While Cook and Whitmeyer suggest that network analysis may be synthesized with (the rationalistically oriented) exchange theory, Mizruchi asks more basic questions about the integrity (and value) of network analysis as a mode of sociological inquiry (and theory). Even those network analysis projects that involve people in the community through direct inquiry (e.g., the Hunter model) tend to focus on identifying powerful individuals (through reputations) rather than examining the actual interchanges in which these people (and others in the community) participate. For a more sustained critique of elite control theory (and reputational studies), see Rose (1967).

28. It also should be appreciated that community-life studies are mammoth undertakings. Thus, another problem encountered by those embarking on these endeavors revolves around the incredible masses of materials that one could collect and the (usually limited) resources of particular scholars to obtain, examine, and synthesize these materials.

29. While Bell and Newby (1971) largely disattend to the human enterprise involved in *forging* community life, they provide a (structuralist) review of several American and European community studies (including materials that I have not cited here).

4 Enduring Tactical Themes

Again, on the subject of peace and war let us use a similar method to obtain our chief kinds of argument. The pretexts for making war on another state are as follows: when we have been the victims of aggression, we must take vengeance on those who have wronged us, now that a suitable opportunity has presented itself; or else, when we are actually being wronged, we must go to war on our own behalf or on behalf of our kindred or benefactors; or else we must help our allies when they are wronged; or else we must go to war to gain some advantage for the city, in respect either of glory, or of resources, or of strength, or of something similar. . . .

. . .If we are trying to prevent a war which is likely to take place, we must first of all find pretexts to show that the alleged grievances either do not exist at all or else are small and insignificant; next we must show that it is not expedient to go to war, dwelling on the disasters that befall men in warfare; and further, that the advantages which conduce to victory (which have just been enumerated) are possessed by the enemy rather than by us. . . . When we are trying to stop a war which has actually started, if those to whom our advice is offered are stronger than their foes, the first point on which we must insist is that sensible men ought not to wait until they have a fall, but should make peace while they are strong; also, that it is characteristic of war to ruin many even of those who are successful in it, but of peace to save the vanquished and to allow the victorious to enjoy the possessions which they have gained in warfare. We must also dwell upon the numerous and incalculable vicissitudes of warfare. Such are the methods by which we must exhort to peace those who are victorious in war. Those who have already met with failure we must urge to make peace on the ground of actual events, and because they ought to learn from their misfortunes and not be exasperated by those who have already injured them, and because of the dangers which have already resulted from not making peace, and because it is better to sacrifice a part of their possessions to an enemy stronger than themselves than to be conquered and lose their lives as well as their property.

—*Aristotle,* De Rhetorica Ad Alexandrum,
1425a–1425b [Forster, trans.]

Whereas chapters 2 and 3 address more conventionalist social science considerations of power, the present chapter broadens the scope somewhat by acknowledging both a deeper historical base and a more pervasive associational dimension than that commonly encountered in the earlier cited literature on power. This material may seem diversionary in certain respects, but it further indicates ways in which notions of power relations extend far beyond most depictions of this phenomenon in the social sciences. At the same time, by attending to some of the more enduring and commonplace features of human relations, chapter 4 may enable scholars to better situate the materials presented in the chapters following.

Acknowledging Early Greek (and Roman) Roots

Aristotle collected the early books on rhetoric, even going back as far as Tisias, well known as the originator and inventor of the art; he made a careful examination of the rules of each author and wrote them out in plain language, giving the author's name, and finally gave a painstaking explanation of the difficult parts. And he so surpassed the original authorities in charm and brevity that no one becomes acquainted with their ideas from their own books, but everyone who wishes to know what their doctrines are, turns to Aristotle, believing him to give a much more convenient exposition. . . .

(I)n Aristotle's day there was a great and famous teacher of oratory named Isocrates; there is known to be a textbook from his hand, but I have not seen it. I have, however, found many treatises on the art by his pupils and by those who carried on his doctrines.

—*Cicero,* De Inventione, *II, II: 6–9 [Hubbell, trans.]*

Because so much of Western civilization is informed by early Greek thought (of which we first start to find preserved, written materials around 500 B.C.),[1] it seems fitting to begin a consideration of human relations with this as a departure point. Not only did the Greeks (also Ionians, Hellenes) possess an extremely sophisticated written language 2,500 years ago,[2] but early Greek scholars were engaged in developing philosophies (and moralities) that would lay the foundations for much contemporary social thought.[3]

Although we have access to only some of the written materials that survived from early Greek and Roman society (c. 500 B.C. to 200 A.D.),[4] it is apparent that the scholars of the day were highly attentive to issues of power (influence and resistance). Not only were they concerned about encounters with other governments and peoples (e.g., conflict, competition, alliances, peace, occupation, trade, technology), but their writings (historical documentaries, analytical texts, courtroom advice, poetry, and theatrical scripts) display an attentiveness to human interchanges across wide ranges of domestic arenas (e.g., political, educational, legal, family life, entertainment, sports).

When our contemporaries discuss early Greece and Rome, they often comment on military conquests and governmental arrangements, architectural accomplishments, poetry and theater, religious themes (especially mythology) and (relatedly) the "superheroes" (such as Apollo, Hercules, and Mercury). Many also observe that early Greece (and Rome, albeit to a lesser extent) is reputed for its contributions to the physical sciences and philosophy. Indeed, most historians would likely acknowledge that Western society has been "enlightened" principally, as a consequence of the Greek and Latin texts (and concepts) that have been preserved over the centuries.

Scholars who focus on the classics (e.g., Herder, 1784; Kennedy, 1963, 1972; Becker and Barnes, 1978; Enos, 1993, 1995) also observe that much Hellenistic and Roman thought did not originate with those whom we may identify as Greek or Roman citizens. They contend that it is difficult to sort out that which is uniquely Greek or Roman from the cultural legacies of the many peoples with whom they have had contact (as travelers, traders, immigrants, instructors, conquerors) over the millennia. What is especially noteworthy, though, is that in developing sophisticated *written* texts and extensive educational forums, the early Greeks and Romans became exceptional scholars (students, observers, adaptors, compilers, articulators, debaters) not only of their own time but also of the practices and wisdoms of the ages. Admittedly, there is much in these early works with which contemporary scholars may find fault (given the base of knowledge [trials, errors, and reformulations] that has been generated over the past two millennia). Still, it behooves us to acknowledge the wisdoms and technologies that have withstood "the tests of human experience over time." Indeed, even when placed (and compared) on a contemporary plane, it is difficult not to be impressed by extended segments of these early realms of scholarship.

Beyond a generalized indebtedness to early Greek scholarship in areas such as science, engineering and architecture, and the humanities, we may also observe that Hellenistic thought has also notably impacted on the social sciences. Tracing the development of social thought throughout recorded history, Becker and Barnes (1978, vol. 1) posit that the early Greek (e.g., Plato, Aristotle) attentiveness to organizational structures, forms of government, organic models, logic, objectivity, and observables represents consequential precursors to contemporary (positivist/structuralist) social theory. Although the linkages to contemporary political science are particularly evident (via Plato and Aristotle), one might (as do Popper [1957] and Gouldner [1965]) also posit that Plato had established the essential foundations for much of what is considered (mainstream) sociology. Likewise, one might observe that Aristotle's emphasis on "examining the experiential essences (both in particular instances and abstract forms) of things" laid the foundation for scientific inquiry more generally.

Like so many other features of Hellenistic culture, early Greek scholarly notions of human experiences (and interchanges) may be best characterized as complex, sophisticated, and conceptually mixed. While some of their writings resonate with various organic, structuralist, functionalist, objectivist, and moralist (and marxist) themes that characterize more conventionalist notions of social science, one also finds within their writings some explicit formulations that are strikingly consistent with the basic position adopted in this volume.

Those more familiar with the Greek classics may quickly acknowledge the relevance of *rhetoric* for a fuller consideration of power, but it is instructive to observe in early Hellenistic scholarship a yet more fundamental appreciation of *language* and *enterprise* for the comprehension of human relations (and power). Indeed, despite the attention given to other aspects of early Greek thought over the centuries, some concepts that are exceedingly vital to a genuine social science have been largely overlooked. Quite directly, in addition to acknowledging the meaningful human enterprise entailed in power relations, the early Greek scholars developed and debated a series of issues revolving around what in more recent times would be termed the philosophy (or sociology) of knowledge.

In contrast to Popper (1957), Gouldner (1965), and Becker and Barnes (1978), who have employed more conventionalist sociological analyses in discussing early Hellenistic society, I approached this literature asking whether the views of human reality with which various of the early Greek (and Roman) scholars worked might parallel an interactionist (Mead, 1934; Blumer, 1969) or socially constructed (Berger and Luckmann, 1966) approach to the study of human group life. The material I have uncovered is notably incomplete, partly reflecting my limited familiarity with what is a major area of study in itself. And, it is likely that I have underestimated the complexity and sophistication of the thought of the early Hellenistic scholars. Still, given the relative neglect of symbolic interactionism (and other interpretivist/constructionist viewpoints) on the part of Popper, Gouldner, and Becker and Barnes, among others, the results of this inquiry were to prove rather intriguing.

I am *not* claiming that the early Greek scholars should be reread as "symbolic interactionists." Indeed, some highly consequential differences are evident. Still, my examination of this literature indicates that some of these scholars were aware (sometimes very explicitly) of what we would now envision as key interactionist (Mead, 1934; Blumer, 1969) concepts.

None of these early scholars, as far as I can tell, had pursued a theory of human interchange along the lines formulated by Wilhelm Dilthey (Ermarth, 1978) or George Herbert Mead (1934),[5] but central figures among *the early Greek scholars appear explicitly cognizant of process, relativism (multiple worldviews and viewpoints), reflectivity, persuasive communication, human enterprise, and the central, enabling features of language,* for instance. Although these concepts are scattered and somewhat fragmentary rather than systematically focused in the early Greek literature, these scholars can be seen to express some rudimentary notions of pragmatism, social constructionism, or interactionist thought.

There is little doubt that these interpretivist images of the human condition have been neglected or obscured by subsequent scholars many of whom (following Plato and Aristotle) adopted more structuralist, objectivist/causal, and moralist orientations (see Rosenfield, 1971). This does not, however, negate the importance of those conceptualizations that have a more interactionist or constructionist emphasis for appreciating the human condition (and power relations) over the course of recorded history.

Interestingly, too, an examination of the writings of the best known authors of this era is particularly revealing in this (interpretivist) sense. Although they are more apt to be associated with contemporary notions of positivist, structuralist, and moralist philosophy than social science, we find in the works of Plato and Aristotle considerable evidence that they were aware of issues (and concepts) related to pragmatist/interactionist/constructionist lines of thought.[6] Still, let us first cast our net a little more broadly as a means of contextualizing the inputs of the early Hellenistic scholars.

As part of the legacy of Greek and Roman scholarship, we have access to some of the earliest recorded histories of the development of governing states and of the relationships of these governments with both their own citizens and the representatives of neighboring governments. Noteworthy here, for instance, are the works of the early Greek historians Herodotus (484–425 B.C.), Thucydides (460–400 B.C.), and Polybius (208–120 B.C.), and the Roman historians Lucetius (96–55 B.C.), Cicero (106–43 B.C.), Julius Caesar (100–44 B.C.), and Livy (59 B.C.–17 A.D.).[7]

While those examining this early literature are often critical of the lapses, claims, and moralities of these early historians, one may still observe an instructive interface of the accounts of various military engagements, interstate relations, and prominent domestic affairs *with* the interpersonal exchanges (and relationships) of the principal participants. Like our contemporary historians, though, none of these early historians appear to have developed a theory of human group life that reflected these interchanges in a more explicit, sustained manner. Nevertheless, the early Greeks and Romans were keenly aware of the importance of people's *communication practices* across wide ranges of human affairs.

How important were persuasive skills to the citizens of the era? The classics historian D. H. Berry likely does not understate the case when he observes:

> To any Roman, military ability was, of course, more important than oratory. . . . Nevertheless, a good general would have to know how to address his

troops, and if he was not an orator he would also . . . find himself disadvantaged in the political arena. (Clarke, 1996: ix)

Of the early Greeks, Aristotle (384–322 B.C.) is often given credit for first articulating the notion that man is a social being, a product of community life:

> *These considerations make it clear, then, that the state is one of those things which exist by nature, and that man is by nature an animal fit for a state. Anyone who by his nature and not by ill-luck has no state is either a wretch or superhuman. . . . Speech, on the other hand, serves to make clear what is beneficial and what is harmful, and so also what is just and what is unjust. For by contrast with the other animals man has this peculiarity: he alone has sense of good and evil, just and unjust, etc. An association in these matters makes a household and a state. (Aristotle, Politics, Book I, 1253a [Saunders, trans.])*

Still, despite his remarkable, wide-ranging competence as a scholar, Aristotle was not alone in recognizing the community and language-based foundations of the human condition or even the first to do so. Thus, somewhat related notions are associated with Protagoras, Socrates,[8] Plato, and Isocrates.

Although most of his writings appear to have been destroyed by Athenian citizens who were displeased that he would not confirm the existence of the Greek gods,[9] Protagoras (490–420 B.C.; often considered the first of the "old sophists"),[10] posits that things are known *only* through (and to the extent of) human experience:

> *Protagoras . . . also holds that "Man is the measure of all things, of existing things that they exist, and of non-existing things that they exist not"; and by "measure" he means the criterion, and by "things" the objects, so that he is virtually asserting that "Man is the criterion of all objects, of those which exist that they exist, and of those which exist not that they exist not." And consequently he posits only what appears to each individual, and thus he introduces relativity. . . .*
>
> *What he states then is this—that matter is in flux, and as it flows additions are made continuously in the place of the effluxions, and the senses are transformed and altered according to the times of life and to all the other conditions of the bodies. He says also that the "reasons" of all the appearances subsist in matter, so that matter, so far as depends on itself, is capable of being all those things which appear to all. . . . And men, he says, apprehend different things at different times owing to their differing dispositions . . . Thus according to him, Man becomes the criterion of real existences; for all things that appear to men also exist, and things that appear to no man have no existence either.*

(Sextus Empiricus, c. 200 A.D.: Outlines of Pyrrhonism, Book I:216–219 [Bury, trans.])

The preceding quote is taken from the Greek skeptic, Sextus Empiricus,[11] but the writings (and teachings) of Protagoras were (much earlier) acknowledged and debated by Plato (427–347 B.C.), Aristotle (384–322 B.C.), and seemingly, as well, by many of their contemporaries (see Aristotle, *Metaphysics*). Plato and Aristotle had their own viewpoints and agendas, but they appear quite aware of human capacities for (a) experiencing (if not defining) situations in diverse manners across individuals and groups,[12] and (b) engaging in persuasive interchange (and resistance).[13]

While only partially conveying the wide-ranging set of conceptions (analytical and moralistic) pertaining to the human condition that Plato has his characters debate in *Theaetetus* (a treatise on knowledge),[14] the following (framentary) extracts suggest a distinct awareness of issues (e.g., relativism, flux, and persuasive interchange) of these sorts on Plato's part:[15]

> *Socrates: Protagoras . . . says, you will remember, that 'man is the measure of all things—alike of the being of things that are and of the not-being of things that are not.' No doubt you have read that. (152a)*
>
> *Socrates: . . . things we are pleased to say 'are,' really are in process of becoming, as a result of movement and change and of blending one with another. We are wrong to speak of them as 'being,' for none of them ever is; they are always becoming. In this matter let us take it that, with exception of Parmenides, the whole series of philosophers agree—Protagoras, Heraclitus, Empedocles—and among the poets the greatest masters in both kinds, Epicharmus in comedy, Homer in tragedy. (152d–e)*
>
> *Socrates: Then just take a look around and make sure that none of the uninitiate overhears us. I mean by the uninitiate the people who believe that nothing is real save what they can grasp with their hands and do not admit that actions or processes or anything invisible can count as real. (155e)*
>
> *Socrates: . . . whatever practices seem right and laudable to any particular state are so, for that state, so long as it holds by them. Only, when the practices are, in any particular case, unsound for them, the wise man substitutes others that are and appear sound. (167c)*
>
> *Socrates: And again in social matters, the theory will say that, so far as good and bad customs or rights and wrongs or matters of religion are concerned, whatever any state makes up its mind to enact as lawful for itself, really is lawful for it, and in this field no individual or state is wiser than another. (172a) (Plato, Theaetetus, 152a–172a [Cornford, trans.])*

Despite the seeming potential (pragmatist/constructionist potency) of the ideas that Plato discusses in *Theaetetus*,[16] Plato fails to sustain an analysis of the intersubjective accomplishment of human group life or the social construction of reality (Berger and Luckmann, 1966).[17]

Apparently, by more completely adopting the viewpoint that "everything is perpetual flux," Plato generally suggests that it is impossible to know and represent the sensate or natural world. As Aristotle observes:

> *After the systems [of thought-RP] we have named came the philosophy of Plato, which in most respects followed these thinkers, but had peculiarities that distinguished it from the philosophy of the Italians. For, having in his youth first become familiar with Cratylus and with the Heraclitean doctrines (that all sensible things are ever in a state of flux and there is no knowledge about them), these views he held even in later years. Socrates, however, was busying himself about ethical matters and neglecting the world of nature as a whole but seeking the universal in these ethical matters, and fixed thought for the first on definitions; Plato accepted his teaching, but held that the problem applied not to any sensible thing but to entities of another kind—for this reason, that the common definition could not be a definition of any sensible thing, as they were always changing. (Aristotle,* Metaphysica, *Book I, 987a–987b [Ross, trans.])*

In developing his own position on being and knowing, Aristotle is much more experientially engaged than many other philosophers of the era. Aristotle also (a) takes the position that the world (that can be known through the senses) is in state of perpetual flux, but he recognizes that (b) change is not a singular or uniform phenomenon, and (c) many changes occur within the context of more enduring human sensations or are subsumed within recurrent or repetitive patterns (as with the life-cycles of specific plant and animal species) of process. As well, Aristotle notes that (d) people (who also are part of this process) not only engage the world as deliberative, causal agents but do so in ways that recognize the more enduring and the more fleeting qualities of some phenomena.

Aristotle interfuses his notions about the human condition with prescriptive agendas that are intended to improve human circumstances, but he very much wishes to dispense with the "know-nothing" philosophies of the day. Accordingly, Aristotle asks about the ways that people learn about the world and do things (pertaining to basic survival and other realms of endeavor).

Both Plato and Aristotle contend that things can be known only in comparison to other things; that knowledge about things would be impossible if everything were unique in all respects. However, in contrast to Plato who argues that (conceptual) forms of objects exist as pure essences regardless of any particular sensate instances that they may be taken to signify, Aristotle posits that forms (as concepts) are derived from (and best known by examining) the particular instances of the phenomena that they are taken to represent.

Likewise, whereas Plato contends that people cannot develop viable knowledge of things through the senses, Aristotle envisions knowing as inevitably rooted in human sensory capacity. Relatedly, too, where Plato turns away from sensate encounters with the world in developing his philosophical pivot point, Aristotle intends to use human sensate contact with the world as the foundation for developing a theory of being and knowing. Moreover, whereas both Plato and Aristotle articulate and promote ideal images of community life and individual moralities, Aristotle intends to assume a stance that is explicitly comparative (across people's practices). Both strive for conceptualizations that are logical and coherent, but Aristotle, who is more attentive to the ways that people (as sensate beings) engage the world, sets out to develop a set of disciplines of wisdom that people (as civilized, community-based beings) might use in pursuing their endeavors.

Because of the immense range of his scholarship, Aristotle's work has considerable relevance for the social sciences. However, since his conceptualizations of the human condition are embedded within other agendas, much of his [social science] must be culled from materials intended for other purposes. Likewise, it is important that the subsequent applications of his works by various scholarly gate-keepers be acknowledged.

As with Western thought more generally, much of the relevance of Aristotle's work has been moderated by religious (especially Christian) theology. Although proportionately more of Plato's writings on morality and religious imagery appear to have been more centrally incorporated into Christian philosophy, Aristotle's depictions of human deliberation and agency were seen by some theologians to provide a dramatic conceptual stage for the struggle of good and evil. While Aristotle's images of the soul imply (a) generalized animal life-energies and (b) more particularized human capacities for deliberation, Christian theologians have recast his writings within the context of a(n eternal) soul to be saved.

Focusing more centrally on what they envisioned as the moral features of Plato's and Aristotle's writings, few theologians, religious studies scholars, or philosophers have given much consideration to the implications of Aristotle's notions of language, human agency, or persuasive interchange for the study of group life more generally.

As well, given Aristotle's emphasis on the (sensate) world, there has been a longstanding tendency to approach his views of reality as objectivist, structuralist, determinist, reductionist, and rationalist in thrust. Although these notions are readily evident in Aristotle's works, attributions of these sorts seem unduly limited. Rather notably, some other analytical themes may be found in his writings (especially his statements on ethics and rhetoric).

Thus (and in a fashion that somewhat anticipates what would later be termed American pragmatism), Aristotle (especially see *Nicomachean Ethics,*

Book III, 1109b–1115a, *Eudemian Ethics*, Book II, 1222b–1228a, *Magna Moralia*, Book I, 1187b–1190a) explicitly acknowledges the human capacity for deliberation (and minded activity). The following extract is indicative:

> *Deliberation is concerned with things that happen in a certain way for the most part, but in which the event is obscure, and with things in which it is indeterminate. We call in others to aid us in deliberation on important questions, distrusting ourselves as not being equal to deciding. . . . Having set the end they consider how and by what means it is to be attained; and if it seems to be produced by several means they consider by which it is most easily and best produced, while if it is achieved by one only they consider how it will be achieved by this and by what means this will be achieved . . . It seems, then, as has been said, that man is a moving principle of actions; now deliberation is about the things to be done by the agent himself, and actions are for the sake of things other than themselves. . . . The object of choice being one of the things in our own power which is desired after deliberation . . . (Aristotle,* Nicomachean Ethics, *Book III, 1112b–1113a [Ross, trans.])*

Much of Aristotle's writings on the practical (human vs. natural) sciences are embedded within prescriptive agendas, but he is nonetheless concerned with the ways that people *do things* (approach, anticipate, strategize, act, assess, and reorient themselves) both on a solitary basis and in concert with others. To this end, Aristotle (in a more pragmatist fashion) directly discusses matters of action, voluntarism, and deliberative choice as well as the related abilities of people to act toward themselves as objects (e.g., treat oneself as a friend) in *Nicomachean Ethics* (Book III, 1109b–1115a; 1168a–1169b), *Eudemian Ethics* (Book II, 1222b–1228a), and *Magna Moralia* (1187b–1190b; 1211a–1213b).

Aristotle (see *Politics,* Book I, 1253a–1253b) also is quite clear in stating that (a) people alone have the enabling quality of speech, (b) that language represents the basis on which people may make meaningful choices, and (c) that the (existing) community assumes a (facilitating/ foundational) priority relative to both the (particular) families and the individuals therein. Aristotle does not grasp (nor is he as concerned about) the fundamentally social essence of "the mind" as thoroughly, consistently, or centrally as do Dilthey ([Betanzos trans.], 1988), Mead (1934), Schutz (1962, 1964), and Blumer (1969), for instance. However, in contrast to most social theorists discussed in chapters 2 and 3, Aristotle clearly acknowledges (also see *Rhetoric, Poetics*) many of the minded features of human action, interaction, and community life that are presently associated with more contemporary pragmatist, interactionist, and constructionist positions in the social sciences.[18]

Although attending to a somewhat different set of matters, Isocrates (436–338 B.C.; who, like Plato, is one of Socrates' students), even more directly addresses the *enabling* features of speech for human group life (and influence):

> *For in the other powers which we possess we are in no respect superior to other living creatures; nay, we are inferior to many in swiftness and in strength and in other resources; but, because there has been implanted in us the power to persuade each other and to make clear to each other whatever we desire, not only have we escaped the life of wild beasts, but we have come together and founded cities and made laws and invented arts; and, generally speaking, there is no institution devised by man which the power of speech has not helped us to establish. . . . With this faculty we both contend against others on matters which are open to dispute and seek light for ourselves on things which are unknown; for the same arguments which we use in persuading others when we speak in public, we employ also when we deliberate in our own thoughts; and while we call eloquent those who are able to speak before a crowd, we regard as sage those who most skillfully debate their problems in their own minds. And, if there is need to speak in brief summary of this power, we shall find that none of the things which are done with intelligence take place without the help of speech, but that in all our actions as well as in all our thoughts speech is our guide, and is most employed by those who have the most wisdom. (Isocrates,* Nicocles *or the Cypians, 3–9 [Norlin, trans.])*

Still, perhaps nowhere is the subject of *influence work* as symbolic communication more systematically developed in early Greek and Roman society than in the practice and study of *rhetoric* (and oratory). Developing an appreciation of the importance of linguistic interchange, variously through the Hellenistic Greek poets (Homer, onward), the playwrights (e.g., Aristophanes),[19] the sophists (and [other] philosophers, educators, orators, and legal speech writers), and the many politicians of their time, Greek citizens appear highly cognizant of the persuasive quality of language (rhetoric and oratory skills) in reference to the fuller participation in Greek political and civil life.[20]

In contrast to most contemporary speech and rhetoric programs that seem primarily focused on the style and structuring of language and the implications of language structure for human thought, the early Greeks and Romans were highly attentive to the *persuasive* potential of language (and other symbolic communication) within the context of human activity (Rosenfield, 1971). Although the importance of rhetoric (and oratory) for political and civil life was recognized long before 500 B.C. (roughly marking the appearance of preserved, written texts in Greece), present-day scholars interested in the *tactical* features of power minimally may recognize some early advice given to rulers and citizens about their roles and relationships with one another, as well as an elaboration of the ways in which people might more strategically (i.e., advantageously) engage one another.

While acknowledging that his *Rhetoric* represents only one of several volumes of written materials on persuasion available (in the marketplace) to Greek citizens at the time,[21] Aristotle's statement attests to the considerable importance that the early Greeks placed on the spoken (and written) word in people's attempts to shape the ways in which others envision and engage the world about them.[22] Viewing rhetoric as a means of achieving persuasion on any subject matter, Aristotle appears to have intended to establish rhetoric as a realm of study on its own. Indeed, Aristotle posits that rhetoric is as indispensable as logic, since all people seem involved in assessing and maintaining arguments as well as defending themselves and condemning others in the course of community life.[23]

Aristotle's *Rhetoric* is a complex, multifocused volume that offers many departure points. Most centrally, it (a) provides a highly sustained analyses of the persuasive features of speech making,[24] but it is also punctuated (and conceptually distracted) by some prominent subthemes. These include (b) a critique of the (misleading and deceptive) rhetorical practices that Aristotle associated with the (mercenary) sophists of the time, (c) an attempt to foster logical and responsible decision making on the part of the citizens at large, (d) an exercise in the grammatical structuring of rhetoric, and (e) an intention to promote personal pleasure and community good as implied by moderation and intellectual discipline more generally.

Still, Aristotle provides many compelling observations on the use of rhetoric for influencing (and resisting) audiences. Distinguishing (1) *ethos* or the character of speakers, (2) *pathos* or the receptivities of the hearer (audience, judge), and (3) *logos* or the speech itself, Aristotle embarks on a sustained, detailed consideration of each of these features of the communication process. Thus, with respect to *the speaker* (Book I), Aristotle considers the ways that people may selectively invoke desired images of the participants in the setting by referencing issues of vice and virtue, accusation and defense, and motivations toward good and evil, as well as matters of injustice, equity, and guilt. Focusing on the concerns (also interests and disaffections) of *judges* in Book II, Aristotle attends to people's receptivities and resistances to speaker presentations. Thus, he addresses topics such as anger and placability, fear, shame, gratitude, pity, indignation, envy, lifestyles, and moral sentiments. Aspects of *the speech* are evident throughout the volume, but the demonstrative features are considered most directly in Books II and III. Here, Aristotle deals with the matters of plausibility, examples, logic, maxims, amplification and extenuation, style, words, metaphors, rhythm, personification, and summary statements.

It should not be surprising that Aristotle's works may invoke images of the sort that our contemporaries would associate with elaborate courtroom drama, for *Rhetoric* seems very much informed by extended observations of, and sustained verbal (and written) interchange regarding citizen participation in the political and legal arenas of early Greece.

Albeit generally less well known than *Rhetoric*, another volume *De Rhetorica Ad Alexandrum* seems no less relevant for scholars interested in the study of power. Allegedly written for Alexander the Great, *De Rhetorica . . .* focuses much more directly on matters of state and how these might be most feasibly accomplished by a political administrator. Following a discussion of public speeches and their realms of application in political arenas, consideration is given to such topics as developing and implementing laws, forming alliances, promoting and avoiding warfare, eulogizing and defending persons in public arenas, and presenting cases to audiences. In contrast to the broader set of prospective users associated with *Rhetoric*, the material in *De Rhetorica . . .* attends much more singularly to expediency (and advantage) of the office holder. At the same time, though (as with the position expressed by Isocrates, following), this volume is also concerned about the viability of the state and stresses the importance of the leader maintaining a competent, supportive citizen base as an enduring resource.

Like *Rhetoric*, *De Rhetorica Ad Alexandrum* is centrally focused on influence work or the practices in which people may engage in attempts to both persuade *and* dissuade others from making certain choices or engaging in particular actions. Hence, it is observed (in some detail) that those wishing to encourage others to do things are apt to benefit by stressing things that are just, lawful, expedient, pleasant, or practical, if not necessary. Those attempting to discourage others from adopting particular lines of action may attempt to show how these matters violate sensibilities of these sorts.

Rhetoric and *De Rhetorica Ad Alexandrum* provide extended illustrations of the (social) construction of influence work. This material is clearly mindful of people's abilities to strategically present themselves (and other things) to audiences as well as resist (critically assess and denounce) the claims and practices of others. In addition to attending to (a) presenters' own appearances, manners and activities, this also means (b) anticipating, defining, discerning, and challenging the viewpoints and practices of others who contend for favorable audience judgements, and (c) anticipating, defining, and adjusting to, the differing receptivities (and resistances) of the particular audiences to whom persuasive endeavors may be pitched.

Intended as a general (political science) discourse on the forms (and variable desirabilities thereof) of governing arrangements, Aristotle's *Politics* is somewhat more structuralist in its overall cast than is *Rhetoric* or *De Rhetorica Ad Alexandrum*. Still, one finds some material here that is more overtly tactical in emphasis. In addition to discussing the "causes of revolution" (and resistance) in various governmental forms (see Book V), Aristotle considers ways in which those pursuing continuity in particular modes of government (e.g., aristocracies, democracies, and tyrannies) might more effectively anticipate, resist, and adjust to others in those settings. It might also be acknowledged that, in setting an agenda for community governing practices, Aristotle's *Politics* assumes a broader tactical (social engineering) dimension (as even more directly do Plato's *Republic* and *The Laws*).

Also addressing the political issues of his time, Isocrates (436–338 B.C.) offers some noteworthy tactical counsel in *To Demonicus, To Nicocles,* and *Nicocles or the Cyprians.*[25] While the first two pieces are directed toward "princes" of sorts, the third is addressed towards a set of subjects. It indicates the roles that citizens might assume in fostering both a viable state and in enhancing their own conditions of living. Approaching the affairs of state in these manners, Isocrates presents some early, but nonetheless instructive guidelines for those holding office (particularly in reference to domestic affairs).

Somewhat like Machiavelli (discussed later), Isocrates cautions princes about their images and reputations as well as their own practices and responsibilities to their subjects. For instance:

> *You must care for the people and make it your first consideration to rule acceptably to them, knowing that all governments—oligarchies as well as the others—have the longest life when they best serve the masses. You will be a wise leader of the people if you do not allow the multitude either to do or to suffer outrage, but see to it that the best among them shall have the honours, while the rest shall suffer no impartment of their rights; for these are the first and most important elements of good government. (Isocrates,* To Nicocles, *15–17 [Norlin, trans.])*

Taken together, or individually, these works (*De Rhetorica Ad Alexandrum, Politics,* and Isocrates' *To Demonicus* and *To Nicocles*) represent highly compelling precursors to the oft-cited writings of Machiavelli. Much more importantly, though, they provide striking evidence of the enduring centrality of symbolic interchange for comprehending [power] at all levels of human affairs, including fundamental matters of state.

While the Greek influence became less prominent with the fall of Alexander the Great, the Greek emphasis on rhetoric (like many other aspects of Greek scholarship) was not only absorbed by the Romans but was spread throughout the Roman-occupied world. The Romans gave particular attention to rhetoric with respect to legal and political exchanges, but they also helped sustain an appreciation of rhetoric as a mode of persuasion in oral and written communication that is relevant across a wide band of public and private forums. Thus, Cicero's (106–43 B.C.) *De Inventione* and *De Oratore* as well as *Rhetorica Ad Herennium* (commonly attributed to Cicero) and Quintilian's (35–100 A.D.) *Institutio Oratorica* represent but a few of the many concerted Roman attempts to articulate, assess, and extend earlier notions of Greek rhetoric.

The early Greek and Roman scholars generally seem quite convinced of the importance of rhetoric for influencing human decisions (and practices) and rather extensively incorporated these into their educational programs (see Kennedy, 1963, 1972; Enos, 1993, 1995). Still, the more explicit analysis of *persuasive activity* (especially as symbolic interchange) has been neglected in most subsequent considerations of human relations (and power). It is particularly surprising that so little of the early Greek and Roman expositions on rhetoric have been incorporated into the study of influence processes in the social sciences (given the persistence of parallel processes in countless, untold settings, across virtually all contemporary settings and throughout the course of recorded history). How this neglect took place is not especially obvious, but a scholarly inattentiveness to the enabling and persuasive features of linguistic interchange clearly is not a uniquely twentieth (or twenty-first) century phenomenon.

Despite their interests in comprehending the human condition, most philosophers have tended to distance themselves from the persuasive aspects of rhetoric, perhaps associating it (variously) with verbal chicanery, the practice of law, the entertainment arts, psychology, political science, or speech and rhetoric programs. At least since the time of Plato, if not the early sophists, philosophers have been concerned with people's experiences of reality (i.e., of being, movement, and order—Rosenfield, 1971). However, relatively little philosophy has been concerned about examining the ways that people engage the world in more direct, active (and interactive) terms. For example, most contemporary philosophers may be cognizant of the phenomenology of Edmund Husserl, but proportionately few seem aware of the works of Mead (1934), Blumer (1969), and the Chicago-school ethnographic research tradition (which has been studying "group life in the making" for several decades). Thus, although Fay (1996) only begins to appreciate the relevance of the interactionist/ethnographic approach for philosophic analysis, his "philosophy of social science" appears relatively ground breaking in this respect.

While some might expect that the psychologists would be intensively engaged in the study of rhetoric (and persuasion processes), this has not happened. Most have been much more concerned about the search for factors thought to determine human behavior than examining influence processes in practice. Although they are less certain about the ways that one might study rhetoric in the course of actual human interchange, Cooper and Nothstine's (1992) and Billig's (1996) critiques of the failure of psychologists to acknowledge the significance of rhetoric for the study of human interchange are instructive here.

Those involved in speech and rhetoric programs have not generated a sustained analysis of actual human interchange either. While grappling with rhetoric-related concepts over the past two millennia, they seem to have emphasized (a) the structuring of language, (b) the ways that the structure of language may shape thought, and (c) the history of rhetoric rather than (d) examining (and conceptually articulating) the ways that people actually use language to influence (and resist) others. As Rosenfield (1971) notes, most rhetoricians have become trapped in the more general philosophic tendency to disassociate theory from action.

The political scientists, generally, also seem to disregard rhetoric as a mode of influence work. Like the philosophers, they readily acknowledge the discussions of government and moral philosophy that one finds in early Greek scholarship (especially Plato's *The Republic* and Aristotle's *Politics*). Many may be aware of passages from *Rhetoric,* particularly those that pertain to government, but they have largely ignored the ways that people use and experience rhetoric in practice. Like most academics in psychology and sociology, those in political science generally have focused on "the factors" associated with particular aspects of political phenomena. Thus, with the exception of fleeting references, they have disattended to the influence (and resistance work) evident in Aristotle's *Rhetoric* or *De Rhetorica Ad Alexandrum,* or Isocrates' *To Demonicus, To Nicocles,* and *Nicocles or the Cypians;* all of which may be seen to constitute (tactical) precursors to Machiavelli's *Discourses* and *The Prince.*

In part, too, many philosophers and political scientists seem to have become more concerned about discerning, promoting, and debating issues of forms of government and morality than developing theory and methods that centrally address the *lived* (and enacted) features of human group life. In all fairness, though, it should be noted that the viewpoints and concepts developed by the early Greek and Latin scholars were not transmitted to subsequent generations in open, well preserved, and complete packages. Thus, tracing the (artificial) separation of thought and action in rhetoric back to Plato, Rosenfield (1971) observes that a great many scholars (including Aristotle, Augustine, Spinoza, Descartes, Kant, and Hegel), albeit in differing ways, jointly contributed to this intellectual misadventure. This practice has been perpetuated by other structuralist thinkers (such as Auguste Comte, J. S. Mill, Wilhelm Wundt, Karl Marx, Max Weber, and Emile Durkheim) who have been more centrally involved in developing the (then) fledgling social sciences.

With the ruptures of early Hellenistic society following the death of Alexander the Great and the eventual demise of the Roman empire, subsequent scholars would very much depend on the earlier infusions of

Hellenistic culture with the Christian, Hebrew, and Arabic life-worlds for the perpetuation of early Greek thought. Our heritage, thus, has been shaped both by the physical ravages of time and by the varying viewpoints and interests of those into whose hands earlier documents may have fallen along the way.[26]

While working with their own agendas (e.g., religious, political, scientific), those engaged in maintaining (Western world) centers of learning through the centuries typically have used Greek and Latin texts to foster literacy, hence, generating (albeit selective) access to both particular and generalized realms of knowledge (Schottenloher, 1968; Rosenfield, 1971; Martin, 1988). In the process, a culturally, politically, and morally, highly diverse (and often disconnected) collection of people became consequential gatekeepers for the distribution of (and emphasis of particular themes within) the early Hellenistic and Roman classics. Building on an uneven and scattered set of interim forums, those developing later institutions of learning (and training) would tap into instances of Greco-Roman thought (and text), more or less continuously supplementing this with localized translations and ever more contemporary (allegedly new and improved) productions.[27]

However, the early Greco-Roman scholarship that pertains most directly to the social sciences constitutes only one small segment of the intellectual legacy handed down to us through the ages. It is worth observing that until the last century or so, most Western world scholars in the humanities would have some training in Greek and Latin, if not more direct exposure to an assortment of the early Greek and Roman classics.

We cannot be certain of what particular social theorists may have read, the materials to which they (or their associates) may have had access, or their notions of relevant concepts. Still it appears that Marx, Weber, and Durkheim, as well as Machiavelli, Hobbes,[28] Rousseau, Hegel, Simmel, Nietzsche, and Dilthey, for instance, had considerable, direct and indirect, exposure to early Greek scholarship, as seemingly also did Peirce, Dewey, and Mead. Thus, even though most of what we presently envision as "social theory" may have been written primarily over the past century or two, it is instructive to acknowledge some of the early foundations of the social sciences and particularly those that pertain to notions of human interchange (and power) across the parameters of the human condition.

Providing Political Advice: Machiavelli and De Callières

Whereas social scientists have only more recently begun to acknowledge the relevance of early Greek rhetoric for analyzing human relations (e.g., Cooper and Nothstine, 1992; Billig, 1996), Niccoló Machiavelli is often referenced in broader considerations of power. Still, a more explicit recognition of the relevance of both Machiavelli's work and that of the Greeks and Romans for human tactical interchange is notably absent in the writings of most of the social theorists cited in chapters 2 and 3. And, most scholars who cite Machiavelli have focused almost exclusively on what they define as a power-usurping, self-serving orientation.

Niccoló Machiavelli

> *(I)t must be understood that a prince, and especially a new prince, cannot observe all those things which are considered good in men, being often obliged, in order to maintain the state, to act against faith, against charity, against humanity, and against religion. And, therefore, he must have a mind disposed to adapt itself according to the wind, and as the variations of fortune dictate, and, as I said before, not deviate from what is good, if possible, but be able to do evil if constrained.*
>
> —Machiavelli, The Prince, *1950 [1513]:65*

Albeit often envisioned as "the tactical guru of power," Niccoló Machiavelli (1469–1527) clearly was not the first to offer textual advice on how kingdoms (*The Prince*) might be maintained. Indeed, Machiavelli may be seen as but one of a great many historical figures who have provided written tactical advice on matters pertaining to government and military practices.[29] Still, Machiavelli's work provides further testimony to some obdurate or generic features of power and human relations across the centuries.

It is quite apparent that Machiavelli (Lerner [1950:xxv–xlvi]) derived considerable inspiration from extended studies of Roman (especially Titus Livius) and Greek scholars who (centuries before) wrote about matters pertaining to conflict, tactical maneuverings, and the maintenance of control and social order. Beyond the comparative materials provided by these earlier scholars, however, Machiavelli drew upon his own experiences in, and observations of, the political settings in which he found himself.

As a secretary (privileged insider) to a senior government official for fourteen years, Machiavelli obtained instructive first-hand observations of the affairs of state. At midpoint in his career, following episodes of political upheaval, Machiavelli was subjected to what would become an extended period of exile from government service. It was at this time that Machiavelli began to produce a series of political commentaries that would eventually form the corpus for *The Discourses*. It was from these statements, too, that Machiavelli would develop *The Prince* (a volume that he hoped would result in an appropriate political appointment).

The term, *Machiavellianism,* is often used synonymously with self-serving pursuits or as a condemnation of ruthless political endeavors. However, whereas *The Discourses* and *The Prince* provide evidence of an author who is deeply interested in issues of power, influence, and control at a historical and conceptual level as well as someone intent on preserving existing social orders, it should not be assumed that Machiavelli was unconcerned with citizen liberties and representation in government (e.g., see *The Discourses*, Book 1, chapters v–viii, xvi–xviii).

For our immediate purposes, though, Machiavelli's work is important because of the attention that he (like the early Greek tactical advisors) gives to the human *enterprise* characterizing political life. Thus, matters of planning, deception, force, good will, reputation, finances, coalitions, loyalties, factions, shifting agendas, tradition, and legislation are brought into sharp, albeit uneven, relief as Machiavelli discusses people's attempts to influence *and* resist one another in an assortment of political arenas.

In contrast to the rational order theorists and those in the marxist nexus, who define power as more or less synonymous with structures and the relative dependencies of the parties involved, Machiavelli emphasizes the dynamic and tactical nature of power relations. Machiavelli's analysis is far from systematic, but (in *The Discourses* and *The Prince*) he outlines a range of tactics (including the selective uses of information, deception, negotiations, legislation, force) that more squarely acknowledge the reflective, strategic, interactive, and adjustive nature of human relations.[30] Given his emphasis on human interchange, Machiavelli's tactical expositions are closer to the present formulation than are the structuralists. At the same time, however, his position is too prescriptive and too fragmented conceptually to provide the essential foundations for an intersubjective theory of influence.

François De Callières

Although relatively unknown to most social scientists, the writings of some other tactical advisors also provide important insight into power as practical accomplishment. One much overlooked and relatively untapped resource is the materials developed by those serving as diplomats, ambassadors, representatives, or envoys to foreign governments.

Assuming a variety of objectives, postures, and interpersonal styles in their "tours of duty," these people typically are expected to provide their "home offices" with wide manners of information regarding the [social] settings to which they are dispatched and reside, often for extended periods of time. This genre of work roles is important, not only because it provides a direct testimony to the fundamental interlinkages of "macro" and "micro" issues, but also because it exemplifies the fundamental interpersonal accomplishment entailed in matters of state (and international relations) more generally.

While the dispatches (extended reports and other messages) directed to ambassadors' home offices (together with the many diaries and notes assembled in the process of pursuing information) and the ongoing task of maintaining viable contacts in the field are reminiscent of ethnographic work in certain regards, the baseline missions that these people pursue are quite different in thrust. Still, it is instructive to attend to accounts of, and instructions regarding, diplomacy as representational activity.

Monsieur François De Callières was clearly not the first person (as evidenced by his own references) to provide written instruction on, and considerations of, diplomatic missions, but in assembling, *On the Manner of Negotiating with Princes* (1716), De Callières provides readers with a wealth of insight on international relations, domestic affairs, and interpersonal relations, as well as a striking appreciation of the fundamental interrelatedness of these ["macro" and "micro"] issues.[31]

François De Callières was over seventy years of age when this volume was published, and it reflects the insights he had gained from serving in a variety of capacities in several foreign offices as well as a careful study of the written accounts of other diplomats' experiences. While intended as a reference manual of sorts for use by his "prince," De Callières' discussions of the various duties, activities, and pitfalls entailed in diplomatic ventures depict a set of life-worlds highly contingent on ongoing reflectivity, enterprise, and interactive adjustments. De Callières' attentiveness to tactical detail (even in what he acknowledges as a sketchy overview) also suggests how much social scientists have yet to learn from "practitioners in the field."

Considerable insight into the affairs of state and particular historical-contextual developments may be gleaned from the writings of other diplomats and envoys, as well as from close study of the often extended dispatches, field notes, and diaries that these people sometimes produced.[32] Unfortunately, except within narrow branches of political science, this literature has been largely neglected. Even in these subtraditions, however, fascinations with "the new diplomacy" or volatile "new situations" have often meant that more basic interpersonal features of diplomatic work have been ignored.[33] Consequently, this material has been applied to the study of power in only a minimalist sense.[34]

Other Purveyors of Advice

Although generally too disattuned to the objective of developing a systematic theory of human relations to be designated as social scientists, a great many other tactical advisors have given extended thought to the ways in which people manage their dealings with others. Intended primarily as practical advice, this literature (if one is to judge by its popularity in the political and public domains) addresses issues considered important to an exceedingly broad cross-section of society.

The tactical advice embedded in this body of writing ranges from matters of coordinating large-scale collective operations to ways of dealing with others in both fleeting and more enduring interpersonal relations. Whether one considers the suggestions presented in these various forums to be valuable and insightful or counterproductive and misguided, this material provides scholars with a fuller appreciation of the tactics (and rationales) that people may invoke in their associations with others. Given the massive nature of this literature, I can do little more than simply point to an assortment of themes that one encounters therein.

One broad set of messages pertain to the "empowerment of people through collective action." These have served as rallying themes for wide ranges of coordinated resistances and more enduring associations. In addition to more isolated instances of protests, riots, boycotts, strikes, demonstrations, sabotage, vigilante activity, and the like, concerns of this sort have been invoked in developing much more sustained resistance in associations of all sorts. In conjunction with this, a great variety of collective stances have been counseled in the literature. These range from violent upheaval to nonviolent confrontation (e.g., Gandhi, 1951; Alinksy, 1971; Sharp, 1973;[35] Nader [Caplan, 1983]), and collective bargaining practices.

Professing to empower groups of people who (are encouraged to) define themselves as disadvantaged in structuralist terms, concerns typically are directed toward the formulation and popularization of troublesome issues, the recruitment of members, and coordination and implementation of (nonviolent) resistance tactics. While authors of these sorts seldom provide scholarly analyses of instances of actual exchange or people's mobilization experiences, their writings may sensitize researchers to some of the processes by which those who become involved in collective enterprises define situations, achieve organizational states, and engage others in the setting.

Included in this broader literature, also, are prescriptions for achieving, maintaining and solidifying leadership or managerial positions,[36] advice regarding negotiation tactics between adversaries,[37] and suggestions for influencing others in the marketplace (on either a generalized, media basis or at the level of interpersonal selling).[38]

Another broad sector of literature in this field has been intended to "empower" people defined as targets or subject to the domination of others. Designed to turn "targets into tacticians," these materials have been pitched at both individual and collective levels. Indicative here are materials on "consumer bewarisms"[39] and "assertiveness training."[40]

Generally much less confrontational in thrust, another broad body of literature revolves around matters of self-control, self-improvement, more

effective presentations of self,[41] interpersonal diplomacy, and the development of more desired relationships. Here, matters of composure, content-
ment, and a sense of direction in life are depicted as the means of more
effectively dealing with, and living more comfortably in a world of, others.
Pitched somewhat at what Goffman (1959) terms "impression management," it is worth noting that at least since the time of Isocrates (436–338
B.C.; in, *To Nicocles*) people have been attentive to the importance of self-
restraint, self-improvement, personal appearances, and the management of
interpersonal comportment in their dealings with others.[42]

In Context

Because it has taken us away from contemporary notions of power in the
social sciences, chapter 4 may seem diversionary in certain respects. At the
same time, though, this material suggests that concerns with power as
denoting *enacted* realms of interchange not only transcend recorded history,
but have widesweeping present and futuristic relevance as well.

As indicated in chapters 2 and 3, a great many social scientists (and
social theorists) have disattended to human agency, enterprise, and interchange in the analysis of power. However, there is little basis, if one is to
judge by the writings of the early Greeks or those providing tactical advice
more generally, for either minimizing the centrality of human agency and
enterprise in the analysis of power or assuming that our contemporaries are
likely to engage one another in ways that are fundamentally different from
the interchanges that took place in "ancient times."

Clearly, my own familiarity with the Greek (and Roman) classics is
limited. However, it is apparent that some of the writings of the early Greeks
(especially some materials associated with Aristotle) resonate notably with
aspects of the pragmatist/interactionist position taken in this volume. Still,
the linkages are far from uniform. Thus, for instance, although Aristotle
(particularly in his work on rhetoric, ethics and politics) is attentive to (a)
some relativist, reflective, engaged, negotiated, and processual features of
human activity (and interchange) within the community setting, his
broader analyses of the human condition are fused with images of (b) an
overarching, universal order, (c) various deterministic features of nature,
(d) some structuralist (personality and organizational) themes, and (e)
prescriptions intended to improve people's circumstances.

Emerging as something of an intellectual "by-product" (i.e., intended
to foster comprehension) of his broader quest for improving the human
condition, Aristotle's [social science] is very uneven, epistemologically
speaking. Clearly, his work lacks the more sustained conceptual and methodological coherence of symbolic interaction (à la Blumer, 1969). Never-

theless, Aristotle's considerations of the human condition predate, if these have not also informed in certain respects, the American pragmatist tradition (as represented by Charles Peirce, William James, John Dewey, and especially George Herbert Mead) on which Herbert Blumer so centrally builds.

While primarily assuming a strategic, often prescriptive (vs. a social science) orientation, the more general corpus of material on "tactical advice" is important to social scientists. Insofar as people "out there" attend to these writings and other orientational endeavor, these notions may be incorporated into their relations with others, as well as denote some centralizing frames of reference.[43] Minimally, though, this literature should help alert social scientists to the great many ways that people may approach situations and the wide scope of practices that may be encompassed by matters of power, control, influence, and resistance at all levels of community life. Although these purveyors of tactical advice offer little in the way of direct, sustained research on human interchange, their writings suggest a great many arenas of community life that would lend themselves to productive ethnographic inquiry.

Chapters 5–8 build on aspects of the literature introduced thus far, but rather than attempt to systematically or thoroughly synthesize the various statements on power introduced to this point, this material conceptualizes power in a manner that is more uniquely and consistently attentive to the ways in which human affairs are accomplished in the here and now.

Envisioning power as a fundamental feature of human relations that may be invoked at *all* levels of analysis and in *all* realms of association, the approach taken from this point more explicitly addresses the ways in which power is defined, experienced, and accomplished within, and across, (ongoing) community life. The chapters following do not presume to offer any solutions to what some might define as the "power problem." However, in "recasting power as intersubjective accomplishment," this material provides a series of departure points for a fuller, grounded (i.e., ethnographic) examination of human interchange and, resultingly, a more adequate appreciation of influence work as an essential feature of the human condition.

Notes

1. The term, *Western civilization* is used primarily as a convenient historical device. While the term distinguishes those traditions more conventionally associated with European influences from Far Eastern (Asian) worldviews, it should be acknowledged that "Hellenistic culture" represents a synthesis of sorts of an assortment of Mediterranean cultures, which, in turn, are rather diversified in East-West (and North-South) terms.

2. It is estimated (see *Cambridge Ancient History*, 1970, Vol. 1, Part 1: 226) that the earliest forms of writing (versus hieroglyphics or pictographic images) may have been developed about 3000 B.C. Readers interested in the development of writing and (relatedly) published text are apt to find Schottenloher (1968) and Martin (1988) particularly relevant.

3. Those wishing general accounts of the history of the development of social thought may find it instructive to consult Herder (1784), Dilthey (Betanzos [trans.], 1988), Bogardus (1960), Becker and Barnes (1978), and the expansive *Cambridge Ancient History*. Valuable overviews of early Greek and Roman rhetoric (sophism and oratory) can be found in Sandys (1920), Freeman (1949), Kennedy (1963, 1972), Guthrie (1971), Enos (1993, 1995), McKirahan (1994), Poulakos (1995), Billig (1996), and Johnstone (1996). My own acquaintance with the classics literature is rather rudimentary, but it is clearly essential that one examine the fuller-text originals (e.g., Plato, Isocrates, Aristotle). While the sources of the former sort are helpful in contextualizing people's writings more generally, these overviews typically disattend to particular but consequential features of the authors whose works they address in more historical sweeps.

4. While Greek culture (which was much more diverse than seems commonly supposed) was to permeate Roman life-worlds (and those of the larger Mediterranean region), most notably with respect to Greek (spoken *and* written) language, the Greco-Roman arenas are much more intertwined than might first seem. See Becker and Barnes (1978,V1: especially 135–256).

5. Given the remarkable competence of early Greek scholarship, a formulation along these lines seems within the range of possibilities, but this [potentiality] may well have been diverted by tendencies on the part of some (e.g., Socrates and Plato) to locate considerations of the human condition within (a) objectivist (abstracted, detached) vs. pragmatist (human lived, engaged) notions of reality, (b) moral directives (idealisms, disaffections, and prescriptions) vs. a sustained, secularized, relativist analysis, and (c) an enduring skepticism of the possibility that humans may know (and represent) the sensate or natural world.

6. Many would concur with the viewpoints that Aristotle (a) articulated the foundations of Western science (e.g., see *Posterior Analytics*) and (b) tried to comprehend the human condition in a scientific manner (i.e., invoking concept-oriented formulations, using rational-deductive logic, attending to observables, and generating systematic, comparative analysis). Still, it should be observed that Aristotle's considerations of human behavior are more explicitly deliberative (rationality as reflective), action-oriented, and interactive (e.g., see *Rhetoric, Eudemian Ethics, Nicomachean Ethics, Magna Moralia, Metaphysica, Poetics,* and *Politics*) than that characterizing a great deal of contemporary (factors-oriented) social science.

Similarly, while idealizing people who are more (a) moderate, rational (logical), and self-disciplined, (b) even-tempered, responsible, and reasonable in their dealings with others, and (c) extensively engaged in the quest for intellectual fulfilment, Aristotle recognizes that people's viewpoints and practices generally fall short of these standards.

Aristotle is inconsistent in his emphasis of the relative importance of biological tendencies, character traits (and learned dispositions), solitary deliberations, and persuasive (influential, accommodative, and resistant) interchanges. Likewise, Aristotle shifts unevenly between (a) presuming that people attend to a pure, objective, or singularistic sensate world and (b) acknowledging that people engage the world by invoking notably different viewpoints, wisdoms, objectives, and modes of tactical interchange (see, for instance, *Rhetoric, Nicomachean Ethics,* and *Politics*) with respect to the things they encounter (and define).

On a methodological note, it may be most fair to say that Aristotle envisions the understanding of human condition (involving language, recollectable memory, deliberation, agency, activity, and strategic interchange) as requiring an approach different from those entailed in the study of inanimate objects and (nonhuman) animals. But apart from a more general, stylistically-invoked, comparative emphasis, Aristotle does not appear to have resolved the issue of the best way to approach the study of human behavior or whether it is fully possible (or even necessary, given his prescriptive agendas) to do so.

7. Readers might appreciate that some of the dates (birth-death) given in this statement are much more approximate than others. Nevertheless, they are useful in establishing chronological sequences of sorts.

8. So far as I know, we have no writings that may be directly attributed to Socrates (470–399 B.C.), but Plato (who appears to have been highly attentive to his mentor) uses Socrates as the central figure (and source of wisdom) in many of his dialogues.

9. Although Hellenistic notions of epistemology are often blended with images of gods (and superheroes), many Greek sophists (and philosophers) appear to have been skeptical of their existence. However, mindful of the experiences of Protagoras, Socrates, and others who incurred the wrath of believers in the community, they may have been hesitant to make their doubts more apparent.

10. The term *sophist* (Freeman, 1949: 341–342) seems earlier to have referred to skilled craftsman and experts as well as the wise and sagely, but following Socrates (see Plato) it also was used to encompass educators, orators, philosophers, legal counsels (speech writers), and "con artists." Defining themselves as "philosophers" (and discerners of truth and good), Socrates, Plato, and Aristotle, amongst others, are severely critical of those they define as sophists, contending that the sophists accept fees for profess-

ing unfounded wisdom and deceptively representing cases in public forums. Assuming roles as self-appointed protectors of the community, Plato (especially) and Aristotle expend considerable effort in their writings (see *Theaetetus* and *Rhetoric,* respectively) attempting to discredit the sophists. Protagoras, who appears to have initiated the practice of charging for imparting his wisdom to others (i.e., a paid educator), was a particular target of their disaffection.

11. In his introduction to a translation of the (substantial) work of Sextus Empiricus, Bury (1933) provides a valuable introduction to classic skepticism. Readers may be interested to observe that the skeptics (who were dubious of all forms of knowing) were quite attentive to what might be termed "cultural relativism" (see Sextus Empiricus, *Outlines of Pyrrhonism,* Book I:135–140 and 163). They also had a long-standing, articulate rejection of the concept of *cause* as "a thing in itself, and causality (as) a real objective quality inherent therein" (Bury, 1933:xxxviii; also see *Outlines of Pyrrhonism,* Book I: 180–186; Book III: 13–29).

12. Albeit of unknown authorship, *Dissoi Logi or Dialexeis* (c. 400 B.C.; from Sprague, 1972: 279–293) provides another, very explicit (sophist) statement on the *relativity* of human definitions of objects and practices. Building on comparisons of both Greek–non-Greek practices and variations of Greek domestic life, the author provides a great many illustrations of contrasting moralities and viewpoints within. As a summary point of sorts, the following quote directly addresses the relativity of human morality:

> . . . *they say that if a group of people should collect from all the nations of the world their disgraceful customs and then should call everyone together and tell each man to select what he thinks is seemly, everything would be taken away as belonging to the seemly things. (Anonymous,* Dissoi Logi or Dialexeis; *Sprague [trans.], 1972:284)*

13. It is not apparent, however, that Plato or Aristotle are particularly concerned about individual versus group viewpoints in some of these debates. Still, both are keenly aware of human capacities for interchange. See, for instance, Plato's *Republic* and *The Laws* and Aristotle's *Rhetoric, Politics,* and *Nicomachean Ethics.*

14. Some related themes are developed in Plato's *Cratylus,* wherein Plato's characters debate about the nature of "names assigned to objects," whether these are matters of convention (given the seeming variations that one encounters from community to community, or groups therein) or whether names reflect some properties that the designated objects somehow possess. Although the matter is left unresolved (and Plato's Socrates assumes the position that we have to go beyond words to examine some more fundamental, stable essences of objects), it is apparent that images of

relativism and "constructionism" run through the dialogues (the passages 384d–385d; 422d; 433e–434a; 438a–438c from *Cratylus* highlight some key points of contention).

15. In *Theaetetus*, Plato particularly attempts to discredit the position of Protagoras ("Man is the measure . . ."), in part by building on Heraclitus's notion that "everything is in perpetual flux." Through (his character) Socrates, Plato ends up at a position in which he argues that there is no viable human criterion for knowing or judging knowledge (about the sensate world).

16. Focusing on Plato's presumptions, categorizations, and inferential practices, Schiller (1908) provides a thoughtful, humanist (pragmatist) critique of Plato's rendering of Protagoras' maxim in *Theaetetus* (also see Burnyeat, 1990:1). Essentially, instead of suggesting that one might examine people's actual practices "in the world out there," Plato moves to a higher level of abstraction and, thus, misses the (human grounded, experiential, accomplishment-oriented) pragmatist turn.

17. Those more familiar with the works of Alfred Schutz (1962, 1964) or Berger and Luckmann (1966) will likely recognize that (*other than* disattending to the ways in which people directly engage [the world]), Plato's *Theaetetus* raises virtually all of the key issues pertinent to a sociology of knowledge. Thus, matters pertaining to diversity (and relativity) of perspectives, persuasive communication, ongoing process, and the problematics of representation (knowing things and sharing information) are evident in this set of dialogues.

Relatedly, some passages in Plato's *Sophist* (Cooper, 1997) also connote a [constructionist] or [pragmatist] viewpoint. Intending to describe and discredit the "sophists," Plato acknowledges a longstanding debate between the idealists and the objectivists about the "essences of reality." Addressing (a) the problematics of defining "that which is" and "that which is not," Plato also considers people's images of (b) stability vs. change and (c) similarities vs. differences, as well as (d) the human capacity for speech and reflectivity. In contrast to the idealistic position that Plato usually takes regarding "the impossibility of knowing about the sensate world," Plato's central spokesperson (pragmatically) insists on locating knowledge claims within the contexts to which people refer.

In *Parmenides*, Plato (Cooper, 1997) not only questions Socrates' "forms" as phenomena that exist beyond the realm of human experience (a position commonly attributed to Plato), but also embarks on an extended consideration of the *relativity* entailed in conceptions of "the one" and "the many," suggesting that matters of these sorts reflect human perspectives.

However, it is Aristotle who more directly and consistently opposes the idealist viewpoints of Socrates and others. Thus, Aristotle's *Metaphysica* invokes sensory-based notions of "being" and "knowing" (also see *On Genera-*

tion and Corruption). Aristotle is considerably more conceptually-oriented, historically-detailed, and experientially-grounded than is Plato.

Aristotle also is both aware of the totalizing relativism of Protagoras' statement and the (related) contradictions that inhere in claiming that either "everything is true" or that "everything is false." As Aristotle observes:

> . . . *those who ask for an irresistible argument, and at the same time demand to be called to account for their views, must guard themselves by saying that the truth is not what appears exists, but that what appears exists for him to whom it appears, and when, and in the sense in which, and in the way in which it appears. And if they give an account of their view, but do not give it in this way, they will soon find themselves contradicting themselves. (Aristotle,* Metaphysica, *Book IV, 1011a [Ross, trans.])*

18. The position articulated here is notably at variance from the heavy structuralist/objectivist emphases generally attributed to Aristotle. Indeed, the more interpretive, enterprising, and interactive aspects of Aristotle's work seem to have been disregarded by even those (e.g., G. H. Mead, 1938) working more centrally in the pragmatist tradition. In part, this may reflect a longstanding scholarly tendency to generalize about the viewpoints and emphasis of the early Greek scholars, using Plato as *the* primary reference point. Relatedly, those focusing on theology, ethics, or moral philosophy seem inclined to cast much of Aristotle's consideration of the human condition within the context of idealist (prescriptive and remedial) dimensions rather than within the broader realm of human endeavor. It appears, too, that Aristotle's *Rhetoric, De Rhetoric Ad Alexandrum, Poetics,* and *Politics* (wherein the more deliberative, tactical, and interactive features of human group life seem particularly evident) have been comparatively neglected by both theologians and philosophers. Although it is not as explicitly attentive to the intersubjective essence of community life as is the present project, Daniel Robinson's (1989) statement, *Aristotle's Psychology* (especially chapter 8 on "the self and social order"), assumes a position somewhat parallel to the one developed here.

19. Those familiar with Aristophanes's plays (e.g., *The Clouds*) may appreciate that notions of relativity, image work, elaborate deception, and multiple, situated definitions of reality were somewhat commonplace in early Greek theater.

20. For overviews of early Greek and Roman rhetoric and oratory, see Kennedy (1963, 1972) and Enos (1993, 1995).

21. Quintilian (Vol I, Book II, I–II) provides a more complete rendering of the early history of rhetoric.

22. Only some of these texts (apparently available in the early Greek marketplace) appear to have survived the passage of time, but *De Rhetorica*

Ad Alexandrum is also indicative of this broader trend. *Rhetoric* and *De Rhetorica Ad Alexandrum* appear to be the most comprehensive of the writings on rhetoric (denoting persuasion work) generally available to the scholars of the time.

23. In addition to concerns with rhetoric as a device enabling one to influence others in the realms of law, finance, trade, and politics, rhetoric was long recognized (see Aristotle's *Rhetoric*) as a facility that could be used in both building and destroying people's reputations in the community (especially around matters of honor and disgrace).

24. Aristotle wants to ensure that people (a) develop rational-deductive reasoning in articulating the positions that they present to others for their consideration and (b) acquire the capacity for discerning deductively viable, irrelevant, and flawed claims that those promoting other positions may make. At the same time, however, Aristotle is highly aware that judges may be influenced by considerations (and tactics) other than those involving rational-deductive argument. Thus, while depreciating these other modes of persuasion in comparative terms, Aristotle deals at some length with the deployment and neutralization of appeals of these (lesser) sorts that people may use to strengthen their positions relative to those assessing the merits of the cases presented to them.

25. A student of both the sophist/orator Gorgias and the philosopher Socrates, Isocrates is credited not only with having written a text on rhetoric, but also with promoting the discipline of rhetoric more generally (Cicero, *De Inventione*, II, II, 7–8).

26. Interestingly, as Schottenloher (1968) and Martin (1988) note, some natural disasters (e.g., volcanic eruptions) have served to preserve (i.e., rendered salvagable) some documents that might be otherwise lost through human disregard and destruction or natural decay.

27. Billig (1996) cites a number of English rhetoricians, such as Lever (1573), Blount (1654), and Smith (1657), who have attended, on an interim basis, to some persuasive features of rhetoric. While instructive in a historical context, these works lack conceptual depth when compared to Aristotle, Cicero, or Quintilian, for instance.

28. As Schlatter (1975:xi) notes, in his introduction to Hobbes's (1629) translation (from Greek) of Thucydides' *The History of the Peloponnesian War,* this volume was not only the starting point for Hobbes's career as a scholar (and philosopher), but reflected a more general Renaissance practice of consulting Greek and Roman historians in attempts to establish reference points for dealing with the political problems of the times. Also see Machiavelli's references to the Roman historian, Titus Livius (Livy).

29. The earliest written Chinese statement on tactical advice that I have been able to locate is Sun Tzu's *The Art of War* (c. 500 B.C.). It is perhaps worth noting, too, that some of the Greek sophists/historians (e.g.,

Xenophon—Delbrook, 1920) also developed texts intended as military advice. The apparently longstanding practice of dedicating tactical manuals to prominent office holders is openly acknowledged by (the Roman) Vegetius in *De Re Militari* (c. 400 A.D.).

30. An attentiveness to these fundamental aspects of human relations is evident in the writings of some other early (pre-Machiavellian) military advisors. See Sun Tzu (c. 500 B.C.) and Vegetius (c. 400 A.D.), for instance.

31. Addressing the human enterprise undergirding affairs of state, De Callière's (1716) work points to some basic weaknesses of those adopting structuralist (e.g., Weber, Marx, Foucault) orientations to the study of power.

32. In addition to matters of access, great care would have to be taken in attempting to authenticate and interpretively contextualize these works. As De Callières (1716) observes, the detailed contextualization of "information" is not new, but rather is germane to the diplomatic exercise in a most fundamental sense.

33. As experts in the field, from De Callières (1716) to Kissinger (1994), underscore, diplomacy and international relations are very much matters of intersubjective accomplishment. For a somewhat limited, but still noteworthy, annotated bibliography that addresses many realms of diplomacy, see Harmon (1971). Although much less extensive, Craig's (1979) statement on "diplomatic history" is also relevant here.

34. The ethnographic potential of inquiry focusing on diplomatic missions and the interchanges involving foreign and home offices is substantial, not only for students of power and affairs of state, but also for those interested in socialization, interpersonal adjustment, relationships, deception, confidence, intimacy and distancing, and the like.

35. For a fairly succinct commentary on Sharp's theory of power (and some related works), see Martin (1989).

36. See, for instance, advice on how to secure political position (Shadegg, 1964; Paizis, 1977; Simpson, 1981; Atkinson, 1984; Schwartzman, 1989), lobby congress (Wolpe, 1990), conduct oneself as an "effective manager" (Kotter, 1985; Argyris, 1993; Lynch, 1993; Wilkinson, 1993; Harrison, 1994), hold "perfect meetings" (Sharman, 1994), or avoid (or contain) prison riots (Useem et al., 1996).

37. For some illustrations of advice on negotiation, see Nierenberg (1968), Lewis (1981), Ilich (1992), and Kennedy (1994).

38. For examples of materials providing advice on media promotions, see Edwards and Brown (1959) and Barton (1970). Suggestions for interpersonal selling tactics are provided by Frank and Lapp (1959), Gross (1959), Ling (1963), Kahn (1963), Girard (1977), and Norris (1982), among others.

39. Wrighter's (1972) exposé of advertising practices is instructive in this regard as is Ralph Nader's (Caplan, 1983) attempts to caution con-

sumers and promote collective resistance to misleading or unsafe marketing endeavors.

40. Although assertiveness training has become more singularly associated with aggressive (confrontational) behavior in popular usage, it originally was intended to foster affectionate as well as confrontational expressions on the part of psychiatric patients (Wolpe, 1958; 1990).

41. Eggert (1992) and Bolles (1998), for example, discuss job hunting and self-presentation in employment-related interviews.

42. In addition to psychological counseling manuals of all sorts, readers are referred to advisors such as Post (1922), Carnegie (1936), Dix (1939), and Peele (1952, 1990).

43. Beyond an extensive, written advisory literature, people also are apt to encounter even more advice on direct interpersonal levels (e.g., consider friends, associates, counselors). Likewise, people may also develop images of influence (and resistance) work from personal observations of exchanges involving others, as well as from exposure to highly diverse portrayals of human interchange in the media (e.g., newspapers, movies, television). While people may face the matters of assessing relevancy, authenticity and viability of any tactical suggestions they encounter, it is important that social scientists appreciate the potentially expansive and multifaceted notions of influence (and resistance) work to which people are exposed through ongoing participation in the human community.

PART III

POWER AS INTERSUBJECTIVE ACCOMPLISHMENT

5 *Attending to Human Interchange*

> *In making the process of interpretation and definition of one another's acts central in human interaction, symbolic interaction is able to cover the full range of the generic forms of human association. It embraces equally well such relationships as cooperation, conflict, domination, exploitation, consensus, disagreement, closely knit identification, and indifferent concern for one another. The participants in each of such relations have the same common task of constructing their acts by interpreting and defining the acts of each other. The significance of this simple observation becomes evident in contrasting symbolic interaction with the various schemes of human interaction that are to be found in the literature. Almost always such schemes construct a general model of human interaction or society on the basis of a particular type of human relationship.*
>
> *—Blumer, 1966:538*

Although many social scientists have written about power and countless others have frequently invoked the term *power* in more casual analysis of the human condition, surprisingly little attention has been given to the essence of power as it takes shape in the course of human group life, as an element of human lived experience.

Further, and no less ironically, while symbolic interactionism (Mead, 1934; Blumer, 1969) frequently has been criticized (especially in mainstream sociological circles) for neglecting power, it is the interactionists who are best able to provide a means of approaching the *study* of power as it is manifested within the human community. Not only is the interactionist viewpoint more amenable to considerations of the ways in which [power] is brought into existence, implemented, experienced, sustained, objectified, resisted, dissipated, and reconstituted in actual practice than is any other approach in the social sciences, but interactionism (by means of ethnographic inquiry) also provides the essential methodology for examining power as an element of human lived experience.

The interactionist tradition is also nonpartisan and while centrally concerned with social change (i.e., ongoing human enterprise and adjustment), it does not attempt to promote or resist any form or substantive realm of human endeavor.[1] Thus, in contrast to those theorists who encourage one or other modes of human experience, the central objective of the interactionist enterprise is to understand the ways in which people deal with one another in all manifestations of the human condition.

Likewise, in opposition to those who emphasize a particular mode of human association such as conflict, cooperation, or compromise in accounting for social order, the interactionist approach attends to *all forms of human association,* directing primary emphasis toward people's actual experiences (considerations, practices, interchanges) in the "here and now" of community life. In contrast to those approaches, then, that might envision power as "the key to understanding community life," the interactionist approach takes the viewpoint that power is best understood within the context (and processes) of ongoing community life. This requires that scholars attend carefully to the ways in which people engage others in all forms and contexts of human association.

This chapter is divided into three sections. The first part provides an overview of the interactionist approach, along with some related conceptual issues. The second section reviews the interactionist literature that more directly addresses power. The last section establishes some further parameters for envisioning power as a definitional, enacted phenomenon.

The Interactionist Paradigm

So that readers might better contextualize the materials presented in this volume more generally, consideration is given to (1) a baseline introduction to symbolic interactionism, (2) some of the more common misunderstandings or misrepresentations of interactionist thought in the literature, (3) subcultural mosaics and intersubjective realities, (4) the ethnographic quest for intersubjectivity, and (5) generic dimensions of association.

Orientational Premises[2]

Addressing four central features of symbolic interaction in the following passage, Herbert Blumer provides an instructive departure point:[3]

> *(1) people, individually and collectively, are prepared to act on the basis of the meanings of the objects that comprise their world; (2) the association of people is necessarily in the form of a process in which they are making indications to one another and interpreting each other's indications; (3) social acts, whether individual or collective, are constructed through a process in which the actors note, interpret, and assess the situations confronting them; and (4) the complex*

interlinkages of acts that comprise organization, institutions, division of labor,
and networks of interdependency are moving and not static affairs. (Blumer,
1969:50)

If one were to quickly locate symbolic interactionism in the broader traditions of academia,[4] it might be observed that although Herbert Blumer introduced the term in 1937, interactionism is very much rooted in the pragmatism of John Dewey (1859–1952), Charles Horton Cooley (1864–1929), and especially George Herbert Mead (1863–1931).[5] While emphasizing the practical accomplishment of human group life, these scholars (particularly Mead) were mindful of the *verstehen* or hermeneutic tradition associated with Wilhelm Dilthey (1833–1911) and others in the interpretivist branch of German social thought. Thus, while emphasizing the study of group life "in the making," the pragmatists are attentive to the differing ways that people (as members of various linguistic communities) make sense of and act toward [things].

Interactionist thought was fused with two other noteworthy analytical themes. One of these reflects the work of Georg Simmel (1858–1918), whose conceptual emphasis on social *process* and the study of society as forms of association resonates strongly with the analytical thrusts of Dilthey,[6] Cooley, Mead, and Blumer. A second, more prominent synthesis involves the merging of the pragmatist/interpretivist tradition with ethnographic inquiry. While most commonly associated with anthropology, the ethnographic tradition that developed in sociology at the University of Chicago (primarily through W. I. Thomas, Ellsworth Faris, Robert Park, and their students) was to provide the essential methodological complement to the then emergent Meadian social psychology.[7]

George Herbert Mead (philosophy department) provided the primary conceptual frame and many others contributed to the interactionist enterprise, but it was Herbert Blumer who most singularly synthesized Meadian thoughts on the human community with ethnographic inquiry. The emphasis was on developing an empirically grounded social science; a science of human behavior that thoroughly (theoretically and methodologically) respects the nature of ongoing community life. It was to be a sustained examination of the ways that people as "community-minded" beings actively engage [the world] about them.

Because readers can refer to more extended discussions of symbolic interaction (Mead, 1934; Blumer, 1969; Strauss, 1993; Prus, 1996b) and its implications for the study of human group life (Prus, 1997b), the following listing of assumptions is intended only to foster shared rudimentary orientations with the reader:[8]

1. *Human group life is intersubjective.* Human group life is constituted through the development of shared, linguistically mediated or symbolically constructed, realities. Since language is the primary enabling feature of the human community, the group precedes the individual for the practical purposes of socialization and the development of cognitive awareness. People develop (and recast) worldviews or perspectives as they (symbolically) interact with one another and engage [the world] in terms of collectively shared symbolic representations (or images) of [the objects] to which they attend.

2. *Human group life is (multi) perspectival.* As groups of people engage the world on an ongoing basis, they develop viewpoints or notions of reality that differ from those of other groups. Still, insofar as members of groups operate (think and act) in particular versions of reality that they linguistically share (albeit somewhat unevenly) with particular communities of others at an intersubjective level, they begin to attach notions of objectivity to their viewpoints and practices. Ergo, the development of "multiple realities" (Schutz, 1962).

3. *Human group life is reflective.* By attending to the viewpoint of "the other" (what Mead [1934] terms, "role-taking"), people are able to attribute meanings not only to other objects but also to their own "essences." In taking the viewpoint of the other into account, thereby becoming "objects unto themselves," people are able to achieve a sense of agency. This enables people to develop lines of action that acknowledge themselves as objects to be acted toward in a world of (socially constructed) objects.

4. *Human group life is activity-based.* Human activity is not the mere expression of various forces or factors exerting themselves on people, but (as Blumer observes) represents an essential formulative process in itself. As reflective, interacting beings, people are centrally involved in the production of meaningful activity (i.e., the doing, constructing, creating, building, forging, coordinating, and adjusting of behavior) in community contexts.

5. *Human group life is negotiable.* While people are able to do some things more extensively their own, a great deal of human activity involves others in more direct manners. Thus, people may endeavor to influence and resist (the influences of) others, as implied in notions such as recruitment, distancing, cooperation, coordination, competition, conflict, and compromise.

6. *Human group life is relational.* People identify and act toward others on a somewhat selective (object) basis, as implied in matters of identities, interpersonal preferences, loyalties, and disaffections.

7. *Human group life is processual.* Human lived experiences (and activities) are viewed as emergent, ongoing, or temporally developed social constructions or productions. Thus, the emphasis on human group life "in the making."

While these premises may seem relatively common-sensical to many, if not most, readers, they have rather profound methodological implications for those studying the human condition. Addressing the human nature of our subject matter, these premises require that social scientists invoke methodological practices that attend to (1) the ways in which people make sense of the world in the course of symbolic (linguistic) interchange, (2) people's capacities for developing multiple viewpoints on [objects], (3) people's abilities to take themselves and others into account in engaging [the world] about them, (4) the enterprising, action-oriented dimensions of the human condition, (5) people's capacities for influencing and resisting one another, (6) the particular forms of association that people develop with others in the course of community life, and (7) process or the developmental sequencing of people's activities (and interchanges).

The implications of these premises for generating theory about the human condition, likewise, are quite substantial. It means that *theory* should be developed from extended, grounded instances of inquiry of human group life in the making. Theory about people should be attentive to the ways that people engage the world about them. Rather than impose a variety of top-down structuralist factors, systems, or rationalities on the human condition, a more explicit appreciation of the premises outlined here implies theory development that attends to people's experiences as they encounter and deal with the world in the meaningful, jointly constructed realms of the here and now.

This will require theory that is not only attentive to matters of human enterprise and intersubjectivity at every point, but that also is more or less continuously adjusted to better approximate an ongoing accumulation of materials obtained through sustained examinations of human accomplishment. Approached in this manner, theory is neither the servant nor the master of research, but an essential informative, integrative, critical, and adjustive component of the social science enterprise, of which ongoing research in the field is the perpetual and necessary corrective. As with the broader human tendency to adjust preexisting images of objects in the world as one engages these things more directly, social science conceptions of the human condition should be adjusted mindfully of the resistances (and surprises) that researchers encounter as they engage the other in the field.

Common Misconceptions

Although I had hoped to launch more directly into an interactionist analysis of power, it should be acknowledged that not all of those in the social sciences are aware of symbolic interactionism and many (even in sociology) have a rather limited familiarity with the interactionist tradition. This includes such textbook theorists in sociology as Zeitlin (1973), Coser (1976), Turner (1978), Alexander (1987), Collins (1989, 1994), and Ritzer (1996), scholars from whom many have derived rather incomplete, if not also distorted, understandings of the perspective.

Although typically well versed in the classics (particularly Marx, Weber, and Durkheim), many of those who have made careers of repackaging theory have poorly represented the interactionist tradition to readers. Not only have they misconstrued the basic positions that Mead and Blumer assume with respect to the fundamentally *intersubjective* and *accomplished* (activity-based) essences of community life, but they have also disattended to the rather substantial body of ethnographic (subcultural) research that has informed those working in this tradition for several decades. More specifically, these theorists have failed to recognize the centrality of the interactionist project with respect to developing theory, methodology, and empirical (ethnographic) inquiry that attends to *all* community life in the making.[9]

Since symbolic interactionism has been described as being subjectivist, micro-level, astructural, ahistorical, atheoretical, or antiscientific by some well known scholars, it may be worthwhile to address these matters so that we might pursue the broader agenda of this volume in manners that are less encumbered by these "ghosts" of misrepresentation.[10]

Given the broader agenda of the volume, it is necessary to deal somewhat directly with these and related issues. At the same time, though, I have contextualized these concerns a little more broadly so that those with little or no exposure to this paradigm may be able to better comprehend both the issues at stake and the interactionist approach more generally.

The Subjectivist Myth

First, in response to the idea that symbolic interactionist is a subjective approach, it should be emphasized that interactionism represents neither a "subjectivist" nor an "objectivist" approach to the study of human behavior. While attentive to the meanings that people (individually and collectively) attribute to objects and the ways in which they act toward and readjust the meanings that they have for things, the interactionists envision the meaning-making process to be fundamentally *intersubjective* in its essence.

Human groups are seen as consisting of people (with selves) interacting with one another in meaningful (linguistic terms), but Mead and Blumer are very clear in assigning priority to the group or community over the individual. Like Dilthey (Ermarth, 1978), they insist that there can be no self without the other. The self is a linguistic (i.e., intersubjective) phenomenon that develops only through symbolic (linguistic) association with others.

Thus, people may invoke "agency" or act in meaningful, intentional ways, but only as a result of adopting (and internalizing) the viewpoint of the (community-based) other. It might also be observed that although people may act on a solitary basis as well as in conjunction with (coordinated interchange) others, all meaningful behavior reflects people's experiences with, uses of, or anticipations of, linguistically mediated images that are acquired through association with others.

As they attain language, people become thrust or immersed into *the obdurate reality of socially constructed experience*. Newborns and other newcomers to the community will be expected (by those in the group whose presence predates them) to come to terms with (what for the newcomers is) a linguistically predefined (thereby "objectified") world.[11] Assuming that newcomers are deemed acceptable or desirable in some manner, those in the community will likely endeavor to share (in varying degrees) their stocks of knowledge with the newcomers.

On acquiring some rudimentary sharing of symbols and meanings (or achieving mutually acknowledged indications) with others, newcomers may begin to experience the world of [objects] in a more socially enduring manner. So long as people implement these shared referents in engaging [the world], they are enmeshed in a world that is clearly not subjective in its constitution. This does not deny or preclude notions of individuality, creativity, or the like, but rather points to the *intersubjective* foundations on which notions of individual consciousness and expression are based. People may develop more particularized and idiosyncratic notions of the world in various ways, but their behaviors (and expressions) are only comprehensible to others insofar as these others achieve a sense of mutuality with these more novel instances. Further, people may work with somewhat particularized definitions of reality and act toward the world accordingly, but they are apt to find that their images or notions of reality (including images of self and other) are more or less continuously tested, revised, and adjusted as they interact with other people and engage other objects in particular setting).[12,13]

The Micro-Myth

Because interactionism recognizes the human capacity for reflectivity and enables scholars to study the ways in which people associate with others in small group settings, it is frequently referenced, often exclusively, as a "micro-level" approach. This viewpoint is also somewhat misplaced. Symbolic interaction is uniquely well suited for the analysis of human relations in small-group settings, but it also can deal effectively with macro-level analysis (e.g., social problems, collective behavior, fashion, political practices, and international relations).

Interactionism entails assumptions and a methodology that are notably at variance from structuralist (and quantitative) approaches to macro issues. Likewise, interactionism is not intended to buttress or substantiate these other theories or methodologies. Thus, an interactionist approach to macro-level matters looks quite different (assumptions, questions, data, objectives) from those with which people approaching group life in more structuralist (e.g., functionalist, marxist) terms may be familiar. This does not invalidate the appropriateness or relevance of interactionist analyses of "large-scale" issues.

Rather, most consequentially, interactionism enables scholars to approach macro issues in manners that directly acknowledge (meaningful) *human enterprise.* This is in sharp variance to those who presume that the human condition is the product of forces that somehow (almost mystically) impose themselves on (and thereby determine) people's social orderings (and behaviors).[14]

Further, acknowledging the full range of human association (e.g., cooperation, conflict, compromise, creativity) and the human capacity for both solitary and joint enterprise, interactionism provides a theoretically and methodologically coherent means of synthesizing broad ("micro" and "macro") realms of human group life. Because of its associational range, methodological groundedness and conceptual coherence, interactionism is highly relevant to the study of *all* realms of human endeavor.

Indeed, if social scientists are to achieve a more viable comprehension of *all* manners of activity that people engage in establishing, implementing, sustaining, resisting, and challenging large organizations, governments, the media, or the military, for instance, then an intersubjectively informed theoretical and methodological orientation is essential. The problem is not that interactionism cannot deal with macro-level processes (e.g., see chapters 7 and 8, for instance), but that many social theorists have so enshrouded macro-phenomena in (mythical) structures that they have overlooked the human enterprise on which "structures" are so thoroughly and extensively reliant for their essences (and resistances).

The Astructural Myth

Another misconception associated with interactionism is that it is astructural. This criticism (somewhat ironically) has been fostered by a subset of interactionists (M. Kuhn, 1964; Meltzer, Petras, and Reynolds, 1975; Stryker, 1980) who have insisted that interactionism should be modeled more directly after Weberian, Durkheimian, or Marxist notions of structure. Their apparent intention was that this viewpoint would somehow pave the way for a greater emphasis on factors, quantification, and notions of external causation. In the process, though, these authors (and others who rely on their works) have lost sight of the more basic interactionist objective of studying group life as *meaningful activity in the making.*

Neither Mead nor Blumer deny structure as an element of human association. Indeed, they have been centrally concerned about the ways in which people structure (i.e., interpret, define, approach, construct, maintain, promote) their life-worlds (e.g., senses of reality, activities, relationships with one another, modes of organizing human activity) on situated, horizontal, vertical, and historical interactional senses. Their emphasis, however, has been on the ways in which people *engage* [the world] as opposed to having people's behaviors (and associations) structured or predetermined by the particular factors (or external phenomena) that some analysts presume to cause people to act in certain ways.

Further, while attending to people's activities in a situated or here and now sense, the Chicago (or Blumerian) interactionists also have emphasized that people act mindfully of their past experiences, as well as any notions of future states that they may invoke. In no way does this deny the existence of practices (e.g., rules, organizations, procedures) that particular people or their predecessors may have "instituted" or "objectified" through use of some sort.[15] However, the baseline recognition is that people act toward all manners of [objects] in terms of the meanings that *they* (interactively and reflectively) associate with those things in the ongoing, particular instances of the here and now in which human activity is accomplished.

Since human behavior is perpetually in the making, it is continuously problematic in its implementation. This does not deny repetition or the stabilization of human behavior or arrangements. Indeed, people may develop wide ranges of routines and arrangements in the process of dealing with [the objects] to which they attend in their life-worlds, and they may act toward particular objects (and situations) in highly consistent ways over time. Likewise, they can endeavor to promote and maintain particular practices both on their own and in conjunction with others.

However, in the course of making sense of (reflecting on) aspects of the world at hand, people may significantly depart from, and alter, earlier behaviors. Whenever people begin to envision objects in other manners, they may contemplate (and possibly implement) other ways of acting toward [these things]. Further, since people are "objects of their own awareness," they may adjust aspects of their own activities in the very process of performing [these activities], possibly changing both their minds and their behaviors in midstream, so to speak.

Notions of interpretation and ongoing adjustment may represent confounding elements to those assuming structuralist viewpoints, but this does not invalidate their centrality for comprehending the human condition. Thus, rather than ignore structures, the interactionist approach readily lends itself to considerations of the ways in which *people* initiate, implement, coordinate, legitimate, extend, encourage, and sustain particular modes of association. This approach enables scholars to attend to the ways that people *engage* these human constructions in practice (including their abilities to disattend to and act back on various modes of social organization).

The Ahistorical Myth

Another confusion sometimes associated with interactionism revolves around the presumption that it is ahistorical. It is the case that those working in the interpretivist tradition have long been skeptical of much of what passes as historical analysis (see Dilthey, in Ermarth, 1978). This cautionary stance reflects inclinations on the part of many historians (and archaeologists) and "social theorists" to (a) impute meanings and motivations to people in the absence of participant-based data and (b) invoke a variety of external rationales and causal structures to account for particular events.

This does not mean, however, that the interactionists are inattentive to historical developments in a more grounded sense. Indeed, interactionist theory and methods are steeped in notions of temporal sequencing, developmental careers, and (more fundamentally) *process*. The difference is this. While these other accounts may be intriguing and suggestive in various senses, the interactionists are deeply concerned that *all* analyses of the human condition be informed by data that attends directly to the ways in which people engage the world in the emergent, here and now situations in which human group life (temporally) takes place.

In some cases, historical (and archaeological) data may be all that we have. Sometimes, too, it is available in considerable depth and handled with great (discerning) care, but this is not an adequate base for building a solid social science. This type of data may alert social scientists to various practices that different people have developed over the years, suggesting both generic themes of association and cautions regarding generalized assumptions. However, because it does *not* allow for participant-researcher interchange, even the very best of this data should not be viewed as a viable substitute for the intersubjective comprehension that can be achieved through careful, sustained ethnographic inquiry. This criticism, thus, is not so much one of the historical enterprise as it is of the practices of those social theorists who attempt to explain social order by linking various social structures or dependent variables with "the forces that seem broadly evident across different historical epochs."

The Atheoretical Myth

It also is sometimes posited that interactionism is atheoretical. If one envisions social theory more exclusively in terms of an integrated set of causal statements or propositions, this viewpoint has some logistic merit. However, if one defines *social theory* as a set of statements intended to (a) explain aspects of the human condition and (b) enable scholars to examine and assess these notions within the context of research on ongoing community life, then symbolic interaction should not be considered atheoretical.

In addition to establishing a clear (in relative, social science terms) set of assumptions regarding the human condition, symbolic interactionism (à la Blumer) also fosters a strong linkage between theory, methods, and research in the field. A related major difference between much social theory and interactionist theory is that the interactionists insist on grounding their theory in people's ongoing enactments of human community life rather than using commentaries on community life as general reference points for developing grand or overarching rationalities that purportedly drive or direct human conduct (and the development of society) or as screens for promoting particular moralities.

The Antiscience Myth

One also encounters allegations that those adopting an interactionist perspective are unscientific or antiscientific. I have left this criticism to the last not because it is inconsequential, but rather because it is sometimes seen as the most devastating critique to which an approach in the social sciences may be subjected. Impressions of a nonscientific or antiscientific orientation appear to revolve around the ways that ethnographers approach the study of the human condition as contrasted with the quantitative (factors, measurements, and variables) methodologies that have more traditionally been associated with the social sciences.

It should be noted that Dilthey, Cooley, Mead, and Blumer, whose works are most conceptually central to what would become known as symbolic interaction, are all deeply committed to the scientific enterprise. They also are concerned that the study of the human condition be approached in a conceptually rigorous fashion. While acknowledging wide manners of accomplishments in the physical sciences, they are concerned that those purporting to study the human condition respect (i.e., examine in close, sustained detail) the subject matter of their focus. They also realize that the task of examining human group life in the making is unattainable through (more traditional, positivist) methodologies of the sort proposed by Auguste Comte and Emile Durkheim in sociology and John Stuart Mill and Wilhelm Wundt in psychology, for instance.

Because survey and experimental research in the social sciences imitate the models and methodologies of the physical sciences, positivist social science may appear "scientific" on the surface. However, as Dilthey and Blumer pointedly emphasize, those adopting stances of this sort effectively neglect the ways in which people engage [the world] in more direct, enacted manners; they ignore or disattend to the scientific requisite of respecting one's subject matter. Envisioning humans as unique, thoroughly intersubjective entities, who act (and interact) in meaningful, reflective terms, the interactionists insist that a *science* of the *human* condition is conceptually and methodologically obligated to attend centrally to these *human* essences.

Clearly, the viewpoint adopted by the interactionists is not one of denouncing the scientific enterprise, but to observe that a different kind of (scientific) approach is necessary for studying the human community.[16,17] There is no attempt to embrace the looseness of "creative" physics or the more speculative theory in astronomy, for instance. Likewise, there is no attempt to reduce human accomplishment in science (and technology) to arbitrary, linguistic, subjectivist relativism as do those affecting postmodernist postures.

While observing that social scientists will be unable to achieve the sort of conceptual and methodological rigor that is commonly associated with the physical sciences, Blumer (1928) concludes that ethnographic inquiry ("sympathetic introspection" [Cooley, 1909]) is the only feasible methodology that social scientists might use to attain a necessary level of intimate familiarity with their (human) subject matter.

Working with a Blumerian orientation, the interactionists not only emphasize direct, first-hand examinations of the empirical social world, but they also strive to develop a set of research-informed concepts that more accurately and completely reflect human group life in the making (Blumer, 1931, 1969). Dilthey and Blumer do not criticize social scientists for adopting a scientific stance, but rather for failing to adopt a scientific stance that is directly and adequately attentive to the unique features of the human condition. Thus, social scientists are beseeched to attend carefully (conceptually *and* methodologically) to the ways in which people engage their lifeworlds in practice.

Subcultural Mosaics and Intersubjective Realities

The preceding considerations of the more overt misconceptions of symbolic interaction are important not only for establishing the conceptual frame on which this volume is based, but also for developing a more viable approach to the human (social) sciences more generally. There is, however, another, much less obvious, seemingly innocuous, misapprehension of the human condition that also merits our attention as social scientists. This pertains to what might be termed, the "cultural problematic" (Prus, 1997b) and revolves around more holistic, integrated, or totalizing images of culture, community, or society.

More global notions of culture, society, and community may be very useful on occasion, particularly when people deal with outsiders in discussing matters such as territorial and identity demarcations or when analysts focus on cultural themes that may be shared across broader groupings or collectivities of people. However, because most community life is accomplished within much more situated, here and now contexts, it is essential that we not lose sight of this fundamental aspect of the human condition.

The term *subcultural mosaics* or the image of community as a subcultural mosaic is used to deal with this cultural problematic or the mythical status of cultural holism.[18] By explicitly acknowledging the multiple life-worlds that constitute particular societies, social scientists are better able to differentiate and examine people's involvements in the many realms of activity entailed in the human struggle for existence as well as any other sets of endeavor in which people may participate.

This is not to deny the thoroughly intersubjective nature of the human condition or the tendency on the part of people to invoke images of "the generalized other" (Mead, 1934) in dealing with one another, but rather to indicate that more global concepts such as society, community, or culture are of limited validity (i.e., operational relevance) when considering the world of human lived experience (and the many realms of human enterprise that this implies).

The development of more particularist life-worlds in any existing community is fundamentally enabled by more common understandings (reflecting shared sets of symbols) that, over time, have come to represent the generally mutual, communicative foundations of that broader collectivity. However, any broader stocks of knowledge that currently exist within communities are derived from and informed by, albeit far from uniformly or centrally, the particular activities and communicative practices that people pursued in implementing earlier and ongoing instances of these multiple, situated life-worlds. Indeed, while people's broader stocks of knowledge may be seen to exist in a dialectic relation with the more particular instances of life-worlds in which they do things, it is to be appreciated that *without these enacted* (particular life-worlds) features of community life, there would be no broader culture, community, or society of which to speak. In the absence of situated applications, language, for instance, would be less than an "empty shell;" it would be a nonentity. It is only as people embark on various (and specific) realms of enterprise that aspects of culture are developed and only within this context are these sustained.

Although broader images of community life are also informed (in the course of ongoing activity and interchange) by these multiple, particularized realms of activity, it should not be assumed that each realm of activity is somehow equally, integrally, or supportively tied to some [hypothetical] cultural center point or that all realms of activity exist in some integrative or holistic relationship to one another.

The people engaging in some activities may intend that their lines of action have clear cooperative, supportive, and integrative consequences for other aspects of community life or for the community at large. In other instances, however, people may embark on practices that they realize may compete with, conflict with, or obstruct the objectives of other people [in the community], perhaps in very central and disabling manners. As well, people may knowingly or openly disregard the concerns of others in some cases or they may embark on particular pursuits without envisioning or anticipating any connections between their activities and those of any others. People (analysts and others) may also draw connections between two realms of activity where none seemed apparent to one or more sets of participants. People also may suddenly, or eventually, dissociate or discontinue practices that may have been linked in clearly supportive or antagonistic terms to other life-worlds in the past.

For students of community life, the danger is one of drawing or inferring links that may be at variance from those invoked by the participants. In the quest to make sense of community life on broader, more holistic cultural levels or to strive for overarching societal or cognitive rationalities, a great many sociologists, psychologists, economists, anthropologists, historians, and others have succumbed to variations of this trap.

The task before us, therefore, involves (a) attending to the various life-worlds or subcultural realms that *the participants* distinguish and (b) establishing intimate familiarity with those participating in these life-worlds so that we might be better able to acknowledge and identify the situated and emergent interlinkages, disjunctures, and irrelevancies that people experience in the course of conducting their affairs. Minimally, this requires that social scientists suspend the pursuit for cultural holisms or overarching rationalities, or at least approach these with exceedingly great caution, even in what may seem the most simplistic of human communities.[19]

Not only does the focus on *activity* (vs. cultural or rational holisms) enable social scientists to study more directly the ways in which humans deal with the fundamental struggle for existence, but it also allows scholars to examine all other realms of human involvement in more sustained, empirically grounded terms.

As indicated elsewhere in more detail (Prus, 1997b), each realm of human enterprise implies a subculture or (social) life-world, wherein people typically (1) develop perspectives or viewpoints on things, (2) devise activities or ways of engaging objects, (3) identify or define one another, (4) develop relationships with one another, (5) experience shared senses of emotionality, and (6) achieve more focused communications (linguistic fluency).

Although in a state of (interactional) flux and adjustment, each of these dimensions of association may be brought into play more or less simultaneously as the people involved in particular life-worlds act toward one another (and other objects) over the duration of their involvements in those settings. Whereas some interchanges are so fleeting that people may not have the time or inclination to attend to all of these notions or develop any of these much at all, other associations may be highly elaborated along one or more of these interactional themes. As well, not only may some participants attend to one or another of these aspects of association much more than the others, but all participants may view any of these matters differently over time.

Further, since people's involvements in any given life-world are far from inevitable, and need not be consistent, in incidence, duration, or emphasis, it is advisable to consider people's "careers of participation" in particular life-worlds. While subcultures are brought into existence only as people interact with one another, thereby implying a certain mutuality of involvement, the participants in any setting may approach and sustain their involvements with different interests and levels of commitment over time. Likewise, since they typically find themselves involved in a plurality of life-worlds, the same people may manage (and experience) their involvements in each life-world in quite different ways.

While participants who enter into preexisting associations often take these for granted, it is important that analysts also recognize "the enterprise entailed in initiating and sustaining particular (subcultural) associations over time."[20] The development and maintenance of any more enduring association requires some ongoing coordinated activity among some of those so involved. Additionally, except for the most fleeting contacts, people in particular subcultures often encounter people from an assortment of other life-worlds in the community.

Because internal (subcultural) coordination typically implies matters of communication, ambiguity, dissension, and adjustment, the internal relations of subcultural associations (large or small) suggest an unlimited set of forums for influence work (and resistance) involving the participants (and the various roles and pursuits they may develop within).

Encountering people outside of the subculture means that members may have to deal with others who (variously) are receptive to, supportive of, antagonistic toward, unconcerned about, or totally unaware of the particular association at hand. Insider views of outsiders, likewise, may be mixed. Insiders may see some outsiders as inconsequential for various reasons but envision others as *targets* (for all manner of influence work) or as *tacticians* (whose endeavors may be thought, benignly or otherwise, to impact on the group at hand).

Reflecting somewhat unique (albeit emergent) configurations of worldviews, activities, identities, relationships, emotionalities, linguistic forms, and coordinated associations, each life-world implies an *intersubjective reality* somewhat unto itself. Each subculture may be interlinked with an assortment of other life-worlds by virtue of some connecting themes, such as overlapping personnel, shared linguistic practices, and commonsense stocks of knowledge, but each subculture also may represent the *paramount reality* in which particular people operate at various time-points or more sustained parameters of engagement.

Notably, people may attend very unevenly to specific subcultural involvements. Some may participate in these settings only reluctantly, perhaps more or less continually reframing situated subcultural experiences from outside viewpoints. But others may intensively assume (particular) subcultural frames, possibly defining issues of life, death, and extended risk-taking activity directly in these contexts. Indeed, some may center their lives extensively and exclusively around particular subcultural involvements.

Representing a vital point of departure from more structuralist cultural modalities and holistic rationalities more generally, the concept of subcultural mosaics (and the multiple intersubjective realities that this notion implies) is highly consequential for those interested in the study of *power.* Locating notions of power within more particularized contexts, the subcultural mosaic draws attention to the necessity of attending to both (a) the situated, action-based implementation of influence (and resistance) endeavors and (b) the variable (operating) realities in which people act or engage the ongoing instances of community life.

Since subcultural life-worlds denote varying viewpoints, objectives, and "practicalities of judgment," the interrelated notions of subcultural mosaics and intersubjective realities also suggest that analysts should exercise considerable caution in invoking broad considerations of rationality with respect to community life. It is essential that analysts be attentive to the (multiple) rationalities that *people* may invoke in embarking on actual instances of activity (and interchange).

Further, while it may be convenient to assume that particular acting units (individuals and collectivities) have singular or overall (e.g., average) viewpoints that they may adopt toward things, social scientists are apt to find it conceptually advantageous to explicitly acknowledge that people (individually and collectively) also may adopt multiple viewpoints on things on a sequential or simultaneous basis. In this sense, it is useful to observe that the same people are often of two (or more) minds (viewpoint-wise) on things. This may be evidenced in people's experiences with ambiguities and dilemmas, but it means that people may act mindfully of one set of concerns while more or less simultaneously considering rationales for acting otherwise. For those endeavoring to act in collective manners (i.e., in teams, in concert), the problem becomes one of defining, sharing, negotiating, and sustaining working sets of viewpoints that enable the participants to achieve certain (joint) lines of action.

The notion of rationality as an ongoing (individual and collective) construction is expressed centrally in the following extract:

> *It is the position of symbolic interactionism that the social action of the actor is* constructed *by him. . . . The actor (let me deal with the individual actor first) is seen as one who is confronted with a situation in which he has to act. In this*

situation, he notes, interprets, and assesses things with which he has to deal in order to act. He can do this by virtue of being able to interact or communicate with himself. Through such self-interaction he constructs his line of action, noting what he wants or what is demanded of him, setting up a goal, judging the possibilities of the situation, and prefiguring his line of action. . . . he may do a poor job in constructing his act, but construct it he must.

The same sort of picture exists in the case of the social action of a collectivity, such as a business corporation, a labor union, an army, a church, a boy's gang, or a nation. . . . The self-interaction of a collectivity is in the form of discussion, counseling, and debate. The collectivity is in the same position as the individual in having to cope with a situation, in having to interpret and analyze the situation, and in having to construct a line of action. (Blumer, 1969:55–56)

The Ethnographic Quest for Intersubjectivity

Once one recognizes that human beings not only operate in intersubjective realities but also actively create, sustain, resist, and reformulate the very life-worlds in which they operate, the task for social scientists becomes one of accessing and comprehending the ways in which people engage the multiple life-worlds that constitute the community at large. Although (unavoidably) minimalist in elaboration,[21] it is hoped that those less familiar with this tradition may still find these comments on ethnographic inquiry helpful in an orientational sense.

In their quest for learning about the life-world of some group of others, ethnographers may build on all manners of knowing (including physical artifacts such as architecture, drawings, documents, and photographs) pertaining to the other. However, the primary or singularly most essential means of achieving intersubjectivity with the other is through sustained linguistic interchange with the practitioners of the particular life-worlds under study. Centrally, this means that researchers assume the task of accessing and immersing themselves in the experiences of the (ethnographic) other in as complete a manner as possible.

Accessing the other observationally, through the "senses" (sight, sound, taste, touch, smell), offers a potentially instructive but very limited sense of the life-world of the other. By enacting roles in those settings that parallel or complement those of the people being studied (i.e., assuming roles as "participant observers"), researchers may gain some more viable appreciations of the viewpoints and practices of the other. This strategy can be especially viable when others provide more extended instruction and other sincere commentary on their viewpoints and practices. However, because humans may interpret any phenomenon (and sensation thereof) in highly diverse manners and in ways that may be quite unanticipated by observers (and even coparticipants), it is only through sustained linguistic interchange (especially open-ended inquiries) with the participants that researchers can hope to achieve a reasonably viable or authentic awareness of the meanings of the other.

Even with sustained interaction, though, the emphasis is on openly and fully attending to, inquiring about, acquiring, and representing the viewpoint of the other; to be receptive to the other in ways that are minimally encumbered by researchers' preexisting viewpoints (and sensibilities). The objective is to develop an appreciation of the experiences of the other in a most fundamental and comprehensive sense. This requires putting one's own orientations in relative states of suspension while questing for any and all interpretations and practices of the other. It means striving for a conceptual oneness with the other in ways that maintain the full integrity of the viewpoint of the other throughout the ethnographic enterprise.

Only in this way, by rather studiously trying to avoid imposing one's insights, advice, and moralisms on the other, may one hope to access "the empirical (i.e., operational, experiential) world of the other." As seasoned ethnographers will readily testify, this is not always easy to do. However, the quest for ethnographic intersubjectivity is contingent on achieving extensive cooperation (and an open sharing of experiences) from the ethnographic other. It is dependent, thus, on researchers applying themselves to this task in more singular or focused respects.

Since there are so many facets of people's life-worlds to which one could attend, another practical problem facing ethnographers is that of settling on a theme for the inquiry. Unlike some ethnographers who may become caught up in other (e.g., structuralist, functionalist, mixed, or more obscure) emphases,[22] those working within the interactionist framework tend to assume a pragmatist focus on activity (i.e., aspects of group life in the making). Thus, the interactionists, generally, concentrate on the ways in which people manage or deal with particular aspects of their life-worlds. While this agenda is still rather encompassing, the underlying attentiveness to the ongoing accomplishment of human activity represents the essential core for approaching the study of the human condition.

Further, focusing on the enacted life-world of the ethnographic other and pursuing detailed (intimate) familiarity with the other through sustained, symbolically informed interchange with the other (probing, testing, and readjusting conceptualizations of the lived experiences of the other), interactionist ethnography is rather firmly grounded in the empirical world of the human community (Blumer, 1969; Strauss, 1993; Prus and Dawson, 1996).

The viewpoint taken here is that ethnography (observation, participant-observation, and *especially sustained interchange*) constitutes the primary methodology for developing a human or social science. This position reflects an attentiveness to the intersubjective (linguistic), multiperspectival, reflective, active, negotiable, relational, and processual features of human community life—and a recognition that a science of the human condition must respect the essences of its (human) subject matter.[23]

Generic Dimensions of Association

> *To speak of a science without concepts suggests all sorts of analogies—a carver without tools, a railroad without tracks, a mammal without bones, a love story without love. A science without concepts would be a fantastic creation.*
> —*Blumer, 1931: 515*

Referring to transsituational or parallel sequences of activity across diverse contexts, generic social processes (GSPs) highlight the emergent, interpretive features of association. They focus our attention on people's activities as they go about doing or accomplishing human group life.

Interactionist concerns about developing processual, cross-contextualized understandings of human interchange can readily be traced back to Simmel's (1917 [Wolff, 1950]) viewpoint that sociology is to be the study of the forms of association. For Simmel, forms of association are abstracted representations or essences that have their existence in particular (i.e., contextualized) instances. This conceptual emphasis would subsequently be fused with the development of ethnographic inquiry at the University of Chicago and the pragmatist concern about studying group life as it is constructed in practice. Thus, one finds an emphasis of the importance of developing process-oriented concepts in the works of Blumer (1931, 1969, 1971), Mead (1934), and Goffman (1959, 1963, 1971), as well as in the writings of many other interactionists.

Still, the quest for an empirically (i.e., ethnographically informed) grounded set of basic or generic processes that would have transcontextual or transsituational validity is particularly explicit in the writings of Glaser and Strauss (1967), Strauss (1970, 1993), Lofland (1970, 1976), Lester and Hadden (1980), Bigus, Hadden, and Glaser (1982), Couch (1984), and Prus (1987, 1994b, 1996b, 1997b).

Recognizing the tentative, emergent nature of scientific endeavor, the interactionists envision generic processes as heuristic devices or sensitizing concepts rather than objective claims or definitive statements of fact. Although there is great concern about attending, in highly detailed fashions, to the developmental features of particular instances of group life, it is also recognized that any attempt to achieve more viable understandings of particular instances of group life requires that researchers have some concepts or reference points with which, and from which, to inquire about, assess, or otherwise make sense of the particular instances one encounters.

Approached in this manner, each contact with the ethnographic other is intended to enable the other to speak to (and speak back to) the researcher (and any existing conceptual formulations). In very fundamental terms, then, actual instances of data retain primacy over the conceptualizations developed to date. Theory is to be more or less continuously adjusted to researchers' encounters with the life-worlds of the other and not vice versa.

It is with these matters in mind, namely the necessity of (a) acquiring (ethnographic) data that is attentive to human group life in the making, (b) developing (process-oriented) concepts that reflect the manner in which instances of community life takes shape, and (c) maintaining the primacy of (intersubjectively informed) data over prevailing conceptual formulations, that attention is directed to the development of generic social processes.

In some earlier work (Prus, 1987, 1996b), I pursued the task of articulating and elaborating a set of processes (GSPs) that seem basic to the accomplishment of ongoing community life. Albeit highly abstracted, it is hoped that the material following will provide readers with a rudimentary sense of this endeavor. This overview of generic social processes is organized around three very broad concepts: (a) participating in situations, (b) engaging subcultural life-worlds, and (c) forming and coordinating associations. These three themes should not be seen as stages or sequences but, instead, represent interrelated sets of processes that people implement on more or less a simultaneous basis as they do things in the community.

This material has been given an ordering, but it should not be assumed (apart from the insistence that the behavior of individuals is meaningful only within a pre-existing community context) that any of these broader themes has particular priority over the others in the course of ongoing group life. Rather, all of these processes may be seen as relevant to human interchange (both generally and particularly) on a more or less simultaneous basis, depending on people's more situated or immediate definitions of (and other modes of involvement in) the particular life-worlds in which they find themselves. As well, because human activity is community-based but takes place only in the specific (and unfolding) instances of the contextual here and now, the conceptual frame referenced here attends to both the enacted and emergent features of human association as well as the more entrenched and enduring aspects of community life.

A. *Participating in Situations (Developing Careers of Involvement)*
The themes sketched out here not only draw attention to the ways (versus causes, motives, factors, or "whys") in which people become involved in, typically multiple, specific life-worlds, but also to the sequential or longitudinal features of people's participation in any realm of endeavor. People may

become involved in situations in many different ways and may approach these settings with a variety of viewpoints, interests, and intensities. Accordingly, it is essential that analysts attend carefully to the things that the (focal) participants *and* their associates do with respect to both the participants' preliminary involvements and their (subsequent) careers of participation in specific situations.

Not only are people's involvements problematic at the outset (and sometimes at variance from their pre-existing interests and reservations), but their participation in specific situations may be much more uneven, partial, ambivalent, sporadic, and distracted than seems evident to outside observers. As well, because people typically become involved in multiple realms of activity on both a sequential and simultaneous basis (i.e., experience multiple careers of participation), people routinely engage in some "juggling of role involvements" within and across time-frames. Hence, even when analysts focus on people's participation in specific settings, it is important that analysts be mindful of these overlapping life-worlds and the ways in which people manage their multiple realms of involvement.

This is not to deny instances of intense, more particularized focusing and dedication, but rather to alert readers to the precarious nature of the enterprise associated with people's participation in any life-world. Thus, very noteworthy themes (detailed in Prus, 1996b:153–156) revolve around the processes entailed in people (1) becoming initially involved (i.e., routings, attractions, reservations) in situations; (2) continuing (and intensifying) particular life-world involvements; (3) becoming disinvolved from specific realms of endeavor; and (4) renewing involvements in particular (previous/related) situations. Focusing on the ways that people approach and sustain careers as participants, these subthemes enable researchers to more effectively comprehend the ways in which those involved in any life-world(s) make sense of, and continue, these ventures over time and amidst a wider, often shifting, backdrop of (multiple) involvements.

B. Engaging Subcultural Life-Worlds

Constituted as two or more people develop associations around particular endeavors, subcultures achieve their essences (and continuity) around the specific people whose careers of participation intersect at certain points in time. Subcultural life-worlds, thus, are realized only as people interact with one another and develop lines of action toward [particular things] in these settings.

Because subcultures can only be formed within the context of people's pre-existing community life-experiences, those associating within these settings rather inevitably share aspects (e.g., language, stocks of knowledge) of the broader community with one another. As a result, and despite their opportunities for all manners of subsequent adjustments (i.e., rejections or modifications of earlier notions, and seemingly new developments), those involved in (more particularized) subcultural associations invariably incorporate a great many aspects of the broader (intersubjective) community into their life-worlds.

Still, regardless of the contents, objectives, endurance, prominence, size, esteem, and so forth attributed to particular affiliational networks in the community, people in all manners of associations find themselves coming to terms with a relatively generic set of processes. These include the matters of: (1) acquiring perspectives; (2) achieving identity; (3) doing activity (performing activities, influencing others, making commitments); (4) developing relationships; (5) experiencing emotionality; and (6) achieving communicative fluency. We may expect that people participating in any setting may be differentially attentive to these dimensions of association on both an overall, collective basis and over time. However, by attending to each of these subprocesses, researchers may more completely approximate the multiplistic features of particular roles (and relationships) that the participants in those settings experience.

Denoting a variety of interactional (and contextual) frames in which subcultural life is accomplished, these features of subcultural interchange (see Prus, 1996b:149–186 for more detail) also indicate pivotal conceptual themes to which scholars may attend when examining influence (and resistance) work of all sorts.

C. *Forming and Coordinating Associations*

Whereas people may (a) develop wide ranges of (individual) careers of participation in specific settings and (b) engage particular life-worlds (and associates) in both similar and highly diverse ways, it is essential that we also consider (c) the emergence, perpetuation, and transformation of subcultural associations. Since subcultures are embedded in community contexts, this means attending to the ways in which the participants (and any outsiders with whom the participants have contact) act to produce particular associational units (interaction, continuity, identity) or generate "organizations in the making."

Because human group life takes place in the course of specific enactments of the here and now, it is of paramount importance that social scientists examine the ways in which those people attend to (i.e., anticipate, initiate, promote, pursue, oppose, disregard) specific group ventures. Highly pertinent here (see Prus, 1996b:160–163 for an elaboration) are the foundational matters of: (1) establishing associations (e.g., involving others, pursuing resources, arranging assemblies); (2) objectifying associations (e.g., developing identity, stipulating justifications, legitimating the group); and (3) encountering outsiders (e.g., making contact, confronting others, protecting the association). Focusing on the activities that people invoke to

(i) develop and sustain particular associations, (ii) achieve greater prominence of the subculture within the community, and (iii) manage (subcultural) relations with others in the broader community, the emphasis here is on the activity (enterprise and interchange) that people engage with respect to the emergence, presence, and associational connectedness of subcultures within and across the broader community context.

D. Experiencing Power Relations

Readers may be somewhat surprised, given the emphasis of the present volume, to find that there was no direct GSP reference to "power." One may notice the term "influencing others" and, perhaps begin to surmise that all of the other processes are relevant to power, but power was not treated as a generic social process unto itself. To qualify as a "generic social process," *experiencing power relations* would not only be envisioned as a transcontextual phenomenon within the human community, and as denoting process of some sort, but to be "social" (in a GSP sense), our notions of power would also directly and fully acknowledge the intersubjective, enterprising, and interactive features of human group life.

In the chapters that follow, particular attention will be given to power as a generic social process—or more accurately, power as an enacted social essence that implies an array of generic social processes. Readers are explicitly cautioned that power is *not* envisioned as the dominant generic social process in society, nor is the study of power as a generic essence viewed as the key to comprehending community life. To the contrary, it is proposed that only in developing a more comprehensive, participant-informed study of community life can we hope to understand "power." Still, mindful of the material in chapters 6–8, we may add the following sub-themes to the earlier formulation of generic social processes: (1) Engaging in Tactical Enterprise; (2) Extending the Theater of Operation; (3) Experiencing Target Roles.

Before pursuing this agenda more directly in the remainder of this chapter and in chapter 6–8, though, it is instructive to recognize some earlier interactionist statements on power and a larger ethnographic literature that addresses [power] as a social essence.

Interactionist Materials on Power

Those who have said that interactionists cannot deal with power are wrong. What they might have said, more accurately, is that the interactionists have not spent much time talking about power. To date, relatively few interactionists have addressed power in more explicit terms and, heretofore, none has provided a highly sustained consideration of this phenomena. However, as will become apparent, a good deal of work in the interactionist tradition deals with aspects of [power] in one or another way. First, though, we should acknowledge the particular relevance of the work of Blumer (1988[1954]), Goffman (1959, 1961, 1963), Klapp (1964, 1969), Hall (1972, 1997), Hall and McGinty (1997), Strauss (1978b, 1993), Couch (1989), and Benford and Hunt (1992) for the more immediate project.[24] While these works are too partial or incomplete as a set to constitute an interactionist theory of power, they have informed the present analysis in essential respects.

Using labor-management relations as a focal point, Herbert Blumer (1954) addresses some essential features of power relations among interest groups. First, he observes that power relations in this context come into effect only when interest groups find prevailing arrangements unacceptable in their dealings with others. Power relations, thus, are marked by a group-based definition of oppositional interests, a willingness of the parties involved to utilize any variety of resources and tactical maneuverings, and the minded pursuit of one's group interests.

In discussing interchanges between interest groups, Blumer encourages analysts to be attentive to "careers" of power relations. He notes that groups tend to develop memories of past experiences and achieve greater senses of tactical expertise as they encounter, experience, and adjust to other groups. He also acknowledges the tasks that interest groups face in maintaining internal organizational continuity and establishing a singularity of direction with respect to external negotiations. Blumer also alerts us to both the fluid, expedient, and tenuous aspects of intergroup relations and the tendency for power struggles involving two or more interest groups to become enmeshed in broader political arenas.[25]

Like Blumer, Erving Goffman (1959, 1961, 1963) recognizes that (a) the human world is a world of images, (b) people act toward objects in the world in terms of the images that they have of those objects, (c) people may assume active roles in shaping the images that others have of things, and (d) people may prefer being viewed (and acted toward) as certain kinds of objects.

Focusing on the world of human lived experience, Goffman draws particular attention to the dramaturgical features of influence work. In *The Presentation of Self in Everyday Life*, Goffman (1959) provides potent insight into anticipated and enacted performances, front and back regions, solitary practices and team work, casual interchanges and dramatic occasions, and disruptive and remedial interchanges. These notions are vital to appreciations of influence (and resistance) work in all manners of contexts, from fleeting dyadic encounters and small teams to large-scale national and international associations (and interchanges). Additionally, while Goffman (1959, 1963) is attentive to people's attempts to attain advantage (via information control) with respect to others (targets, competitors), he also acknowledges people's attempts to maintain respectability relative to their associates and to manage threats to, or losses of, esteem or acceptance within their communities (especially see *Stigma*).

Albeit developed with a somewhat different cast, Goffman's (1961) work on "total institutions" also deserves recognition in considerations of power. Like his (1959) work on impression management, *Asylums* is only partially ethnographic in thrust. At the same time, however, it recognizes the abilities of people (targets, patients, inmates) often thought severely disabled or disoriented both to pursue desired senses of self (and self-defined interests) under conditions clearly intended to foster conformity (to institutional routines) and to resist (or act back on) those promoting "totalizing" systems of control.

Working in a related venue, Orrin Klapp (1964, 1969) also has contributed valuable insights into the power phenomenon as a dramaturgical and enacted essence. In *Symbolic Leaders* (1964), Klapp deals with the images (projected, interpreted, and adjusted) associated with people's careers as celebrities (heroes, villains, and fools) in the community. Focusing on matters such as becoming a symbol, experiencing dramatic encounters, encountering image trouble, role reversals, and hero stuff, Klapp addresses aspects of image projection, spread, resistance, and ongoing (dialectic) adjustments. These themes are relevant across the realms (e.g., entertainment, religion, politics, military) of human enterprise (and influence work).

In *The Collective Search for Identity*, Klapp (1969) adds another vital dimension to the power phenomenon. Attending to people's involvements in the arenas of fashion, cults, and crusades, this volume considers a variety of forms of mass-oriented influence work and people's receptivities (and resistances) to an assortment of collective endeavors.

Applying basic interactionist notions such as emergence, process, voluntarism, symbolic communication, self-reflectivity, collective behavior, and negotiation directly to the study of politics, Peter Hall (1972) also argues for the necessity of envisioning power as social enterprise. Hall outlines four areas of emphasis for people interested in the study of political power, namely: (a) bargaining over material resources; (b) [engaging in] political talk, impression management, and definition of the situation;[26] (c) [managing] control of information flow; and (d) [attaining] symbolic mobilization of support.

Building, in part, on the work of Estes and Edmonds (1981) on policy as process, and their own fieldwork in an educational arena, Peter Hall and Patrick McGinty (1997) focus attention on policy as a dynamic, collectively shaped, and experienced phenomenon. Envisioned thusly, policy may reflect particular intentions, but its operational content, practices, and consequences are matters of (ongoing) intersubjective accomplishment.

In another recent statement, Hall (1997) identifies five realms of organizational practice pertinent to the power process. These involve (a) strategic agency, whereby people endeavor to control the lines or flow of organizational activity, (b) the rule (or convention) making process, (c) the structuring of teams and organizational agendas, (d) the development of organizational language and rationalities, and (e) people's experiences with the delegation process. By focusing on these themes, Hall draws attention to the ways in which people engage organizations *in order to* pursue and accomplish (social) action.

Another interactionist who grapples with aspects of [power] is Anselm Strauss (1978b, 1993). While Strauss's (1978b) *Negotiations* focuses on power more directly through a consideration of "negotiation contexts," his (1993) *Continual Permutations of Action* provides a more extended recognition of multiple human life-worlds and the ways that these intersect within ongoing community (societal, national, and international) arenas.

Observing that negotiations (bargains, agreements, deals, trades) are generic across human communities (and contexts within), Strauss (*Negotiations*) draws attention to a number of contingencies that researchers should consider in developing an appreciation of negotiated orders as situated activity. Indeed, as Strauss (1978b:5) emphasizes, ongoing social orders are more or less continuously in a state of reconstitution (reviewed, reevaluated, revised, reworked, and renewed, as well as terminated and modified by the influx of new considerations). While attending to issues such as the number of negotiators involved in a setting, their relative experiences in negotiations, and the nature of their representation (self or others), Strauss (1978b:238) also asks whether negotiations are solitary events or whether they are interconnected through repetition, sequencing, and the like. He also acknowledges people's respective stakes (risks and opportunities), the visibility of the transactions at hand, the number and complexity of the issues involved, and the sorts of options that people consider for maneuvring with and avoiding particular interchanges. As Strauss points out, his volume very much represents a starting point for an analysis. Still, by examining organizational arrangements in the making, we begin to appreciate the processes that undergird (the surface appearances of) structure.[27]

Strauss's concerns with negotiated orders are less prominent in *Continual Permutations of Action* (1993), but he addresses power-related issues on an even more compelling plane. Taking issue with those who tend to homogenize culture, society, community, government, and the like, Strauss alerts social scientists to the necessity of explicitly acknowledging the multiple life-worlds in which people live, think, act, and interact. The study of community life, Strauss says, not only requires an attentiveness to people's experiences within the many social worlds in which they may find themselves, but also necessitates an examination of the ways that people engage one another within the contexts of overlapping and intersecting life-worlds.

Thus, as Strauss (1993: 215) observes, we need to examine how *these subworlds originate, evolve, maintain themselves, distinguish themselves from others, break apart in further segmentation, also decline and vanish, and so on.* For Strauss, community life takes place through an ongoing set of interchanges (cooperation, conflict, competition, alliances, distancing, and so forth) within and across the various social worlds that people engage on a day-to-day basis. Pursuing an interactionist (Mead, 1934; Blumer, 1969) agenda, Strauss (1993) is attentive not only to the definitional and enacted features of human relations but also to the necessity of developing theory that is ethnographically grounded in human interchange.

Although focusing on "charisma" rather than power per se, Carl Couch (1989) very squarely locates this phenomenon in process terms. Observing that charismatic leaders typically emerge in arenas of extensive shared discontent, Couch draws our attention to the following processes: (1) the ways in which people acquire reputations for effectively articulating discontent; (2) the development of forums and meetings featuring the leader's expressions of discontent; (3) the formation of a new solidarity around particular issues of discontent; (4) the emergence of a new set of definitions regarding the reality of the present; and (5) the portrayal of a utopian future. Acknowledging the developmental sequencing of events and the enterprise (and resistance) that charismatic movements entail, Couch's statement emphasizes the collective, processual dimensions of the positions that (those who become known as) charismatic leaders attain with respect to their supporters.

The Benford and Hunt (1992) statement is a partial derivative of a number of related attempts to apply Goffman's notions of "impression management" (1959) and "frame analysis" (1974) to the study of social movements.[28] Here, more than in other works, though, we are presented with a set of framing techniques that more directly enter into the accomplishment of power relations.

Viewing those involved in social movements as producing dramas in various life-world domains, Benford and Hunt delineate four processes that appear to have considerable relevance across fuller instances of collective public confrontations or displays. Events of these sorts often appear spontaneous to outsiders and, indeed, are often characterized by considerable ambiguity on the part of the participants, as well as denoting emergent, situated adjustments. However, those involved in social movements may plan to make their position apparent (sometimes under the guise of spontaneity) to others by more extensively engaging in scripting, staging, performing, and interpreting activities.

Scripting refers to the preparatory aligning activities that people engage as they work out definitions of problems, develop prognoses of various sorts, work out rationales for participation, and plan strategies. Denoting activities intended to provide presentational forums for dramatic confrontations, *staging* entails matters such as choosing settings, moving materials and props around, casting roles and rehearsing performances, and attracting and assembling audiences. *Performing* refers to the actual enactment or presentation of the event to audiences in attendance and reflects a wide range of presentational matters (including Goffman's [1959] notions of dramaturgical loyalty, discipline, and circumspection). The matter of (audience) *interpretation* is both consequential and problematic. Thus, even when participants try to pitch their messages toward anticipated audience sentiments or otherwise adjust their routines to maximize appeal to particular audiences, they are ultimately dependent on these (interpretive) others for eventual effects. Likewise, as Benford and Hunt observe, concerns with scripting, staging, performing, and audience interpretation often represent points of considerable (and sometimes irreconcilable) influence work among those involved in particular social movements.

Noting that the framing concept with which Benford and his associates have been working has been adopted rather quickly by those in the social movement literature, Benford (1997) has written a very thoughtful (insider) critique of the more common uses of this notion among scholars in this sector of academia. More specifically, Benford alerts readers to unwarranted tendencies to (a) invoke framing concepts in the absence of empirical research, (b) develop more elaborate framing typologies (in the absence of research), (c) envision frames as static properties rather than enacted (processual) features of situations, (d) reify analyst-invoked frames to the relative neglect of human agency and enterprise, (e) reduce frames to attitudinal and motivational (vs. intersubjectively constructed) essences, (f) emphasize the framing practices of "elite" sectors to the relative neglect of other participants in the setting, and (g) apply framing notions in manners that approximate centralizing factors as opposed to acknowledging the multiple, complex, shifting and ambiguous aspects of human interchange. Benford's statement applies most directly to those assuming structuralist approaches to the study of social movements, but his critique further underscores the necessity of social scientists venturing out into the community of the other and attending in direct, sustained manners to the ways in which people engage one another in the various life-worlds that constitute community life.

For their part, the interactionists also have conducted few ethnographic studies of social movements, political arenas or other explicitly defined instances of "power." Among the more noteworthy, though, are studies of relations among congressional staff (Kinsey, 1985) and recruitment by those involved in unions (Karsh et al., 1953), peace movements (Benford, 1987, 1993a; Hunt, 1991), political parties (Grills, 1994; Atkinson, 1995), and feminist movements (C. Wolf, 1994). Also pertinent is D. Wolf's (1991) portrayal of the internal politics of biker gangs. However, much insight into the power phenomenon (and influence process) can be gleaned from other ethnographic considerations of influence work, resistance, and negotiation processes in a wide variety of life-worlds. Indeed, because the interactionist literature is so extensively grounded in the study of ongoing human association, it represents the most consequential literature available for examining instances of human influence (and resistance).

Even the earliest instances of subcultural or life-world research, such as Anderson's *The Hobo* (1923), Shaw's *The Jack Roller* (1930), Waller's *The Old Love and the New* (1930), Cressey's *The Taxi-Dance Hall* (1932), and Sutherland's *The Professional Thief* (1937), are instructive here, They provide materials that indicate ways in which people (individually and in groups) attempt to pursue, maintain, enhance, or protect their interests with respect to the assortment of other people that they encounter in their day-to-day circumstances.

While providing only a very partial listing of both the realms of involvement that have been approached in this manner and of the studies embarked upon by those assuming an interactionist orientation, the following materials are suggestive. Some instances of influence work (definitions, negotiations, resistances) revolving around health, illness, and the hospitalization experience can be found in Goffman (1961), Roth (1962), Davis (1963), Glaser and Strauss (1965), Haas and Shaffir (1987), and Charmaz (1991). Some research depicting interchange (and resistance) on skid row are provided by Bittner (1967), Rubington (1968), and Wiseman (1970). Likewise, one gains valuable insight into influence work in religious subcommunities by examining the studies of Lofland (1966), Shaffir (1974, 1993, 1995), Rochford (1986), Ebaugh (1988), and Van Zandt (1991). Materials dealing with negotiations, recruitment, and worker-client relations are also evident in studies of cab drivers (Davis, 1959), factory workers (Bensmen and Gerver, 1963), musicians (Becker, 1963; Stebbins, 1990; and MacLeod, 1993), lawyers (Blumberg, 1967), and insurance claim adjustors (Ross, 1980). Some other instructive insight into influence work, recruitment processes, and control concerns can be attained through depictions of people's involvements in [deviant] life-worlds (e.g., see Becker, 1963; Lesieur, 1977; Adler, 1985; Steffensmeier, 1986; Faupel, 1991), and the ways in which people attempt (formally and informally) to regulate these activities (Brown, 1931; Ray, 1961; Lemert, 1962; Biernacki, 1988).

In addition to the interchanges depicted in the interactionist literature more generally, the present volume is also informed by a set of ethnographic studies in which I have been centrally involved. These have dealt with persuasive exchanges in bars (Prus, 1978, 1983; Prus and Irini, 1980) and hotel security work (Irini and Prus, 1982); the influence work entailed in an assortment of marketing and sales settings (Prus, 1989a, 1989b; Prus and Frisby, 1990) and economic development (Prus and Fleras, 1996); the deceptive influences characterizing card and dice hustling (Prus and Sharper, 1977) and the production of magic (Prus and Sharper, 1991); the persuasion work involving clergy and their congregations (Prus, 1976); and people's involvements as targets and tacticians in consumptive behavior (Prus and Dawson, 1991; Prus, 1991, 1993a, 1993b, 1994a, 1997a). Although these ethnographic inquiries are substantively diverse as a set, matters of influence *and* resistance emerged as consequential matters of concern time and time again. Readers more familiar with these studies will recognize a relatively enduring emphasis on people's activities (solitary and coordinated), careers of involvements, impression management and deception, deviance and control, and influence work (and resistance). These themes also have been more or less continuously interlinked with the broader interactionist literature by virtue of an emphasis on transsituational or generic social processes.

Envisioning Power in Interactionist Terms

Power may be tentatively defined by instances in which people (individually and collectively) attempt to shape the behaviors and experiences of others in particular ways,[29] but *some important qualifications must be made if we are to understand power as a dynamic or enacted feature of human relations.* It is here that we address the definitional and processual essences of power along with some other problematic aspects of people's experiences with power.

Power as Definitional

In contrast to those who envision power as denoting objectively definable states of affairs that inhere in the possession of certain resources or the existence of particular structures,[30] the position taken here is that *power is always contingent on human definition and enterprise for its essence.* Power is ubiquitous in the sense that it may be brought into existence in any variety of situations, but it is *not* a necessary element of any situation.

Power implies *an intent and a capacity on the part of a person or collectivity to influence, control, dominate, persuade, manipulate, or otherwise affect the behaviors, experiences, or situations of some target.*[31] However, as a quality imputed to a situation by some audience, *power is brought into existence only when someone defines the situation in power or influence (and resistance) terms of some sort.* Definitions or imputations of power may reflect the viewpoints of the people actually involved in particular situations as well as those of outside third parties, but until definitions or inferences of these sorts are made, notions of power are not relevant in any particular case.

Thus, rather than positing that power inheres in some situation or comparative context, we begin with the recognition that, like beauty, morality, and deviance, power is a quality attributed to a situation by some audience. This means that *the essential starting point for any analysis of power hinges on the definitions that people make,* however tentatively, of specific situations in reference to matters of influence, control, domination and the like. In the absence of definitions implying power dimensions, the interchanges or situations in question may be defined in many other ways, such as play, fun, fascinating, work, frustrating, confusing, boring, instructive, educational, challenging, cooperative, helpful, and so forth.

Further, even when one party begins to define the situation in power terms, this does not guarantee that the others will do likewise or that the first party will sustain this definition over time. This is why it is essential that analysts (as third parties) be *extremely cautious* about their own tendencies to define and objectify situations in power terms. In particular, scholars should be concerned that their definitions of situations as analysts *reflect* the definitions invoked by the participants in the settings under consideration.

At a very elementary level, one may distinguish between *target* and *tactician* viewpoints on power—recognizing that these viewpoints (and the "roles" implied therein) must themselves be defined (i.e., perceived, attributed) to be brought into existence. This is not to imply any evaluation of target or tactician roles, but merely to point to an orientational distinction of self as a recipient of action initiated by others as opposed to self as an initiator of action directed toward others.[32] Still, analysts should approach even this distinction with caution.

First, while people may envision and implement target or tactician roles in highly rather singular ways in some cases, they also may adopt mixed (i.e., pluralistic, contradictory, ambiguous) viewpoints of the roles they assume as targets or tacticians. Because of this, it is most important that analysts be attentive to the capacity of people to invoke a *multiplicity of perspectives* in their dealings with others on a sequential as well as a simultaneous basis; to acknowledge the differing (and mixed) ways that people may define their roles as targets or tacticians in the instances of [power] that they experience.

Notably too, people not uncommonly invoke roles as *both* targets and tacticians in their encounters with others. As analysts, we cannot talk about everything at once, but it is essential to recognize people's abilities to assume an *interchangeability of standpoints,* to acknowledge that participants in a setting may assume roles as *both* targets *and* tacticians in particular interchanges, on either a sequential or simultaneous basis.

Approaching the study of power as a "definitional feature" of human lived experience enables analysts not only to ask when and how people are more or less apt to consider situations in "power terms," but also to examine people's experiences with influence, control, and the like as matters that may be *intended, anticipated, implemented, experienced, objectified, coordinated, sustained, extended, resisted, negotiated, neutralized, dismissed, forgotten, and resurrected* overtime. Only in this way, may we begin unraveling (processually) the various facets of power dynamics that people experience in their interchanges with others.

Power as Processual

By viewing power in emergent or dynamic terms (and attending to its definitional base), all instances in which notions of power are invoked become amenable to a *natural history* or *career* analysis. Thus, we may ask when and how people (on both more individualized and more coordinated bases) are likely to first define situations as denoting aspects of influence or control, and when these definitions are likely to persist, intensify, dissipate, and possibly resurface at later points in time. Relatedly, once participants define situations in control-related themes, we may ask about the ways in which they develop lines of action mindful of those definitions. This means being attentive not only to people's preliminary and shifting definitions of the situations at hand, but also to their anticipated lines of action and the ongoing, adjustive strategies they invoke in dealing with others.

Additionally, it should be appreciated that tacticians need not know or be able to predict exactly what actions on their part will generate the particular experiences or behaviors that they might desire in others. Hence, while people may develop customary, habitual, and preferred styles of pursuing cooperation from others, they also may experience considerable ambiguity and uncertainty in developing tactics for dealing with others as situations unfold. Some strategies will reflect people's "first choices," but other tactics may well represent ongoing adjustments or denote instances of "closure" (Lemert, 1953; Prus, 1978; Prus, 1989a:183–209) or "last resorts" (Emerson, 1981) when more acceptable lines of action appear unfeasible or ineffective. Analysts need to attend to the options, anticipations, ongoing assessments, dilemmas, and reservations that people may experience regarding the implementation of particular tactics, both in immediate contexts and on an ongoing basis.[33]

Although people seem differentially willing and able to influence others, it is important to appreciate that *the success of people's attempts to shape the behaviors of others generally depends on the target's willingness to cooperate with the agent or tactician in the situation at hand.* Consequently, it is imperative that analysts attend to the ways in which the "targets of influence" act toward those they envision as tacticians of sorts.

Tacticians (and analysts) may presume or anticipate levels of tactician influence over others, but tactician efforts are subject to ongoing interpretations, assessments, and adjustments on the part of the targets whose behavior they are trying to influence. And, even when agents appear successful in invoking particular lines of action on the part of others, compliance may have been attained on grounds other than those that agents had intended. The targets may have had other objectives in mind and, in some cases, may engage in (seemingly) cooperative behavior *despite* their disregard of, or disdain for, the efforts of the agent.

Further, when considering the influence process, it should not be assumed that those who might be defined as "targets" will inevitably wish to resist the influence efforts of those that outsiders might be inclined to define as tacticians. Indeed, targets may deliberately, sometimes eagerly, seek out the influences of particular others, especially those people whom they define as helpful, knowledgeable, congenial, sympathetic, or fascinating in some respect.

Acknowledging target definitions and interpretations, target senses of receptivity and vulnerability, and target capacities for resistance and encouragement, an adequate "theory of influence" implies a "theory of being influenced." Still, because so much influence work involves minded interchange between the parties involved, something more is required: an explicit, sustained appreciation of interchangeability of viewpoints. This means attending to the potential of *all* participants to assume roles of *both* targets and tacticians. That is, even when people clearly define themselves as targets of influence, it should be recognized that these (same) targets also may assume roles as tacticians in their own right. This means that *agents of influence may become (or often are) targets of influence for the very people whose lives they intend to shape.*[34]

Associated Problematics

Part of the reason that analysts have had difficulty coming to terms with the concept of power is that power exists not as an inherent (structural) state or quality of a situation, an actor, or an act, but reflects people's *activities* (and interpretations) as they work their ways through the situations at hand. Although warranting much more attention than they have been given here, the following discussions of unilaterality, unboundedness, and violence may help clarify the continued emphasis on the definitional, enacted, and processual features of human relations.

Acknowledging Unilaterality

Although most instances of power appear to be interactive or dialectic in their essence, we should recognize three relatively unilateral or one-way variants of the power phenomenon. These reflect (a) secretive tacticians, (b) self-defined targets, and (c) third-party definitions.

First, people (as tacticians) sometimes deliberately attempt to shape the experiences of others without those others being aware of these efforts. Tactician intentions may range from benign to malicious with respect to particular targets, or they may be oriented toward the development of more general conditions or principles that may only incidently affect particular people. In any case, these objectives maintain a unilateral thrust insofar as they are pursued without explicit recognition on the part of the target(s) involved.

On the flip side, people sometimes may envision themselves to be targets of influence or control on the part of others, even though the alleged tacticians may neither be attempting to influence the self-defined targets nor be aware of these attributions. Under these conditions, one may encounter wide ranges of behavior singularly inspired by these self-defined targets. In many cases, these targets may experience senses of apprehension, distrust, anxiety, or anger, anticipating that others (alleged tacticians) might dominate, control, or act toward them in some undesired manner.[35] Self-defined targets may also embark on a variety of tactics (e.g., avoidance, aggression) designed to enable them to deal with (their definitions of) the situation. Occasionally, as well, people may subject themselves to considerable hardship (including physical injury), presupposing that this is how [tactician] others might like them to behave.

In a third variant, outsiders (e.g., witnesses, benefactors, moralists, analysts) may define situations, acts, or actors, in control terms, thereby "generating instances of power" unbeknownst to those engaging one another in the settings under consideration. These third parties may, but need not, intercede in these situations. Should they secretly intervene in these settings, third parties (now acting as tacticians) may be seen to pursue a variant of the first version of unilateral power.

In each of these cases, the role that human reflectivity assumes in these definitions of power is strikingly consequential. As objects unto themselves, people not only are able to define situations in terms of power, control, influence, domination, and the like, but they also may initiate activities that reflect their (private) definitions of the situation. However, once people (agents, targets, or third parties) disclose or otherwise make their definitions of the situation known to others in the situation, then the power process may take on a more explicitly shared, interactive quality.[36] While disclosures regarding power definitions may come about in many ways, and may be pursued with widely varying degrees of intensity on the part of one or more parties in the situation, *it is when people disclose their definitions to others, that power achieves fuller recognition as a social (relational) process.*[37] Still, unilaterality of tactician, target, and third party roles warrants ethnographic attention, with researchers focusing on (a) the ways that those assuming unilateral stances approach and define their positions relative to others, (b) the things they do within these definitional parameters, (c) their concerns and practices regarding secrecy, and (d) their tendencies toward, and manners of, revealing their definitions (and activities) to others.

Unbounded Power

Since unilaterality of power-related enterprise is by no means devastating in itself, it is important that we give some attention to what might be termed *unbounded power* or the notion that tacticians may invoke exceptional licence in developing lines of action toward others.

On a broad level, one may envision people who appear to have absolute control over the lives and deaths of large numbers of others as having unbounded power. Military dictators, such as Stalin, Hitler, Mussolini, and Hussain, may come readily to mind, as might images of sovereign monarchs and heads of superpower nations (with major armaments at their disposal). Particular concern is often expressed over what may be seen as tendencies toward, or potential for, capricious, unpredictable, irrational, and highly malicious behaviors, as well as the seeming lack of restraint or accountability that these people may be able to achieve on a more immediate (and sometimes a more sustained) basis. Even here, however, some qualifications are in order.

People may come to occupy "positions of unbounded power" in highly diverse ways, but these situations are typically much less individualistically achieved and sustained than might first seem.[38] Broader (e.g., national, regional) instances of unbounded power generally entail extended levels of enterprise and the continued cooperation on the part of a significant sector of people in the community, as well as a more generalized symbolic receptivity to these figureheads among the population at large.[39] In addition to those over whom these people seem to have absolute power, "power barons" are typically dependent on an assortment of others not only to implement their wishes but also to ensure the continuity of their positions and their own physical well-being on a day-to-day basis. Outsiders (targets and potential targets) sometimes live in considerable fear of military dictators and other power barons and may effectively pursue their demise, but history is replete with accounts of the (insider) destruction of leaders who fell into disrepute within their home communities.

While one may tend to envision instances of unbounded power as operative on more extended (e.g., regional or national) levels, it is also important to acknowledge that people in much smaller communities, including neighborhoods, school yards, family settings, and other casual contexts may also endeavor to establish themselves as power barons or unbounded aggressors of sorts, even though they would appear to be subject to various "rules of the land."[40] By disattending to normal restrictions (e.g., concerns with community propriety, legal accountability, personal well-being) for shorter or longer periods of time, tacticians may assume postures of unbounded power with respect to their associates.

In instances of these sorts, it is important that analysts not become so engrossed with the "power mystique" that they fail to consider (a) the ways in which people try to acquire and sustain positions of control within particular settings, (b) the fascinations that people may develop with particular positions or missions,[41] (c) people's willingness to assume (even short-term) liberties in imposing their interests on others, and (d) the ways in which others (supporting casts, outside third parties, and targets) deal with these people and their associates.[42] Indeed, each of these notions represents an essential research theme to be explored by those attending to the concept of unbounded power.

Regardless of whether instances of unbounded power are associated with unilateral tactical ventures, isolated dyadic interchanges (in which tacticians lack supporting casts or even third-party audiences), or multiple party contexts, all instances of power are best located within the (intersubjective) context of the community life-worlds in which they emerge and are sustained. This is fundamental for overcoming the power mystique. It is in this sense, too, that it is generally so much more instructive for analysts to focus on the *production* of situated (and more systematic) instances of activity as opposed to vilifying and exalting particular actors or reifying power structures.

Violence as a Definitional Essence

In order to focus on the power phenomenon in a more direct, analytical fashion, it is important to differentiate power from violence.[43] Because images of violence commonly invoke notions of human fragility, loss, and suffering, amid concerns with human agency and culpability, they are frequently associated with fear, distrust, indignation, sympathy, fatalism, and intrigue. Relatedly, because some people are more able than others to impose certin kinds of injury on others, violence is often associated with power.

Without denying the losses and injuries that people may experience as a consequence of the acts (and intentions) of others, it is exceedingly important that analysts maintain a very clear sense of the particular phenomena they are trying to explain. Whereas some instances of enacted power (tactical enterprise) may be intended to cause people injuries, losses, discomforts, and the like (and should be acknowledged as such in considerations of power), other instances of tactical enterprise may entail no actual or implied physical injury or other loss on the part of targets, and other instances of tactical enterprise, yet, may be intended to protect, benefit, enable, educate, or entertain targets.

As with power, it is also essential that analysts attend to the *definitional* features of [violence]. In particular, it is important that one not try to explain one set of people's (individual or group) behaviors by invoking definitions proposed by parties other than those engaging in the activities at hand. That someone disapproves of, or is considered to be harmed by, some activity does nothing to explain the enacted features of human behavior. The definition of injury, loss, or victim status, for instance, entails a different set of processes than does the formation of some tactician line of activity. The task facing social scientists, thus, is one of developing comprehensions of situations that build directly on the viewpoints and experiences of all of the participants in the setting, while being mindful of exactly whose behaviors one is trying to explain at each point in the interchange.

Although it also requires an interpretivist, ethnographically informed approach, the study of violence extends far beyond matters of power and vice versa. In all cases, though, it is essential to be mindful of the definitions that the various participants in the setting employ as their situations unfold; to attend to the ways people invoke, sustain, drop, or reinvoke definitions of self, other people, and other [objects] in the course of accomplishing particular instances of human interchange.

In Perspective

In contrast to the materials introduced in chapters 2–4, the interactionist approach enables us to focus much more directly on power within the context of ongoing human association. If we are to understand power as intersubjective or pragmatic accomplishment, it is essential to acknowledge the definitional, processual, enterprising, and interactive foundations of human relations. To ignore these features of human association is to conceptually short-circuit or hopelessly obscure an adequate comprehension of power as humanly experienced.

Chapters 6–8 build on the premises, research, conceptual framing, and analytical insights derived from interactionist literature introduced in this chapter. Quite simply and directly, I intend to provide a frame for conceptualizing and studying power as an *enacted* phenomenon that may be utilized across the width and breadth of community life.

Notes

1. The notable exception, of course, pertains to the ways in which social scientists approach the study of human behavior. While one could

also study academic productions as instances of particular life-worlds in the making (i.e., ethnographically study these realms of activity in the same way one might study religious or political endeavors, for instance), the interactionists have been critical, of those versions of social science that do not respect the *social* essences of the human condition.

2. This discussion is necessarily cryptic and should not be taken as a substitute for more extended theoretical statements (see Mead, 1934; Blumer, 1969; Laurer and Handel, 1977; Strauss, 1993; Prus, 1996b, 1997b), more detailed discussions of methodological practices (e.g., Becker, 1970; Bogdan and Taylor, 1975; Jorgensen, 1989; Lofland and Lofland, 1995; Prus et al., 1997), or the array of Chicago-style ethnographies that have been developed over the past century (see Prus [1997b] for a partial review).

3. As will be apparent to readers more familiar with this tradition, the present volume draws heavily on the work of Herbert Blumer (1969).

4. Prus (1996b) provides a fuller elaboration of the historical (theoretical and methodological) roots of symbolic interaction.

5. Readers may recognize affinities of these scholars with the works of William James (1842–1910) and Charles Peirce (1839–1914), but the impact of the latter two pragmatists on symbolic interaction is notably less direct.

6. It is worth noting that (the more senior) Wilhelm Dilthey and Georg Simmel were colleagues at Berlin and that their works display a number of conceptual affinities regarding the field of sociology.

7. An elaboration of the development of ethnographic research in both sociology and anthropology is provided elsewhere (Prus, 1996b).

8. For a more detailed consideration of affinities and contrasts of the interactionist approach with both positivist (structuralist) and postmodernist (poststructuralist) orientations to the social sciences, see Dawson and Prus (1993a, 1993b, 1995), Maines (1996a, 1996b), Prus (1996b), Prus and Dawson (1996).

9. These textbook writers may have achieved some mystique in sociological circles by studiously affiliating themselves with some European masters, but when compared against the basic reference point of this volume (namely, Do these scholars attend to the world of human experience or the ways that group life is accomplished in practice?), it becomes apparent that, however eloquent or objectified their formulations may seem, the writings of these theorists (and those they enshrine) are of limited relevance for those interested in learning about the ways in which people actually engage one another in the here and now of community life.

10. Readers are referred to Blumer (1969), Strauss (1993), and Prus (1996b) for a fuller consideration of these matters. In developing this immediate discussion of common misconceptions, I have benefited consider-

ably from Maines's (1977, 1988) very thoughtful commentaries on these and related matters.

11. For an appreciation of objectification as a social process, see Berger and Luckmann (1966), and Prus and Dawson (1996).

12. While positing that people act toward [objects] in terms of the meanings that they have for them, the interactionists also observe that whenever people engage objects in reflective (intersubjectivity informed) manners, they may revise their earlier conceptions of those objects in ways that are attentive to their experiences (e.g., successes or resistances) of acting toward those things in that manner. Likewise, people's interpretive practices are not simply (anticipatory) preludes to behavior but may be invoked during (engagement) and after people's encounters with objects. See Blumer (1969) and Prus and Dawson (1996) for a fuller sense of the interactionist notion of "obdurate reality."

13. The capacity for reflectivity implies that people are objects of their own awareness or may develop lines of action that take themselves (as objects) into account, but it is important to explicitly recognize that people also may act toward (and back on) one another as objects. Further, people's contacts with others need not be continually sustained (co-present, co-impinging or even perpetually conscious of others) for people to be reminded (memories, anticipations) of both their embeddedness and own *object* essences (as potential or actual recipients or targets) within the community.

14. Elsewhere (Prus, 1996b), the term *paratheory* (suggested by Robert A. Campbell) is used to refer to the secondary *theory* that is constructed to account for whatever particular correlations or other associations that those employing structuralist variables invoke in trying to draw connections between "structures" and human behavior.

15. The interactionist position here is quite consistent with Schutz (1962, 1964) and Berger and Luckmann (1966).

16. This is not to challenge or deny the viability of positivist science as this pertains to the study of physical and physiological matters that may affect the human condition. But it is observed that whenever human definitions of objects are involved, some appreciation of human interpretive practices, enterprise, and interchanges are appropriate for comprehending the broader phenomenon at hand. It is instructive to attend to the behaviors and judgments of all of the people involved in these situations. In dealing with those [physiological] conditions over which the participants seem unable to exercise any control (in incidence or recovery, for instance), we would not only be concerned about the ways in which those experiencing symptoms of various sorts may note, define, and deal with these but also the ways in which any others (e.g., close associates, diagnosticians, treatment

providers, researchers, technicians, analysts, publicists) also make sense of and act toward instances of these phenomena over certain time frames.

17. What is entailed, as Dilthey (Ermarth, 1978; Betanzos [trans.], 1988) and Blumer (1969) make explicit, is a different notion of (human-interpretive) science; a paradigm shift in Thomas Kuhn's (1962) terms.

18. Given the agenda undertaken in the volume, it simply is not possible to elaborate on these points herein. However, the matter of "community as a subcultural mosaic" is developed in more detail in Prus (1997b). Readers also may appreciate affinities with the notions of subcultural life-worlds as used herein and Strauss's (1978a, 1982, 1984, 1993) writings on multiple social worlds. A somewhat parallel viewpoint is developed in Hannerz (1992).

19. Once analysts look past their own technologies, it should become apparent that the struggle for human survival implies a challenging, multi-faceted set of endeavors, even under the most benign geographical conditions. The idea of a "simple" human community is clearly mythical.

20. For a fuller discussion of the tasks entailed in forming and coordinating associations, see Prus (1997b).

21. Some excellent descriptions of ethnographic research practices can be found in Becker (1970), Bogdan and Taylor (1975), Jorgensen (1989), and Lofland and Lofland (1995). The collected editions of Shaffir et al. (1980), Shaffir and Stebbins (1991), and Emerson (1988) are also valuable in this regard. For more extended indications of my own thoughts and practices regarding field research, see Prus (1980, 1991), and Prus et al. (1997a,b). Interactionist statements that deal more directly with the interrelationship of theory to methods can be found in Blumer (1969), Strauss (1993), and Prus (1996b, 1997b).

22. This uneven mix of ethnographic foci represents a major obstacle to those attempting to develop comparisons and contrasts (e.g., generic social processes) across the anthropological literature (see Prus, 1996b: 104–112).

23. For a more extended indication of existing ethnographic studies that reflect this subtradition of the social sciences, see Prus (1997b).

24. The works of Luckenbill (1979) and Altheide and Johnson (1995) are also relevant in a more general sense. Some other interactionist material pertinent to power has been introduced in chapter 3, in the discussion of collectivist approaches.

25. Although Blumer (1971) does not define his statement on "social problems as collective behavior" explicitly in power terms, this material draws attention to the importance of matters of process, perspectives, definitions, enterprise, coordination, negotiation, resistance, and ongoing adjustment in the forging of social problems in the broader community. Focusing on the community quest for propriety (and embedded attempts to

shape the directions of community life), Blumer provides an instructive conceptual framework for envisioning consequential aspects of the power phenomenon.

26. Albeit somewhat tentative (i.e., removed from first-hand or ethnographic inquiry), readers may also refer to Hall's (1979) discussion of the presidency and impression management. McGinniss (1969) provides a related, but clearly journalistic account of "selling a president."

27. Some other conceptual material on negotiation (and labeling processes) can be found in Lemert (1951, 1962, 1967), Garfinkel (1956), Goffman (1959, 1963), Klapp (1962, 1964, 1971), Prus (1975a, 1975b), Emerson and Messinger (1977), and Maines (1977).

28. For other materials that Benford, Hunt, and their associates have developed, see Snow (1979), Benford (1984, 1993a, 1993b), Snow et al. (1986), Snow and Benford (1988, 1992), Hunt (1991), Hunt and Benford (1994).

29. This preliminary definition is largely consistent with the positions assumed by a number of scholars addressing power, including French and Raven (1959), Weber (1968), Emerson (1972), Hall (1972), Giddens (1976, 1984), Luckenbill (1979), Wrong (1988), and Lawler (1992), among others. It implies an ability on the part of people to shape the behaviors and experiences of others, but it may be extended to the recognition of people's abilities (i.e., human agency) to control (predict, manipulate, utilize) other (physical) aspects of their environment as well.

30. The position adopted here is notably at variance from structuralist viewpoints that tend to claim that power is determined by virtue of people's positions in (economic and other) social orderings. Those in the marxist nexus and others (e.g., functionalists, exchange theorists) who objectify power in this manner effectively violate the fundamental hermeneutic essence of human group life.

31. While it is important to distinguish people's intentions from their eventual successes in achieving influence or control with respect to one another, to ignore people's intentions, limitations, implementations, adjustments, and the like (by alleging that power is the ability to influence others) is to lose track of, and consequentially obscure, a great deal of the reflectivity and enterprise that people invoke in the course of implementing, engaging, experiencing, and dealing with the power phenomenon.

32. In general, people seem more likely to adopt the role or viewpoint of *targets* or become more concerned about others being the targets of control efforts when they (a) define situations in adversarial (or competitive) terms; (b) anticipate more consequential outcomes; and (c) envision other people [tacticians or agents] to be more intent on, and capable of, shaping target situations in manners consistent with their [tactician] own preferences. Those defining situations from the viewpoints of *tacticians*

seem more apt to envision situations in power terms when they (a) see themselves as desiring or requiring the cooperation of others in pursuit of some objective; (b) discern ways of shaping the situations, behaviors, or experiences of others in desired manners; and (c) contemplate resistance (obstacles, competition) on the part of others. However, these notions of target and tactician roles are best viewed in process terms and mindful of people's abilities to take (i.e., invoke) the roles of *both* targets and tacticians on sequential, concurrent, and intermittent bases.

33. Even when the parties involved intend to cooperate and communicate rather freely, they often have difficulty coordinating their behaviors with others. However, when the people involved are unable or reluctant to communicate with one another, or attempt to do so largely within atmospheres of adversary, competition, distrust, or hostility, any preliminary concerns that interactants have with power (e.g., control, disruption, ensuing losses, or embarrassment) may readily become intensified. Consequently, people seem apt to find one another's actions more unpredictable, evasive, and unsettling when they operate within contexts of suspicion and distrust (see Lemert, 1962; Hunt and Hunt, 1977:191–220; Prus, 1989a: 234–254).

34. People occupying "management" roles as parents, teachers, religious leaders, work supervisors, prison guards, physicians, baby-sitters, and the like, generally realize that although they may appear to be in situations of control with respect to their role (supervisee) associates, they are very much dependent on the cooperative behavior of those with whom they work. Not only are those (presumably) being monitored, directed, instructed, or supervised able to resist a great many of the influence endeavors they experience, but the "managers" with whom they deal may be subject to extensive instances of influence work from these other "tacticians."

35. It should not be assumed that self-defined targets envision themselves only as recipients of undesired influence. Self-defined targets may also see themselves as subject to positive or personally desired attempts of influence of which the presumed tactician is unaware. Under these circumstances, self-defined targets (now presuming the viewpoint of the other) may "treat themselves very well," assuming that is how those they have in mind would like them to act. On learning of these matters, the unwitting "tacticians" may subsequently respond positively to these presumptions in some cases, but in other instances they may find the [self-defined target's] behavior out of place, possibly resulting in confusion and embarrassment on the part of one or both parties.

36. There is no guarantee that others will accept these definitions. Likewise, even the perpetrators of power-related definitions may cease thinking and acting in these terms at some point after they have disclosed these to others.

37. Karsh et al.'s (1953) account of "the union organizer and his tactics" is especially instructive in outlining some ways in which third parties may attempt to maneuver within interactional contexts.

38. In *The Rise and Fall of the Third Reich,* Schirer (1959) provides an elaborate account of the webs of supporting casts (through loyalty and fear) involved in establishing an extended military dictatorship. Representing a political microcosm of sorts, Wolf's (1991) account of outlaw bikers also provides a very instructive case in point. While leaders and other members of certain groups may sometimes delight in terrorizing (i.e., imposing themselves on) others in undesired and seemingly capricious or irrational manners, one develops a much fuller appreciation of both the roles of "supporting casts" and the relative inabilities of leaders to sustain their positions over time on their own. Indeed, leaders may become so indebted to particular supporters for their initial and ongoing assistance that they may find that they are obligated to extend considerable latitude to these supporters even when they consider the behavior of their supporters objectionable on other grounds. Machiavelli's (1950:194–196) statement on, "showing that the Roman Generals were never punished for any faults they committed, not even when by their ignorance and unfortunate operations they occasioned serious losses to the republic," suggests a somewhat similar concern about avoiding side confrontations with those assigned the task of supporting central community (in this case military) objectives.

39. Klapp's (1964, 1969, 1971) and Couch's (1989) depictions of the dynamic processes surrounding the attainment and maintenance of leadership or celebrity status and the development of social movements are much more compelling in this sense than is Weber's (1968; Bendix, 1960:298–328) more structural (and persona focused) portrayal of charisma.

40. Felony homicides (Dietz, 1983) are among the most extreme instances of situations of this type, but a great deal of unbounded violence may be exhibited in casual settings when people situationally, temporarily, or systematically disattend to or disregard the applicability of laws and other community restrictions to themselves (see, Prus, 1978; Athens, 1980, 1989; Prus and Irini, 1980; Wolf, 1991). It also should not be assumed that the particular interchanges that result in homicides are more intense in intended injury and experienced suffering than many that do not.

41. This would include, as well, fascinations that tacticians develop with respect to specific kinds of experiences involving others. Beyond using (any of a variety of) others to achieve certain outcomes, people may develop interests in subjecting particular others to certain kinds of treatment. In the latter case, the most extreme instances are those involving "targets of enhancement" and "targets of misery." Here, people develop more sustained (agendalike) fascinations with particular target reactions. At one extreme, tacticians may encourage happiness and pleasure and the like, while at the

other tacticians may endeavor to make people's lives miserable, watch them suffer, or relentlessly pursue retribution or "justice," for instance.

42. Rather than reduce solitary instances of unbounded power to psychological characteristics, it is proposed that attention be directed toward the ways in which people develop particular interests and the ways in which they pursue these notions on their own (including the management of covertly veiled association with others) over time. Apart from the difficulty of accessing and attaining the cooperation of people developing and pursuing fascinations with particular [power] themes, this realm of inquiry should be amenable to ethnographic research, particularly in the form of extended, open-ended interviews. Research of this type should also be attentive to solitary instances of [power] that analysts (and others in the community) may define as more benign as well as more sinister in thrust.

43. For some other interactionist analyses of violence, see Prus (1978), Athens (1980, 1989, 1997), and Dietz (1983). Other ethnographic materials that deal with violence in group (subcultural) settings can be found in Keiser (1969), Prus and Irini (1980), and D. Wolf (1991).

6 Engaging in Tactical Enterprise

So magic, basically, is, you take the reality and you change it, and the way you impose your interpretation is by not allowing the audience the ability to sort of form alternate theories. Now the reason they can't form alternate theories is, they don't know what's about to happen. When you structure the trick, they don't know what to pay attention to. When I say I'm imposing my interpretation, in a sense I'm editing what things they pay attention to, right? If I keep it very narrow, they have to come to these conclusions. . . .

You have to do it this way, because if they can follow the events the same way you do, there will be no illusion. See, and that's a method thing, it doesn't have a lot to do with the presentation. What is the audience thinking at this point? What are they interested in at this point? How do I change things to create the illusion? You have to go through the trick and figure out each point what they want to know, and that's a method. On the presentation side, you have to go through the trick and say, "Why is the audience interested at this point and how do I keep their interest?" If I have to deal the cards out twenty times they're going to get bored, so what do I do?[1]

—*Prus and Sharper, 1991:256–257*

$\mathbf{F}$ocusing on an assortment of baseline tactical orientations and practices that people may invoke in attempts to deal with and influence other people (individuals or groups), chapter 6 is the first of three chapters intended to outline an interactionist approach to the study of power. While providing only a partial picture of power as an enacted phenomenon, this chapter focuses on the processes by which people attempt to "get their own way" in encounters with others. The immediate objective is to sketch out the dimensions or parameters of these practices and indicate ways in which these essences might be examined in the course of ethnographic inquiry. ?

Before embarking more directly on this task, though, it is important to recognize that people may engage human targets with a wide range of stances. Thus, tacticians may sometimes envision themselves as exceedingly advantaged relative to the other, as implied in notions of being in total control, being resource-laden, having authority, being revered, or being able to apply extended sanctions to the other. At other times, tacticians may see themselves on comparatively equal grounds relative to those they encounter, or they may see themselves as both advantaged and disadvantaged relative to the targets they plan to engage. In still other instances, tacticians may view themselves as greatly disadvantaged or essentially powerless relative to prospective targets. On some occasions, too, people need not even be concerned about these things; they may just want to influence or impact on the target in some way.

Some scholars may be tempted to map out grids that depict typologies of tactician-target relationships along the lines just indicated, but the approach taken here is concerned more fundamentally with the ways that any tactician may engage any target. Consideration will be given to a variety of stances that people may assume relative to one another, but rather than presume particular structures or advantages at the outset, the emphasis is on the range of things that tacticians may implement in practice.

While tacticians often (a) seek outcomes that are to their own advantage or (b) the mutual advantage of their targets and themselves, tacticians also may primarily intend to (c) advantage targets or third parties or (d) influence targets in ways that acknowledge or foster some (group-related) mission, principle, or office (including things that may be somewhat at variance from tacticians' own personal preferences).

Those adopting tactician roles frequently engage (individual or group) targets in more solitary (autonomous) capacities, but tacticians may also represent (or act on behalf of) other individuals or groups. Further, tacticians may act collectively (as groups, teams, coalitions) in an attempt to influence some individual or group target.

Likewise, while tacticians may have highly focused, very singular objectives on some occasions, they may have more nebulous or possibly mixed viewpoints and goals at other times. Sometimes, too, tacticians direct their activities toward very specific people, but at other times they may pursue their interests amid a more diffuse or diverse set of targets. Similarly, people may deal with some targets on a highly immediate (perhaps instantaneous) basis, but work with much broader time parameters in other situations.

On a related note, people may develop more favored or habitual forms of dealing with others, but need not approve or even contemplate tactics that others might use often or freely. The same tacticians also may be quite willing to approach certain targets in particular ways, but deem these practices highly inappropriate for engaging others.

Variations in tactician stances along these lines represent important aspects of the power phenomena, but even more central is the recognition that *all influence work connotes activity in the making*. Mindful of the agenda of enabling researchers to examine power as an enacted phenomenon, this chapter gives explicit consideration not only to the matter of (1) people assuming tactical orientations toward others but also to people's involvements in (2) enhancing practices, (3) focusing procedures, (4) neutralizing strategies, (5) leveraging tactics, and (6) autonomizing tactics, as well as the related concerns of (7) exercising persistence and experiencing tactical openness.

This listing of topics was developed primarily from the interactionist/ethnographic literature referenced in chapter 5, but it also reflects an attentiveness to the broader literature on tactical practices,[2] as well as a great many other, more casual, observations. Both the actual terms (and categories) used and the ordering in which these topics are presented are somewhat arbitrary, but the underlying forms of enterprise that they address are essences that appear to have endured across societies and over the course of recorded history. While people may develop particular orientations and practices in more elaborate and crystalline forms in some settings and pursue these in more explicit fashions at specific times, the processes outlined here appear to have a broad transcontextual or generic relevance across human groupings. We can make these claims most readily about contemporary western societies and particularly those groups that have been studied in greater ethnographic detail (see chapter 5), but we should not assume that the interactional life-worlds of other peoples (including those lacking written language) are vastly underdeveloped compared to our own.

In some earlier drafts of this chapter, I had tried to generate a more exclusive or singularistic listing of tactics than what I have to offer here. However, I came to realize that people typically "attempt to accomplish things" rather than "implement particular tactics." This is not to suggest that people do not invoke specific tactical practices, for indeed they may do so on many occasions. Still, tactics achieve their essences only as people implement or apply these to the situations at hand. Tactics may be discussed, envisioned, and practiced in more abstract terms, but they enter most prominently into people's influence work when they are employed within some (operational) context.

Not only is it essential for scholars to envision influence work (and tactical enterprise) as *enacted,* but to recognize, as well, that tactics are generally invoked (i.e., embedded) *within* people's ongoing roles, relationships, and encounters. It is one thing to list or identify a series of different tactics on a more abstract level, but this is not the same as acknowledging the ways in which *people bring tactics into play in dealing with others.* Indeed, most of the [tactics] that tacticians use in engaging targets build on wider sets of antecedent, concurrent, or anticipated circumstances (objectives, experiences, activities) involving the same or other people. People may concentrate their efforts in certain regards, emphasizing one tactical orientation or set of practices relative to others, especially at particular times or in certain kinds of situations. However, even in highly fleeting encounters, people's tactical endeavors tend not to be as distinct or exclusive as might first seem.

Thus, rather than attempt to establish frequency comparisons of influence practices or to argue for the relative importance or worth of specific tactics, the immediate emphasis is on (1) depicting the essences of particular modes of influence work, (2) indicating strategies people may invoke along these lines, and (3) suggesting some practical limitations that tacticians may encounter. In the process, I have tried to set out discussions of these matters in ways that would more readily lend themselves to ethnographic inquiry and cumulative (comparatively informed) conceptual understandings. Still, I do worry that I have been unduly presumptive and sketchy at times and too obvious and detailed at others, at least relative to certain readers.

Readers also are cautioned that although the following material has a presentational flow, tacticians may engage targets in fashions that are much more partial, fragmented, and erratic, as well as more simultaneous and intertwined, than this sequencing of topics suggests. The processes outlined here are not intended as mutually exclusive categories, but rather represent a conceptual scheme for considering a relatively vast set of activities that appear pertinent to people's endeavors as tacticians.

The material introduced here cuts across (and informs) many of the notions of power developed in chapters 7 (Extending the Theater of Operations) and 8 (Experiencing Target Roles). However, because chapter 6 does not adequately depict people's involvements in the broader communities in which they find themselves, the influence processes discussed here provide only a partial foundation for an understanding of power as intersubjective accomplishment. I have endeavored to be attentive to target viewpoints and practices in developing chapter 6, but a more extensive acknowledgment of target roles (chapter 8) is essential for an adequate analysis of power relations. Likewise, while not all instances of influence work involve third parties (e.g., referrals, coalitions, media), a great deal of persuasive enterprise involves participants other than the tacticians and targets in a more singular sense. This is not to minimize the significance of more isolated dyadic tactician-target interchanges, but to observe that a fuller, more accurate conceptualization of influence work requires sustained attention to these other dimensions of community life.

Before embarking on a more concerted consideration of tactician practices, though, one further qualification is necessary. Just as it is vital to attend to the differing ways that people define situations with respect to power, it is also essential to appreciate that people (as tacticians, targets, or third parties) may imbue seemingly identical behaviors and practices with diverse intentions and meanings.

Since people may engage in seemingly similar activities with variable and potentially shifting intentions (many of which are not "influence oriented"), efforts to code or define influence tactics by reference to behavioral indicators are exceedingly ill-founded. Accordingly, the material following attends to the *intentions* with which participants invoke particular practices. As a result, some seemingly identical activities may be discussed in more than one context as we sort through the ways in which people embark on influence work.

Assuming Tactical Orientations

While it is often supposed that people who endeavor to influence others are doing so because of personal interests or the prospects of personal gains, it is instructive to consider not only the differing ways in which people may assume roles as tacticians in specific instances but also when and how people are apt to maintain tactical orientations in these situations.

Albeit a tentative guide for the present purposes, the interactionist literature indicates several ways in which people become involved in situations.[3] The most common of these are represented by notions of seekership, recruitment, and closure, but one may also recognize some instances of inadvertent or accidental involvements. Whereas inadvertent or accidental involvements acknowledge occasions in which people have little or no (minded) control over the situations in which they (or others) find themselves, the other routings (seekership, recruitment, and closure) provide testimony to the relevance of human agency, as does the somewhat related matter of dealing with one's reservations.

Seekership (Lofland, 1966; Klapp, 1969) implies a self-defined interest, allure, or fascination that people associate with some form of involvement. The idea is that people would not only be receptive to venues of this sort but would voluntarily seek out or pursue situations of these (favored) types on their own or in conjunction with other people. *Recruitment* reflects people's attempts to involve others in particular situations. The preliminary motivation or encouragement for participation, thus, derives from the efforts of these [tacticians] rather than prospective participants. The term, *closure* (Lemert, 1953) acknowledges the sense of obligation and (sometimes) desperation that people may associate with achieving (or avoiding) certain outcomes. Under these conditions, people may knowingly become involved in situations that they might otherwise consider inappropriate or undesirable. These routings are not mutually exclusive and people often find themselves considering particular involvements amid combinations of these themes.

While people experiencing closure may engage in activities that they might otherwise wish to avoid, it also is important to acknowledge the *reserva-*

sense of decontextualized; actors out of social
organization, institutions, etc

tions that people have about engaging in particular situations. Instead of a route to involvement, though, people's reservations may represent obstacles to particular involvements. Consequently, any hesitations or dilemmas that people experience around moralities, risks, costs, or other complications that they link to particular involvements, may enter prominently into their reluctances to engage in activities (even those that might seem appealing, popular or encouraged, or advantageous in other respects).

Further, while people may define particular situations in specific (or more mixed) ways at the outset, the interactionist literature also indicates that people commonly reinterpret their (potential and eventual) involvements over time as they reflect on these matters, both on their own and through association with others.

The implications of these notions for the study of tactical involvements are highly consequential. Because people's involvements in influence work are much more multifaceted than commonly implied in the social sciences literature, the preliminary matter of people's definitions of, and willingness to pursue, roles as *tacticians* in particular situations merits considerable ethnographic attention.

In addition to examining the ways that people might envision tactical activities on their own, we would also want to attend to the roles that people may play in encouraging (and discouraging) one another's tactical involvements both at the outset and over time. Approached, thusly, we move past tendencies to reduce power to individual attributes, attitudes, or motivations even at a preliminary level. By acknowledging participant viewpoints, we may begin more fully to comprehend the ways (interpretive processes and emergent behaviors) in which people become involved in and sustain these efforts in actual cases. We may also better understand people's tendencies to avoid roles entailing tactical endeavor.

Enhancing Practices

Generally viewed as precursors to other influence work directed toward targets, enhancing practices represent "stage-setting" activities that people may use in pursuing more focused objectives. Tacticians may implement these practices at various points in interchanges with targets, but tacticians also may embark on these enabling activities in advance of any contact occasion, as well as dispense with such matters on other occasions.

Consideration is given to four broad, but somewhat interrelated, sets of enhancing practices that tacticians may invoke: (a) formulating plans and making preparations, (b) attending to target circumstances, (c) shaping images of reality, and (d) cultivating relationships.

Formulating Plans and Making Preparations

Sometimes, people so quickly engage targets in tactical manners that they seem to dispense with thoughts of options and outcomes. Still, these anticipatory themes have considerable relevance in many other instances. This is not to suggest that people attend to as many things as they might desire or that they anticipate outcomes with any particular degree of accuracy. Still, for the researcher, an important task is one of ascertaining preliminary tactician viewpoints *and* activities as people anticipate influencing others.

Thus, researchers may begin to ask about the ways that tacticians attend to options (i.e., noting, contemplating, articulating, assessing, comparing, initiating, exploring, testing, and dismissing possibilities) for dealing with targets. While these reflective, anticipatory, or sometimes partially enacted, aspects of action are commonly ignored by those relying on behavioral indicators of tactical engagement, they represent vital lines of inquiry for scholars concerned about the ways in which influence work materializes in practice.

Relatedly, although tacticians will sometimes implement (and pursue) particular lines of action in highly singularized manners, they may reinvoke preparatory or anticipatory frameworks at any number of times during their engagements with targets. Indeed, people may consider other options as well as make secondary adjustments to their immediate activities in the midst of pursuing particular lines of tactical engagement. While some instances of tactical engagement may be concluded almost as quickly as they are begun, tacticians may attend to the matters of planning and preparation on an ongoing basis in more enduring tactician-target encounters. Because notions of planning and preparation cut across many facets of human interchange, researchers are apt to find it highly productive to focus on these anticipatory aspects of the influence process across particular episodes of tactical endeavor.

Attending to Target Circumstances (information / intelligence

In developing lines of action toward others, tacticians often presume that targets have certain interests (fascinations, requirements, or vulnerabilities) as a consequence of (a) their knowledge of "the generalized other" (Mead, 1934) or (b) attributing tacticians' own interests to targets. However, tacticians also may learn that individual targets have more particularized desires, limitations, and sensitivities. Some of this information may come about inadvertently and may never be explicitly crystalized in the tactician's mind, but it may be strategically deployed in other cases. In other instances, still, tacticians may deliberately embark on monitoring and probing practices to uncover particular target interests and other "soft spots" or vulnerabilities.

Tactician's concerns and strategies along these lines can vary immensely, as may the time and effort that even the most calculating agents have to devote to these exercises. While the accuracy of any information (or inferences) that tacticians employ is problematic, tacticians may use this (insider) material as a base for planning and implementing a variety of other behaviors (and tactics).[4] Whereas some probing may assume the more secretive, outreaching dimensions associated with spy or espionage activity, tacticians may also acquire information about the other through open inquiry, naturalistic observation (watching, listening, deducting), and target-initiated revelations.[5,6]

Although addressing only one aspect of influence work, this is a realm of tactical endeavor to which analysts of power might pay much greater attention. Detailed examination of the occasions under which and the ways in which people acquire *and* use information about targets would not only shed valuable light on some of the more subtle aspects of the influence process, but would also foster a general understanding of human interchange.

Shaping Images of Reality (and Invoking Deception)

Since human group life is based on images (impressions, perceptions, interpretations), people involved in attempts to shape or reconfigure the symbolic realities that others experience (and act upon) may be seen to engage in a rather fundamental form of influence work. Only some tacticians may explicitly envision themselves as attending to "image work" but most people see themselves engaged in some form of communication with those they wish to influence. Even those employing physically oriented tactics to affect others' experiences (and activities) generally intend or assume some conscious acknowledgment of their messages (or activities) on the part of targets. Viewed thusly, the matter of shaping images is relevant to an exceedingly wide cross-section of tactics that people may invoke in attempts to influence others.

Image work may revolve around any aspect of human experience. It encompasses the representation of objects in the very broadest sense (physical entities, activities, concepts, spiritual essences). Recognizing that people may endeavor to influence others by shaping the ways that others experience things,[7] we turn directly to the notion that influence work entails a dramaturgical production (Goffman, 1959, 1963; Klapp, 1964).

While Goffman's (1959) discussion of impression management is most centrally related to "the presentation of self" (qualities, characters, personas) that people try to convey to others, his work also addresses the ways that people shape images in their broader theaters of operation. As Goffman indicates, people (on their own and in teams) may go to great lengths in their attempts to create particular impressions for others. This means, for instance, attending to front and back regions, settings and props, appearances and manners, casting and scripting, practice and composure, teamwork and loyalty, consistency and discretion, and mistakes and remedial interchanges.

Although performers are ultimately dependent on the interpretations and acknowledgments of their audiences, the underlying implication is that people who are more able to shape presented realities will be more able to gain control over subsequent target activities. There is some good ethnographic evidence of the viability (and the limitations) of the dramaturgical frame, as indicated in work by Edgerton (1967), Prus and Sharper (1977, 1991), Haas and Shaffir (1987), Prus (1989a, 1989b), Sanders (1989), D. Wolf (1991), and MacLeod (1993).

Still, because (a) tacticians do not continually invoke or uniformly sustain concerns with impression management, and (b) tacticians are dependent on audience interpretation of tactician endeavors, it is important to distinguish (1) images that people "project with the intention of influencing others" from (2) images that they may "project with other concerns in mind" (e.g., expressing preferred self-images, pursuing other missions) and (3) any images they may "unintentionally give off" as they go about their (other) activities in the setting. Centrally, too, (4) once tacticians' enter into the awareness contexts of targets (and other audiences), they are subject to a different set of processes, wherein tacticians efforts may be interpreted in manners quite different from any that they had intended.

In order to attain a shared sense of reality with the other (i.e., achieve intersubjective realization), the images that tacticians project (sincere or otherwise) have to invoke in the recipient or audience the meanings that the sender had intended. Because people both act toward the world as they know it to be, and yet are dependent on the images of the world given off by others, those who are more able to tap into other people's interpretive frameworks or existing notions of the world seem apt to achieve higher levels of (shared) realism or authenticity.

The problem in all communication is one of agents being able to achieve some goodness of fit of their messages relative to recipients' existing stocks of knowledge and the things that recipients might reasonably anticipate or be able to accommodate within those parameters of thought. Agent sincerity does not guarantee that recipients will achieve or sustain a sharedness of definitions with the agent. However, this same capacity for achieving shared meaning(fulness) with the other means, rather simultaneously, that people are open to messages that may be intentionally (as well as inadvertently) deceptive in thrust.

While much, if not most, image work seems sincere, benign, or expressive in intent, it is critical that analysts acknowledge people's (reflective) capacities for selectively shaping (by revealing and concealing, emphasizing and minimizing, falsifying and objectifying) the images that they present to others. Because deception may involve altered representations of any aspect (e.g., tacticians, targets, other people, or any other object) of the situation under consideration, deception may be integrated into wide ranges of tactical endeavor. Further, since tacticians may engage in similar practices with a variety of objectives and orientations in mind, it is essential that analysts ascertain tactician viewpoints rather than either imputing motivations to those in the setting or relying on target (or other recipient) interpretations of tactician intentions.

As with other communications, the "magic" entailed in all instances of successful deception is fundamentally rooted in targets' willingness (however temporarily this might be) to accept the images or versions of reality offered by the initiators or tacticians.[8] Because people contextualize incoming images within their broader notions of reality, deception seems most effective when targets more readily are able to substantiate other aspects of the situation to which tacticians lay claim. In this sense, it matters not whether the illusions generated are intended to maintain the image that "nothing unusual is happening" or to generate the image that "something unusual is happening," or whether these notions are combined in particular misrepresentations. However, for deception to be successful from the tactician's viewpoint, the images have to be accepted for as long as the tactician intends and targets have to respond to those images in the manner desired by the tacticians.

Although all influence tactics may be seen to entail minded activity, human capacities for deception (and concerns with truthfulness) acutely attest to the reflective nature of the human interchange. In addition to Goffman's work on "impression management" (1959) and "stigma" (1963), other valuable insights into deception may be found in ethnographic studies of lawyers (Blumberg, 1967), hustlers and thieves (Sutherland, 1937; Prus and Sharper, 1977; Prus and Irini, 1980), magicians (Stebbins, 1984; Prus and Sharper, 1991), the mentally retarded (Edgerton, 1967), and medical students (Haas and Shaffir, 1987). However, the practice of deception (e.g., covering, concealing, dramatizing, lying, tricking, cheating) appears both commonplace and significantly understudied by social scientists. The human capacity for deception (and the reflective and interactive nature of image work more generally) also requires dramatic revisions to the ways in which power has been conceptualized (and studied) in the social sciences.

From this viewpoint, a theory of deception would have the following elements. First, we would ask about the "perspectives," interpretive frameworks, or belief structures in which people conceptualize, present and experience deceptions or illusions. Within this notion of perspectives, we next ask about the

definitions of self, other, and the situation that the "perpetrators of the decep-
tion" invoke. What are their interests, preliminary considerations, plans, prepa-
rations, and attempted presentations? Likewise, we would attend to the "au-
diences," asking how targets receive presentations of illusions. What are their
interests, and what sorts of interpretations and adjustments (influences and
resistances) do they make to performers as their mutual encounters transpire?
Fourth, we would ask about the ways in which performers and targets view each
other (identities) and the types of relationships or bonds that develop among
themselves as their encounters take place. Fifth, the theory would be processual;
we would try to follow the sequence along, as it was developed, experienced, and
modified by the parties involved. Viewed in this manner, deceptions are
social constructions. *They may entail creativity and resourcefulness and may*
be implemented with any variety of interests or motives in mind, but they are
developed in anticipation of audience reactions and only through audience
reactions can they hope to achieve a sense of viability. (Prus and Sharper,
1991:301)

The implication is that social scientists may learn much about image
work (and the influence process) by attending in extended detail to (a)
tacticians' initial definitions of (and objectives within) the situations at
hand; (b) tacticians' considerations of the particular options (sincere and
deceptive) they might pursue; (c) tacticians selections of, preparations for,
and projections of particular images vis-à-vis designated targets; (d) targets'
interpretations of and responses to the tacticians they encounter; and (e)
tactician assessments and adjustments to target responses (including any
subsequent target interchanges with tacticians).

Analysts concerned with power may be more intrigued by the potential for deception in influence work, but the processes by which tacticians
communicate images (sincere or deceptive) are very much the same. Moreover, since influence work often involves mixes of sincere and deceptive
messages (and is ultimately dependent on target interpretations), the entire
set of processes outlined here would seem to warrant extended consideration on the part of social scientists. Clearly, too, concerns with the images
that tacticians project do not stop here. Indeed, the subsequent discussions
of influence work build centrally on tactician representations and target
(re)interpretations of the world.

Cultivating Relationships[9]

Because people are usually thought more able to influence those with
whom they have achieved stronger or more intimate bonds, the practice of
cultivating relationships has long been seen as a significant mode of shaping
the behaviors of others (e.g., see Isocrates [436–338 B.C.]). Thus, expres-

sions such as "getting on people's good sides," "acting friendly toward others," or "currying favor," point to the potential associated with deliberately contrived or fabricated relationships. Additionally, recognizing that others may invoke strategies along these lines, there are long-standing cautions about "people being used by others," "that others are only pretending to be friendly," or that one (after Helen of Troy) should "beware of Greeks bearing gifts." However, amid these tactical encouragements, contrived enactments, and skepticisms is also the rather pervasive recognition that people often intend to build relationships with others that reflect genuine contexts of friendship, affection, and benign regard for the other. Noteworthy too (given the earlier noted skepticisms), is the awareness that these latter efforts may be subject to sinister interpretations on the part of recipients. Further, most people desire, if not genuinely require and benefit from, relationships that are cultivated or developed in benign (e.g., friendly, helpful, caring, accommodative) fashions.

While people sometimes find themselves privileged relative to particular others because of the ways these others view them, people also may endeavor to generate associations that other people would find more agreeable. People's motives or interests for engaging particular others may be quite varied, but the emphasis here is on the ways that people try to win favor or consolidate themselves with others.

Since people with diverse interests and applications may approach relationships in similar manners, it is important to outline some of the ways people endeavor to build bonds with others. Thus, consideration is given to the matters of getting noticed, acknowledging tactician mystique, expressing empathy, spending time (associating) with others, helping and protecting others, complying with others' desires, encouraging trust, fostering loyalty, and encountering practical limitations. While some analysts may be more intrigued by "manipulative" endeavors, it should be emphasized that the people involved need not use these practices to particular advantage in their dealings with others, in either the short or long term. Likewise, an attentiveness to all endeavors along these lines, irrespective of intention, is important for achieving a fuller appreciation of influence as a social process.

Getting Noticed
Sometimes, people are thrust into others' presence in ways that these others would find difficult to miss. In other cases, a first task that those wishing to cultivate relationships with particular targets encounter is that of "establishing presence" or achieving preliminary target awareness or recognition.[10] Even when they aspire for heightened levels of acknowledgment and influence, many people anticipate that they are unlikely to achieve desired lines of action from targets until they at least become noticed. The implication is

that once tacticians become more distinct objects in the minds of those targets,[11] these others might be more willing to attend to them in the future. For researchers, noteworthy questions revolve around the matters of how people attempt to obtain the attention (or more explicit recognition) of others and how they deal with various setbacks (including targets who disregard or become disaffected with their efforts).

Acknowledging [Tactician] Mystique

As used here, "mystique" reflects notions of esteem, intrigue, charisma, or other prominent images, awes, or auras that audiences attribute to others (individuals, groups, or categories of people). People who provide unencumbered assistance to others may sometimes find that the recipients of their assistance accord them a degree of mystique or aura,[12] but there are many other bases (e.g., popular esteem, appearances, possessions, skills, missions, even promises) on which particular people may be envisioned as having an alluring or exceptional presence. Whereas positive auras may be seen as pertinent to influence work, negative auras (particularly those envisioned as engendering fear or intimidation) also may be very effective in some instances.

Although there may be a tendency for analysts to associate mystique, charisma, or aura more exclusively with widely acclaimed public figures, somewhat parallel fascinations, enchantments, or other engrossments may develop around people in smaller communities and in two-person groupings. These intrigues may develop through sustained contact with others or from a distance. They may be largely one-sided or more dualistic (as in mutual admiration or reciprocated animosity) in thrust. Particularly consequential, though, for our purposes, is the recognition that those accorded mystique by particular targets may more readily be able to influence those targets.[13]

Whereas (a) tacticians are sometimes advantaged at the outset because of the qualities that particular people attribute to them and may use this as a basis for encouraging certain behaviors on the part of these targets, (b) tacticians (individuals and groups) may engage in considerable impression management in attempts to promote more compelling images of self (Goffman, 1959; Klapp, 1964; Lofland, 1966; Prus and Irini, 1980; Haas and Shaffir, 1987; Prus, 1989a, 1989b; Sanders, 1989; Prus and Sharper, 1991; Van Zandt, 1991; MacLeod, 1993; Grills, 1994; Prus and Fleras, 1996).

Regardless of whether they focus on the mystique associated with people in large-scale or dyadic settings, scholars interested in power as a community phenomena may learn much by carefully examining (a) the processes by which people attribute auras (e.g., intrigue, affection, fear) to others, (b) the enterprise in which tacticians engage in attempts to have themselves envisioned in certain fashions, (c) the manners in which tacti-

cians endeavor to utilize current imputations of mystique, and (d) the ways
that their targets view and deal with these practices.

Expressing Empathy

While empathizing generally refers to people developing an awareness of
the viewpoints of others, our focus, more centrally, is on the practice of
indicating affinities of interest, understanding, or emotional experience
with others. Tacticians adopting this strategy attempt to convey a sharing or
mutuality of viewpoints with the other. Not everyone who comprehends
the viewpoint of the other will make indications that comfortably resonate
with that other. Indeed, some may use these understandings to disadvantage targets (as in ransoms, teasing, or overt cruelty). There are also
those who may make seemingly appropriate indications, but are not seen by
others as adequately informed or sincere. Still, whether addressing notions
of (a) loss, fear, suffering, and sympathy; (b) boredom, frustration, and
endless toil; (c) success and accomplishment; or (d) excitement, adventure,
or novelty, for instance, those able to convey a sense of affinity that is
acknowledged by the other would appear to gain some insider relevance
with that other.

Spending Time (Associating) with Others

Whether by intent or more natural circumstance, those who associate with
others over longer time frames have greater opportunities to develop more
meaningful relationships with these others. Although recreational, playful,
and other more pleasurable times together may contribute to greater senses
of bondedness, it should be appreciated that other interrelated activities
and experiences may also contribute to people's notions of affinity.

   In addition to expressing an openness or receptivity to the other by
making oneself more available to the other, we should recognize the sense
of interrelatedness that people often experience as they do things together,
especially as coordinated (vs. same setting but more individualized, parallel) activities. The sharing, and especially the joint construction, of events,
activities, and experiences contribute to a sense of closeness (and often
interdependency) with the other. Thus, while people may naturally "hang
around with others" on some occasions, those wishing to become privileged
insiders may assume considerable enterprise (sometimes in settings that
they find discordant in other ways) in attempts to become accepted as
insiders of sorts. Still, as with those trying to be noticed, people may have
difficulty gaining access to those with whom they might most like to consolidate themselves.

Helping Others

The notion of assisting or helping others suggests a wide range of volun-
teered activity. Consider such things as suggesting options, offering advice,

providing tutelage, facilitating, lending, doing favors, and gifting, as well as endorsing, sponsoring, representing, and championing. Helping also may involve more direct or explicit exchanges or trades as well as more subtle anticipations of reciprocity, but those cultivating relationships in this manner need *not* intend, imply, or require an exchange or repayment of any sort.

When people operate as gatekeepers or control points of access to various outcomes that others might desire (or desire to avoid), they may build stronger bonds with others by selectively using these offices or resources to advantage these others. Beyond these other modes of assistance or consideration, people sometimes make implied or direct promises, anticipating that these notions of help might serve to endear them to others.

Another variant of the helping role revolves around the matter of protecting others from difficult times, threats, losses, and villains of sorts. Regardless of their motives, those providing aid, especially on timely or more desperate occasions (as Klapp, 1964 observes), seem more apt to be accorded some heroic status by grateful others.

In addition to instances of assistance that are tactician-generated, people who are asked to help others either by prospective recipients or third parties may also find that these helping occasions lend themselves to tactical advantages along the way. Some consideration is given to the ways in which people (as tacticians) may seek help from others later in this chapter, but it should be recognized that people who are asked for help may be advantaged in "cultivating relationships" with particular others, should they avail themselves of these options.

Complying with Others' Desires

In addition to the helping roles just discussed, people may pursue favor with others by (a) acknowledging the other or (b) otherwise creating desired effects. "Acknowledging the other" ranges from things such as recognizing the other person in a more general sense, to indicating tolerances or acceptances of them, to expressing consensus or agreements with their thoughts and activities, to providing more direct, positive significations (e.g., compliments, esteem). While practices along these lines are sometimes envisioned as flattery or ingratiation practices, recipients play an essential role in defining the significance (i.e., sincerity, relevance, and appropriateness) of these acknowledgements.

People sometimes try to please others by "creating desired effects." In addition to gifting (and other forms of assisting or honoring others), people may attempt to present themselves (Goffman, 1959) in ways that others might find appealing. Here, in addition to generating settings or creating scenes that others might more readily prefer, people may adjust their own appearances, demeanor, and activities. In some cases, tacticians may try to orchestrate the appearances, manners, and activities of others in the setting, so that these others too, might contribute to desired effects.

Encouraging Trust

Because people who trust or put more confidence in the intentions and abilities of others are seen more likely to act in line with the suggestions of these others, there may be an incentive on the part of some to generate an enhanced sense of confidence. Often, people are accorded some degree of trust by virtue of the mutualities associated with the relationships that they cultivate with others in other ways. Still, where people do not believe that they are accorded appropriate confidences on general levels or in some realms that they might more particularly desire, they may more directly attempt to generate trust.

Two themes seem particularly consequential to attributes of trust. First, is the tactician thought to have the target's interests in mind. Second, is the tactician thought able to act effectively in this area. Not everyone will explicitly make these inferences, but tacticians often try to indicate that they have the targets' best interests in mind by representing themselves as concerned, personable, competent, knowledgeable, and the like. Salespeople (Prus, 1989a:102–130), for instance, frequently attempt to consolidate themselves with targets by (a) conveying tactician integrity, (b) establishing definitions of quality pertaining to objects (goods, people, concepts, lines of action) being promoted, or (c) providing evidence of minimized target investments (inconveniences and liabilities).[14]

If we are to understand trust more thoroughly as part of the influence process a great deal of work remains to be done. This involves field research not only (a) on the ways in which tacticians endeavor to encourage trust (and the practical limitations that they encounter), but also (b) on target interpretations of these situations and the ways in which they incorporate trust and other considerations into their subsequent lines of activity.[15]

Fostering Loyalty (and Dependency)

Although many of the preceding practices may generate some loyalty (or more enduring commitments) from others, tacticians may attempt to establish a variety of other dependencies on the part of targets. Thus, for instance, people may encourage targets to (a) adopt tactician-related perspectives (viewpoints, ideologies, moralities), (b) develop identities that are more closely tied to tacticians, (c) acquire dependency on tactician-related activities, (d) establish bonds with others who are affiliated with particular tacticians, and (e) make more extensive, especially irretrievable, commitments to tacticians.

Tacticians need not attend to all of these strands or interlinkages, but each represents a theme that might either be used (1) to encourage targets to seek out or otherwise favor the influences of these tacticians or (2) as a leverage point in pursuing target commitments. Where targets are bonded in more manners to tacticians, the potential for influence would seem greater. Still, although some people may be more dedicated to their associates than vice versa, relatively mutual interdependencies and loyalties are evident in many settings (e.g., between partners, family members, friends).

Loyalty is pertinent to a wide assortment of influence contexts, but for some ethnographic depictions of tactician promotions of (and participant experiences with) bondedness, readers are referred to studies of religious recruitment (Lofland, 1966; Prus, 1976; Van Zandt, 1991), vendor practices (Prus, 1989a: especially 210–233; Prus and Frisby, 1990), bar staff (Prus and Irini, 1980; Prus, 1983), street gangs (Keiser, 1969), outlaw biker gangs (D. Wolf, 1991), and feminists (C. Wolf, 1994). While people may knowingly generate dependencies on the part of others, the (seeming) targets may be willing partners (and sometimes initiators) of these relationships. Rather than dismissing tactician attempts to foster sustained target involvements as instances of "mind control" or "brainwashing," or, conversely, viewing loyalty as "weak mindedness" or "fanaticism," researchers are apt to find that these more enduring interchanges represent consequential realms for inquiry into people's participation in subcultural life-worlds.

Encountering Practical Limitations
Although it often denotes a tactical endeavor, the matter of cultivating relationships is most appropriately located within the more general context of human association and audience definitions. Clearly, some people are greatly advantaged over others at the outset (e.g., preexisting acquaintances, mystique, more enduring co-presence) and may do very little to achieve high levels of target attentiveness and compliance. At other times, people may work extensively at cultivating relationships (genuine or otherwise), possibly with minimal or even negative impact on the other.

Sometimes, recipients are inattentive to, or clearly opposed to, tacticians' attempts to establish congenial relations with them. In addition to other interests and disaffections, targets may be distracted by the prospects that third-party relationships represent to them. Indeed, third-party others (as competitive tacticians) may also strive for recognition, mystique, and loyalty from the recipients under consideration.

For those interested in the study of power, the practices introduced here provide a plethora of departure points for research on tacticians and targets (and their relationships). In addition to outlining a series of conceptual notions that may be applied to an endless variety of human contexts, we may ask how people learn about practices of these sorts, when and how they invoke these strategies, how they deal with any resistance (and competition) they encounter, and how they move from enhancing tactics of the sort just discussed to more directive or focused forms of influence work and commitment.

Focusing Procedures

A great many focusing practices build on or incorporate enhancement tactics of the sort just discussed, but focusing tactics differ from the latter with respect to the greater sense of direction that they imply. Whereas those engaging in stage-setting or relational activities may achieve greater target receptivity than other tacticians, influence work normally presupposes an expression or indication of some preferred lines of target activity on the part of tacticians. Targets may miss or be oblivious to these indications in some cases and may misinterpret or ignore them in other instance, but overt expressions are important. Not only do they usually suggest some line of activity for the target to follow, but once acknowledged by targets these expressions typically involve tacticians in more direct or enacted relationships with targets.

Indicating Lines of Action

The overt indications that tacticians make to targets may assume the forms of commands, directives, suggestions, questions, requests, or observations. They may be very limited or extensively developed, and may be presented in highly emotional, highly subdued, or more mixed tones. Indications directed toward targets may, but need not, imply any sanctions or other target considerations.

Although some instances of influence work may be effectively realized (defined, acknowledged, enacted, and deemed satisfactory) on the basis of one indication, other messages may be little more than entry points into more complicated, potentially unpredictable, assortments of tactical interchange. Thus, in addition to the ways in which targets interpret and deal with tactician indications, researchers may attend to the sorts of indications that tacticians provide, the concerns that tacticians have (and the ways they articulate and express these to targets), and any adjustments that tacticians make to their indications (e.g., more abrupt, less detailed, more emphatic) over time.

Promoting Target Interests

In an attempt to foster receptivity to particular lines of action, tacticians sometimes endeavor to establish a sharpened interest or relevancy base for targets. These activities commonly involve such things as (a) presenting rationales, (b) embellishing aspects of the situation, (c) encouraging targets to sample things, and (d) generating discontent with current target circumstances.[16]

In *presenting rationale,* tacticians explain concepts to targets or outline the benefits (for targets or others) associated with particular lines of action. Whether they also see themselves as justifying target practices or redefining situations for targets, tacticians presenting rationale attempt to convince targets of the viability or wisdom of acting in certain respects by sharing their perspectives, stocks of knowledge, and assessments of the situation with these targets. Although tacticians may alter their own strategies when straightforward explanations or justifications do not seem adequate, our consideration of explanatory tactics should not end here. Rather, it would be very instructive to examine the ways in which people actually formulate and present rationale to others, how they deal with any target resistance(s) they encounter, and when they switch off to other tactics (and possibly return to explanatory endeavors).

Somewhat relatedly, tacticians may pursue cooperation by encouraging target allures or fascinations in the objects or situations at hand. Intended to prompt targets to define things as more compelling, this involves *embellishing* things or presenting products, concepts, agendas, and lines of action in ways thought to be more appealing to targets. Tacticians may pursue this objective in highly ad hoc manners or they may engage in extended preparations or stage-setting activities.

Tacticians also may encourage preliminary forms of *target participation* as a means of making certain things more evident to targets. Thus, tacticians may attempt to have targets sample, test, or experience particular items or practices. The hopes are (variously) that targets might develop preferences for these lines of action, overcome earlier hesitations, make (even partial) commitments to particular lines of activity, or become more accustomed to or dependent on some aspect of the experience.

A related strategy involves attempts to verbally *generate disenchantment* with the target's present circumstances. Here, tacticians endeavor to sharpen the contrasts between current and more desirable sets of target circumstances. Tacticians typically attempt to create discontent on the part of targets by emphasizing discrepancies or incongruities between current (undesirable, more mundane) target situations and "the more desired conditions" that the tacticians are promoting.[17]

The matter of developing target interest in tactician agendas is very much overlooked by those promoting structuralist or resource orientations to power relations, but the practices outlined here can be exceedingly consequential for shaping target behavior. Thus, although tacticians are dependent on targets acknowledging, internalizing, and acting in conjunction with these frames of reference, researchers may gain much by attending to the ways that tacticians envision, develop, assess, readjust, drop, and return to one or another of these persuasive endeavors as they attend to target capacities for minded behavior.

Neutralizing and Debasing Strategies

Often combined with enhancing and focusing practices, neutralizing and debasing tactics are generally intended to counter options (other objects, including people, activities, situations) to which targets may attend. While tacticians may approach targets with varying degrees of intensity, diplomacy, tolerance, and the like, neutralizing and debasing practices are initiated to encourage targets to define the people or other things under consideration as inconsequential, undesirable, offensive, threatening, and the like. Thus, tactician practices commonly include the minimizing, discounting, challenging, denigrating, disparaging, and vilifying of options. Often, as well, tacticians justify their claims by invoking reference points or standards that their targets are thought (or thought ought) to consider appropriate, desirable, or ideal in some respect. Tacticians frequently embark on these discrediting activities on their own, but they may also attempt to involve others (e.g., as collaborators, witnesses, judges, or audiences) in order to convince targets of the viability of their viewpoints.

Neutralization tactics seem frequently employed when tacticians encounter targets who are reluctant to act in ways that tacticians deem appropriate. To this end, tacticians may attempt to uncover and dispense with any reservations that targets might have about those lines of activity. Sometimes, tacticians are aware that targets have long-standing fears, hesitations, or reservations and may plan to neutralize these in advance. At other times, tacticians may subsequently learn about these from target disclosures, personal observations, or third-party comments. In still other instances, tacticians may inquire about any reluctances that they suspect targets might have. Some tacticians appear unconcerned about such things, but others see these queries and ensuing neutralizations as ways to foster influence work.[18] Likewise, although some tacticians may endeavor to be diplomatic in their inquiries, others may be more blunt or insistent ("Why not? What's wrong with you?").

Tacticians may also engage in neutralizing practices when they see themselves or their ideas, programs, missions, and the like threatened or put at risk by the choices that targets might make. Some neutralizing practices are directed toward the objective of discrediting people (especially competitors, disreputables, or enemies) that tacticians dislike or oppose. In other cases, but sometimes concurrently, tacticians may attempt to disqualify ideas, activities, products, or appearances that they consider inappropriate. These are, it seems, rather common practices as suggested by people expressing (and contesting) all sorts of preferences (e.g., food, clothing, customs, knowledge, moralities).

More explicit or extensive denigrations or other debasing practices may be used as neutralization devices (wherein tacticians attempt to discourage certain kinds of target viewpoints or other involvements), but condemnations also may be used more pointedly to incite targets to act against those things (people, practices, circumstances) that tacticians define in adversarial or oppositional terms. Here, tacticians may cast any variety of aspersions on particular objects (people or other things) in attempts to invoke moral indignation on the part of the targets they are trying to influence. The anticipation is that by more extensively disgracing or chastizing the referenced objects, the targets to whom these messages are directed may, more "righteously" and with greater intensity, embark on negative treatment of those things that (now) offend their moralities and other sensibilities.

When human targets are involved, those at whom these denigrations are directed may, but need not, be present. Thus, in addition to (a) those encounters in which the people (or representatives of the things) being discredited are the only audiences present, we may also consider (b) instances in which the debased parties are absent (i.e., the messages are pitched to other audiences), and (c) those in which both the denigrated parties and others are present. Those subjected to neutralization or condemnation practices may, but need not, have opportunities to contest or otherwise resist these imputations even if they are present.

Lest some readers assume that neutralization and debasing practices are recent inventions, they are reminded that Aristotle (*Rhetoric*) proposed that a discipline be developed around claims-making and neutralization practices. He observed that rhetoric was essential as logic for comprehending the human condition.

As well, there is no indication (e.g., from Socrates [see Plato], onward) that those who envision themselves as more ethical, good, or moral are in any way freed from these practices compared to others. Indeed, as Klapp (1962, 1964, 1969, 1971) observes, the "forces of good" achieve viability and vitality by emphasizing the threats of evil. Although only some neutralization practices may be intended to foster large-scale crusades or missions, one may observe parallel tendencies in the long-standing practice of malicious gossip as well as in more structured degradation ceremonies and tribunals.[19]

Whether directed at human targets (individuals and groups) or any other objects, sustained examinations of neutralizing or debasing practices (and the ensuing interchanges) are apt to shed much light on power relations in a great many realms of human enterprise.

Leveraging Tactics

When tacticians are more esteemed by targets or where targets have developed interests that are more consistent with tactician proposals, targets may willingly act in accordance with tactician indications, possibly with the slightest of suggestions. Occasionally, too tacticians may be so besieged with applicants, volunteers, and other interested parties that they face the dilemma of making choices between eager candidates.

Often, though, commitment is not as readily forthcoming and it is here that tacticians may turn to leveraging tactics. These procedures are intended to enable tacticians to obtain target commitments or lock targets into certain lines of activity. In addition to (1) establishing consensus and (2) usurping agency, other noteworthy leveraging practices include (3) using inducements and treatments, (4) bargaining with targets, and (5) tapping into existing relationships and community affiliations.

Establishing Consensus

While tacticians sometimes have only to acknowledge target inclinations to achieve a firm mutuality of focus relative to target activity, the pursuit of consensus may entail extensive tactician enterprise even when targets seem somewhat disposed in those directions.[20]

In some cases, it may be sufficient for tacticians to merely ask targets if they would like to make commitments to tactician agendas, but tacticians also may be more directive. Here, they may request or insist that targets make commitments at certain times or select from a specified range of options (all of which may be favorable to tacticians). Attempts to "close" targets into particular lines of action may involve other modes of influence work as well. Thus, for example, tacticians may provide additional justifications for making specific commitments, emphasize the tentative nature of the commitments (possibly) being made, or point out the shortcomings apt to be experienced by those who do not commit. In some cases, too, tacticians may presume consensus on behalf of targets. Tacticians may allow targets to resist these definitions but, unless challenged in some manner, tacticians act as if particular lines of action are acceptable (i.e., denote mutuality) to targets.

Although practices of these sorts may seem rather subtle compared to some other leveraging endeavors, researchers are apt to find it highly instructive to examine the ways that tacticians pursue (and targets resist) consensus along these lines in the many arenas that constitute everyday life.

Usurping Agency

The term, *usurping agency* refers to those situations in which tacticians impose their wills (agency) on targets in more direct fashions. Whereas tacticians operating from other modes of influence tend to acknowledge target capacities for responding to agents in some meaningful or minded respect, tacticians who usurp agency intend to deal with [people] in more unilateral, objectlike manners.

Since people live and act in a world of symbolically constituted objects, all activity directed to humans implies some object status (i.e., people act toward other people and themselves as objects as well). This reflects people's broader capacities for dealing with (defining, using, fixing, improving, being entertained by, moving, disposing of) any manner of objects.

While operating as minded entities, themselves, people usurping agency disattend to, or distance themselves from, the [unique mindedness of human targets]. In Goffman's (1959) terms, they treat these [people] as "nonpersons." Those usurping agency may focus more exclusively on this tactic or they may combine these practices with other leveraging tactics. However, as a procedure unto itself, the emphasis is on achieving control over objects (that happen to be human) rather than trying to affect minded changes on the part of human targets.

In their purest forms, tactics of this sort are invoked in highly unilateral (noninteractive) terms, with targets having no opportunity or ability to challenge these activities. In some cases, targets may be completely unaware of impending or actual tactician activities. However, even when targets are cognizant of these efforts, they may be unable (or unprepared) to resist these.[21] The practice of usurping agency need not preclude the possibility of targets acting back on tacticians and, in some cases, people may assume bilateral roles (as in military contests),[22] each endeavoring to usurp agency (or commitment-making capacities) on the part of the other. Nevertheless, it is the generalized sense of human fragility (and the implied, often unknown, dependency on tactician others) along with the apparent, presumed, or intended inability of human targets to defend themselves from tacticians that represents the basis of concern (fear) of this tactical orientation.

Assuming or usurping agency means that tacticians presume, make, or totally disregard commitments on behalf of target others. In some more extreme cases, for example, assassins and terrorists may assign or make commitments to death on behalf of human targets or more completely disregard the [essential humanness] of targets. Although less dramatic, somewhat parallel impositions may be noted in reference to such things as robbery, burglary, or theft, wherein people are seen primarily as objects to be managed in more direct ways.

Beyond "doing others in" by physically imposing one's agency (will) on them, people also may usurp agency as a means of protecting or caring for targets who are thought unable to manage their own circumstances. Likewise, tacticians may believe that unless they presume agency in

other instances, targets or others may experience considerable loss or disadvantage. In some cases, as well, people may adopt impositional practices when other modes of influence work have failed (i.e., as "last resorts," Emerson, 1981).

People also may usurp agency when they envision themselves obliged
to enforce some [impositional] role to which they have been assigned (or
that they assume) within the broader community. Roles such as judges,
police officers, prison guards, and executioners, as well as politicians,
and religious leaders, may be more obvious in this respect, but consider
people who also engage humans in other official (also objective, righteous,
dispassionate) ways. Even in trying to be "fair" and "consistent," people
commonly invoke agency on the part of those who come under consideration. Thus, many public service and private sector employees, as well as
parents and others who are endeavoring to balance notions of justice and
equity or to ensure the rights of multiple parties may find themselves more
extensively usurping agency on behalf of others than they might have
desired or anticipated.

Instances of people usurping agency on the part of others may seem
more intriguing when these practices physically jeopardize the lives or circumstances of those who innocently have become targets for tacticians
pursuing personal or group missions of various sorts. Still, it should be
noted that people frequently usurp agency when they (a) attempt to
discredit or vilify others as in neutralizing and debasing practices or (b) try
to explain other people's behaviors without consulting them.

Also, albeit under the guise of presenting the news and other informative and entertainment venues, those producing the media generally usurp
agency on behalf of the people whose personas and activities they purport
to represent. Somewhat relatedly, the question may also be raised whether
social scientists, despite their academic objectives, are exempt from the
practice of usurping agency on the part of others?

Because they invoke dependent and independent variables (typically
some distance removed from considerations of human agency) to explain
human behavior (or related conditions), those engaged in quantitative
analyses (demographics, surveys, experiments) may seem particularly apparent in this regard. However, those involved in grand-level theorizing
routinely impose broad sets of impersonal forces on members of the
community as even more extensively do those academics who also impose
their moralities (or politics) on others. In purporting to tell people in the
community what causes human behavior, why they do things, or what
they should do, many social scientists also appear to disregard or impose
agency on the part of those of whom they speak. Even those who engage
more fully in ethnographic research (i.e., attend more completely to participant viewpoints) make some choices that presume agency on the part of

others. Somewhat relatedly, it seems impossible not to at least partially presume or usurp agency in making classroom presentations or in attempting to simultaneously converse with multiple people in other settings. While some roles and activities may be more impositional than others, few realms of endeavor may be exempt.[23]

As with most of the other tactics examined here, it appears that the practice of usurping agency is much more commonplace than one might first assume. Likewise, people may impose agency on others with a variety of intentions and degrees of community tolerance (from explicit rejection to explicit encouragement).

Still, because people are sometimes thought to impose themselves on [targets] in ways that others consider abrupt, undesired, or threatening, much general attention (and fascination) revolves around these episodes and people's reactions to these situations. It is most appropriate for researchers to examine the after-the-fact reactions of targets and others to these situations, wherein one considers matters such as defining trouble, identifying victims and culprits, mobilizing for perpetrator control, pursuing restitution, and fostering deterrence in the future. However, this is only a part of the analytical picture.

Rather directly, we also need to attend to the imposition of agency as an *enacted* phenomenon. It may be tempting, in certain regards, to divide considerations of this sort along the lines of good and evil intentions or life-threatening and relatively innocuous activities (or outcomes), but it is much more productive to examine a great many instances (and varieties) of imposed agency in extended detail and to develop comparisons (similarities and contrasts) across the fuller range of circumstances that one might encounter in community life.

The task facing social scientists is one of carefully examining these instances of human endeavor relative to (a) the ways that people define [human targets] in given situations or applications, (b) the manners in which tacticians implement particular lines of activity with respect to [human objects], and (c) the roles that others (targets, other audiences) assume in these immediate cases and their aftermath, including interchanges with tacticians and other people.

Likewise, although it may seem to shift the focus away from usurping agency, analysts are apt to achieve a more complete sense understanding of this process by (d) acknowledging the flip-side question of when people more explicitly attend to (and accommodate) the viewpoints of others when they engage these others. The matters of disregarding and attending to others may suggest polar variants, but (as with parents both attending to and disregarding their children's viewpoints, or vice versa), it is apparent that the same tacticians may implement both sets of practices in relating to the same targets in the same settings. Thus, scholars may find that the two are much more intertwined in practice; that tactical orientations of the one sort may only be effectively understood in conjunction with the other.

Using Inducements and Other Treatments

In elaborating on the use of leveraging tactics, it is most instructive to consider the ways in which tacticians attempt to objectify or structure relations with others through the use of inducements (threats and promises) and other treatments (behaviors or practices intended to impact on others' experiences in more compelling or direct, explicit experiential manners).[24] While inducements differ from other treatments in the sense that they centrally imply futuristic target gains or losses, inducements may be envisioned as treatments for most analytical purposes. Indeed, like other treatments, the viability of inducements as experiential events rests on targets' willingness to acknowledge "the realism" or authenticity of tactician endeavors. That some inducements may employ deception does not differentiate these practices from treatments more generally. Further, despite a tendency on the part of many people (analysts included) to focus on the more physical or material aspects of inducements and treatments, it is essential that scholars concerned with the study of human relations be keenly attentive to the *meanings* that both tacticians and targets assign to these phenomena.

Treatments (and inducements) do *not* exist as objective states, even when they seem based entirely on physical or material conditions. Tacticians may maintain fairly consistent definitions of particular treatments over time, but they may also assume differing views of specific treatments prior to, during, and after implementing these or other treatments. That tacticians often fall short of their objectives in using treatments is not of central consequence for our purposes, although this may result in some tactician redefinitions of and subsequent adjustments to particular target treatments. What is important is that analysts obtain intimately informed senses of what tacticians experience over time as they (1) consider, (2) implement, (3) assess, and (4) adjust the treatments that they direct toward particular targets.[25]

Although tacticians sometimes administer particular treatments to targets (a) to encourage conformity to tactician agendas or foster morally desirable group practices on the part of targets, tacticians also may implement treatments (b) to please others (targets or third parties), and (c) to express personal or group satisfaction or discontent.[26] On other occasions, treatments may be employed as (d) "default options" when tacticians, for example, face pressing time restraints, try to minimize other costs, or cannot think of more viable alternatives.

The treatments that tacticians direct toward others seem virtually unlimited. Nevertheless, the matter of what constitutes "treatment" in particular cases is somewhat elusive. In addition to (a) things intended as strategic in their deployment, we should also recognize that (b) tacticians often "act" toward others in ways that they do not intend as consequential in treatment terms. Tacticians may assume that targets effectively differentiate treatments from the other things that tacticians do, but it is not apparent that targets will (c) distinguish treatment and nontreatment themes along the lines envisioned by tacticians or (d) interpret either set of events (treatment and nontreatment) in the ways in which they were intended. Even when the intentions of treatments are clearly communicated to targets, treatments may be accorded meanings by targets that differ substantially from those that tacticians had intended (e.g., tactician identified "assistance" may be interpreted as irrelevant, bothersome, embarrassing, or threatening by recipients).

When inducements and treatments are directed towards groups or categories of people, their meanings (and effectiveness) are even more problematic. Not only may tactician communications be subject to highly diverse and shifting interpretations on the part of the targets (as individuals) involved, but any interaction among the targets (and outsiders) also may generate definitions of the treatments (and tacticians' objectives) that substantially alter their intended effects.[27]

Extended, in-depth (ethnographic) studies of both (a) tacticians' contemplation and implementation of inducements and treatments and (b) targets' experiences with these situations are required if we are to comprehend these rather basic aspects of human interchange. In this way, researchers may move past more singularistic or psychologistic notions of sanctions to a recognition that all treatments represent objects (and activities) that are experienced by both targets *and* tacticians.

Like other things, treatments are subject to ongoing definitions, interpretations, and adjustments on the part of both targets and tacticians as they attend (in their own terms) to notions of the past, present, and future. While an appreciation of target interpretations of, and actions toward, treatments is essential for a fuller understanding of this phenomena, researchers can add much to our understanding of power relations by asking "when and how tacticians are more likely to implement (i.e., envision, initiate, sustain, intensify, assess, discontinue, and reinstate) particular treatments." These elements acknowledge a reflective, adjustive, historical flow that is highly consequential for understanding the implementation of treatment (and control) programs.

Bargaining with Targets

The terms *bargaining* and *negotiating* are sometimes used to encompass all modes of interpersonal influence (i.e., that group life is negotiable), but it is useful to consider bargaining as a tactic somewhat unto itself. Thus, the immediate reference is to the more explicit practice of "making deals," wherein two or more parties envision themselves as tacticians with the potential to enter into exchanges or trade with others for specific considerations.[28] This involves tacticians making concessions to others or offering targets things in attempts to obtain desired forms of cooperation (and other objects) from those targets. However, this strategy assumes that tacticians have (or can convince targets that they have) something of interest to targets. It is worth noting, too, that people may develop bargains in response to earlier modes of influence (e.g., developing interest, providing treatment) or they may embed deals within, or use these in conjunction with, other tactical endeavors (e.g., deception, generating trust, usurping agency).

The items to be exchanged may be of any sort imaginable, from physical objects to services, concepts, entertainment, and symbolic references (ranging from money to other forms of signification, including affection, respect, and acknowledgment).[29] Typically, one party will anticipate a trade before the other has given the matter any consideration. However, for a bargain or exchange to take place (be completed), there must be some *mutuality* of focus and some shared visions of an interrelated (if only short term) future; an understanding or acknowledgment on the part of the parties involved that each will do or provide something for the other once they have settled on the terms of the exchange.

The ways that people represent the items of exchange as well as the procedures by which they make and receive offers (to make deals) may vary along several dimensions. For instance, the participants may embellish the items they possess, disparage the possessions of the other, simply announce object availability, or make highly direct offers to exchange things with others. Not only may people be differentially concerned about the potential gains and losses that trades might entail, but they are also apt to vary in the ways that they represent their situations to others and resist the definitions (and offers) of others.[30] Likewise, bargains may range from highly explicit, quick, open, and direct exchanges to those that (variously) are only vaguely formulated, highly complex, or characterized by much hesitation, concealment, debate, counteroffering, or discontinuities, for instance.[31]

While dyadic bargains occasionally become quite complex, exchanges may more readily become complicated when the parties entering negotiations are representatives for other parties (individuals or groups). In the process of working out deals with the immediate other, these tacticians may be faced with the task of attending to (home-front) accountability with respect to those they represent.[32] Representatives may invoke (sincerely and deceptively) images of accountability as a tactical lever in their immediate dealings with targets, but they also may more or less simultaneously engage in other instances of influence work (possibly involving secondary agendas and any variety of tactical maneuverings) with those whom they are purporting to represent.[33]

Some exchanges or other target commitments may be realized more directly or immediately, but others imply futuristic activities or other considerations on the part of targets. Under these latter conditions, tacticians may be willing to accept a variety of target expressions (e.g., promises, contracts, head nods) as indications of mutual understanding. Regardless of the ways that target commitments are obtained or expressed, though, tacticians may later endeavor to use these indications as levers to ensure compliance from the targets in question. The implication is that people who fail to receive appropriate considerations from others would be justified in making claims against these targets or embarking on other activities designed to balance the earlier agreements made with them.

Tacticians anticipating failures may seek greater leverage in shaping target behaviors by extracting commitments that seem more enduring or binding. Hence, tacticians may attempt to obtain irretrievable investments or build other contingencies into the agreement, possibly specifying secondary activities to be pursued should the parties fail to live up to their primary obligations.

Although more explicit and irretrievable commitments may be seen to provide "safety nets" for one or other of the parties, it is important that social scientists look past the more formal or technical features of agreements and focus more broadly on the ways that people may (a) propose, articulate, negotiate, endorse, and fulfill all manner of commitments that they make to others; (b) overlook, ignore, or avoid their commitments; and (c) pursue nonhonored commitments, make claims against targets, and work out secondary arrangements with targets. The suggestion is not that scholars ignore any mode of commitment that people make to others but that researchers examine all commitments within these fuller parameters.

For students of power relationships, bargaining suggests a variety of subprocesses or activities that are worthy of further inquiry. These include attending to the ways that people (1) indicate an openness to deal; (2) suggest objects of trade; (3) embellish and discredit objects; (4) conceal and express interests and vulnerabilities; (5) resist and increase offers; (6) broaden and delimit the scope of objects involved; and (7) consider, imply, or pursue external bargaining options. Other noteworthy themes pertain to participants (8) assessing the credibility of trading partners and (9) developing modes of arranging for exchanges.

Where people enter into exchanges on behalf of others, researchers would also want to consider the ways in which tacticians (10) reference and juggle notions of accountability to third parties (implying another set of relationships, limitations, interests, vulnerabilities, and the like) in the immediate bargaining context, as well as (11) manage current and subsequent relations with those they purport to represent.

Finally, irrespective of the range of people involved in striking particular bargains or their earlier interchanges, researchers are apt to find it instructive to examine the ways in which people (12) consolidate their agreements, (13) fulfil or disregard their commitments to one another, and (14) deal with one another when their agreements have not been honored.

Appealing to Existing Relationships and Community Affiliations

Before leaving this discussion of leveraging tactics, we should acknowledge appeals that revolve around (a) tacticians' personal relationships with targets and (b) targets' broader senses of embeddedness in community life.

Assuming Privileged Relationships

Because they reflect people's existing bonds or networks, the strategies discussed here are somewhat de-limited, targetwise. Further, these appeals are generally dependent on targets voluntarily accepting the appropriateness of these claims for the situation at hand. Still, tacticians may use a wide array of relationships with others as levers for influence work.

Tacticians *asking for help* may adopt a variety of styles in preestablished relationships. Where tacticians have achieved some mystique relative to targets, tacticians may merely express or hint at their interests so that these targets may learn of them. At other times, tacticians may engage in straightforward requests, or they may direct, demand, or command targets to do certain things. Tacticians also may plead, cry, or become overtly angry in attempts to obtain assistance from others. In each instance, though, there seems to be a presumption, anticipation, or hope, that targets will succumb to these requests as a consequence of acknowledging some preestablished relationship or bond between the two parties.

In another variant, tacticians may *emphasize targets' relational obligations to them.* This involves more explicit references to the expectations one might associate with [targets] having certain affiliations or bonds with the tacticians. Here, tacticians draw attention to the affections, loyalties (see enhancing practices), or other obligations that one might somehow associate with parents, spouses, relatives, friends, and the like, as they attempt to induce compliance on the part of these targets.

Somewhat relatedly, tacticians who envision themselves to have done things for targets in the past may attempt to *invoke senses of "reciprocal indebtedness"* on the part of targets. Targets may be reminded of favors or assistance of various kinds that have not yet been repaid or returned in like manner. Here, tacticians may endeavor to generate guilt, reaffirm principles of fair play, or establish bargains on a delayed basis.

On some occasions, tacticians may also attempt to influence targets by *distancing themselves* from targets or otherwise threatening to diminish their relationships in some way. Although the effectiveness of this tactic (as a treatment) seems highly contingent on targets' valuings of these relationships, tactician practices may range from casual distancing and more overt expressions of disaffection with the other to abrupt, possibly hostile withdrawal from the relationships at hand. The implication is that cooperative behavior on the part of the target may result in a fuller restoration of the tactician-target relationship.

Finally, in contrast to distancing practices, tacticians sometimes endeavor to *intensify or restore relationships* with targets as a means of influencing them. People who have had more distant or disruptive associations with others may endeavor to generate (or rebuild) closer relationships in anticipation of influencing those targets. Restorations may be accompanied by explanations, apologies, promises to make amends, expressions of affection, gifting, and the like but may be largely motivated by concerns with the subsequent influence opportunities that these renewed relationships may provide.

Since much influence work occurs between people who have various preexisting relationships with one another, extended examinations of these seemingly mundane tactics (and the ensuing interchanges) may offer social scientists a great deal of insight into the ways that power is accomplished in practice.

Emphasizing Community Ties

Beyond the more personalized leveraging strategies just outlined, tacticians may also make appeals that build on target embeddedness in the broader community. While these strategies may be invoked in the absence of any third party witnesses, these requests presume (or hope) that targets will act as "responsible and caring members" of their immediate communities.

One way that tacticians may appeal to both more enduring acquaintances and relative strangers is by *referencing group-based principles*. Since all human groupings, from very large nation states and international associations to the smallest (dyadic) groups of some duration establish claims or understandings concerning their normative frameworks or principles of operation, these objectifications (Schutz, 1962; Berger and Luckmann, 1966) represent conceptual levers that tacticians may use in attempts to influence targets.[34] The tempo and tone of people's appeals can range greatly, from very diplomatic hints or straightforward comments to dramatized assertions, complaints, challenges, threats, and treatments. Still, the objective is the same, to shape the behaviors of the other by invoking any collective understandings that tacticians think might fit the situation at hand.

Beyond references to group-based principles, tacticians also may attempt to shape the behaviors of members of the community by *appealing to desired target identity claims or images*. Whether tacticians pitch to target concerns with past, present, or futuristic identities, appeals to desired images are contingent on the targets accepting the authenticity and relevancy of those notions for the situations under consideration. Thus, for instance, targets who would like to be envisioned as "fearless" may find themselves closed into pursuing activities that tacticians more explicitly define as entailing (target) acts of bravery.[35] Likewise, targets desiring to appear "fair" may find themselves feeling obliged to attend to situations in which matters of equality, integrity, or honor are made prominent (and related to target selves) by tacticians.

In a third variant of community-based appeal, tacticians attempt to invoke *generalized sympathies (and related senses of obligation)*. Here, targets are more directly asked to acknowledge concern for disadvantaged others in the community. This may include the tacticians, mutually known others, or even only vaguely defined others on whose behalf tacticians may be seeking assistance.

To learn more about the ways that appeals to one's associates or more general community ties are developed, it is instructive to consider not only (a) when and how tacticians invoke (anticipate, conceptualize, implement, and persist with) strategies of these sorts, but also (b) when and how targets acknowledge the viewpoints under consideration and accord definitions of relevancy to these appeals (versus other personalized interests, group values, or collective wisdoms). Not all requests along these lines will be acknowledged by the targets, much less fulfilled, but these references to preexisting relationships and other community ties further indicate that people need not be "resource laden" to accomplish influence work in a great many cases.

Pcrne, fom

Autonomizing Endeavors

In addition to the things that people may do to influence others in more direct respects, it also is important to acknowledge those things that people may do in attempts to free themselves from the influence of others. Since autonomizing tactics are intended to minimize people's accountability to others, people sometimes use these practices to distance themselves from undesired target roles. However, people may also use autonomizing tactics to enhance personal freedom or to avoid accountability for their tactical endeavors.

Some tactician quests for autonomy may be relatively unobtrusive vis-à-vis targets. Thus, people may engage in a variety of distancing practices, some of which may never be recognized by the targets in question. Likewise, people may endeavor to reduce their own dependencies on others, possibly by endeavoring to redefine their interests, diversifying their activities, or trying to become more self-reliant. Tacticians may also become more secretive in their activities and more vague or elusive in their dealings with others. As well, tacticians may threaten to sever relationships if not granted the freedoms they desire.

In other cases, tacticians may go to some length to minimize accountability and undesired reactions from others. Some of these efforts may reflect after-the-fact neutralizing practices on the part of tacticians, but tacticians may also attempt to attain greater operating autonomy for certain of their activities by seeking various permissions, exemptions, understandings, or collaborations. In some instances, too, tacticians may find themselves juggling existing problems in accountability in the midst of related tactical pursuits.

As well as examining (a) any concerns that tacticians might have about accountability and (b) the things that tacticians might do on their own to achieve greater autonomy, researchers would likely find it instructive to consider (c) tactician attempts to obtain assistance from others (e.g., representatives, benefactors, supporters) with respect to autonomizing endeavors, (d) the roles that others (targets or other third parties) assume as they deal with tactician accountability, and (e) the ways in which the tacticians incorporate concerns with accountability and autonomy into their ongoing ventures.

Exercising Persistence and Experiencing Openness

Although the tactics outlined in this chapter have been given a flow of sorts, it is important to reemphasize the occasional, sporadic, repetitive, enduring, and uneven (if not also the mixed, multiplistic, fractured, distracted, aborted, and renewed) aspects of influence work. Throughout, I have tried to acknowledge the meaningful and enterprising aspects of human interchange, as well as its persistently problematic and potentially negotiable nature. The following themes briefly draw attention to some related, but relatively neglected, issues.

Exercising Persistence

The term, "persistence" lacks the specificity that one commonly associates with influence tactics, but it merits consideration because of its implied, sustained focus (and enterprise) on instances of influence work. While people sometimes seem highly motivated to pursue certain modes of influence work at the outset, these initiatives are not always sustained and may be dropped or redefined more often than is commonly acknowledged. At the same time, people may pursue objectives that they deemed much less compelling at the outset.

While tacticians are apt to find that they are able to influence targets along desired routings in many cases, it is also evident that targets can resist tacticians in a great many ways. We will be dealing with target roles (and resistances) more directly in chapter 8, but it seems instructive to ask when and how people are likely to persist with specific strategies or objectives.[36]

On some occasions, those exercising persistence may be willing to involve any number or variety of people in their pursuits, caring less about who they may involve in their ventures than in accomplishing their objectives. In other cases, persistence may be directed at very specific targets, possibly because these targets are seen as essential sources or key access points to the objectives that the agents have in mind. In instances of this latter sort, targets seem more apt to experience multiple facets of influence work as tacticians pursue target compliance by embarking on an extended barrage of similar or diverse tactics. Even if exercised only in a quasi-explicit manner, this persistence may still frustrate or "wear away" targets to the point that they give in to tactician requests.[37]

Because of their potentially engulfing tendencies, some other aspects of persistence warrant attention. First, tacticians sometimes become so singularly focused or engrossed in pursuing particular objectives that they neglect other aspects of their situations. Although this need not be seen as a problem to the tacticians involved, tacticians who become more engrossed, fascinated, or resolute with respect to attaining particular objectives may embark on a series of activities that others define as troublesome, risky, dangerous, treacherous, or unbounded with respect to community morality or the well-being of others (and, perhaps, the tactician in question).[38] While audience standards and tolerances vary considerably, persistences that are seen as threats by targets or others may engender heightened concerns about controlling (and possibly excluding) these tacticians. Under conditions like these, tacticians may become targets for considerable moral indignation and extended control efforts (Lemert, 1962).

Perseverance is no guarantee of success, and it may engender considerable resentment on the part of targets and others. However, by acknowledging this concept, researchers may begin to track (a) the development of tactician interests and objectives, (b) the deployment of particular tactics over time, (c) ongoing tactician assessments of their situations (objectives, tactics, resistances, gains and losses), and (d) other emergent tactician and target experiences, including the development of tactical stocks of knowledge on the parts of the participants and the ongoing adjustments that people (targets and other parties) make to their circumstances in light of these developments.

Experiencing Tactical Openness

Assuming that tacticians can sustain contact with targets, there may be no particular restrictions on the number or variety of strategies that tacticians may invoke, how often they might invoke particular tactics, in what orders they might do so, or over what period of time they may persist in any realms of influence work.

As researchers, it is important that we acknowledge tacticians' sense of openness; attending, in this respect, not only to the options that tacticians consider but also their notions of sequencing and adjustment, goals and compromises, and ambiguities and dilemmas. Noteworthy, too, are tacticians' concerns with other involvements, particularly as they find these distracting or intensifying relative to particular realms of tactical enterprise.

As suggested throughout chapter 6, the tactical openness and fluidity of human interchange indicates some consequential limitations of most "theorizing" about power. The human capacity for reflectivity and enterprise (i.e., interpretation, definition, anticipation, selectivity, goal-directed activity, self and other monitoring practices, and ongoing interchange and adjustment) requires that theory about power relations be much more attentive to the *symbolically enacted realities* (i.e., the instances thereof) in which people conduct their affairs. Although the aspects of interchange discussed to this point may seem especially amenable to inquiry in dyadic settings, these matters also represent foundational themes for comprehending the human interaction that occurs in greatly extended contexts. Focusing on the ways in which influence work may be pursued and resisted across a wide range of social arenas, chapters 7 and 8 build centrally on the material introduced herein.

Notes

1. In addition to his own practice of magic, the magician speaking here is actively involved in the creation and sale of magic tricks of several varieties—propped or apparatus-based, naturalist, and mentalist.

2. Although their analyses are embedded with prescriptions and remedies, I found the depictions of influence work developed by the tactical advisors cited in chapter 4 helpful in articulating these themes. While I also benefited from considerations of tactical procedures by Jones (1964), Marwell and Schmitt (1967), Wood et al. (1967), Tedeschi and Bonoma (1972),

Finley and Humphries (1974), Clark and Delia (1976), Falbo and Peplau (1980), Kipnis et al. (1980), Rule et al. (1985), and Howard et al. (1986), these statements concentrate on isolating the factors (e.g., tactician or target characteristics) associated with the incidence of particular tactics, as opposed to examining the ways in which people attempt to influence others in more processual terms. The interactionist frame utilized here is much more attentive to the *enactment* of human interchange.

3. A fuller notion of career contingencies would not only include initial involvements (as seekership, recruitment, closure, and reservations), but also the matters of continuity, disinvolvement, and reinvolvement. See Prus (1996b) for an elaboration of these concepts and references to a much broader interactionist/ethnographic literature that goes back to the 1930s.

4. This is one reason that Goffman (1959, 1963) envisions "information control" as an element exceedingly central to impression management and respectability.

5. For some instances of undercover work in the ethnographic literature, see Karsh et al.'s (1953) portrayal of union organizers, Prus and Sharper's (1977) depiction of the practices of road hustlers, Adler's (1985) account of drug dealing, and Jacobs (1992a, 1992b) study of undercover police officers. In attempting to "qualify" customers, salespeople (Prus, 1989a:81–88) sometimes engage in extended, open-ended inquiry. Although their interest in learning about the other is quite different in purpose, ethnographers can readily relate to these various modes of learning about the situations and interests of the other.

6. Insofar as it draws attention to a wide variety of tactical applications, as well as the multiple ways in which one may learn things about the other, De Callières (1716) depiction of diplomacy as enterprise is very suggestive.

7. Although notions of computerized virtual reality (Chayko, 1993) have existed for some years (acknowledging the capacity of people to technologically alter people's sensations of "the world"), the matter of shaping the images that others experience is as fundamental as the development of human symbols. The concepts (and "technologies") entailed in other human productions such as dramatizing, lying, magic, the printed word, theater, radio, television, computer networks, and the like, thus represent analogues with awesome potential for shaping people's images of reality, as do other aspects of influence work considered here. On a more mundane note, even the notion of children "playing games" denotes the fundamental aspects of invoking multiple realities or achieving multiple viewpoints on the world (see Mead, 1934) and shaping the realities of one's associates.

8. This statement on deception is very much based on Prus and Sharper (1991). Ethnographically portraying the practices of hustlers and magicians, and comparing these with the influence work of those in market-

ing and sales activity, this volume outlines a theory of deception and considers the implications of deception for influence work more generally.

9. I attribute this term to Bigus (1972) who provides us with an ethnographic account of "the milkman and his customers." Some other ethnographic work on cultivating relationships can be found in studies of cab drivers (Davis, 1959), a religious cult (Lofland, 1966), card and dice hustlers (Prus and Sharper, 1977), the hotel community (Prus and Irini, 1980), congressional staff (Kinsey, 1985), marketing and sales activity (Prus, 1989a, 1989b), outlaw bikers (D. Wolf, 1991), and musicians (MacLeod, 1993).

Readers will note some affinities of these materials with the writings of Goffman (1959), Klapp (1962, 1964, 1971), and Jones (1964), but the term *cultivating relationships* seems to better capture this aspect of the influence process than do the concepts of "impression management," "symbolic leaders," or "ingratiation tactics," respectively.

10. Klapp (1964) suggests that "color" (more obvious distinctions of any sort) is essential to being noticed and remembered, but those intending to achieve heroic status might also be mindful of the significance of doing things alone, being more engaging, and becoming involved in dramatic events. Still, Klapp acknowledges the ultimate dependency of tacticians on audience interpretations and the related, often uncontrollable, matters of relevancy and timing.

11. While people may use the media to present products, generate trust, reduce reservations, and the like (Prus, 1989b:200–242), a first and sometimes major objective is that of making contact or creating an awareness on the part of prospective buyers. Likewise, "hookers," "exotic dancers," and other entertainers in bars sometimes complain about patrons not taking notice of their presence or performances (Prus and Irini, 1980). Further, while some try to achieve more provocative or compelling presentations of self, this does not ensure even the preliminary attention they might desire.

12. Unencumbered assistance may be associated with positive auras (e.g., affection, trust, respect) in some cases, but in other instances benignly intended generosity may result in negative attributions (e.g., resentment revolving around notions of not helping more, "showing off," or self-serving pretensions) from recipients.

13. It is this personal mystique that Weber (1968:1111–1157) addresses in his discussion of charismatic leaders. However, Goffman (1959, 1963), Klapp (1962, 1964, 1971), and Couch (1989) provide much more instructive conceptualizations of the *processes* by which people become (and lose their standings as) "symbolic leaders" on an intersubjective level. Noteworthy too, are some other statements that examine the processes by which people acquire identities as discredited, stigmatized, and the like (see Aris-

totle, *Rhetoric;* Garfinkel, 1956; Becker, 1963; Prus, 1975a, 1975b; Prus and Irini, 1980).

14. Some other ethnographic examinations of vendors' attempts to develop trust on the part of prospective buyers are provided in Henslin (1968), Bigus (1972), Browne (1973), Sanders (1989), Prus and Frisby (1990), and Roznaczuk (1998). Somewhat relatedly, studies of hustlers and magicians (Sutherland, 1937; Prus and Sharper, 1991) and undercover officers (Jacobs, 1992) also provide instructive insights into the development of trust.

15. Some flip-side examinations of buyer (target) definitions of, and experiences with, trust (Prus and Frisby, 1990; Prus, 1991; and Roznaczuk, 1998) indicate that while trust generally fosters compliance, trust is very much a quality attributed to people (tacticians in this case) by others. Not only may trust-inducing work not be acknowledged as intended, but targets need not even attend to matters of trust as thoroughly, consistently, or as wisely as they, themselves, might like. Still, when targets define tacticians as more trustworthy, they may relinquish considerable decision-making potential to those tacticians.

16. While one can find evidence of these practices in many ethnographies (e.g., Lofland, 1966; Prus, 1976; Sanders, 1989; D. Wolf, 1991; Grills, 1994; C. Wolf, 1994), these notions are most explicitly developed in considerations of marketing and sales activity (see Prus, 1989a, 1989b; Prus and Frisby, 1990; Prus and Fleras, 1996). However, the practices depicted here build most directly on Prus (1989a:89–98).

17. Although a common tactic in the sales setting (Prus, 1989a: 94–98), the strategy of invoking discontent is frequently employed by those promoting religious involvements (Lofland, 1966; Prus, 1976; Van Zandt, 1991), as well as union formation and membership drives (Karsh et al., 1953).

18. The matter of neutralizing target reservations seems relevant across a variety of contexts, but it often appears in a more elaborated or crystalline form in the sales setting (Prus, 1989a:131–162).

19. In addition to Aristotle's *Rhetoric* and *De Rhetorica Ad Alexandrum,* readers may refer to Garfinkel (1956), Goffman (1959, 1963), Klapp (1962, 1964, 1971), Lyman and Scott (1989), and Prus (1975a, 1975b) for analytical considerations of neutralization and debasing processes.

20. For an ethnographic examination of "closing practices" in the sales setting, see Prus (1989a:163–182). For indications of elusiveness on the part of shoppers, see Prus and Frisby (1990) and Prus (1994a, 1997a).

21. The inability of targets to act back on these tacticians may have several foundations. On some occasions, targets may be physically incapacitated or destroyed by tacticians' activities. Even if able to respond, targets may be taken by surprise or have little time to react, establish defenses, or

seek support; they may lack the physique, technologies, or other materials that they might use to fashion defense or offense; they may be unable to identify, locate, or access the tacticians involved; or they may experience reservations pertaining to physical fears, community standards, or personal embarrassment, material losses, or inconvenience.

22. Tacticians who usurp agency may also attempt to ensure that they have generated defenses or resistances that targets who might oppose their efforts are unable to overcome. Here, tacticians may acknowledge target vulnerability (e.g., human fragilities, defenses, resources) but simultaneously endeavor to maximize their invulnerability relative to those who might resist their efforts.

23. Because people are "objects unto themselves" (Mead, 1934) and act toward themselves as objects, they, too, can impose (as tacticians) particular viewpoints and treatments on themselves, sometimes without allowing themselves (as targets) to resist the viewpoints they have invoked (e.g., consider suicide, sacrifices made to "the cause," or personal goals or resolutions).

24. The term *treatment* is used in lieu of sanction since the latter tends to be viewed more directly in terms of costs and rewards. There may be times in which the primary purpose of invoking treatment may be one of generating costs and rewards or varieties of pain and pleasure, but tacticians, targets, and third parties may view treatments in many other ways (e.g., education, rehabilitation, tribute, expressing community sentiments).

25. For some considerations of tacticians deciding against more severe target treatments, see Bensmen and Gerver (1963), Bittner (1967), Robert Emerson (1969, 1994), Prus and Stratton (1976), and Meehan (1992). The matter of "tactician discretion" in selecting, implementing, sustaining, and adjusting particular treatments is worthy of considerable ethnographic attention.

26. Although presumably directed toward target-recipients, treatments also may be used to send messages to a variety of others who may be aware of the setting. Thus, treatments may be used to express satisfaction and dissatisfaction; maintain generalized images of moral order within the community; "restore justice" in the community; or foster tactician relations with third parties who want targets treated in more specific manners.

27. Roth's (1962) examination of the redefinitions and negotiations of treatment in a tuberculosis center is relevant here as is Bensmen and Gerver's (1963) consideration of "tapping" (prohibited activity) in an airplane factory.

28. The matter of "making deals" is central to "exchange theory" (Homans, 1958, 1961; Blau, 1964), but as indicated elsewhere (Prus, 1989b:58), their notions of exchange are too presumptive and limited to match up effectively with ongoing human association.

On another note, some interactionists (e.g., Hall and Hall, 1982; Strauss, 1978b) have attempted to define "conditions conducive to exchange." As Couch (1979) observes, however, in discussing Strauss's (1978b) work more specifically, this sort of orientation is not particularly attentive to the ways in which exchanges actually take place.

29. Readers may note that little direct attention has been given to money as an element of consequence in the bargaining process. To a large extent, the position taken here very much resonates with that of Georg Simmel, who states:

> *Money is the purest form of the tool . . . it is an institution through which the individual concentrates his activity and possessions in order to attain goals that he could not attain directly. The fact that everyone works with it makes its character as a tool more evident. . . . The nature and effectiveness of money is not to be found simply in the coin that I hold in my hand; its qualities are invested in the social organizations and the supra-subjective norms that make this coin a tool of endlessly diverse and extensive uses despite its material limitations, its insignificance and rigidity. . . . (Simmel, 1978 [1907]:210)*

> *Inasmuch as interests are focused on money and to the extent that possessions consist of money, the individual will develop the tendency and feeling of independent importance in relation to the social whole. He will relate to the social whole as one power confronting another, since he is free to take up business relations and cooperation wherever he likes. (Simmel, 1978 [1907]: 343)*

Despite its remarkable utility in the marketplace, money has no intrinsic value. To the extent that money assumes any value, this worth derives from, and is sustained by virtue of, its embeddedness within the human community (i.e., as a socially acknowledged and enacted phenomenon). The integrity and worth of any (instance of) money, thus, becomes objectified by whatever people (at that time) are willing to offer to its possessors in exchange.

Further, as Simmel so cogently observes, money also represents a liberating device. Most notably, because of its generalized acceptance in the marketplace, money provides its possessors with flexibilities, options, and capacities for influence that they might not otherwise be able to achieve. Still, money denotes only one aspect of human interchange and, like all other objects, its relevance (and resource value) is contingent on the definitions of those in the setting at hand.

Thus, in contrast to those who see money as an evil or oppressive force, money is envisioned as but one of a great many objects that people may use in developing interchanges with others. In no way does this deny people's concerns about acquiring, possessing, or using money to pursue diverse interests, nor does this in any way preclude ethnographic consideration of these matters (e.g., see Prus, 1997b: especially 93–96; 107–109). Instead of fostering mystiques around "the power of money," it is proposed that considerations of money as an aspect of the influence process be thoroughly and fundamentally embedded in the study of the ways in which people engage particular activities (acknowledging, anticipating, trading, transforming, deploying, and resisting objects) in conjunction with others across a wide range of settings.

30. Most bargains also introduce or imply some notion of temporality, whereby exchanges are to be completed or managed within some, if only vaguely defined, time-parameters. This time frame may be particulary consequential in some instances, as people may find themselves making or gaining various concessions as a consequence of the situated notions of urgency experienced on the part of one or more of the involved parties.

31. Retributions represent noteworthy but peculiar forms of exchanges in which people envisioning themselves as grieved or harmed targets endeavor to balance out exchanges by making others pay for their suffering and losses. Since these activities may be quite one-sided in some cases, those embarked on retribution agendas would need to make their aligning activities known to others for a bargain to take place in a more complete sense.

32. In addition to the research (laboratory studies of negotiations involving representatives of various sorts) conducted by Couch et al. (1986a, 1986b), readers may also wish to examine the work of Hall (1972) and Strauss (1978b) which focus largely on negotiations in organizational contexts. Although the present paper has benefited from their analyses, all of these scholars have assumed positions that are more structuralist in their orientations. They have been less attentive to power as definitional, reflective, interactive accomplishments than is the position taken in the present statement. A much overlooked participant-informed account of the diplomat (De Callières, 1716) provides many valuable insights into the many roles assumable by those representing others in matters of state.

33. Diplomats (De Callières, 1716), company purchasing agents (Prus, 1989b:133–172), insurance adjustors (Ross, 1980), lawyers (Blumberg, 1967), police officers (Meehan, 1992), and high school disciplinary officers (Emerson, 1994), amongst others, commonly find themselves in the roles of "double agents" as they attempt to strike deals that are acceptable to both outsider targets and the insiders (targets) they represent.

34. This discussion is also informed by Simmel's (1950:250–267) very insightful statement of "subordination under a principle."

35. For some ethnographic research pertinent to the matter of pub-

licly displaying "heart" or fearlessness, see Keiser's (1969) study of street gangs, Haas (1972, 1977) depiction of high iron steel workers, and Wolf's (1991) account of outlaw bikers.

36. Researchers also are apt to find it worthwhile to examine the ways that tacticians define resistances and setbacks, as well as to consider the ways that notions of progress or success are synthesized into people's tactical stocks of knowledge or used in anticipating subsequent encounters with the same or other targets.

37. Although children may utilize a variety of strategies in dealing with their parents, even the least sophisticated tactics (as most parents will attest) may become compelling if pursued with persistence.

38. Lesieur (1977) uses the term *encapsulation* to refer to a somewhat parallel sense of engrossment experienced by heavy gamblers.

7 Extending the Theater of Operations

Revolutions in democracies are generally caused by the intemperance of demagogues, who either in their private capacity lay information against rich men until they compel them to combine [i.e., establish an oligarchy - RP] *(for a common danger unites even the bitterest enemies), or coming forward in public stir up the people against them . . .*

Much in the same manner the democracy at Megara . . . was overturned; there the demagogues drove out many of the notables in order that they might be able to confiscate their property. At length the exiles, becoming numerous, returned, and, engaging and defeating the people, established the oligarchy . . .

[S]ometimes the demagogues, in order to curry favour with the people, wrong the notables and so force them to combine;—either they make a division of their property, or diminish their incomes by the imposition of public services, and sometimes they bring accusations against the rich that they may have their wealth to confiscate.

—Aristotle, Politica, *Book V: 1304b–1305a [Jowett, trans.]*

Should tacticians consider themselves unable or unwilling to deal with targets on a one-to-one basis, they may involve others in attempts to shape the situations and behaviors of those targets. There is no guarantee that third parties will automatically support the tacticians in question, but by involving others in their influence endeavors tacticians may centrally alter the relationships they have with targets. Targets sometimes envision third-party involvements as indications of tactician weakness or ineffectiveness, but a more consequential element may be the subsequent dependency that tacticians develop with respect to third parties and their own subsequent vulnerabilities to third-party interests (see Emerson and Messinger, 1977).

Further, as Simmel (1950:135–169) so astutely observed, the addition of a third party suggests all sorts of interactional possibilities (e.g., mediator, arbitrator, advantaged player, "troublemaker," and eventual conqueror of both parties) beyond those implied in dyadic relations. Thus, although the practice of involving others in the theater of operations may be seen as a "quick fix" in the pursuit of influence work, these additional parties generally add new complexities and unpredictabilities to the situation.[1]

209

There are several ways in which tacticians may extend their influence endeavors. These involve: (1) working with third-party agents; (2) developing collective influence ventures; (3) generating (and enforcing) policy; (4) pursuing positional control; (5) using the media; and (6) developing political agendas (governmental forums, military operations, and control agencies).

While some readers may be inclined to envision some of these processes more exclusively at "macro" levels (possibly involving national and international endeavors), a great many of these same processes may be implemented in much smaller settings wherein three or more people may be involved (e.g., consider events occurring within classrooms, departments, or families). Matters of communication, coordination, and decision making may become more complicated in interchanges involving larger populations, and there seems greater uncertainty regarding the eventual directions that larger-scale events may assume, but even these episodes must be understood in reference to the *human interchange* that occurs within all collective events.

In acknowledging a broader theater of operations, it should also be appreciated that people assuming tactical stances may not only involve other people in their ventures in varying degrees of secrecy or openness with respect to targets, but may assume other strategic maneuvers in both overt and covert manners. Since neither targets nor analysts may know (a) which parties (identities or scope) may be forming alignments, (b) the nature of any action taken or contemplated, or (c) the sorts of arrangements worked out by the parties involved, the matter of coordinated (oppositional) activity takes analysts into more complex realms of information control, strategy, trust and distrust, advantage and vulnerability, and influence and resistance work. It is essential, therefore, that analysts consider people's (tacticians and targets) situations in manners that are mindful of the variants that these interchanges may assume.

Working with Third-Party Agents

Third-party agents, here, refer to people (individuals or groups) who maintain a relatively autonomous identity in the course of dealing with (initial or primary) tacticians and their targets. There are four major ways in which tacticians involve third party agents in their influence endeavors. First, tacticians may tap into these people's stocks of knowledge as consultants of sorts. Second, they may attempt to obtain their assistance as agents in more active senses; to act on their behalf, as representatives, in more, direct, target-focused manners. Third, tacticians may attempt to use third parties as control agents, wherein they refer troublesome cases to them so that third parties might assume some or all of the tasks of dealing with targets. Fourth, tacticians may seek assistance in dealing with targets by pursuing adjudication. On the surface, tacticians involving third parties in these varied manners would seem differentially situated with respect to the autonomy they experience with regard to influence work, but in actual practice these seemingly distinct roles (especially the activities they imply) may blend or shift in ways quite unanticipated by the tacticians at hand.

Consulting with Third Parties

Generally speaking, the practice of discussing situations with, or seeking advice from, third parties appears to be a relatively low-risk option for tacticians. These encounters may provide valuable opportunities for those contemplating influence work to consider and evaluate a wider range of strategies with the benefit of a third party's experience and counsel. However, any time that third parties become involved in situations, the dynamics can change dramatically.

Even at very casual or tentative levels, tactician-consultant interchanges denote "teams at work." Thus, as Goffman (1959) suggests, "dramaturgical loyalty" can be both highly consequential and precarious. Like other team members, consultants (and confidants) are in ideal (privileged) positions to destroy the integrity of tacticians or to expose their vulnerabilities to others. Even well-intentioned third parties may inadvertently disclose consequential information to others or pursue lines of action that tacticians might deem undesirable. Notably too, third parties may embark on their own agendas or provide advice that need not be in the best interest of those seeking their counsel. Still, third party consultations seem relatively common events in the community. Regardless of the ways that tacticians and consultants make contact, these interchanges offer scholars a valuable window for sustained ethnographic inquiry.

Obtaining Representatives (Agents)

Although consultants may be seen to extend agent capacities by sharing their experiences with tacticians (and providing forums for tacticians to consider and articulate their thoughts on influence work), tacticians also may induce others to represent them in more direct, participatory manners. These agents or representatives may assume a variety of roles, including champions, defenders, ambassadors, promoters, recruiters, spies, negotiators, aggressors, saboteurs, managers, trainers, and accomplices.[2]

Tacticians (or their supporters) may compensate agents for their services on many occasions, but representatives may also engage in these activities as a consequence of loyalty, affection, or other senses of obligation, or because of personal intrigues or interests. While it should not be assumed that the agents involved will conduct these activities with uniform loyalty, competence, or enthusiasm, they represent noteworthy, sometimes vital, extensions of the tactician self. As with third-party consultations, these modes of representation merit extended research on the part of analysts, as do the relationships that develop between the primary tactician and these secondary (tactician) agents.

Making Third-Party Referrals

Another way that tacticians sometimes endeavor to influence targets is by referring or turning targets over to third parties. Although referrals or "turn-overs" often reduce or alter tactician contacts with targets, this tactic is typically initiated to gain control over targets with whom tacticians have had difficulty dealing on their own.[3,4]

If we examine referrals in process terms, it is quite apparent that people may seek assistance from others at any time in their dealings with targets.[5] Third parties, thus, may be involved from tacticians' first concerns (or, in some cases, third parties may initially draw tacticians' attention to "problems"), or at any point in the career of the "troublesome situation" (Emerson and Messinger, 1977). However, a great many referrals come about when tacticians find themselves uncertain about appropriate lines of action or deem themselves unable to influence targets in other ways. People sometimes contact third parties very quickly to deal with troublesome targets, but often they will have tried other things on their own and may only reluctantly involve third parties.

In general, tacticians seem more likely to seek assistance from third parties (both informally and formally) when: (1) they consider third parties to be (a) more accessible, (b) more ready to believe their accounts, and (c) more likely to act in their interests; (2) they perceive troublesome situations as (a) more identifiable, (b) more persistent, (c) more offensive, (d) more threatening, and (e) more difficult to control; (3) they consider revelations of trouble to be less personally costly (e.g., reputation, friendship) to themselves;[6] (4) they hold targets in lower esteem (disclosers are less concerned about any subsequent costs or injuries that targets may incur as a result of the revelations); and (5) they envision third-party disclosures as likely to have the effect of negatively sanctioning targets. Although both the referral process and related tactician–third party interchanges deserve much more ethnographic attention, considerable insight into the influence process may also be gained by more pointedly examining the ways in which the third parties (who also represent tacticians in their own right) deal with the situation at hand, including their relations with the primary tacticians.[7]

Pursuing Adjudication

While third parties sometimes (a) find themselves imposing judgments on people who seem unwilling or unable to settle things in other ways,[8] those invoking roles as tacticians may attempt to deal with targets (b) by asking third parties to act as mediators when they have reached impassés with their associates or (c) by alleging that targets have violated situational proprieties that fall under the jurisdiction or field of responsibility of the third parties to whom claims are presented.

In many respects, attempts to pursue adjudication may be seen as a subset of the referral process. However, in contrast to referrals that, once acknowledged, largely focus on the disposition of the target, tacticians seeking third-party judgments typically expect to benefit in a more direct manner from the mediation process or the other claims they present to adjudicators. In pursuing adjudication, tacticians often have greater opportunities to participate more fully in the subsequent processing of targets than in referrals (where third parties are more apt to handle things on their own).

In contrast to mediation, which generally assumes a greater degree of mutuality on the part of the involved parties, those making more unilateral claims against targets typically proceed in more adversarial manners. The contexts in which allegations of target impropriety are made may vary greatly in formality, dramatization, the recognized authority of the adjudicator, and the adjudicators' abilities to enforce any sanctions implied in the eventual decision. However, since adjudicators sometimes exercise discretion in the claims they entertain, a tactician's first objective may be one of formulating charges in ways that would encourage participation on the part of prospective decision makers. Those invoking claims may also find that once the process is begun, adjudication proceedings may become intractable. Not only may tacticians find themselves accountable to the adjudicators to whom they had appealed, but also that the adjudicators expect the tacticians to respect their decisions.

Regardless of the sincerity with which allegations are made, tacticians invoking this option not only put targets in defensive postures vis-à-vis [the tribunal] at hand but typically disrupt target activities (if not also possibly embarrass targets in the process).[9] Adjudication, thus, at the outset at least, appears to advantage the initiators.

Denoting adversarial measures, claims-making proceedings dramatize particular aspects of tactician-target relations and tend to polarize the two (tactician-target) entities. Since these events are apt to generate distancing, distrust, and resentment on the part of those drawn into these episodes as targets, adjudication becomes a risky endeavor for tacticians who wish to maintain viable long-term relations with particular targets.[10] As with the referral process more generally, much insight into the adjudication process may be gained through ethnographic examinations of these episodes, regardless of the realms in which, or the formalities with which, these interchanges take place.

Developing Collective Ventures

When tacticians are unable or are unwilling to manage targets on their own, they may establish alliances or other team-like arrangements to pursue these missions. These cooperative alignments may be fleeting or more enduring in their composition, and may be eagerly pursued or only reluctantly developed by the parties involved. Like those consulting with, making referrals to, or pursuing adjudication through third parties, tacticians developing alliances with others may forgo some control over the directions that their dealings with targets assume.

While some of those forming coalitions or alliances may assume equal roles in the association, other collective ventures may be much more uneven in constitution. Further, the membership of some alliances or teams may remain small in number, but other collective endeavors may become quite massive with varying levels of internal organizational complexity (possibly with more central participants overseeing extended organizational units of their own).

Also, whereas some collective efforts involve singularly focused attempts to shape target practices, experiences, moralities, or life-styles in certain respects, other influence concerns may be more multifaceted. For example, in some cases, those forming coalitions may begin to act on targets in very immediate and direct fashions. In other instances, those forming associations may assume the preliminary task of pursuing the support of a secondary set of targets (with respect to such things as endorsements, funding, and other assistance) so that their primary target agendas may be enacted more effectively.[11] In associations of these latter sorts, both realms of influence work are important for understanding the pursuit of control within the community context.[12]

When those involved in alliances pursue multiple influence (sets of targets) objectives over time, elaborate sets of routines or organizational themes may be developed around each of these tasks.[13] In these settings, it is not uncommon to find various service specialists (e.g., campaign directors, salespeople, counselors, rule enforcers, lobbyists, strategists) whose full-time work revolves around the active pursuit of cooperation from particular subsets of targets (individuals or groups).

Similarly, while some alliances will be generated specifically to deal with particular target situations, other collective influence ventures may develop within associations that have been established with quite different purposes. In contrast to fledgling associations that are built more directly from the "grassroots" up, tacticians who pursue new realms of influence work within preexisting associations are often in positions to access a variety of resources (money, technology, human networks and skills, objectifications) in much shorter time-frames. It need not be assumed that these secondary influence ventures are consistent with the primary purpose of the association. Indeed, some of these subagendas may become consequential points of distraction and confrontation within preexisting associations.

Despite considerable variations in both target emphasis and the organizational foundations of particular alliances, the subprocesses that collective ventures entail are fairly generic across substantively diverse associations. In many respects, it matters not whether tacticians (a) see themselves as developing coalitions, alliances, teams, arrangements, associations, clubs, agencies, gangs, cartels, committees, unions, or parties, and so on, (b) intend these ventures to deal with targets in offensive or defensive manners, (c) view the influence work directed toward the targets in question as a primary or secondary agenda within the group, (d) focus on one or multiple sets of targets, or (e) represent newly constituted associations or are embedded within existing associations, the processes involved in developing and sustaining collective enterprises seem rather parallel across a range of settings. Still, researchers interested in influence work should more specifically acknowledge the differing and often multiple sets of targets that particular instances of collective enterprise address.

Many of these ventures will be short-lived, while others may be much more extensively developed. Nevertheless, three major subprocesses seem relevant in a great many cases. These are establishing associations, objectifying associations, and encountering outsiders.[14] Albeit denoting a conceptual overview, the following material suggests a great many focal points for research and analysis of collective ventures.

Establishing Associations

Regardless of how particular associations are envisioned (e.g., as an alliance, group, team, organization, crew, mob, band, tribe, or cult), analysts should be attentive to all of the enterprises involved in incorporating people into collectively focused entities. People involved in more fleeting alignments may circumvent or truncate some of the following processes, but researchers interested in the alliance-making process are apt to learn much about the development of associations by attending to activities of the following sort:

- *Anticipating the value of collective enterprise*
- *Involving others in the venture (recruitment, screening, minimizing reservations)*

- *Justifying the group (developing perspectives, moral viewpoints)*
- *Celebrating the venture (witnessing, recognizing, emphasizing—within the group)*
- *Defining the team (membership criteria, positions, responsibilities)*
- *Establishing communication forums (interpersonal, media)*
- *Pursuing resources for the group*
- *Arranging member assemblies (encounters, practices)*
- *Providing instruction for members (perspectives, techniques)*
- *Monitoring members*
- *Assessing member performances*
- *Motivating and disciplining members*
- *Rejecting and reinstating members*
- *Facing internal upheaval (splintering, factions, challenges from within)*
- *Facing generalized loss of interest*
- *Dealing with dissolution*
- *Attempting to revitalize cooperative ventures (Prus, 1996b:161)*

Objectifying Associations

While the coordinators of some groups may intend to operate more casually or in more limited capacities, others may be interested in establishing a prominence that is more obvious to both members and outsiders within the community. It is here that one may speak of the task of objectifying associations.[15] Even those subcultures who wish to "go undercover" for a variety of reasons still may adopt practices intended to make their groups appear "more real" (i.e., evident, vital, authentic) to their members. Those desiring greater recognition within the broader community may be even more out-reaching in their efforts.

Beyond the enterprises in which members might engage that serve to establish these associations within the community more generally, a variety of outsiders may also contribute to the objectification process by the ways in which they focus attention on these associations. Not all researchers may be able to examine the objectification processes from the perspectives of both insiders and outsiders, but those who spend more time in these settings may be able to address a variety of objectification processes from one or both vantage points.

As *insiders*, people interested in objectifying or having their (subcultural) associations envisioned as more viable elements either within particular segments of the community or the community at-large may engage in practices of the following kind:

- *Developing a group identity (name, logo, flag)*
- *Stipulating justifications for existence and operations*

- *Creating identity markers for members (uniforms, appearances, signs)*
- *Defining exclusiveness (selectivity, oaths, codes, jargon)*
- *Establishing a public presence (announcements, advertising, displays, rallies, protests)*
- *Legitimating the group publicly (endorsements, credentials, charters, licences)*
- *Demarcating territories and jurisdictions (buildings, places, locations) (Prus, 1996b:162)*

Outsiders (e.g., opponents, supporters, media producers, general public) may have rather diverse interests (e.g., curiosities, fascinations, entertainment, knowledge, fear, condemnation, control, elimination) with respect to the association in question. However, when they identify, talk about, and act toward particular groups as if they were more unique, more prominent, more consequential, and the like, outsiders also may be seen to contribute to the visibility and realism of particular groups. Thus, outsider activities of the following kind seem particularly noteworthy in generating a profile for particular (subcultural) associations:

- *Defining a set of people as constituting a group or interactive entity within the community*
- *Associating (assigning, acknowledging) specific names (and other identity markers) with the group*
- *Attributing particular properties (qualities and evaluations) to the group*
- *Discussing (talk, rumor, media messages) the group with others in the community*
- *Making more concerted effort (reflecting curiousities and fascinations to condemnations and control concerns) to attend to, or deal with, the group as an entity within the broader community (Prus, 1996b:162)*

Encountering Outsiders

As entities endeavoring to achieve viability within the community, members of groups often become involved in influence work with an assortment of outsiders. While some outsiders may be viewed more incidentally (ambiguously or vaguely) or as relatively irrelevant, insiders may envision other people in a variety of target or tactician capacities.

Some outsiders may represent the central or primary targets of influence work for the focal group or organization's enterprises (e.g., prospects, clients, customers, patrons, cases, suckers, marks, patients, and inmates). Other outsiders may be viewed as potential partners for cooperative ventures, as implied by terms such as traders, agents, representatives, assistants, volunteers, coworkers, and team members. Still others may represent obstructions of sorts, possibly as tacticians to be feared and avoided and/or targets to be neutralized or destroyed (i.e., troublemakers, competitors, adversaries, and enemies) en route to more desired (insider) life-world arrangements.

While the focal association's interests in particular individuals and groups can be quite wide-ranging, much can be gained by ethnographically scrutinizing insider practices along these lines:

- *Representing the organization('s interests)*
- *Making contact with outsiders (establishing co-presence, making the scene)*
- *Defining the theater of operation (places, objectives, strategies)*
- *Identifying outsiders (targets, cooperators, witnesses, nobodies)*
- *Pursuing associational objectives through the others (cooperation, influence work)*
- *Confronting outsiders (challenges, competitions, conflicts)*
- *Protecting (sometimes concealing) the association from the outsiders*
- *Readjusting group routines to more effectively deal with the outsiders (Prus, 1996b:163)*

Reflecting extended and diversely focused instances of human enterprise, the matters of forming associations, objectifying associations, and managing encounters with others offer a series of conceptual pivot points. Not only do these themes suggest activities to be considered in the course of pursuing particular instances of ethnographic inquiry, but they also represent a grid around which to assess and develop more precise, empirically grounded conceptualizations of collective ventures.

Generating (and Enforcing) Policy

Another means by which people may pursue control over others is through the development of principles, rules, or policies designed to shape behavior within particular settings (i.e., groups, organizations, communities). Typically intended to encourage target cooperation or compliance by establishing guidelines for behavior and frameworks for holding people accountable for their actions, these policies (understandings, agreements, rules, laws, etc.) imply endorsement, if not enforcement, on the part of sponsors within associational contexts.

Many organizational "arrangements" are generated within small groups (e.g., families, friendship dyads, work groups), but others may be pitched at much broader sets of targets (e.g., cities, regions, nations). They may be intended as maxims (e.g., honesty, fairness, equality) or may be developed with respect to specific realms of human activity (e.g., living arrangements, foods and beverages, religion, business practices, recreational pursuits). Likewise, associational principles may range from very fleeting understandings, or those applied to specific people, to those intended to be infinite in duration, or universal in effect. In some cases, these policies may be systematically promoted, protected, or enforced by formalized (and possibly multi-layered) control agencies, but, in other instances, any control efforts may be fleeting, situated, or informal in thrust.

Sometimes, by virtue of positions that they have been able to access (inherited, appointed, elected, or otherwise achieved) within particular settings, certain people are able to establish guidelines that others appear prepared to accept, endorse, or help enforce. While more stereotypic notions of structural power may be useful in predicting the source of group principles for certain settings and periods of time, it should not be assumed that the underlying processes are as coherent as they may appear from the outside or that the policies in question are unilaterally conceptualized, developed, and maintained. Thus, even with the most sustained, despotic conditions, scholars would seem advised to attend not only to people's capacities for reflectivity, initiative, and resistance but also to the multiple sources of (human) support that may be entailed in "policy production" beyond that implied in more formal channels or structures.

Although the development of policies and application of treatments may entail a considerable amount of influence work (and resistance) in some smaller group settings, the achievement of consensus on these matters can readily become problematic in larger contexts. Thus, the emergence of other principles may reflect the efforts of those involved in crusades, missions, or other collective ventures within specific organizations or the community more broadly. On occasion, those attempting to establish particular policies may achieve their objectives in relatively short time spans, but other endeavors of this sort may result in long, complicated, and nebulous undertakings with partial successes, at best.[16]

As with all tactics of control involving the cooperation of people beyond the immediate targets of influence, it is essential that analysts be attentive to the sets (often multiple and highly diverse) of secondary targets with which tacticians may have to deal en route to their primary (target) objectives. Indeed, tacticians may encounter so much resistance establishing guidelines in some settings that the intended primary targets of influence may be only modestly, if at all, affected by tactician efforts to create and enforce control through these organizational restraints. This is not to deny the effective development (or zealous application) of some principles, but rather to draw attention to obstacles that tacticians may encounter in these preliminary respects.

Overall, it appears that parties promoting particular policies are more likely to be successful in having their proposals accepted by others in the community when those to whom they appeal accept or assume notions that:[17] (1) the situation under consideration is morally undesirable; (2) the situation represents an immediate, powerful, and active threat to both the public good and widespread individual well-being; (3) the definitions proffered have the support of prominent, respected, and knowledgeable persons and groups in the community at hand; (4) any opposition is defined as ill-informed, irresponsible, self-serving, or otherwise suspect of motive; and (5) the proposed control efforts could be implemented with a minimum of disruption (money, inconvenience, suffering) to community members.

Relatedly, tacticians seem more apt to be successful in promoting particular principles when they are able to (6) generate, dramatize, and sustain media attention regarding the situation at hand; (7) develop coalitions with other groups and agencies who are also willing to express their moral indignation about the situation in question; (8) establish and maintain control agencies focused on these matters;[18] and (9) make people in the community who are more concerned with public accountability appear personally responsible for the deplorable circumstances being depicted.

Those who are more successful as moral entrepreneurs (Becker, 1963) may not only (a) establish organizational principles, but also (b) promote "working definitions of deviance" mindful of those policies, (c) determine the ways in which deviants are categorized and explained, and (d) generate and shape regulatory agencies and practices.

While the preceding points depict some themes that tacticians may pursue in endeavoring to establish and consolidate particular principles within group settings, researchers still need to attend to the interchanges that take place as people in various moral arenas *engage* one another (i.e., define, propose, legitimate, resist, mobilize, compromise, intensify, or cease to encourage particular principles). Thus, while it appears that particular policies are more apt to be accepted when tacticians are able to convince others of the desirability (or necessity) of these lines of action, we are left with the question of *how* tacticians pursue influence work (around whatever issues they promote) in practice and how all of the parties involved deal with or otherwise adjust to these endeavors over some time frame.

Even when moral entrepreneurs encounter little resistance in defining principles at the outset and are able to develop mechanisms for their enforcement, they may still find that the matter of *implementation* neutralizes their hopes for effective control. Beyond ignorance, misunderstandings, and mistakes, as well as more deliberate evasiveness and overt resistance on the part of intended targets, analysts should be attentive to the emergent features of enforcement activities.

Not only may rule enforcers have difficulty monitoring targets and accurately defining instances of trouble, but they, too, may make mistakes as well as deal with situations in more elusive ways, perhaps attending to matters of organizational expediency, strategic short cuts, and personal opportunism. Some agents also may more directly resist the principles they presumably represent.[19]

As Blumer (1971), Estes and Edmonds (1981), and Hall and McGinty (1997) observe, "policy" is very much an emergent phenomenon. Or as stated by Hall and McGinty (1997), "Policy is . . . a transformation of intentions where policy content, practices, and consequences are generated in the dynamics across time and space."

Envisioned in operational terms, the quest for control by establishing policy seems fraught with uncertainty. Yet, because people pursue the development and enforcement of principles across wide varieties of community (and subcommunity) contexts, researchers have an almost endless set of opportunities to examine these aspects of "power" in practice.

Beyond the influence (and resistance) work that is (a) more directly associated with intended targets, researchers may examine the various realms and forms of influence (and resistance) work involving (b) the assortment of insiders (e.g., rule creators, administrators, staff, volunteers, internal security) involved in matters of policy. Further, those who embark on missions to establish and enforce principles often have to contend not just with targets and a variety of insiders, but also with (c) an assortment of outsiders (some of whose efforts, missions, and senses of righteousness, may parallel their own). For researchers in the field, this means not only attending to those who make and pursue particular policies, but also to others who (individually or collectively) appear on the scene at various points and encourage, endorse, support, resist, challenge, redefine or dramatically recast these efforts.

Pursuing Positional Control

Where organizations have already been established, people may try to influence others by pursuing what they envision as "power sites" within these associations. Those attempting to situate themselves as prominent or dominant figures in organizations may also be initiators or early sponsors of those associations, but tacticians may strive to secure particular positions in preestablished associations so that they might avail themselves of the advantages that they associate with "the powers of office."

People sometimes assume prominent offices with little effort on their part, but access is often more challenging. Likewise, while it may be tempting to assume that those occupying central positions have sought out these situations, it is important that analysts avoid imputing unwarranted motives to office holders.[20] More generally, it is essential that researchers attend to the *collective dimensions* (e.g., personal enterprise, encouragements, resistances, negotiations, debts, coalitions, contests, upheavals) of attaining office.

Although numerous historical (and many autobiographical) accounts exist of people's attempts to situate themselves in "power sites," maintain those positions, and use those offices to control or shape the life-worlds that others experience, by no means are these endeavors limited to power barons, charismatics, or celebrities. The quest for positional control may occur whenever people form any association.

Because those wishing to occupy office are typically highly dependent on insider acceptances, a fundamental concern revolves around the matter of consolidating oneself with these people (i.e., establishing oneself as a consequential member of the group). I can only briefly sketch out some of the activities that tacticians may pursue in the quest for office. Clearly, not all tacticians will be concerned about these matters and, even those that are, need not engage these activities in any sustained manners.[21]

Still, in a great many cases, processes of the following kind seem highly central: (1) cultivating relationships with insiders; (2) cultivating networks of supporters; (3) assuming strategic assignments; (4) attending to leadership images; (5) neutralizing competitors; (6) extending nodes of influence; (7) becoming entrenched in the organization; and (8) becoming absorbed in power motifs.

Since the matter of *cultivating relationships* with others has been dealt with at some length in chapter 6, it may be sufficient to observe that some of those pursuing positional control will be differentially advantaged relative to others in the setting as a consequence of the relationships they have managed to cultivate to that time. Whether their efforts have been more natural or (specifically) contrived with leadership (or other offices) in mind, any auras or other preferences that candidates have acquired suggest interpersonal loyalties that may help them achieve meritorious considerations relative to competitors. Still, should tacticians wish to continue along these lines (i.e., cultivating relationships), they may face decisions pertaining not only to the specific strategies they might invoke but also about those on whom they might most productively concentrate their efforts.

In many respects, the task of *cultivating networks of supporters* seems to parallel that of cultivating relationships more generally. However, the strategic potential of these coalitions, as a resource to be implemented (or from a competitive viewpoint, a force with which to be reckoned), adds another realm of complexity to tactician routines. A two-person alignment in a group of three can dramatically change the operational field, but even relatively small networks within larger associations can be quite consequential.

The primary tactician (PT) may use any manner of influence tactics in appealing to prospective members of networks. Although the matter of tactician concerns and practices in assembling teams merits extended study, the most capable associates need not be sought out. Indeed, some attention may be given to the less capable or those thought apt to become extensively and exclusively dependent on the PT; people who may have more to lose if things do not go well for the PT.

Those questing for organizational control may also *pursue and assume strategic assignments* in the organization. Whether these represent high-profile matters or organizational "grunt work," tacticians may engage a variety of tasks and opportunities en route to more consequential positions in the association. These activities may be envisioned as (a) establishing tacticians as more dedicated, integral, and knowledgeable members, but they may also (b) provide tacticians with opportunities to develop dependencies and indebtedness on the part of others. In addition to becoming more central to the background operations of the organization, these activities may (c) enable tacticians to access a variety of resources within the organization, including opportunities with which to cultivate various individual and network relationships.

In *attending to leadership images*, the primary tacticians (or their supporters) lay claim to PT skills and viewpoints that transcend the ordinary member. Although people's efforts may be quite diverse, partial, or nebulous at times, leadership claims commonly revolve around three emphases. Thus, effort may be directed toward exhibiting that the PT is (1) a competent, reliable, dedicated team member; (2) helpful, fair, honest, and tolerant in dealing with insiders; and (3) someone who represents the organization to outsiders in ways that bespeak integrity and fearlessness as well as shrewdness and competence. Sometimes, as well, there is a concern (4) that PTs achieve a noteworthy presence relative to outsiders who are thought more consequential vis-à-vis the association.

While only some offices may be contested (e.g., others may be assigned or assumed by default), PTs may also face the task of *neutralizing competitors*. Typically, this implies embarking on neutralizing and debasing tactics of the sort discussed in chapter 6. In some cases, tacticians may do this more exclusively on their own, but PTs who have cultivated more extensive relationships with particular supporters (especially networks), may find that these others are willing to attack challengers as well as protect the PT from the challenges of others. Whether PT supporters assume these initiatives on their own or are encouraged by the PT to do so, they may enable PTs to maintain "clean hands" and other images of relative civility.

In striving for control, PTs sometimes become involved in *extending nodes of influence*. In one major variant, PTs endeavor to consolidate their interests within the organization by encouraging those in supportive networks to fill all offices within the association. The intention, thus, is to occupy all points of influence as completely as possible with PT supporters. If successful, the result is an organizational monopoly of sorts.

On some occasions, PTs may be able to make appointments along these lines, but in other instances they may encourage, endorse, and support particular candidates, often in conjunction with others in their broader networks. PTs may be concerned, as well, that those who occupy these positions not become too independent; that they realize their indebtedness to the PT and consult with the PT prior to assuming lines of action that might negatively impact on the PT. By controlling more nodes of influence, PTs may not only disadvantage any competitors they might have at the time, but also encourage a greater sense of dependence of the members at large on the PTs (and their supporters).

The second scheme involves attempts on the part of PTs to pursue positions of influence outside the immediate association. This may be done alone or with the assistance of others in the network. This may enable PTs and supporters to access various resources on the outside as well as attain greater external recognition. Should PTs be able to achieve or oversee gatekeeping functions in these other organizations, this may provide PTs with greater realms of maneuverability within and across multiple organizations.

In like manner, PTs may also attempt to extend their scope of influence by developing bonds with people in other organizations who might be receptive to becoming power players in these other settings. While typically building on some overarching sense of affinity (e.g., ideological sympathies, common enemies), PTs may support these others in various manners. However, as with those within the home organization that the PT assists, these people, too, are expected to exhibit PT loyalty in return.

In all of these cases, we begin to appreciate the collective nature that the struggle for positional control may assume. It becomes more evident, too, that by embarking on collective enterprise of this sort, the PTs and their network associates have opportunities to "be somebody" in ways that they might not have been able to approximate through their own works within the organization. At the same time, they also become more tied into relationships with one another and more obligated to tolerate the practices of each other, even when they might be inclined to think and do otherwise.

Since the pursuit of office often represents a consequential, if not also dramatic, event in many organizations, those vying for key positions may strive to *become entrenched in the organization*. Effectively, the more embedded that someone is, relative to the membership at large (and especially more extended networks, within), the more difficult it becomes to dislodge that person as a candidate, office holder, or informal source of influence. In many settings too, it becomes more challenging, if not also riskier, for insiders to challenge PTs who are well entrenched in the organization. Those resisting these PTs are faced with the prospects of neutralizing a collective subfield of the membership (and all that the PT supporters may bring into the contest in the way of resources and enterprise from both inside and outside the immediate organization).

Regardless of the ways in which, and the objectives with which, people initially assume office, they also may *become deeply caught up in the power motif*. Somewhat like Lemert's (1951, 1967) notion of "secondary deviation," once people acquire organizational images as [power players] and begin to see themselves in these terms, it may be difficult for them to disentangle themselves from these practices even should they desire so to do. Whenever people are acted toward as if they were more important, they may begin to experience fascinations with these acknowledged senses of self.

If they are to be successful as [power players], people generally have to organize their lives around influence work. However, the very things (e.g., enterprise, networks, encouragements, strategizing, campaigning, endorsing, the action, excitement, and personal mystique) that enable PTs to be successful in these arenas also represent things that they may not wish to forgo. In some cases, PT ventures very much revolve around enhanced images of themselves as [power players]. In other cases, PTs may be involved in missions or ideological associations that presumably extend far beyond their own interests, but, even here, they may become occupied with more expansive senses of self.

While rather rudimentary in its formulation, the preceding materials suggest an intriguing array of research themes that revolve around the quest for, and maintenance of, office. In addition, by focusing on the activities in which primary tacticians and their associates may engage in attempts to achieve, consolidate, and implement their interests in associational contexts, it becomes apparent that valuable opportunities to learn about these processes abound in a wide range of group settings.[22] Minimally, it is essential that researchers move beyond the "organizational" and "personality" mystiques that often typify analyses of people attaining positional control and attend carefully to the collective enterprise (often denoting multiple realms of influence and resistance) that these ventures entail in actual practice.

Promoting Totalizing Associations

While many of those involved in generating policy and pursuing positional control may be quite intense in their efforts and may plan to have a broad impact on various targets, it may be useful to envision some of these efforts as yet more encompassing or engulfing in thrust. Although people may become rather fully or centrally involved in *any* subcultural pursuit (e.g., gambling, drinking, drug use, music, business or other work, or recreational involvements), those promoting *totalizing associations* (TAs) intend that these organizations will assume centralizing and encompassing senses of direction in the lives of those involved therein.

Whereas all subcultural life-worlds denote some sense of distinctiveness or focus within the broader subcultural mosaic of the community, TA coordinators seek to provide adherents with a pervasive orientational emphasis that extends across a wide range of activities.[23,24] Still, it should be noted that whereas coordinators may attempt to impose TAs on others in some cases, and recruit them into these ventures in other instances, people may also seek out particular TAs as the central, meaningful themes in their lives.

TAs denote moral frames of various sorts, but only some of these associations have a distinctively or predominantly religious orientation.[25] Others may assume nationalistic, political, military, or remedial orientations, for instance. In all cases, though, TAs represent fairly broad centering frames of reference for people deemed to fall under their jurisdiction. Because of their more encompassing realms of application, these associations both provide the cognitive frameworks for shaping broader sectors of human behaviors and connote the arenas in which more direct, often intensive, influence work and interchange occurs.[26]

As entities in broader social contexts, these associations may be massive or have very few adherents. Likewise, they may be highly conventionalized or revered (as elite organizations) within community contexts or be viewed as strange or unacceptable by most people in the larger community. TA coordinators may assume or strive for broad regional, national, or international memberships in some cases, but other TAs may be highly localized, selective, or exclusionary. Likewise, more localized "chapters" may be embedded within, or interlinked through, larger, more particularized or transregional TAs.

Like people concerned about fostering subcultures more generally, those promoting totalizing associations may attempt to (a) establish people's worldviews (ideologies, moralities), (b) define people's identities in the community, (c) outline procedures for accomplishing activities, (d) describe the sorts of relationships adherents might have with others, (e) indicate the sorts of emotionalities that participants might reasonably experience and express, and (f) formulate the language (and concepts) that participants use in communicating with one another.[27] Still, it should not be assumed that TA personnel are attentive to all of these processes or are particularly effective in realizing objectives along these lines.

Because they may intend to engulf people's life-worlds so extensively, totalizing associations signify a potential for influence work that seems unparalleled in many other contexts. At the same time, though, like *all* policy applications, TA precepts are subject to variable *implementation* (definition, promotion, acknowledgment, enactment, resistance, negotiation, and adjustment) in the actual, situated instances in which human life takes place.

Thus, while some TAs may be so massive, or have existed for so long, that they seem invulnerable to change or resistance (even to many insiders), those involved in attempts to coordinate the activities of those falling under their domains are likely to see things quite differently. Since focused associations do not sustain themselves spontaneously, those tending to the viability (short and long term) of TAs are apt to become involved in a fuller range of the activities entailed in establishing associations, objectifying associations, and encountering outsiders. This means tending to things such as recruiting and sustaining members, instructing members on the proprieties of group conduct, monitoring and assessing people's practices, encouraging devotion, regulating disruptive behaviors on the part of members, dealing with outsiders, and focusing adherents' commitments and activities around any missions (internally and externally oriented) that may be deemed consequential for the organization at hand.

Those participating therein, thus, represent targets who are expected to adhere to organizationally established precepts generally and contribute to particular organizational missions more specifically. While some members may be much more righteous, devoted, and dependable than others, it should be recognized that all may cooperate with those representing the organization in some ways, and all, also, may resist certain kinds of situations, possibly assuming tactical roles that are explicitly intended to act back on, and shape in very different ways the experiences (and life-worlds) of those trying to influence them.

Indeed, because they address so many arenas of human endeavor, totalizing associations become vulnerable to resistance (disregard, rejection, alteration) at each of these same points. While outsiders often tend to assume homogeneity or singularity of emphases on the part of those involved in TAs (as they may do with more particularized subcultures as well), it is instructive for analysts to be attentive to the differing ways that insiders may engage (envision, implement, assess, resist, alter) various aspects of TA life-worlds.

Since TAs typically entail multiple realms, levels, sites, and styles of influence (and resistance) work, there is much that social scientists might learn from detailed examinations of the enterprise and interchange that takes place in these arenas. Hopefully the materials introduced in chapters 6–8 may provide a conceptual tool kit of sorts for embarking on studies of the ways in which people encourage, shape, and resist influence work with respect to these collectivizing realms of tactical endeavor.

Using the Media

Despite commonplace discussions of "the power of the media,"[28] social scientists have given surprisingly little direct (ethnographic) attention to the ways in which "the media" is developed, used, and or experienced by people.[29] Most basically, the media (also mass media, mass communications) refers to a set of communication processes that achieve their existences only as people *engage* one another and the products of their enterprise. From the tacticians' viewpoint, the media denotes the forums through which they may attempt to convey messages to larger audiences or "the masses out there." These messages may be aided by acoustic engineering, the emergence and proliferation of written languages, the development of print and electronic technology, and the like, but group assemblies and rumor transmissions may be seen as early prototypes of the mass media. Thus, while the following analysis attends to the media as a realm of tactical endeavor, these notions are to be juxtaposed with the experiences (and activities) of targets (and other recipients).

Likewise, while the mass media may be used to promote marketplace activity, these forums also may be used for any variety of political, religious, educational, or recreational pursuits. Indeed, part of the allure of, and fear associated with, the media revolves around the recognition that the media can be used across wide realms of influence contexts and endeavors.[30] Encompassing communications ranging (on a contemporary plane) from television and radio broadcasts, to computer and telephone networks, to photos and films, books, newspapers, fliers, catalogs, signs, product packaging, and mass mailings as well as assemblies and rumors, the media can be used as a tool for communicating all manners of messages to wide varieties of audiences.

Clearly, the media is *not* an entity unto itself. Rather, "the media" takes on its essence as a meaningful phenomenon (phenomena, more accurately) as a consequence of the many different ways that *people* (including analysts) engage aspects of the communication process.

Because of both the extensiveness of people's exposure to the media and their ongoing interactions with others (who have also been exposed in many ways to the media), it becomes virtually impossible to separate any singular effects of the media from other modes of information to which people are exposed. Indeed, since people in contemporary society make such extensive use of a great many forms of the media, the media has become assimilated into almost every realm of people's lives, including education, family life, entertainment, work, religion, and politics.

Given the general usefulness of the media (as promotional, entertainment, and information forums), people are both exposed to *and* seek out wide ranges of media messages on a more or less continual basis. People may be the intended targets and eventual recipients of much unwanted media exposure, but most also are active, selective users and pursuers of the media as well as the interpreters of all messages to which they attend.

One also might observe that, insofar as media messages typically (a) provide generalized as opposed to personalized messages, (b) are pitched to nebulous audiences out there, (c) entail great ambiguities regarding the ways in which these messages are acknowledged and interpreted by those prospective recipients, and (d) offer much less potential for interactive adjustments on the part of communicators than do interpersonal communications, media messages lack some of the persuasive potential of interpersonal communication. At the same time, however, the media provides a potential for amplifying, conveying, spreading, and sustaining messages that generally supersedes the abilities of unaided individuals to reach broader audiences. Further, many of these communications are explicitly designed to strike targets as interesting and entertaining, if not highly compelling, action-oriented experiences. It is beyond the scope of this statement to consider matters of media effectiveness or efficiency more fully,[31] but, more centrally, we can ask how people deal with the media as both tacticians and targets.

Like people trying to shape target behaviors more generally, those *using the media to influence target activities* may attempt to (a) encourage initial target involvements or compliance in situations; (b) foster longer-term participation in certain lines of action; (c) deter disinvolvements from particular lines of action; and (d) (where this has gone astray) encourage target reinvolvement along desired lines.

As suggested in a study of marketing and sales activity (Prus, 1989b: especially 201–242; 1989a: especially 234–254), people may use the media to make contact with others, establish credibility, introduce things, embellish products, focus interest, pursue commitments, and neutralize resistance, as well as encourage loyalty and generate reinvolvements. Further, tacticians may pursue these objectives in ways that parallel interpersonal encounters. Since marketing is a relatively generic practice, it seems possible to extrapolate from this study to other situations in which people use the media in attempts to shape "object" images (e.g., religious, political, remedial programs, volunteer agency work). Minimally, this material provides a base for dialoguing with research on the use of the media in other contexts.

The matter of *target experiences with the media* is given central consideration in Blumer (1933), Blumer and Hauser (1933), and Prus (1993a). While exposure to the media is both problematic and subject to interpretation along a great many lines (intended and otherwise), the messages received may enable recipients to develop a greater awareness of objects and situations in a general sense (i.e., often add to people's stocks of knowledge or awareness) and may be responsible for the development of more focused lines of interest in particular situations (perspectives, products, people, practices, and the like). However, in all instances, media messages are subject to interpretation as recipients contextualize (and recontextualize) communicated images both on their own and through interaction with others.

Both people's initial interpretations of media messages and those that they develop over time may take them in directions quite different from those intended by the tacticians (sponsors and producers). However, even when media messages are interpreted more in line with the images desired by the communicators, matters of credibility (and skepticism) can be highly consequential. Sometimes targets will openly, directly, and centrally attend to media messages, but as with other communications, media messages are apt to be judged against recipients' senses of relevancy, their existing stocks of knowledge, and any endorsements or counterclaims expressed by others with whom they have contact.[32]

Beyond more routine (and from their viewpoints, more inadvertent) exposure to media messages, people also may assume highly active roles in both selecting and disregarding various mediums and the realms of information available through these mediums. Indeed, people may assume very direct (tactician) roles in searching out, selecting, screening, assessing, comparing, emphasizing, appreciating, disattending, discounting, rejecting, and resisting media materials on both solitary and interactive levels (see Blumer, 1933; Blumer and Hauser, 1933; Frazer and Reid, 1979; Altheide, 1985; Prus, 1993a).

Analysts sometimes shroud the media in mystique, seemingly envisioning it as an omnipresent, omnipotent, source of influence. However, the media (a) rests centrally on human enterprise [and a great variety of organizational accomplishments]; (b) often entails competitive, if not conflicting, messages; (c) is fundamentally dependent on interpretations [and reinterpretations] by recipients and those with whom they associate; and (d) is subject to considerable selective attention [seekership and rejection] on the part of "consumers."[33]

If we are to achieve a more viable understanding of the media, it will be necessary not only (1) to embark on sustained ethnographic inquiries of the ways in which people engage "the media,"[34] but, in doing so, (2) to recognize the plurality of actors involved in the media process, and (3) to attend carefully to the activities (and experiences) of each category of participants in the media process and the interrelatedness of each of these activities with those of others. As indicated in Prus (1997b:151–152), themes of the following kind require sustained attention on the part of researchers who wish to understand the media as an aspect of influence (and resistance) work:

Developing, Maintaining, and Using Communication Concepts and Technologies
Developing Communications Concepts

Creating (e.g., making, financing, assembling) Prototypic Communications Devices

Testing, Revising and Dropping Communications Concepts and Prototypes

Promoting Communications Concepts, and Products

    Encouraging others to use particular forums, concepts, services

    Servicing users (providing third-party support for tacticians)

    Encountering resistance (from financiers, businesses, consumers)

    Dealing with competitors (with similar and alternative products)

Using Mass Communication as Forums for Influence[35]

Directing Messages to Multiple Others

Generating Public Assemblies and Theaters

Using the Print and Electronic Media

    Developing specific media forums, formats, and messages

    Employing media forums and technologies

    Generating and formatting media messages

    Sending and assessing (evaluating, comparing efficiency of) media messages

Experiencing the Media as Targets

    Encountering, Interpreting, and Attending to Particular Media Material

    Seeking, Managing, Disregarding, and Avoiding Media Materials

    Using Media Materials for One's Own Purposes

If people lived out their lives more exclusively as "media-logues," entities whose viewpoints, stocks of knowledge, and experiences were primarily determined by media exposure, the argument that "you are what you witness in the media" would be more compelling. However, because people not only routinely operate in multiple life-worlds (i.e., a subcultural mosaic as opposed to a singular cultural world) and *engage* those particular life-worlds in a variety of manners (activities, interactions, relationships) that extend beyond any media materials that they may encounter, it is essential that media messages be located *within* these broader (mosaical), lived (and enacted) notions of community life. This observation is not intended to divert attention from more sustained examinations of the media, but rather to encourage researchers to embark on research that attends more directly and fully to *the ways that people experience the media* within the more situated realms of human enterprise and interchange that constitute community life.

Developing Political Agendas

Hearken and hear then, said he [Thrasmachus]. *I affirm that the just is nothing else than the advantage of the stronger . . . (S)ome cities are governed*

by tyrants, in others democracy rules, in others aristocracy . . . And each form of
government enacts the laws with a view to its own advantage, a democracy
democratic laws and tyranny autocratic and the others likewise, and by so
legislating they proclaim that the just for their subjects is that which is for
their—rulers'—advantage and the man who deviates from this law they
chastise as a lawbreaker and a wrongdoer. This, then, my good sir, is what I
understand as the identical principle of justice that obtains in all states—the
advantage of the established government . . .

    Now, said I [Socrates], *I have learned your meaning, but whether it is true*
or not I have to try to learn . . . I too admit that the just is something that is of
advantage—but you are for making an addition and affirm it to be the advan-
tage of the stronger, while I don't profess to know—we must pursue the inquiry.
        —Plato, Republic, *Book I: 338c–339a [Shorey, trans.]*

While some may contend that political agendas (and interchanges) take
one into uniquely macro-societal realms of analysis, the considerations of
political endeavor developed herein rest centrally on the modes of influence discussed so far (particularly in chapter 6 and the present chapter).

    Much of the enterprise entailed in developing political agendas has
already been outlined in the preceding considerations of influence work.
Thus, for instance, (1) wide variations of enhancing, focusing, leveraging,
and neutralizing and debasing tactics are pertinent, if not central to political endeavor. Likewise, the processes entailed in (2) developing collective
ventures (establishing associations, objectifying associations, and dealing
with outsiders) are extremely important for comprehending political life-
worlds, as are (3) people's concerns with developing communitywide
agendas (principles and constraints) and (4) pursuing strategic (positional)
control in organizational contexts. Because much political enterprise rests
on broader levels of communication, an appreciation of (5) the media also
is highly pertinent.

    As indicated at some length in chapters 2 and 3, social scientists,
generally, have disattended to the human *enterprise* that undergirds power
(and politics) in community life. In addition to producing volumes of
learned discussions about politics, political scientists and political sociologists also have generated a great deal of survey research (and opinion poll-
ing) designed to tap into attitude formation and other factors allegedly
affecting people's voting practices. Still, these scholars have contributed
very little to the study of political life in the making.

    Encompassing regional, national, and international arenas of various
sorts, the realm of political endeavor covers a great deal of conceptual and
substantive territory. This does not mean, however, that it is best understood
through conventional macro-societal analysis. What is required, instead, is a
notably different approach: one that enables social scientists to more

rigorously and directly examine the great many instances of human interchange (activities, relationships, organizations) that constitute political life, to examine political phenomena as a set of interlinked realms of human enactment.

To provide readers with a more definite sense of the sorts of issues that ethnographic research might address with respect to political processes, three subthemes are introduced: (a) *implementing governmental forums,* (b) *invoking military operations,* and (c) *establishing control agencies.*[36] The statements outlined here will prove rather partial and limited when researchers examine actual realms of political endeavor more closely, but they do point to the great variety of subprocesses that these matters entail. Most importantly, they offer a means of dealing with political interchange on a clearly processual, intersubjectively informed, and empirically grounded basis.

In addition to delineating a series of consequential themes for future research, this material also suggests focal points for integrating (comparing, assessing, synthesizing) ethnographic research in "political arenas" with research in other realms of human endeavor in which similar processes come into play (e.g., street gangs, corporations, religious groups). This is not to imply that political agendas and related matters are omnipresent in human associations, but rather to comment on the transcontextual parallels of human association (i.e., generic social processes) that transcend political and other spheres of community life, such that research on the political process may be used to inform these other realms of activity and vice versa.

Implementing Governmental Forums[37]

> [Athenian:] *As these larger homesteads are in process of growth from the smaller and most primitive, each of the smaller groups will bring along with it its patriarchal ruler and certain private customs of its own; private, I mean, because the groups are isolated from each other, and the several groups have been trained by their different progenitors and fosterers in different habits of conduct towards gods and fellow-men, in more orderly habits where the ancestors have been more orderly, in more valiant where they have been valiant. Thus each group comes accordingly, as I say, into the larger settlement with special laws of its own, and prepared to imprint its own preferences upon its children, and their children after them . . . And of course each group unavoidably gives its approval to its own laws, and only in the second place to those of the others.*
> —Plato, The Laws, *Book III: 681 [Taylor, trans.]*

Although human groups sometimes develop very explicit and extensive governmental forums and practices, the matters addressed herein revolve around the relatively basic concerns of *coordinating, representing, and regulating group members.* In many respects, these pursuits are rather unexceptional.

They appear to take place in all more enduring community contexts ranging from family and play groups to all manners of formal organizations including massive national and international forums.

Political forums, thus, at base only represent the more explicit, presumably more encompassing arrangements that members of communities (or subcultures) develop for making decisions pertaining to the collectivity under consideration.[38] Much may be learned about influence processes in any setting (educational, recreational, familial, business, religious) in which people interact. However, because they connote somewhat enduring instances of regulatory mandates that are dynamically applied across broader community settings, governments also denote highly consequential and intriguing realms of study on their own.

While governments may be developed at any variety of community levels, from small group associations, to "city halls," to regional, federal, and international arrangements, neither political scientists nor political sociologists have generated much research that depicts the ways in which people in any context, forms, or levels of government actually accomplish their tasks on a day-to-day basis. What is required is a research agenda that attends to human experiences and endeavors in the collective spheres of the community under consideration. This will entail replacing an emphasis on factors, surveys, and learned speculation with ethnographic data that examines the ways in which political behavior is implemented on a day-to-day, here and now, and more sustained basis.

Some earlier, interactionist informed, statements by Sutherland (1950), Blumer (1954, 1971), Becker (1963), Klapp (1964, 1969, especially 257–314), Hall (1972), and Gusfield (1981, 1989) contribute to a more general understanding of governmental forums, but research in sociology that focuses explicitly on the ways in which people directly engage governmental processes has been very limited to date.

Among the more pertinent ethnographic ventures are Cressey's (1932) study of legislation pertaining to "taxi-dance" halls; Karsh et al.'s (1953) examination of the unionization process; Milbrath's (1963) study of Washington lobbyists; Kinsey's (1985) depiction of relations among congressional staff; D. Wolf's (1991) account of the political life of biker gangs; Benford and Hunt's (1992) and Hunt and Benford's (1994) analysis of public confrontations,[39] and Grills's (1989, 1994) study of the development and recruitment practices of a national (religiously inspired) political movement.[40]

Mindful of the desirability of establishing a research agenda for studying political life-worlds, six aspects of the larger governmental process are outlined. These involve the matters of (1) developing and maintaining governing arrangements, (2) encountering and dealing with resistance and competition, (3) assessing community conditions and implementing policy,

(4) developing and sustaining foreign policy, (5) challenging existing governing practices, and (6) engaging political life-worlds (managing careers as participants). Notably, these themes are interlinked and people may embark on activities of these sorts in concurrent, intermittent, and recurrent manners.

Developing and Maintaining Governing Arrangements
 Developing Visions of Governing Arrangements
 Promoting, Initiating, and Coordinating Governing Associations
 Objectifying (consolidating, formalizing, legitimating) Governing Arrangements
 Financing Governmental Activities
 Sustaining Governing Forums and Practices
 Extending Jurisdictions and Realms of Influence
 Establishing and Maintaining (internal) Subagencies[41]
Encountering and Dealing with Resistance and Competition
 Facing Challenges from Community Members
  Seemingly supportive insiders / Opponents within the community
 Mediating among Competing and Opposional Factions in the Community
 Encountering Foreign Offensives (see foreign policy, military agendas)
 Resisting, Adjusting, Compromising while in Office
 Relinquishing Office / Dissolving Government
Assessing Community Conditions and Implementing Policies[42]
 Defining Situations as Troublesome / Legitimating Problems
 Mobilizing (concerned parties) for Action / Forming an Official Plan
 Implementing the Official Plan
  Establishing agendas and control agencies (and enforcers)[43]
  Encountering resistance / Assessing and adjusting policies and practices
Developing and Sustaining Foreign Policy
 Recognizing Outsider Governments (also agencies and spokespeople)
 Establishing Foreign Policy Agencies (e.g., trade, diplomacy, military)[44]
 Implementing Foreign Policy / Adjusting to Outsider Governments

Whereas the preceding themes deal with government arrangements primarily from the viewpoint of those involved in the implementation and maintenance of existing arrangements, the next set of topics focus more directly on those within the community who resist the current governing arrangements (i.e., policies, practices, personnel).

Challenging Governing Practices from within Communities
 Defining Discontent with Present Governmental Practices

Initiating and Objectifying Challenges
  Embarking on individual resistance / Engaging in collective
  ventures[45]
Encountering Resistance from Governing Agencies (and other parties)
Achieving Success (attaining desired arrangements/positions)
  Consolidating arrangements / Defending against others

The last theme in this section deals with people's careers in the political arena. As such, it encompasses the involvements (and activities) of everyone, who in some way, endeavors to shape the political arenas in which they and others in the community find themselves. Approached thusly, political careers engulf the somewhat interrelated and often overlapping notions of leaders and followers, contenders and supporters, distracters and mediators, promoters and voters. Although this may seem unduly broad to some, it should be appreciated that people's careers as office holders, candidates, sponsors, voters, or resisters of various sorts, need not begin or end with these particular points of engagement. Thus, it is instructive to attend to people's prior experiences (and activities) as well as their anticipations of the future. Beyond enabling researchers to focus on the careers of "politicians" as office holders, it is hoped that this broader emphasis on multiple realms of people's involvement in governmental forums may also encourage researchers to consider the ways in which people both engage and shift their locus of involvement in these realms of political endeavor.

Engaging Political Life-worlds (any level, arena, capacity)[46]
  Becoming Involved / Sustaining and Intensifying Involvements
  Becoming Disengaged / Renewing Involvements

Invoking Military Operations[47]

> (I)t is an intellectual tragedy that sociological research has given so little attention in recent years to military affairs or to the closely related areas of arms control, peacekeeping, and international cooperation. It makes very little sense, either for science or for public policy, to separate "peace studies" from "war studies."
>
> Williams, 1984:192

Although military agendas or enterprises may seem like tactical endeavors in themselves (and they are in a general sense), these realms of human endeavor represent arenas of inquiry and analysis that are as diversified and challenging as any other. Indeed, if these ventures are to be understood in ways that reflect the actualities of human interchange, then it is essential that social scientists and researchers attend carefully to the socially constructed nature of the military enterprise.

It also should be emphasized that the matter of defending, maintaining, or asserting one's community vis-à-vis others is by no means limited to military involvements. Military confrontations may assume priorities in some instances and programs, but such involvements may be viewed as last resorts in other cases. Matters of diplomacy, trade, humanitarian appeals, and other tactical maneuverings may be seen as alternatives to, and resources to be used in conjunction with, military involvements in the "pursuit of presence." Indeed, scholars attending to intergroup relations may find it most instructive to consider all of the ways in which people in oppositional groups opt for, pursue, and adjust their activities along multiple realms and lines of endeavor over time.

Still, military agendas may be most centrally defined by community (or subcommunity) based use of physical force (and related resources) to defend, maintain, or assert one's interests with respect to others.[48] This definition encompasses a wide range of adversarial or confrontational stances, many of which are rooted in, or interlinked with, governing practices and policies by means of direction, coordination, and resource allocation.

Given the enduring, albeit situated and sporadic, involvement of humans in intragroup conflict, it should not be surprising to find that a vast literature has developed around military, war, diplomacy, and related matters. Although one finds fragmentary ethnographic observations within this broader literature, this material is largely prescriptive, moralistic, historically sweeping, or technological, in thrust.[49] It is hoped that by depicting aspects of military operations, in even the broader processual terms outlined here, that researchers may be able to embark on more precise, more sustained ethnographic examinations of what minimally represents a recurrent theme in human relations.

Attending to Defensive and Expansionary Concerns
    Defining Problems or Objectives that entail (offensive or defensive) Military Agendas
    Envisioning, Promoting, and Establishing Military Programs and Policies
Developing and Maintaining Military Agencies (and Technologies)
    Recruiting and Staffing Military Organizations
    Generating Funds / Obtaining Supplies, Equipment, Facilities
    Establishing and Maintaining Centrality of Command
    Establishing and Consolidating Communication Channels
    Developing Military Technologies and Tactics / Providing Training
    Achieving Order within Military Agencies and Operations
Pursuing Military Agendas
    Maintaining Internal Security (citizen discretion and loyalty)
    Dealing with Collective Civil Unrest and Resistance
    Deploying Military Agencies (confronting outsiders)

Encountering Military Initiatives from Outsiders
    Defining and dealing with adversaries
    Invoking tactics and making ongoing adjustments
  Generating Allies (and coordinating activities with allies)
  Defining and Dealing with Success, Resistance, and Failure in the Field
  Managing Accountability (and resistances) on the Home Front
  Sustaining Desired Images in Outside (hostile, supportive, judgmental)
  Communities
  Reaching Terms (settlements) with Adversaries (and mediators)
  Disbanding (and Reconfiguring) Military Agencies
Engaging Military Life-Worlds (Careers of Participation)
  Becoming Involved / Sustaining (and Intensifying) Involvements
  Becoming Disinvolved / Renewing Involvements

As with those conducting research in various political life-worlds, those embarking on ethnographic inquiry in military arenas will find it helpful to attend to the various tactics outlined in chapters 6 and 7 that people may invoke in attempts to influence others. While some may be tempted to concentrate on the practice of "usurping agency" (chapter 6), a fuller consideration of people's practices in the military theater is apt to reveal not only how very partial and limited this tactic is (even in this setting), but how very much military endeavor may be accompanied by, or replaced with, other modes of influence work.

Establishing Control Agencies

Control agencies are organizations within the community that have been established with the intention of regulating some aspect of people's lives. A great many control agencies (e.g., police, courts, parole offices) are specifically developed within the context of governmental regulatory mandates, but others are considerably more diffuse or autonomous in thrust. While many other agencies also pursue governmental funding (and other support) for a wide variety of influence, remedial, and reform programs, some other regulatory associations may arise rather independently of, and perhaps in opposition to, the agencies sponsored by the prevailing government. As well, because they may pursue a broad range of agendas, control agencies not infrequently work at cross-purposes to one another.

It also may be useful to recognize the fear often engendered by images of governments (e.g., totalitarian regimes or repressive states) that more extensively use control agencies to regulate the life experiences of the citizenry. The implication, here, is that control may be so singularly focused, concentrated, and enforced that the fate of the people caught up therein rests entirely on the whims of those in charge.

Images of more complete and unrelenting domination are commonly associated with notions of state-legitimated biological reproduction, pharmaceutical intervention, psychological conditioning, totalistic surveillance, severe tribunals and inquisitions, information control, and the ability to inflict suffering and end human lives. Further, some would observe that ongoing developments in technology make this an increasingly ominous possibility. Minimally, images of pervasive state control generally do not sit comfortably with the populace at large. Indeed, considerable skepticism may be directed toward government control agencies of all sorts.

However, despite widespread concerns about avoiding or encouraging situations of this sort, one encounters a great many (large and small) protest, prohibition, censorship, or reform movements that encourage the extended use of control agencies to achieve particular versions of morality. Some of these missions of control are focused on more isolated [troublesome] individuals, but others may be directed at broad categories of people within the community. While characterized by their own notions of benign intentions, it appears that many advocacy positions would be realized only if more totalizing or repressive agendas and measures were implemented.

Because existing governmental control agencies are thought more readily able to provide surveillance, enforcements, and treatments of all kinds, it is not uncommon to see those promoting particular moralities attempting to use these agencies to enforce their own agendas. In the process, they may pressure government office holders to either extend the mandates of existing control agencies or to develop new agencies and enhanced technologies to regulate more realms of community life.

At the same time, many people, often including those who seek heightened governmental control in certain arenas, attach considerable esteem to those "champions of the public" who seem able to generate greater freedoms in other realms of community life. Likewise, some attribute a mystique to those innovators, rebels, and outlaws who challenge or "beat the system" in other terms. In the quest for particular moralities and desired life-styles, thus, one frequently witnesses wide assortments of community tensions and contradictions as politicians, control agents, moral spokespeople, and the public at large, deal with varying notions of propriety and trouble, control and resistance, and restraint and freedom of expression.

It is intriguing, in certain respects, to talk or debate more broadly about concerns with morality and control relative to matters of freedom and resistance. Likewise, we can recognize that such matters warrant sustained consideration on the part of those centrally concerned with notions of liberty, mutuality of freedom, and democracy, for instance. However, it is instructive for social scientists to more modestly, but more directly, focus on people's experiences with control agencies across a range of particularized settings. It is within these instances of the here and now that the actualities of human experience are enacted.

By attending to the ways that (a) people establish, staff, implement, and readjust control programs of various sorts, as well as the manners in which (b) people experience (encounter, assess, accept, resist) control efforts as targets, social scientists should be able to provide more sustained, empirically (i. e., ethnographically) grounded insights into the control and resistance work that occurs in regulatory settings. This would include those agencies that are explicitly more totalizing in control terms as well as those that purport to be more protective, remedial, or benignly reconstitutive in emphasis.

The following material draws attention to various realms of enterprise in which people may engage in the course of establishing, implementing, and experiencing control agencies. While this material has been developed mindfully of government-established or government-sponsored agencies, the themes outlined here seem applicable across the range of organizations that assume the mandate of regulating people's lives in some manner.

Consideration is given to four features of control agency activity: (1) establishing and maintaining control agencies, (2) developing careers in control agency work, (3) implementing office (as control agents), and (4) encountering control agencies as targets.[50] Whereas the first three of these topics are developed from the viewpoint of those approaching control agencies as regulators (promoters, coordinators, and staff), the fourth puts the emphasis more squarely on those who experience control agencies as targets.

Establishing and Maintaining Control Agencies[51]
    Setting up Control Agencies
        Conceptualizing control agencies (and defining general agendas)
        Legitimating (justifying, gaining acceptance for) control agencies
        Obtaining funding (and other resources) for control agencies
        Locating, training, and maintaining personnel
    Operating Control Agencies[52]
        Developing (and changing) routines
        Accessing cases / Classifying cases / Processing cases
    Maintaining Control Agencies
        Assessing effectiveness / Maintaining internal order
        Experiencing accountability / Displaying competence
        Dealing with (outside) competition
Developing Careers in Deviance Regulation (Control, Rehabilitation Work)
    Becoming Involved / Sustaining (and Intensifying) Involvements
    Becoming Disinvolved / Renewing Involvements
Implementing Office (Performing Activities) as Control Agents

Acquiring Perspectives of Office / Engaging in Preventative Work
Monitoring Prospective and Designated Cases / Investigating Trouble
Handling Things Informally / Providing (official) Treatment
Encountering Target Resistance / Adjusting to Targets
Experiencing (internal) Accountability / Displaying Competence
Attending to the Control Agency Community (insiders)
Encountering Difficulties with Outsiders

Although the introduction of materials dealing with those targeted for control in various manners entails a shift in emphasis, it should be acknowledged that (as "the grist for the mill") target involvements (experiences and activities) fundamentally contribute to a comprehension of the broader control agency subculture (in which multiple staff and target subcultures may be embedded). It should be fully appreciated, as well, that those targeted for control work may assume a variety of *tactician* roles as they (a) relate to other targets, (b) act back on the control agents they encounter within the setting, and (c) deal with any outsiders.

In addition to acknowledging the multiple subcultures that targets may become involved within particular control agency settings, it should be recognized that these targets often participate in multiple life-worlds outside of the agency. Some outsider associates may actively encourage targets to pursue control agency objectives, but other outsider affiliates may disregard, if not more entirely oppose, agency agendas. Consider, for example, the distracting associations of those undergoing treatment for drug use (Brown, 1931; Ray, 1961), tuberculosis (Roth, 1962), alcoholism (Wiseman, 1970), gambling (Lesieur, 1977), or those involved in religious orders (Lofland, 1966; Ebaugh, 1988).

Encountering Particular Control Agencies as Targets[53]
    Developing Preliminary Images of the Agency / Making Initial Contact
    Making Sense of the Situation
Encountering Agency Treatment
    Experiencing (defining, seeking, accepting, and resisting) "Treatment"
    Pursuing and Avoiding other Considerations in the Setting
Attending to the Community of Others (agents, other targets, outsiders)
Acknowledging Posttreatment Experiences
    Becoming Disengaged from Agency Contact
    Abstaining from, and Relapsing into, Agency Proscribed Activities[54]
    Considering and Encountering Other Remedial Practices

In Context

Acknowledging the capacity for tacticians to involve others in their attempts to shape target situations and behaviors, this chapter has outlined a number of realms of collective enterprise. By approaching the study of power in definitional, interactional, and implementational terms, the more complex grids of human interchange are opened up in ways that become more directly amenable to research. Thus, we may begin to examine, more directly, the processes by which people work with third-party agents, develop collective ventures, pursue office, promote totalizing associations, use the media, or develop political and military agendas.

Although some theaters of operation are more complex (e.g., media, government, military) and enduring than others, the key to studying collective interchange is to recognize that *all human associations* are envisioned, defined, enacted, sustained, resisted, and altered by *people as they* engage one another in the course of ongoing community life. The facets of collective endeavor addressed here represent relatively uncharted areas for ethnographic inquiry, but the generic emphasis (theoretical orientations, methodological practices, and conceptual cross-contextual comparisons) of Chicago interactionism seems singularly advantaged over existing approaches to the study of these more complex human relations. Still, the present statement can only sketch out some of the parameters of the conceptual and empirical work that remains. By focusing on a variety of target roles, chapter 8 further extends the theater of operations.

Notes

1. Clearly, not all third-party involvements are solicited by tacticians. Third parties may also intervene at their own initiative, at the request of targets (who, in doing so, assume a tactical stance themselves), or at the solicitation of yet other (third) parties.

2. As De Callières (1716) indicates in his portrayal of diplomatic work, agents in the field commonly adopt a plurality of stances in attending to their missions. For another indication of the ways in which representatives' agendas may differ from those of the tacticians employing them, see Blumberg's (1967) account of criminal lawyers.

3. For some illustrations of "turnovers" in the sales setting, see Prus (1989a:170–171).

4. On some occasions, "tattling on" or reporting targets denotes instances of spite or retribution on the part of tacticians. Here, tacticians commonly work on the assumption that third parties (as secondary tacticians) would deal more effectively with targets than could the (primary) tacticians themselves. Also some (primary) tacticians may not wish to be bothered with the "dirty work" that control or punishment entails.

5. The third parties to whom referrals are made may be seen as sec-

ondary targets for tacticians. Once approached in this manner, though, the third parties effectively assume the roles of tacticians, themselves, with respect to *both* the primary tactician (soliciting their help) and the primary target(s) of that tactician.

6. These disclosures (truthful or otherwise) may in some cases be very productive for the "troubled" individuals, enabling them to restore or achieve esteem by indicating the obstacles they have encountered, their suffering, their relative innocence in the venture, and the like.

7. For fuller conceptual discussions of the roles that third parties play in the emergence, resolution, and intensification of disputes, see Simmel (1950:145–169), Goffman (1961), Bittner (1967), Blumberg (1967), Emerson and Messinger (1977), and Prus (1978).

For some ethnographic portrayals of third-party involvements, readers are referred to Emerson (1969, 1994), Prus (1978), Prus and Irini (1980), Ross (1980), Prus (1989a, especially 171–182; 183–209; 1993b), D. Wolf (1991), and Meehan (1992).

8. Consider, for instance, the involvements of third parties (e.g., parents, referees, peace officers, judges in court cases, bar staff, teachers) who seek to control relations between two or more interactants in settings for which they assume some responsibility.

9. For an insightful consideration of the contingencies affecting the success of degradation ceremonies, see Garfinkel (1956). Readers interested in the claims-making (and defense) process will likely find Aristotle's *Rhetoric* and *De Rhetorica Ad Alexandrum* highly instructive as well.

10. Interestingly, while tacticians utilizing this option may seem only to be availing themselves of practices that may be recognized within the community, people who implement adjudication practices (more or less simultaneously) may be seen to violate community notions of respecting the citizens at large. This may foster a more widespread community distancing and distrust of tacticians (i.e., "troublemakers") who invoke adjudication proceedings.

11. A great many control agencies find themselves in this latter situation as their representatives attempt to establish and maintain (financially and otherwise) the agency in the community in order that they might pursue their alleged primary objectives of attending to particular sets of troublesome targets.

12. Those agencies able to display earlier instances of success with troublesome targets may be better able to achieve support from sponsors should they wish to intensify or expand their domains of influence.

13. Volunteer organizations (Marks, 1990) provide an interesting instance as these associations not only (a) target those (clients) allegedly in need of their services, but also direct influence work toward (b) their paid staff, (c) existing and prospective volunteers, and (d) various sources of

funding (government, corporate, citizens at large) as they pursue their purportedly central mission of assisting a particular set of targets.

14. For some ethnographic depictions of these processes, see Sutherland's (1937) professional thieves; Karsh et al.'s (1953) union organizers; Lofland's (1966) and Van Zandt's (1991) examinations of religious cults; Rubington's (1968) study of bottle-gangs; Shaffir's (1974) examination of a Lubavitch hasidim (religious) community; Prus and Sharper's (1977) account of road hustlers; Adler's (1985) portrayal of drug dealers; Prus's (1989a, 1989b) examination of marketing and sales activities; Prus and Frisby's (1990) analysis of home party plans; Keiser's (1969) depiction of street gangs; Wolf's (1991) consideration of outlaw bikers; MacLeod's (1993) study of dance bands; Grills's (1994) and Atkinson's (1995) inquiries into political party recruitment practices; and Prus and Fleras's (1996) portrayal of economic development officers.

15. While informed by Schutz's (1962, 1964) and Berger and Luckmann's (1966) work on typification and objectification, this statement attempts to locate these notions more squarely in an emergent, associative context.

16. Gusfield's (1963) depiction of the American Temperance Movement as a "symbolic crusade" and his (1981, 1996) considerations of the drinking-driving problem attest to the frustration that many attempts to control people's behavior engender on the part of moral entrepreneurs. Zurcher et al.'s (1971) account of two "antiporn" movements makes a similar point, as does Wiseman's (1970) examination of skid row agency practices.

17. This discussion builds on the works of Cressey (1932), Sutherland (1950), Karsh et al. (1953), Garfinkel (1956), Becker (1963), Klapp (1969), T. Kuhn (1970), Blumer (1971), Gusfield (1981, 1989), the Best (1989) collection, and others.

18. Beyond representing the potential for full-time employment and career development for some individuals, these associations may also serve as (a) central reference points for claims-making activities, (b) agency benign sources of "expertise," and (c) ardent pursuers of financial support.

19. It is worth noting that even people who create and enforce rules of their own designs, may be remiss in pursuing these on a sustained basis. Parents represent an instructive case in point. They seldom seem able to pursue their own rules as effectively as they might desire, especially when they attempt to deal with multiple children or accomplish other tasks at the same time. They, too, have been known to question and repeal their own rules.

20. The earlier discussion of routings and careers of tactician involvement (chapter 6) is highly relevant here.

21. In developing this material, I found the Karsh et al. (1953) account of union organization tactics particularly valuable, along with Klapp's (1964) statement on symbolic leaders, D. Wolf's (1991) study of outlaw bikers, Grills's (1994) examination of a political party, and C. Wolf's (1994) work on feminism.

22. Indeed, although less spectacular in many respects, the situations that are more immediately and intimately accessible to social scientists are apt to afford them much better data for understanding people's experiences in pursuing and holding office than are the accounts that are generally available on more prominent figures.

23. Keiser's (1969) ethnographic account of street gangs and Daniel Wolf's (1991) examination of outlaw biker gangs offer instructive portrayals of totalizing associations as do field studies of religious associations conducted by Lofland (1966), Shaffir (1974, 1993), Rochford (1986), and Van Zandt (1991). Charlotte Wolf's (1994) consideration of feminist subcultural involvements and Grills's (1994) study of a religiously inspired political party illustrate the potential that associations of these sorts offer as totalizing organizations.

24. It may be argued that some of these associations do a poor job in these respects (consider, for example, those Christian religious denominations that appear to have only a Sunday or "going to church" relevance to the life-worlds of their adherents). Still, this should not obscure either the aspirations that leaders may have for a more comprehensive member effect or coordinators' abilities to pursue certain kinds of missions with these same memberships.

25. Although religious (social) movements are often defined by an attentiveness to the supernatural, our concern here is not whether particular associations or organizations are religious in this sense or not. Thus, any association that articulates (and sustains) a more encompassing philosophy of life, claims a privileged source of legitimation and knowledge, emphasizes ingroup solidarity, and attempts to organize people's lives around group agendas and routines may be seen as totalizing or cultlike (also see Klapp, 1969) for our purposes.

26. Readers familiar with Goffman's (1961) *Asylums* will recognize numerous parallels with what he calls "total institutions." Thus, the close ethnographic study of more secluded total institutions such as mental hospitals, prisons, convents, military outposts, and the like would offer a great many viable comparison points with detailed examinations of other totalizing (e.g., religious, political) associations that operate in the community at large. Indeed, while acknowledging some differential emphases (e.g., membership, participation, mobility, surveillance, regimentation) across those associations that are intended to be more totalizing in thrust, it also seems

instructive to compare and contrast) the influence and resistance work that one encounters across much broader bands (i.e., more totalizing and more partialized) of association.

27. For instance, see Plato's *Republic*. More developed statements on generic dimensions of association can be found in Prus (1996b, 1997b).

28. See the earlier discussion of "Mass Communication Themes" in chapter 3.

29. This discussion draws heavily on ethnographic accounts of people's experiences with the media. Most notably, this includes accounts of adolescent encounters with movies (Blumer, 1933; Blumer and Hauser, 1933), vendors' use of the media (Prus, 1989b:201–242) in conjunction with other sales-related practices (Prus, 1989a, 1989b), as well as the use of the media (and other promotional practices) by economic development agencies (Prus and Fleras, 1996) and consumer encounters with the media (Prus, 1993a). Also noteworthy are some ethnographic portrayals of media constructions by Altheide (1974), Tuchman (1978), Fishman (1980), and Ericson et al. (1987, 1989). Although only minimally ethnographic in thrust, some other interactionist considerations of the media can be found in the work of Altheide and Snow (1979), Altheide and Johnson (1980), and Altheide (1985).

30. Concerns with community wisdom, morality, and the media (via rhetoric, oratory, and theater, as well as written text) can be found in early Greek and Roman literature. See Aristotle's *Rhetoric*, for instance. Also see Freeman (1949), Kennedy (1963, 1972), and Enos (1993, 1995).

31. This matter is given some preliminary but explicit attention in Prus (1989b:237–241). However, as suggested in the present statement, concerns with media effects should be envisioned and qualified within much broader frames of human engagement.

32. Even children, who are commonly envisioned as highly vulnerable to television commercials and store displays, for instance, generally attend with differing levels of interest to the media. Consider, for instance, advertisements and displays featuring toys and candy as opposed to the promotion of cars, banks, or antiperspirants. Children may become curious about these latter items, but are apt to attend to very different aspects of these promotions from those that tacticians had intended as consequential. Similarly, after eating some cereal found distasteful, children may be less enthusiastic about insisting, the second time around, that their parents buy the cereal box with the "fun" characters on the front or the "neat favors" inside. Sometimes, too, children will heed (in advance) their parents' advice about products that might seem appealing in other ways.

33. A close reading of Aristotle, who addresses matters of persuasion in public forums in *Rhetoric*, indicates that he was clearly aware of these processes as they pertain to the communications developed in these set-

tings. Unfortunately, these notions appear to have been largely neglected by scholars over the years (also see Billig, 1996).

34. So-called, content analysis and postmodernist renderings of the media are most inadequate for developing appreciations of the socially constructed essences of the media. While often cast in quantitative terms, content analysis typically reveals much more about the orientations of the analysts than it does about the viewpoints and activities of those involved in generating or consuming aspects of the media. Postmodernist analysis is less readily defined but, at its core, one usually finds some variant of a marxist critique (oppression thesis) of western society. In neither case are the analysts apt to be privileged (i.e., participant informed) insiders with respect to those involved in the production of the media or those consumers who purportedly experience these materials. Both content analysis and post-modernist statements may be relatively quick and easy to generate, but these speculative ventures (however entertaining they may seem on occasion) are poor substitutes for sustained ethnographic inquiry into aspects of the media process.

35. The matter of using the media for persuasive endeavor requires greater analytic (and methodological) detail when third-party agents or service providers are involved (e.g., as script writers, producers, agency personnel, market researchers).

36. While some "control agencies" (e.g., vigilantes, protest groups, terrorist groups) exist in clear opposition to government policies and practice, a great many others reflect government mandates or would likely cease to exist without government funding or subsidies. Still, whether funded by, approved of, or viewed in oppositional terms, by broader community governments, each control agency may be seen as engaged in the activity of trying to shape, direct, or govern, the lives of some or all members of the community.

37. This statement on "implementing governmental forums" is derived from Prus (1997b).

38. Even the notion of being "more encompassing" generates definitional problems as in cases, for example, where religious themes are presumed ultimately to overrule human governing practices.

39. These statements build on earlier ethnographic work on the peace movement by Benford (1987) and Hunt (1991).

40. Although only at a preliminary stage of development, Atkinson (1995) has begun to lay out a research agenda for the study of national and local, democratic political processes.

41. Some of these subagencies may be primarily supportive of the government in a more internal sense (e.g., accounting, personnel, internal security), but many others (i.e., most control agencies) assume regulatory tasks pitched at the populace more directly.

42. The points listed in this section are derived from Blumer's (1971) discussion of "Social Problems as Collective Behavior." As Blumer observes, many issues to which governments attend are rooted in much earlier and broader realms of community enterprise and interchange.

43. Control agencies represent consequential developments within larger-scale governing bodies, but regulatory agencies may be developed in many spheres other than those signified by government mandates. See the later consideration of "establishing control agencies."

44. While reflecting first-hand experiences rather than ethnographic inquiries per se, social scientists interested in matters of foreign policy may find it highly instructive to attend to the accounts of those engaged in diplomatic roles (e.g., De Callières, 1716; Kissinger, 1994) as well as to begin embarking on field research in this realm of endeavor.

45. For some ethnographic materials on collective challenges to prevailing governing bodies, see Benford and Hunt's (1992) and Hunt and Benford's (1994) depictions of peace movements as well as the works of Grills (1994) and Atkinson (1995) on the problematics of establishing and maintaining political parties. D. Wolf's (1991) account of the internal governing practices of outlaw biker gangs is also instructive in this regard. The earlier statement in this chapter on "developing collective ventures" is highly pertinent here as is material in chapter 8 on target roles ("assuming competitive stances" and "participating in collective events").

46. More conceptual and reference material on career contingencies (involvements) can be found in Prus (1996b). For some ethnographic work pertaining to people's careers in politics, see Milbrath's (1963) depiction of lobbyists, Kinsey's (1985) study of congressional staff, and Grills's (1994) inquiry into the recruitment practices of political parties.

47. This discussion of military agendas and agencies builds on materials developed in Prus (1997b).

48. Conflict within communities may also assume military proportions. Consider, for instance, the postures and practices of street gangs (Keiser, 1969) and biker gangs (D. Wolf, 1991). Likewise, one sometimes encounters militaristic images in the tactical orientations of competitors in the marketplace, sports arenas, and entertainment sectors, as well as among moral crusaders of various ilks (Becker, 1963; Klapp, 1969).

49. For some valuable ethnographic work on the military, see Zurcher's (1965) study of sailors aboard ship, Cockerham's (1979) work on heroic symbolism among the Green Berets of the U.S. Army, Ingraham's (1984) account of "the boys in the barracks," Charleton and Hertz's (1989) account of security specialists in the U.S. Air Force, and Faulkner and McGaw's (1977) study of the reentry transition of Vietnam veterans. Instances of ethnographic research on parallel (career contingency) processes in other contexts can be found in the sources cited in Prus (1996b, 1997b).

50. This discussion of control agencies builds on material developed in Prus (1997b:140–146).

51. For a greater sense of the range of control agencies that may be found in our own society, see Prus (1997b:161, fn 64).

52. Compared to many other realms of human endeavor, a considerable amount of ethnographic work has focused on control agencies (see Prus, 1997b: especially 162, fn 66, for some pertinent sources).

53. Schmid and Jones (1991, 1993) provide valuable insights into the incarceration experience, while Fishman (1990) offers an account of the experiences of prisoners' wives. For some other depictions of people's circumstances as they undergo treatment and experience posttreatment adjustment, see Goffman (1961, 1963), Peyrot (1985), and Herman (1993). For other materials on target roles, see chapter 8.

54. As indicated in Brown (1931), Ray (1961), Wiseman (1970), and Lesieur (1977), abstinence and relapse cycles are common experiences on the part of those undergoing treatment programs.

8 Experiencing Target Roles
(with Lorraine Prus)

> [T]o "victimize" someone instructs others to understand the person as a rather passive, indeed helpless, recipient of injury or injustice. While this can be situationally useful . . . "victimizing" a person "dis-ables" that person to the extent that victim status appropriates one's personal identity as a competent efficacious actor.
>
> —Holstein and Miller, 1990:119

While depicting a great many of the reflective, enterprising, and inter-active features of the "power phenomenon," chapters 6 and 7 focus much more on tactician activities than those of the targets (individuals, small groups, nations, etc.) that tacticians are purportedly trying to influence. This emphasis is clearly consistent with the larger literature on power, but target roles have been vastly understated and understudied. That is, despite frequent claims to recognize (and, sometimes, dramatize) target concerns, social scientists typically have envisioned targets of influence work as relatively passive, helpless pawns; as people seemingly caught up (often as "victims") in various power structures.[1] In contrast, this chapter draws attention to the wide variety of roles that "targets" may assume in human inter-change and suggests themes for future research that acknowledge this diversity.

Some appreciation of these multifaceted aspects of target roles can be gleaned in the ethnographic literature,[2] but the neglect of target *activities* represents a serious flaw in the works of most scholars who have discussed power. In part, this omission may reflect the enduring tendency on the part of social scientists to rely on structuralist explanations of power rather than examining power as intersubjective accomplishment.

Assuming Target Roles

Generally speaking, targets tend to be defined by virtue of some agent (i.e., as a tactician) acting on them. However, it should be emphasized that *one is not a target in a more complete sense until one takes on the role of the target.* This

should be elaborated
more detail in fairly ch 14

means defining oneself as a recipient of some activity on the part of another and acting mindfully of that definition. This is not to deny tactician intentions and practices, but rather to (a) direct attention to the centrality of [target] interpretations of the situation at hand and (b) recognize that those defining themselves as "targets" (or nontargets) need not share viewpoints with alleged tacticians in arriving at definitions of their situations. Some other qualifications are in order, as well.

Although particular targets or tacticians may define their roles in more singular target or tactician terms and act more exclusively in these manners, it is essential that analysts be attentive to both the interchangeability and multiplicity of the target and tactician roles that people may assume in any context. First, even in more isolated, dyadic settings, both parties to an interaction sequence may assume tactician *and* target roles. This is not to claim equality or even mutuality of focus within or across interactional contexts. Indeed, a great many encounters may be highly skewed interactionally, with people assuming (or not assuming) stances as targets and/or tacticians. However, the interactants may engage both of these roles sequentially, or more or less concurrently, as their interchanges take place.

When more people are involved in the setting, any two interactants may not only assume roles as targets and tacticians with respect to one another, but they may also find themselves involved in a plurality of relationships with others. As a result, they may experience multiple roles as (both) targets and tacticians with respect to one another and the other parties in the setting.[3] Because of the ways in which people's involvements and activities spill over into particular interactional contexts, it is essential for analysts to recognize people's potential for invoking (and assuming) a multiplicity of target and tactician roles in any setting.[4]

It is also instructive for analysts to distinguish specific from more generalized targets. Whereas some influence work may be focused on highly particularized individuals (as in instances of "eye-to-eye, belly-to-belly selling" or children attempting to "work on" one or both parents), other attempts to shape target experiences may be more diffusely directed (as in media promotions or in classroom lectures). While people may be subjected to highly intense levels of influence work in one or both regards, analysts would find it instructive to attend to the differing levels of attention and accountability experienced by the people who as targets encounter (define and deal with) persuasive endeavors along these lines.

Likewise, although people may be the subject of much undesired influence work on the part of others, analysts should not assume that all "influence work" is undesired. Indeed, where others are seen as engaged in interesting or worthwhile endeavors, people [targets] may seek out their company, advice, or other influences, perhaps desiring very much to become more like, or influenced by, these [tacticians]. People may also re-define the desirability of particular influence endeavors on the part of others over time, such that undesired influences might later be viewed in positive terms, and vice versa.

Defining Self as Subject to Influence

Although many instances of influence may seem obvious to outside ob-servers, it is essential to recognize that *the participants* may envision situations in a wide variety of ways and that only some of these definitions may imply notions of influence, direction, or control. Indeed, people may very un-evenly define particular situations as "instances of influence work" (or themselves as targets) as they orient and reorient themselves to assortments of here and now activities (and interchanges).

Further, even though people's situations may seem relatively constant to outside observers, the participants may pursue, disregard, or resurrect any variety of interests (and disaffections) both as they engage situations in more immediate senses and in later considerations of their experiences therein. Participants may pursue or play out certain interests in more direct, obvious ways, but they need not act on all of their concerns, including some that they may consider to be very important. Thus, analysts would find it instructive to attend to the ways in which people:

Define the Broader Situations at Hand
Define the Roles (viewpoints, practices, interests) of the People in the Setting under Consideration
Define "Influence Work" (as a relevant concept) in the Setting[5]
    Identify tacticians (including self) / Identify targets (including self)
    Encounter definitions of influence work from others
Invoke and Act on Notions of Influence
    Monitor and define the activities of others
    Embark on, monitor, and adjust one's activities
Revise Earlier Definitions of the Situation (including self roles)

While the preceding notions could be applied to both targets and tacticians, the materials following focus more centrally on the ways in which people (including those who identify themselves primarily as tacticians) envision the *target* component of *their* roles.[6] It is here that we attend to *all* partici-pants' considerations of receptive, vulnerable, restrained, and elusive selves.

Acknowledging the Receptive Self

As used herein, the notion of a receptive self refers to those situations in which people envision themselves as willing or ready to take cues from others in the setting. While some indication, suggestion, inducement, command, or other encouragement from the other (or inference thereof) is the typical precondition for defining the situation in more mutual or interactive terms, people also may invoke receptive selves when they act in ways that they anticipate the other might appreciate. The notion of a receptive (target) self, thus, acknowledges a generalized readiness (and sometimes acute desires) to act mindfully of others' inclinations.[7]

Beyond (a) people's senses of affection toward, fascination with, or closeness to, particular others, we should be attentive to people's (b) interests in (or fascinations with) things that specific others may be seen to offer, and (c) concerns about obtaining help from others in dealing with dilemmas or problems. Still, even when targets experience inclinations to "go along with the other," they may find that they are not able to overcome the reservations or other obstacles (e.g., resources, skills, acceptability) they associate with particular activities or outcomes. Thus, the following themes seem pertinent to people envisioning themselves as more willing to comply with [tacticians]:

Experiencing attraction(s) toward the [Tactician]
Having Interests in [Tactician] Situations or Suggestions
Envisioning [Tactician] Situations or Suggestions as Resolving Difficulties
Feeling Less Restrained about [Tactician] Situations or Suggestions

Experiencing the Vulnerable Self

In contrast to images of a receptive self or someone who more willingly attends to the desires or interests of the other, the focus here is on those instances in which targets feel obliged to acknowledge tactician suggestions (requests, directions, commands, or inferences thereof) because of self (target) defined dependencies or limitations.

None of the following points guarantee compliance, and targets may actively resist tacticians despite acute senses of vulnerability in some cases. Nevertheless, these are matters to which targets may attend in defining the situations in which they find themselves:

Acknowledging Dependencies on the Tactician Other[8]
   Defining oneself as dependent on things controlled by the tactician
   Valuing long-term relations with the tactician
   Encountering third-party encouragement to comply with the tactician
Attending to Target (self) Limitations in the Setting
   Envisioning the tactician as strategically (i.e., resources, skills) advantaged
   Defining the tactician as more persistent, relentless

Envisioning the tactician as less constrained (e.g., desperate, ruthless)
Lacking alternatives to the tactician
Defining resistance as riskier or costlier
Viewing resistance as futile (e.g., ineffectual, defenseless)

Developing a Restrained Self

Regardless of whether people may be tempted to pursue activities that tacticians encourage or experience senses of vulnerability, they may also engage tacticians in ways that they anticipate will be more limited or constrained in nature. [Targets] may knowingly put themselves in contact with those they envision as very competent tacticians, but, in doing so, they typically hope that they will be able to limit the scope (and consequences) of these involvements. Relatedly, when people expect that they will be able to exercise some control over the ensuing interchanges, they may eagerly seek out (e.g., as entertainment, thrills, challenges, tests, learning experiences) encounters with tacticians that they might consider quite formidable in other terms.

Denoting anticipatory postures of sorts, there are at least three major ways in which people minimize risks in encounters with others. The first denotes an assessment that one is somehow immune or invulnerable to the influence work of others. A second viewpoint is contingent on some predefined limits that one plans to invoke in the setting. The third form reflects a preplanned openness, an anticipation that one will engage the other but will do so in ways that maintain viable "routes of escape."

Defining Self as Resilient to Tactician Inputs
Envisioning self as more impervious to the tactics of others
Viewing self as more confident (wiser, more capable than the tactician)
Adopting a skeptical (distrusting) orientation toward the tactician
Considering the other to be relatively inconsequential, ineffectual
Feeling less incentive to cooperate with the tactician
Imposing Limitations (prior to encountering tacticians)
Predetermining one's own interests in anticipated encounters
Preestablishing maximal commitment levels
Planning to Maintain Openness Beyond Tactician Encounters
Entertaining alternative lines of action or options outside of the setting
Postponing or avoiding commitments in the setting

In addition to examining the orientations (e.g., receptive, vulnerable, restrained) with which people might envision themselves, research along these lines may also consider the ways in which those targets adjust their definitions of self over time as they encounter, engage, and possibly reengage particular tacticians.

Deploying the Elusive Self

Although perhaps most readily associated with a sense of vulnerability, people more generally encountering undesired attention from others may invoke an assortment of evasive postures or defensive maneuverings in attempts to avoid complying with tacticians.[9] People may develop more characteristic modes of averting influence work on the part of others, but they need not consider particular strategies at the most opportune times. Likewise, targets may be unwilling to implement particular tactics for a variety of reasons (e.g., concerns about self-images or impressions that they might convey to others).[10] We may expect considerable variation in the tactics that targets invoke in practice, but by examining instances of target-tactician exchange along the following lines, researchers may be better able to dialogue with the "essences of elusiveness" in a more comparative-informed sense:

Invoking Distance
   Disclaiming seriousness regarding subsequent involvements
   Being more abrupt with tacticians
   Minimizing information provided to tacticians
Expressing Limitations and Contingencies that Deter Subsequent Involvements
   Indicating uncertainty (i.e., "the necessity" of thinking things over)
   Finding fault with (aspects of) the situation
   Expressing personal (target-self) limitations (problems, shortcomings)
   Implying options outside the immediate situation
   Drawing attention to external (third-party) accountability
   Stipulating parameters (or terms) of influence
Negotiating (and Renegotiating) Positions with Tacticians
Disengaging from (or avoiding) Situations Involving Tacticians

Invoking the Tactician Self

Although the discussion to this point has acknowledged some tactical or strategic features of target roles, the following subthemes depict a more explicit set of "role reversals" with respect to target-tactician encounters. Whether people (a) assume initiative in encounters with tacticians or (b) act back on tacticians (on either a solitary or collective basis), the focus is on those [targets] who deliberately engage [tacticians] as they (targets) pursue influence work of their own.

    Since these target activities *entail tactician roles*, it is most instructive to return to the earlier material in chapters 6 and 7 for a fuller consideration of the forms and limitations that these ventures may assume. At the same time, however, so long as people envision themselves to be, or are envisioned by others as, "targets," it is important to consider the ways that they bring target-related identities into play around interchanges with those viewed as tacticians. The following material draws attention to three, somewhat interrelated, features of tactical target roles, namely: (a) initiating activity, (b) resisting tacticians, and (c) invoking target-status.

Initiating Activity toward [Tacticians]

There is no reason that people who are cast into target roles (by others or themselves) may not embark on activities that they intend to affect those who are defined as tacticians in the same equation. People may use existing "target" identities as "screens" for implementing behaviors that effectively reverse the roles into which they seemingly have been cast, but many of these ventures will reflect relatively straightforward attempts on the part of those defined as targets to gain desired outcomes that involve particular [tacticians]. As with other tacticians, these targets may assume a wide variety of stances (e.g., reflecting fascinations and benign intentions to disaffections and malicious intentions) relative to [tacticians]. Similarly, these "targets" may entertain multiple and possibly shifting objectives vis-à-vis others over some time frame. Among the objectives that targets may initiate with respect to [tacticians], the following themes seem especially noteworthy:

Seeking Attention (or acknowledgement) from [Tacticians]
Pursuing Involvements in [Tactician] Activities or Situations
Involving [Tacticians] in Target Ventures
Encouraging [Tacticians] to Engage in Outside Activities
Pursuing Concessions from [Tacticians]
Altering [Tactician] Activities or Experiences (for any reason)
Achieving (and Maintaining) Autonomy from [Tacticians]

In addition to attending to the variable objectives that targets may pursue in dealing with tacticians, each of these subthemes suggests realms of study that hinge on the ways in which those cast into target roles may initiate or direct influence work toward those thought to be esteemed, advantaged, in control, or to occupy superordinate statuses of some sort.

Resisting Tacticians

In contrast to [target] initiatives, the emphasis here is on those instances in which people engage in activities that they define more directly as "reactions against" the earlier activities of tacticians. Typically, then, these behaviors are intended to oppose, challenge, or disrupt tactician agendas and enterprises.

While people may invoke a variety of motivational themes (e.g., in-group values, personal integrity, impending losses) in resisting tacticians, it should be appreciated that motivational motifs are best studied in reflective and interactive terms. This means examining (a) the ways that people (individually and collectively) develop these viewpoints and (b) how these are invoked (also resisted, and adjusted) in practice. Still, like targets who initiate activity toward [tacticians], those acting back on tacticians effectively assume tactician roles of the sort referenced in chapter 6 and 7.

Whether they act on a more solitary basis or in conjunction with others, targets (as *initiators* or *resistors*) may engage in enhancing tactics, focusing procedures, neutralizing and debasing strategies, leveraging tactics, and autonomizing tactics; and they, too, may exercise persistence and experience tactical openness. Similarly, targets may *extend the theater of operations* by working with third parties, developing collective ventures, establishing policy, pursuing positional control, using the media, and developing political agendas (including governmental forums, military agendas, and control agencies).

This is not to imply that tacticians and targets are to be viewed as synonymous entities for all purposes. Notably, specific self and other definitions of people (as "targets" or "tacticians") may have important implications for the ways in which (and effectiveness with which) the people involved work out their particular tactical exchanges.

Claiming Target Status

In addition to other ways that they may engage tacticians, some people may consider it beneficial to more explicitly identify (or let themselves be identified) variously as subordinated, disadvantaged, wronged, or victimized.11 Only some [targets] may attempt to invoke identities of these sorts and not all that endeavor to do so will be successful either in being acknowledged in these terms by others or experiencing clear benefits for adopting postures of this type.

Whether people seek or are assigned "target status" on a solitary or a broader, collective basis, they may use target status in attempts to (1) benefit from encounters with tacticians, (2) appeal to outsiders for assistance, and (3) foster the pursuit of internally defined group agendas. Somewhat more specifically, researchers may find it instructive to examine the ways in which people engage in processes of the following sort:

*Using "Target Identity" for Advantage in Interchanges with [Tacticians]*12
  Emphasizing dependency / Requesting desired objects
  Assuming liberties / Denying accountability
  Proclaiming helplessness / Justifying incompetence

Appealing to Outsiders (for sympathy, support, defense)
  Presenting self as innocent, vulnerable, suffering
  Claiming (and dramatizing) mistreatment by [tactician]
  Emphasizing relative disadvantages [to tactician]
  Discrediting [the tactician] more generally (i.e., in other ways)
Encouraging Tactically Focused Activity Within the Target Collectivity
  Emphasizing mutuality of suffering (victim status) of the collectivity
  Condemning [the tactician] for the problems of the collectivity
  Stressing the imminent danger of [the tactician] to the collectivity
  Promoting an alternative vision (perspective, morality) for the collectivity
  Generating an alternative leadership to represent the collectivity
  Presenting an alternative agenda for the collectivity
  Focusing on individual member responsibility for the collectivity
  Emphasizing the protective and uplifting potential of the collectivity
  Celebrating accomplishments associated with the collectivity
  Providing occasions for collective assemblies and activities
Discouraging Opposition from Within the Target Collectivity[13]
  Dismissing resistors as incompetent or ill-informed
  Denigrating resistors as violating the morality of the collectivity
  Discrediting resistors as disloyal to the collectivity
  Stressing the threat of internal resistance to the collectivity

Assuming Competitive Stances

Although there will be situations in which people (a) do not define others who pursue identical, mutually exclusive objectives as competitors, or (b) are unaware that others may be pursuing the very same (exclusive) objectives, once people begin to define others in competitive (adversarial or contestlike) manners, they may embark on a series of practices that are intended to protect themselves from, or advantage themselves relative to, these others.[14] Competitors may define themselves primarily as targets or tacticians vis-à-vis others or as both targets and tacticians in their quest for some object, but the notion of a competitive self provides another vantage point from which to more fully consider target roles.

In addition to those that they envision as (a) *competitors,* people may also be concerned about (b) *allies* (partners, supporters, facilitators) of particular competitors and (c) *judges* (also selectors, referees, or controllers) who may affect the outcomes experienced by the competitors. In some cases, too, competitors may direct more attention to these third parties than they do toward other competitors or the particular objectives they had intended to pursue.

While only some interchanges that people have with [competitive others] involve third parties, the following material has been developed in ways that allow for the possibility of these more complex associations. Thus, we begin with the matters of people defining competitors and adopting adversarial stances toward these individuals or groups. The next topic, dealing with third parties, recognizes particular competitors' inclinations to form alliances as well as monitor their competitors' tendencies in these regards. It also acknowledges the assortment of roles that competitors and judges may develop in reference to one another. Those assuming third-party roles as allies or adjudicators may play very active roles in the ensuing interchanges, possibly fostering levels of desire, intensity, or adversity that would not have existed otherwise. Finally, whereas competitors are often defined in polarized or mutually exclusive terms, the last set of processes draw attention to some further complexities of [power] relations that characterize the actualities of human lived experience. Viewed thusly, the following themes suggest some lines of inquiry that should enable analysts to develop more viable conceptual appreciations of competitive interchanges (in the making) across wide ranges of substantive contexts, including sports, military, trade, academic, political, religious, entertainment, and family arenas, for instance.

Defining Others as Competitors
   Noticing limitations or setbacks associated with [competitive others][15]
   Encountering challenges, claims, or comparisons from [competitive others]
   Experiencing comparisons or preferences initiated by third parties
   Assessing self with respect to [competitive others]
Developing Adversarial Stances Toward [Competitive Others]
   Monitoring [competitive others]
   Distancing oneself from [competitive others]
   Seeking advantages over [competitive others]
   Encountering distancing or disruptions attributed to [competitive others]
   Acknowledging vulnerability (and timidity) because of [competitive others]
   Experiencing closure (urgency, desperation) because of [competitive others]
   Engaging [competitive others] in direct contests
      Invoking tactical actions against [competitive others]
      Experiencing tactical actions attributed to [competitive others]
Dealing with Third Parties
   Forming alliances with third parties (to advantage self vs. competitors)
      Considering/Pursuing/Implementing third-party alliances

Managing/Sustaining/Disengaging from third-party alliances
Monitoring third-party alliances with [competitive others]
Anticipating/Discouraging third-party alliances with [competitive others]
Encountering and adjusting to third-party alliances with [competitive others]
Attempting to disrupt existing third-party relations with [competitive others]
Envisioning and attending to third-party judges
Defining adjudicator concerns (interests, preferences, vulnerabilities)
"Pitching" performances (and self) to judges
Endeavoring to discredit [competitive others] relative to judges
Acknowledging Benefits of [Competitive Others] in the Setting
Appreciating adjudicator distractions because of [competitive others]
Benefiting from adjudicator comparisons with [competitive others]
Minimizing personal losses because of losses by [competitive others]
Letting [competitive others] test risky situations
Learning from [competitive others]
Cooperating with [competitive others] to deal with outside threats, targets
Developing affective bonds with [competitive others]

Participating in Collective Events[16]

While the preceding discussion of competitive roles suggests some ways in which targets, tacticians, and third parties may engage one another in practice, as to some extent does the material more broadly presented in chapters 6–8, it is hoped that the following consideration of collective events may provide another instructive vantage point from which to examine target-tactician interchanges.

By drawing attention to the processual features of people's encounters with others, in the more situated or enacted instances in which they occur, collective events enable scholars to consider the senses of clarity and purpose as well as the ambiguity and confusion that people may experience as they encounter, make sense of, participate in, coordinate, resist, and subsequently assess interchanges with others.

Only some collective events may be appropriately cast in power terms (i.e., are so defined by the participants) and even fewer of these events have an explicit political or governing thrust. Still, an appreciation of collective events is fundamental to a fuller consideration of power as a matter of practical accomplishment. Instead of attempting to account for the outcomes of human exchanges by virtue of (vague) structures, historical forces, and the like, it is much more productive to examine the ways that particular human interchanges are worked out (cooperation, resistance, competition) by the people involved.

At the same time, because collective events denote settings in which people may work out a variety of interests with others, any episode may readily become the site of multiple [power] considerations, possibly to the extent that other matters of influence (and resistance) overshadow the original or presumed main theme for the collective occasion.

Many collective events revolve around relatively routine occurrences, such as family meals, encounters with service specialists, or adolescents "hanging around" after school. Other instances of collective events are implied by terms such as festive occasions, confrontational episodes, contests, honorific ceremonies, public presentations and performances, assemblies, recruitment and other influence ventures, and responses to emergency situations. Although the preceding categories may suggest more specific research sites for the study of collective events, the emphasis, here, is on the ways in which people experience collective events in a more basic or transcontextual sense. Whereas people often expect that these events will proceed in a more manageable, if not predictable, manner, it is essential that analysts attend to the problematic, emergent, enacted nature of all of these episodes.

Some of these events (both more routine and more exceptional) may be highly planned and extensively coordinated throughout the duration of the event, as people attempt to assemble, script, and engage others in detailed precision. In some other cases, the basic themes may be fairly well defined at the outset, but subsequent interactions may be only vaguely planned. In still other instances, people may find themselves in settings in which they may have great difficulty just comprehending and articulating any dominant themes.

Collective events are often intended to have centralized themes, but larger or more enduring focal events are often embedded with subsets of collective events. Sometimes, these subevents are incorporated by design. For instance, many present-day national or regional competitions may include media sessions, precontest receptions, and award ceremonies. Notably each of these subevents may encompass a variety of subthemes as well. Likewise, military or political campaigns typically include vast arrays of planned collective subevents, many of which (e.g., recruitment, honorific ceremonies, fund raising) take place some distance from sites of confrontation with adversaries and may involve entirely different sets of people.

In these and other instances of collective behavior, we could also attend to any variety of subevents that may develop as the participants in particular settings pursue other (than the intended main event) agendas, become embroiled in disputes, encounter disasters, and the like. On some occasions, as well, these [other events] may significantly distract from, compete with, or effectively destroy what formerly was intended as the focal event.

Beyond (1) the potentially shifting parameters of collective events and (2) "the trans-emergence" of interconnected or embedded subevents within the focal event, scholars also would find it productive to attend to (3) the unevenness of people's involvements therein. Not only may the "participants" be (a) differentially aware of specific (major and secondary events), but they may (b) enter situations with wide assortments of interests, (c) adopt a variety of (more central and more peripheral) roles as collective events take place, and (d) become more and less caught up in the central spirit of the occasion as events transpire. Relatedly, they may (e) encounter, develop, or pursue all manners of (secondary) agendas as they interact with others in the setting.

Likewise, it is important that analysts centrally appreciate (4) the human enterprise (and ambiguity) entailed in matters of promoting (defining, assembling, coordinating, maintaining enthusiasm) collective events as well as people's manners of opposing, concluding, and assessing (primary and secondary) collective events. The following listings draw attention to notions of this sort (and some of the options they entail), but sustained, ethnographic examinations of particular collective events are essential if social scientists are to arrive at more adequate (i.e., substantiated, qualified) understandings of these aspects of community life.[17]

Becoming Aware of, and Involved in, Collective Events
    Finding oneself in the midst of collective events begun by others
    Being recruited by others who are initiating or encouraging collective events
    Seeking out collective events begun by others
    Initiating events intended to involve others in the community
Coordinating and Sustaining Collective Events[18]
    Developing (and articulating) a sense of purpose or mission
    Promoting the collective event to others[19]
    Generating agendas (plans of action) for collective events
    Developing (and encouraging) associations to support particular events[20]
    Accessing funding and other supplies for collective events
    Encountering isolated, widespread, and coordinated resistances
Making Sense of Collective Events[21]
    Defining events as (essentially) familiar or novel forms
    Obtaining definitions of events from others
    Sharing (and comparing) definitions with others
    Dealing with multiple (diverse) themes or definitions of the situation

Watching events take place over time
Making inferences about other participants (presence, activities, objectives)[22]
Engaging the situation at hand
Attending to the reactions of others to self
Becoming Caught Up in Collective Events
Attending to the enthusiasm of others
Encountering encouragement from others to participate
Anticipating and experiencing intriguing (fascinating) aspects of the situation
Feeling a sense of obligation to participate in the event
Encouraging (successfully) others to participate in the event
Feeling freed up from external restraints (or prohibitions)
Developing affective bonds with enthusiastic participants
Making commitments (personal and public) to the event at hand
Assuming More Central Roles in Collective Events
Assuming greater initiative or responsibility
Being assigned positions of prominence
Being acknowledged for commitments and accomplishments
Withdrawing Participation from Collective Events
Experiencing reservations about participating in the central event
Being distracted from central events by others in the setting
Being disregarded, discredited, or rejected by participants
Being distracted from collective events by outsider associates and obligations
Finding ways (and opportunitites) to minimize participation
Resisting Collective Events (also Particular Themes, Activities, and Others)
Putting limits on the scope of one's own involvement
Resisting collective events on a solitary basis/with others
Concluding Collective Events
Being informed of event endings by others
Announcing conclusions to events
Facing funding and other operational limitations
Becoming weary (e.g., bored, fatigued)
Witnessing gradual dispersal (e.g., waning interest) of participants
Encountering resistance or competition from external sources
Reviewing, Redefining, and Readjusting to (Particular) Collective Events
Dismissing or disattending to (the aftermath of) collective events
Reassessing collective events, alone and with others
Experiencing controversy regarding collective events
Attending to matters of accountability and culpability
Making adjustments following collective events
Attempting to resurrect (revise) collective events

Trying to neutralize (earlier) collective events for others

Given both the vast array of activities that collective events may entail and the large and often geographically dispersed sets of people who may participate in some of these episodes, the study of collective events can be most challenging.

It appears impossible to study large-scale events in their entirety, even with fairly extensive teams of researchers. However, small teams, or researchers working alone, may still contribute significantly to our understandings of aspects of these processes when they engage (some of) the participants in careful, extended ethnographic inquiry. Likewise, by putting the emphasis on *social process* rather than trying to account for the entirety of any particular large-scale event,[23] we may arrive at much more viable analytical appreciations of collective events as researchers accumulate, compare, and assess materials gathered on a wide assortment of human enterprise (and interchange) mindful of generic subprocesses of the sort suggested here.

Also, by looking past the aura or mystique that is often associated with large-scale events, researchers may be able to locate endless instances of smaller (but processually parallel) collective events. Because the latter are more manageable, ethnographically, these microcosms may afford more comprehensive empirical appreciations of basic social processes. By examining, in extended ethnographic detail, the ways in which people engage larger and smaller collective events, researchers will be better able to comprehend the vast assortment of target and tactician roles that these interchanges entail. They will also develop a more substantial base for appreciating the ways in which all sorts of collective events (and the subevents they encompass) develop, are sustained, dissipate, and become reconstituted within community contexts.

In Perspective

Albeit focused more directly on target roles, this chapter contributes to a dynamic, adjustive view of [power] in the making. While acknowledging the more obvious recipiency quality of target roles, this statement centrally attends to the interpretive and enacted essences of human interchange. Addressing a multiplicity of viewpoints that [targets] may assume, the material presented here recognizes [target] abilities to invoke a variety of *recipient* and *tactical* orientations. Beyond self-definitions of target vulnerability, attention is also given to notions of receptive, restrained, and elusive target selves as well as more overt tactician (target) selves (whereby, on a solitary and collective basis, targets may initiate activity with respect to alleged tacticians and resist tacticians who try to influence them).

This chapter also extends target and tactician roles by locating these within the context of competitive stances and emergent collective events. Given the sparsity of ethnographic research on people's roles as targets, the social processes outlined here suggest a series of reference points for those interested in studying the ways in which people experience and engage influence work. By making explicit vital aspects of target roles that have been taken for granted or ignored in most discussions of human interchange, chapter 8 more completely establishes the foundations for a much needed reconceptualization of power, a framework that attends centrally to [power] as an *enacted* feature of community life.

Notes

1. As Holstein and Miller (1990) indicate, those who have developed the "victimization" literature with its emphasis on the conditions, consequences, and correlates of victimization have done little to recognize the socially (reflective, enterprising, interactive, processual) constituted nature of human interchange (and victimization as an intersubjective essence more specifically).

2. The notion of targets assuming *active* roles in their encounters with tacticians seems appropriate across a wide range of substantive sectors. See, for instance, Blumer's (1933) and Blumer and Hauser's (1933) studies of adolescent encounters with movies; Lofland's (1966) work on the recruitment experiences of people involved in a religious cult; Davis's (1961), Goffman's (1963), and Edgerton's (1967) depictions of people's encounters with stigma; Roth's (1962) portrayal of bargaining on the part of tuberculosis patients; Emerson's (1969) depiction of juvenile probation agencies; Wiseman's (1970) examination of client and staff encounters in skid-row agencies; Prus's (1989b) considerations of vendors dealing with their suppliers; Sanders's(1989) portrayal of people's involvements with tattoos; Prus and Frisby's (1990) account of the multiple (differing) targets in home party plans; Prus and Dawson's (1991) and Prus's (1993a, 1993b, 1994a, 1997a) work on consumer behavior; Wolf's (1991) study of outlaw bikers; Dietz and Cooper's (1994) study of "blue chip" athletes; and Grills's (1994) examination of the recruitment practices of political parties.

3. As noted specifically in Prus (1989b: 316–321), although retailers are ordinarily considered the tacticians (with respect to consumers) in the marketplace, they too are subject to a variety of target roles, including influence work from stockholders, staff, property managers (e.g., malls), government officials, suppliers, competitors, advertising agents, and consumers. Similarly, all of the people involved in "home party plans" (Prus and Frisby, 1990) as dealers, hostesses, and guests may be seen as both targets

and tacticians in their dealings with one another. Perhaps, this plurality of target and tactician roles is even more evident in a study of "the hotel community" (Prus and Irini, 1980), wherein hookers, dancers, bar staff, and patrons engage one another in a variety of ways, on a more or less concurrent basis.

4. For some indications of the multiple (and shifting) tactician and target roles that people may engage in the course of pursuing actual performances, see ethnographic research on factory workers (Bensman and Gerver, 1963), ballet dancers (Dietz, 1994), hustlers (Prus and Sharper, 1977), hookers, strippers, and bar staff (Prus and Irini, 1980), business people (Prus, 1989a, 1989b; Prus and Frisby, 1990; Prus and Fleras, 1996), police officers (Bittner, 1967; Meehan, 1992), bikers (D. Wolf, 1991), engineers (Kunda, 1992), politicians (Grills, 1994), medical students (Haas and Shaffir, 1987), and musicians (Becker, 1963; MacLeod, 1993). Indeed, many roles that people assume imply that they will invoke and experience an assortment of tactical procedures as these people shift (and juggle) a plurality of tactician and target roles.

5. It is worth noting that both targets and tacticians may be recipients of [objects], may do things for others, may exhibit compliance, may engage in behaviors they dislike, and may be subject to criticism. Since matters of these sorts are inadequate for distinguishing targets from tacticians in themselves, concern should be directed to the ways in which (and perspectives from which) those participating in particular settings apply these and related notions to others and themselves in defining the directions of any influence work they envision as occurring within those contexts.

6. Some people may not envision themselves as targets in any sense, but this formulation allows participants to make that definition rather than have analysts "usurp agency" by presuming participant (self-identified tacticians included) definitions.

7. Elsewhere (e.g., Prus, 1996b, 1997b), the term "seekership" has been used to refer to people's interests or fascinations in pursuing certain situations, experiences, or objects. For some ethnographic work that more explicitly illustrates seekership, see Lofland (1966), Lesieur (1977), Prus and Irini (1980), Prus and Sharper (1991), and Prus and Dawson (1991).

8. The materials in this section address variants of "closure," wherein people experience senses of obligation and urgency to act in ways that they might otherwise consider inappropriate. Other explicit discussions of closure can be found in Lemert (1953), Prus and Sharper (1977), Prus and Irini (1980), and Prus (1989a, 1989b), but this notion seems relevant to a great many cases of reluctant involvement.

9. For a more detailed ethnographic consideration of "elusive targets," see Prus's (1994a; 1997a) examination of consumer behavior. Although shoppers are often faced with the prospects of developing lines of

action under less than ideal circumstances (e.g., time constraints, ambiguities of product use, stock limitations, potentially misleading vendor claims), shoppers are much more creative, resourceful, and tactically oriented than seems commonly supposed in the literature.

10. Tacticians encountering particular evasions also are limited by their thoughtfulness and reservations. Still, like targets learning to be more evasive as a consequence of their earlier experiences with tacticians, tacticians who have encountered earlier instances of evasiveness by different or the same targets may develop a repertoire of responses designed to offset some of these practices. The tactical adjustments of hookers, entertainers, and bar staff (Prus and Irini, 1980), salespeople (Prus, 1989a, 1989b), hustlers and magicians (Prus and Sharper, 1991), and college athlete recruiters (Dietz and Cooper, 1994) are noteworthy here.

11. Among other sources, this discussion of invoking target-status has benefited considerably from Cressey's (1932) portrayal of taxi-dance halls, Karsh et al.'s (1953) study of union organizers, Klapp's (1962, 1964, 1971) work on "heroes, villains, and fools," Lemert's (1962) account of "paranoid" relationships, Goffman's (1963) rendering of stigma, Couch's (1989) statement on charismatic leaders, Klapp's (1969) consideration of crusades, Holstein and Miller's (1990) analysis of victimization, D. Wolf's (1991) portrayal of outlaw bikers, and C. Wolf's (1994) account of women's involvements in feminism. Also see Aristotle's *Rhetoric* and *De Rhetorica Ad Alexandrum*. In contrast to those who concentrate on elaborating on the structural conditions or consequences of "victimization," these authors centrally address the interactionally constituted (and problematic) nature of challenged (and disadvantaged) identities.

12. Although those invoking target identities are dependent on confirmations of these notions on the part of tacticians, more explicit identity claims may allow "targets" to assume greater liberties and achieve more privileges than might otherwise be the case.

13. Internal resistance may take a wide variety of emphases and forms, introducing any manner of analytical focal points. While some concerns may revolve around the identification of outsider [tacticians] and the articulation of appropriate lines of action to be directed toward those [tacticians], other matters may reflect concerns with existing policies and procedures, internal leadership, the coordination of groups and the timing of activities, and the like. Benford's (1993a) consideration of the internal dynamics of the peace movement is pertinent here. No less centrally, analysts would likely find it most productive to consider instances of resistance within target collectivities as denoting still other arenas of influence work, with other sets of (insider) target and tactician roles (identities and aligning practices) being invoked therein.

14. This statement on the competitive self has benefited considerably

from Cressey's (1932) examination of taxi-dance halls, Scott's (1981) study of women's basketball players and coaches, Haas and Shaffir's (1987) work on medical students, Smith's (1989) study of auctions, Wolf's (1991) portrayal of outlaw biker clubs, Kunda's (1992) consideration of an engineering subculture, MacLeod's (1993) study of musicians, Dietz's (1994) consideration of ballet, Dietz and Cooper's (1994) examination of the recruitment of "blue chip" athletes, Grills's (1994) statement on the recruitment practices of political parties, and Snyder's (1994) depiction of shuffling among senior citizens. It also is informed by some ethnographic research conducted on the recruitment practices of clergy (Prus, 1976), the practices of card and dice hustlers (Prus and Sharper, 1977), the activities of those engaged in the hotel community (Prus and Irini, 1980), the work of those involved in marketing and sales (Prus, 1989a, 1989b; Prus and Frisby, 1990), and the recruitment practices of economic developers (Prus and Fleras, 1996).

15. The term [competitive others] has been bracketed to emphasize the problematic nature of this status. Clearly, people need not achieve mutuality in reference to the levels of intensity with which they pursue competition or the specific realms of competition that one or other parties might envision. Further, some people may not see themselves engaged in any sort of competition with particular others although these others may be quite definite about the competitive frame that they have invoked. Likewise, while some people may pursue competitive stances toward specific others, these [target] others may endeavor to discourage framings of this sort. Finally, whereas people may compete with others in certain regards (even on a mutually acknowledged basis), these same parties may have no interest in competing with one another in other arenas (and may readily form alliances of sorts in other realms of endeavor).

16. This statement has been adapted from Prus (1997b). Accordingly, some of the points discussed here receive further elaboration in that statement.

17. Although it has been necessary to represent collective events in more prototypic forms for conceptual purposes, ethnographers in the field will encounter (and should carefully attend to) *the collective events that emerge or are embedded within larger collective events*. While many of these embedded events will be implemented because of, and take orientational shape from, more encompassing collective events, these subevents can both contribute to, as well as detract from (and, in some cases, effectively replace) earlier, more central events.

18. For some ethnographic depictions of the extensive background work involved in producing collective events, see Karsh et al.'s (1953) account of union organizers; Prus's (1989a, 1989b), Sanders's (1989), Prus and Frisby's (1990), and Prus and Fleras' (1996) portrayals of marketing and

sales ventures; D. Wolf's (1991) consideration of outlaw bikers going on a "run;" Kunda's (1992) study of an engineering subculture; MacLeod's (1993) depiction of music bands and their performances; and Grills's (1994) account of political recruitment.

19. Influence work represents a vital feature of "coordinating and sustaining collective events" at almost all stages (see chapters 6 and 7).

20. The matter of "forming and coordinating (subcultural) associations" is exceedingly central to the matter of sustaining collective events. It should be appreciated, though, that associations may be developed prior to particular collective events, as well as during and following specific collective events. Analysts attempting to comprehend particular instances of collective events should be especially mindful of people's preexisting and emergent associations.

21. For related materials on sense-making activity, see Prus (1997b, especially "acquiring perspectives" [62–63] and "achieving intersubjectivity" [88–96]).

22. People may be working with very incomplete stocks of knowledge as they attempt to sort their way through particular collective events. Indeed, people's experiences of ambiguity and tentativeness may greatly overshadow their sense of predictability.

23. The idea of adequately accounting for a large-scale collective event (i.e., "Why did it happen?") on any motivational (social or psychological) basis seems highly untenable. At best, we can try to indicate how various people experience and contribute (knowingly and inadvertently) to particular aspects of the process as these subsequently are experienced and engaged by (potentially vast assortments of) others. In this way, we may begin to piece together more of the human enterprise (and interchange) that constitutes "the event," or at least begin to recognize that large-scale events are generally plethoras of (sub)events, many of which may be somewhat, if not almost entirely in some cases, detached from one another. People sometimes endeavor to generate and coordinate the main themes of events, but any successes they have are very much dependent on others acknowledging these efforts and focusing their activities accordingly. Typically, too, events are seen and engaged in different ways by the participants. Once collective events are seen as constituted of ongoing sets of (often) more isolated and more interlinked involvements (and activities) versus structurally (e.g., culture, class, organizational, or psychological) motivated causes, questions of the type "Why did it happen?" become starkly simplistic and unrealistic. There is no one event to be explained. Rather, somewhat like the term "society," references to specific large-scale events represent short-hand designations for countless (embedded) subevents and activities.

9 Engaging the Power Motif

> *Most academics, sociologists and what not, they haven't paid their dues! If you're a criminologist or somebody in deviance, say, and you haven't been out on the streets, you haven't paid your dues. . . . But it's not just them, it's the whole field, actually. Now maybe you can exempt someone like Parsons or Merton, say, because they're kind of special. They've done other things. But most other people, they haven't paid their dues. . . . It's been the interactionists, mostly, who've gone out there. They go out and study things. It's been them and their students. They have a tradition of doing that, that goes back to the Chicago School. These people, they've pretty well all paid their dues, but they're a minority. Most academics just haven't paid their dues. They might talk a good line, and some of the stuff they do is pretty sophisticated, and you have to give them credit for other things they've done. They work hard, most of them. But they've not gone out there and gotten involved with the people out there.*
>
> *—retired sociologist*

Implying the potential for people to be placed under the control or direction of others, power represents an enduring theme across time and place. However, because notions of power also denote realms of fascination, allure, and intrigue, as well as frustration, apprehension, and fear, a great many people have become caught up in both *the power motif* and *the power mystique.*

The themes that appear within the seemingly endless conversations and textual discourses about power, domination, control, and the like are multifaceted indeed. Thus, it is not uncommon to find people who talk about power within the contexts of: (a) condemning its use,[1] (b) proposing moralities (and agendas) to deal with its implementation, (c) endeavoring to raise consciousness regarding power relations, (d) "empowering" targets, or (e) using power relations as entertainment themes of sorts. Other statements abound that deal with (f) ways of, and technologies for, gaining and maximizing advantage in all sorts of encounters or arenas. Additionally, a considerable literature exists that is directed toward (g) a scholarly analysis of power, wherein notions of domination, control, influence, negotiation, and the like become the objects of study.

Focused on the ways in which people (individually and collectively) engage those whom they encounter in their own theaters of operation, the present statement most directly addresses this latter concern. At the same time, this volume has been critical of a great many scholars who have endeavored to analyze power. While questioning neither the general sincerity of these other authors, nor, most certainly, their abilities, this literature has been subjected to one primary criterion—does it attend to power as a matter of intersubjective accomplishment; *does the approach* (theoretical viewpoint, conceptual scheme, methodology) *under consideration enable us to envision and study the ways in which human interchange is worked out in the ongoing instances of the here and now in which community life takes place?*

As noted in chapter 1, this emphasis represents the primary anchorage or reference point in dealing with what otherwise is a massive, complex, and highly diffuse literature. It also becomes a rather severe criterion for assessing existing statements on power. For reasons about which I can only guess, most social theorists have disregarded the fuller consideration (i.e., analysis, study) of group life *in the making*. As a result, despite an incredible array of materials that deal with power in one or another way, very little of this literature attends to the ways in which people accomplish power relations in practice.

Rather than attempt to summarize this volume, I would like to use the remaining pages to emphasize the importance of social scientists engaging their human subject matter in more direct terms. By this I do not just mean the study of power relations, but the study of *all* realms of human endeavor (processes, levels, contexts). If we can do that, then we will better understand "power."

Power does *not* exist as "something out there," as an objective phenomenon unto itself. And, power does not drive society or community life. People may engage all manner of [physical objects] in relating to one another, but power most fundamentally is a social, meaningful enacted essence. It is dependent on people for its conceptualization, contextualization, implementation, resistance, adjustment, and impact. Power is *not* the key to understanding society. Instead, only as we develop more in depth understandings of the ways in which people accomplish community life more generally, will we be better able to appreciate power as a (social) essence.

Given the popular condemnations, fascinations, moralities, fears, advocacy positions, and dramatizations that surround the [power] phenomenon, many analysts have had difficulty sustaining stances that are divested of evaluative themes along these lines. Still, another persistent obstacle in the study of power relations revolves around the tendency to objectify power; to assume that people might approach the study of power as a reality that transcends (or even renders irrelevant) human experience and human enterprise. This orientation seems predicated on the insistence, on the part of some, that social scientists model themselves after the methodologies that have been so successfully applied by those in the physical sciences. The inference is that power could be studied in ways that somewhat parallel the manners in which others approach physics or chemistry, for instance, wherein the things being studied are (in themselves) devoid of symbolic interchange, meaningful activity, and collective enterprise.

Although some notions of intersubjectivity (e.g., language, relativity, reflectivity) can be traced back to the early Greeks (chapter 4), these have been largely ignored in most considerations of power, even to the present time. Instead, the quest for more finite answers (e.g., forces and factors) to "the power question" and ongoing tendencies to disregard human activity (and interaction) have prevailed over the centuries.

Perhaps, too, it is noteworthy that all peoples (about whom we have this sort of information) seem aware of the importance of sharing information with newcomers and others through linguistic interchange (and asking others about things when they would like to know about something or learn how others do things). Indeed, symbolic interchange represents the very *foundation* of all socialization and educational processes (concepts, practices, and programs). Still, this fundamental feature of the human condition has generally been regarded as having little scientific potential when it comes to learning about human community life. How odd! Yet, only since the early 1900s, and then only in some relatively small sectors of the social sciences, have (ethnographic) practices been more systematically used to examine the ways in which *people* accomplish community life (Prus, 1996b:103–140). Otherwise, as with scholars working in so many other areas of human endeavor, those analyzing power appear to have been most reluctant to *talk to people,* in extended detail, about their experiences in dealing with one another.

It may be challenging (and frustrating at times) for people to put their own moralities or other popular sentiments in suspension and to examine each and every instance of human interchange as a *participant-informed occurrence* unto itself. Likewise, some scholars may be reluctant to "mingle with the masses;" perhaps, to assume the posture of students there to learn from those who may have less formal education than themselves. Possibly, too, some are shy or would feel uncomfortable approaching others (who may not be particularly interested in the research venture at hand) or spending time in unfamiliar settings. However, unless analysts maintain a concerted focus on power as a humanly enacted phenomenon (of which the *power mystique* is but a part),[2] then they, too, are apt to contribute to, and further objectify the power mystique.

Relatedly, it is a mistake to assume that power relations are essentially conflictual or cooperative in their essence, or that power relations are determined by certain structures or overarching rationalities. In the quest to achieve generalized accounts of the human condition, it may be tempting to

propose sweeping historical, cultural, organizational, or psychological motivations of various sorts. However, such views are clearly inconsistent with the
ongoing formulation or accomplishment of human group life. It is not the
case that notions of structure and rationality are inconsequential. Indeed,
people routinely try to order their life-worlds so that these might be more
manageable. Still, like any other matters to which people may attend, these
"orderings" become consequential to people when (and in the ways in
which) *they* acknowledge, define, implement, promote, or resist working
formulations along these lines. Unfortunately, it is precisely this situated or
"here and now" human engagement of the socially constituted world that
has been so generally neglected in the literature.

As social scientists, we can be grateful for each instance of human
interchange that we are able to examine in great detail (assuming participant-informed data), regardless of the circumstances, intentions, directions, or outcomes of the case at hand. At the same time, if we are to develop
more viable comprehensions of the human condition, it is necessary that we
actively pursue the study of as many instances (and variations thereof) of
human interchanges as possible.

Because interactionism is attentive to community life in the making, it
enables scholars to study [power] relations across the endless instances of
interchange that comprise community life. Particularly consequential in
this respect are explicit recognitions of (a) the intersubjectively constituted
realities in which people (meaningfully) act, (b) the multiple realms of
activity in which people participate, and (c) people's capacities to (mind-
edly or reflectively) engage other people (and other objects) on both a
solitary and a collective basis.

The approach presented in this volume may imply a substantial paradigm shift for many, but it enables social scientists to realign their theoretical and methodological viewpoints in ways that more closely match the
experiences (and practices) of those (analysts included) who interactively
constitute the human community. This conceptual reframing does *not* ren-
der the ensuing study of power unscientific or undisciplined.

Insofar as the objective of any realm of science is to generate knowledge that is informed by close, sustained examinations of the essences of the
phenomenon at hand, then the interactionist approach is particularly appropriate for developing a science of human community life. By placing the
focus on the enacted features of human interchange, this volume not only
indicates ways of envisioning power in *process* terms, but it also highlights a
number of analytically strategic points at which much needed ethnographic
work on aspects of the [power] phenomenon may be pursued.

Beyond asking when and how people define interchanges with others
in power (and other) terms, this volume gives consideration to the ways in
which people become involved in instances of influence work and how they

engage these enterprises as both tacticians and targets. In addition to addressing various strategies that people may invoke in dealing with others on a more exclusively dyadic basis, attention is directed toward the processes and problematics of embarking on an assortment of collective influence endeavors. Consideration is also given to the plurality of roles that people may adopt as [targets] and relatedly to people's participation in competitive arenas and other collective events. Rather centrally, this statement acknowledges human capacities for anticipating and adjusting to the other as well as assuming an interchangeability of *enacted* standpoints (that the same people may adopt both tactician and target roles on a sequential and a concurrent basis).

The material presented here recognizes the senses of continuity (and objectified reality) that people associate with notions of familiarity, repetition, routines, and organization, including the things they experience on more physical planes. Indeed, because instances of human interchange are inevitably contextualized, people invariably take [traditions] and [physical entities] into account in forging lines of action, both in more individualized and more directly interactive terms. Still, the recognition that people *may invoke* some of these things as (more enduring) reference points should not, in any way, obscure or deflect attention from a sustained examination of the *formulative aspects* of human behavior (and associational practices).

Space limitations preclude a fuller consideration of the processes and problematics of conducting ethnographic inquiry and the development of an intersubjectively grounded social science (also see chapter 5). However, it is worth noting that, in addition to representing the essential methodology for learning about group life as it is actively constituted, ethnographic inquiry is, itself, very much an exercise in human interchange. It places researchers in circumstances that parallel, in a great many ways, the situations that others encounter in pursuing cooperation from their associates.[3]

Like many other activities, sustained ethnographic inquiry is a laborious, demanding undertaking. It entails a great deal of ongoing cognitive adjustment and a considerable amount of persistence, mental alertness, and physical stamina. But, it typically also requires that scholars assume the initiative of making contact with, and maintaining close working relations with, an assortment of other people who may have little, if any, preliminary interest in the research project. To learn more fully about the viewpoints and practices of others, it also will be necessary for researchers to suspend their own moralities and more personalized notions of rationality and wisdom so that they might more openly and completely attend to the lifeworlds (and activities) of the other.

Ethnographic encounters with the other can be extremely productive, substantively and conceptually. Like other instances of human association, these interchanges are often congenial, interesting, and insightful. Nevertheless, researchers' encounters with others are also apt to be notably ambiguous, frustrating, and disconcerting at times, if not more unsettling on occasion. Still, however variable these experiences might be, it is essential that researchers achieve and maintain a presence that is not only acceptable to others in the field, but also one that enables ethnographers to access a variety of front and back regions. Often, too, this means diplomatically dealing with an assortment of others whose relationships with one another may be quite mixed, if not highly volatile, at times. Quite directly, though, there is no viable substitute for the information that one may gain by pursuing intersubjectivity through extended, interactive contact with the humans "out there."

Although informed by the existing ethnographic literature, the present volume is intended to foster ethnographic examinations of power relations in the human community. It is, however, only a preliminary step in that direction and should not be viewed as an alternative to that research. Indeed, unless social scientists examine notions of power (and other enacted facets of community life) as these are implemented by those engaged in particular instances of human interchange, there will be no opportunity for "the people out there" to inform (and *resist*) scholarly conceptualizations about their life-worlds. We will remain mired, variously, in conceptual and methodological misrepresentations of community life, moralisms and agendas for reform, and endless, speculative discourse. Only by engaging "the other" in direct, sustained, and open interchange, may we more effectively permeate the power mystique and more adequately comprehend (and conceptualize) power relations as these are accomplished in the here and now of community life.

Notes

1. Some people might wish, somehow, to dispense with notions of influence (and resistance). However, such hopes seem entirely unfeasible. Given people's tendencies to impinge on one another in the course of community life, it is impossible to eliminate [power] considerations from human association. Thus, beyond any concerns about influencing others as this pertains to more fundamental human struggles for physical existence, the acquisition of particular objects, or the active pursuit of other interests at a more personal or collective level, any attempt on the part of individuals or collectivities to establish routines, policies, or moralities both within and beyond particular groups (and communities) or, relatedly, to assert individual freedoms or collective tolerances, almost inevitably takes people into the realm of power relations.

2. Similarly, much may be learned about the human condition by examining *the power mystique* as a socially constructed phenomenon. To this

end, social scientists also are encouraged to attend to the ways in which people in various life-worlds develop images (and evaluations) of power related phenomena and how the participants therein promote (and resist) these depictions.

3. Indeed, since ethnography puts researchers in situations in which they are highly dependent on sustaining working relations with some set of others, the research role offers scholars a rather simultaneous occasion not only to learn about ways in which people relate to one another in particular life-worlds, but also to reflect on the influence and resistance processes that researchers experience in a more direct sense as they engage (*and* are engaged by) other people in the field.

References

Adler, Patricia. 1985. *Wheeling and Dealing*. New York: Columbia University Press.

√ **Agger, Ben.** 1992. *The Discourse of Domination*. Evanston, IL: Northwestern University Press.

Alexander, Jeffrey C. 1987. *Twenty Lectures: Sociology Theory Since World War II*. New York: Columbia University Press.

Alinksy, Saul D. 1971. *Rules for Radicals*. New York: Vintage.

Altheide, David L. 1974. *Creating Reality: How TV News Distorts Events*. Beverly Hills, CA: Sage.

————. 1985. *Media Power*. Beverly Hills, CA: Sage.

Altheide, David L., and John M. Johnson. 1980. *Bureaucratic Propaganda*. Boston: Allyn and Bacon.

————. 1995. "Symbolic Interaction, Power and Justice." Paper presented at the Stone Symbolic Interaction Symposium, Drake University, Des Moines, IA.

Altheide, David L., and Robert P. Snow. 1979. *Media Logic*. Beverly Hills, CA: Sage.

Altschull, J. Herbert. 1984. *Agents of Power: The Role of the News Media in Human Affairs*. New York: Longman.

Anderson, Nels. 1923. *The Hobo*. Chicago: University of Chicago Press.

Andrews, Florence Kellner. 1983. "A Case Study of Two Types of Officer-Inmate Interaction in a Correctional Establishment." *Symbolic Interaction* 6:51–68.

Argyris, Chris. 1993. *Knowledge for Action: A Guide to Overcoming Barriers to Organizational Change*. San Francisco, CA: Jossey-Bass.

Aristotle (384–322 B.C.). *De Rhetorica Ad Alexandrum*. Trans. by E. S. Forster. Vol. 11 of *The Works of Aristotle*. W. D. Ross (ed.). London: Oxford University Press (1946).

————. *Ethica Eudemia*. Trans. by J. Solomon. Vol. 9 of *The Works of Aristotle*. W. D. Ross (ed.). London: Oxford University Press (1915).

————. *Ethica Nicomachea*. Trans. by W. D. Ross. Vol. 9 of *The Works of Aristotle*. W. D. Ross (ed.). London: Oxford University Press (1915).

————. *Eudemian Ethics*. Trans. by J. Solomon. Vol. 2 of *The Complete Works of Aristotle*. Jonathan Barns (ed.). Princeton, NJ: Princeton University Press (1995).

————. *History of Animals*. Trans. by d'A. W. Thompson. Vol. 1 of *The Complete*

Works of Aristotle. Jonathan Barns (ed.). Princeton, NJ: Princeton University Press (1995).

———. *Magna Moralia.* Trans. by St. George Stock. Vol. 2 of *The Complete Works of Aristotle.* Jonathan Barns (ed.). Princeton, NJ: Princeton University Press (1995).

———. *Metaphysica.* Trans. by W. D. Ross. Vol. 8 of *The Works of Aristotle.* W. D. Ross (ed.). London: Oxford University Press (1928).

———. *Metaphysics.* Trans. by W. D. Ross. Vol. 2 of *The Complete Works of Aristotle.* Jonathan Barns (ed.). Princeton, NJ: Princeton University Press (1995).

———. *Nicomachean Ethics.* Trans. by W. D. Ross, revised by J. O. Urmson. Vol. 2 of *The Complete Works of Aristotle.* Jonathan Barns (ed.). Princeton, NJ: Princeton University Press (1995).

———. *On Generation and Corruption.* Trans. by H. H. Joachim. Vol. 1 of *The Complete Works of Aristotle.* Jonathan Barns (ed.). Princeton, NJ: Princeton University Press (1995).

———. *Poetics.* Trans. by I. Bywater. Vol. 2 of *The Complete Works of Aristotle.* Jonathan Barns (ed.). Princeton, NJ: Princeton University Press (1995).

———. *Politica.* Trans. by Benjamin Jowett. Vol. 10 of *The Works of Aristotle.* W. D. Ross (ed.). London: Oxford University Press (1921).

———. *Politics.* Trans. by B. Jowett. Vol. 2 of *The Complete Works of Aristotle.* Jonathan Barns (ed.). Princeton, NJ: Princeton University Press (1995).

———. *Politics* (Books I and II). Trans. by Trevor J. Saunders. New York: Oxford University Press (1995).

———. *Posterior Analytics.* Trans. by Jonathan Barnes. Vol. 1 of *The Complete Works of Aristotle.* Jonathan Barns (ed.). Princeton, NJ: Princeton University Press (1995).

———. *Rhetoric.* Trans. by W. Rhys Roberts. Vol. 2 of *The Complete Works of Aristotle.* Jonathan Barns (ed.). Princeton, NJ: Princeton University Press (1995).

———. *Rhetoric To Alexander.* Trans. by E. S. Forster. Vol. 2 of *The Complete Works of Aristotle.* Jonathan Barns (ed.). Princeton, NJ: Princeton University Press (1995).

———. *Rhetorica.* Trans. by W. Rhys Roberts. Vol. 11 of *The Works of Aristotle.* W. D. Ross (ed.). London: Oxford University Press (1946).

Arnold, William R. 1970. *Juveniles on Parole.* New York: Random House.

Aronson, Ronald. 1995. *After Marxism.* New York: Guilford.

Athens, Lonnie. 1974. "The Self and the Violent Criminal Act." *Urban Life and Culture* 3(1):98–112.

———. 1977. "Violent Crime: A Symbolic Interactionist Study." *Symbolic Interaction* 1(1):56–70.

———. 1980. *Violent Criminal Acts and Actors: A Symbolic Interactionist Study.* Boston: Routledge and Kegan Paul.

———. 1989. *The Creation of Dangerous Violent Criminals.* New York: Routledge.

———. 1997. *Violent Criminal Acts and Actors Revisited.* Urbana: University of Illinois Press.

Atkinson, Max. 1984. *Our Masters' Voices: The Dynamics of Political Speech-making.* New York: Methuen.

Atkinson, Michael. 1995. "Toeing the Party Line: An Ethnographic Study of Political Parties and the Political Process as Human Lived Experience." Paper presented at Qualitative Research Conference. McMaster University, Hamilton, Ontario.

Avineri, Shlomo. 1969. *The Social and Political Thought of Karl Marx.* New York: Cambridge University Press.

Bagdikian, Ben H. 1990. *The Media Monopoly.* Boston: Beacon.

Barton, Roger. 1970. *Handbook of Advertising Management.* New York: McGraw-Hill.

Baudrillard, Jean. 1983. *Simulations.* New York: Semiotext(e).

———. 1988. *Jean Baudrillard: Selected Writings.* Edited and Introduction by Mark Poster. Stanford, CA: Stanford University Press.

Becker, Howard and Harry Elmer Barnes. 1978. *Social Thought: From Lore to Science* (3rd. ed.). Gloucester, MA: Peter Smith.

Becker, Howard S. 1963. *Outsiders.* New York: Free Press.

———. 1970. *Sociological Work: Method and Substance.* Chicago: Aldine.

Bell, Colin and Howard Newby. 1971. *Community Studies.* London: Allen and Irwin.

Bendix, Rhinehard. 1960. *Max Weber: An Intellectual Portrait.* New York: Doubleday-Anchor.

Benford, Robert D. 1987. Framing Activity, Meaning, and Social Movement Participation: The Nuclear Disarmament Movement. Doctoral Dissertation, University of Texas, Austin.

———. 1993a. "Frame Disputes within the Nuclear Disarmament Movement." *Social Forces* 71(3):677–701.

———. 1993b. "'You Could be the Hundredth Monkey': Collective Action Frames and Vocabularies of Motive Within the Nuclear Disarmament Movement." *The Sociological Quarterly* 34:195–216.

———. 1997. "An Insider's Critique of the Social Movement Framing Perspective." *Sociological Inquiry* 67:409–430.

Benford, Robert D., and Scott A. Hunt. 1992. "Dramaturgy and Social Movements: The Social Construction of Communication of Power." *Sociological Inquiry* 62(1):36–55.

Benford, Robert and Louis A. Zurcher. 1990. "Instrumental and Symbolic Competition among Peace Movement Organizations." Pp. 125–139

in Sam Marullo and John Lofland (eds.), *Peace Action in the Eighties.*
New Brunswick, NJ: Rutgers.

Benhabib, Seyla, Judith Butler, Priscella Cornell, and Nancy Fraser. 1995.
Feminist Contentions: A Philosophical Change. New York: Routledge.

Bennett, W. Lance. 1988. *News: The Politics of Illusion.* New York: Longman.

Bensmen, Joseph, and Israel Gerver. 1963. "Crime and Punishment in the
Factory: The Function of Deviance in Maintaining the Social System." *American Sociological Review* 28:588–598.

Bentley, Arthur F. 1908. *The Process of Government.* Chicago: University of
Chicago Press (Reprinted 1967, by Harvard University Press, Cambridge, MA).

Berger, Charles R. 1985. "Social Power and Interpersonal Communication."
Pp. 439–499 in Mark L. Knapp and Gerald R. Miller (eds.), *Handbook
of Interpersonal Communication.* Beverly Hills, CA: Sage.

Berger, Charles R., and Steven H. Chaffee. 1987. *Handbook of Communication
Science.* Beverly Hills, CA: Sage.

Berger, Peter, and Thomas Luckmann. 1966. *The Social Construction of Reality.*
New York: Anchor.

Best, Joel. 1989. *Images of Issues: Typifying Social Problems.* New York: Aldine
de Gruyter.

———. 1995. "Lost in the Ozone Again: The Postmodernist Fad and Interactionist Foibles." Pp. 125–129 in Norman K. Denzin (ed.), *Studies in
Symbolic Interaction,* Vol. 17. Greenwich, CT: JAI.

Biernacki, Patrick. 1988. *Pathways from Heroin Addiction: Recovery without
Treatment.* Philadelphia: Temple University Press.

Bigus, Odis E. 1972. "The Milkman and His Customer: A Cultivated Relationship." *Urban Life and Culture* 1:131–165.

Bigus, O. E., S. C. Hadden, and B. G. Glaser. 1982. "Basic Social Processes."
Pp. 251–272 in R. B. Smith and P. K. Manning (eds.) *Handbook of
Social Science Methods, Vol. 2: Qualitative Methods.* Cambridge, MA:
Ballinger.

Billig, Michael. 1996. *Arguing and Thinking: A Rhetorical Approach to Social
Psychology.* New York: Cambridge University Press.

Bittner, Egon. 1965. "The Concept of Organization." *Social Research* 32:230–
255.

———. 1967. "The Police on Skid Row." *American Sociological Review* 32:699–
715.

Black, Donald J. 1970. "Production of Crime Rates." *American Sociological
Review* 35:733–747.

Black, Donald J., and Albert J. Reiss, Jr. 1970. "Police Control of Juveniles."
American Sociological Review 35:63–77.

Blalock, Hubert M., Jr. 1989. *Power and Conflict: Toward a General Theory.*
Newbury Park, CA: Sage.

Blau, Peter. 1964. *Exchange and Power in Social Life.* New York: Wiley.

Blount, Thomas. 1654. *The Academy of Eloquence.* Menston, UK: Scholar Press (1971).

Blumberg, Abraham. 1967. "The Practice of Law as a Confidence Game: Organizational Cooptation of a Profession." *Law and Society Review* 1:15–39.

Blumer, Herbert. 1928. Method in Social Psychology. Doctoral Dissertation. University of Chicago.

———. 1931. "Science Without Concepts." *American Journal of Sociology* 36: 515–533.

———. 1933. *Movies and Conduct.* New York: Macmillan.

———. 1937. "Social Psychology." Pp. 144–198 in Emerson P. Schmidt (ed.), *Man and Society.* New York: Prentice-Hall.

———. 1939. "Collective Behavior." Pp. 220–278 in Robert E. Park (ed.), *An Outline of the Principles of Sociology.* New York: Barnes & Noble.

———. 1951. "Collective Behavior." Pp. 166–222 in Alfred McClung Lee (ed.), *New Outline of the Principles of Sociology.* New York: Barnes and Noble (Subsequent editions in 1955, 1969).

———. 1954. "Social Structure and Power Conflict." Pp. 232–239 in Arthur Kornhauser, Robert Dubin, and Arthur M. Ross (eds.), *Industrial Conflict.* New York: McGraw-Hill.

———. 1960. "Early Industrialization and the Laboring Class." *Sociological Quarterly* 1:5–14.

———. 1964. "Industrialization and the Traditional Order." *Sociology and Social Research* 48:129–138.

———. 1966. "Sociological Implications of the Thought of George Herbert Mead." *American Journal of Sociology* 71:535–548.

———. 1969. *Symbolic Interaction.* Englewood Cliffs, NJ: Prentice-Hall.

———. 1971. "Social Problems as Collective Behavior." *Social Problems* 18:298–306.

———. 1988. "Social Structure and Power Conflict." Pp. 326–336 in Stanford M. Lyman and Arthur Vidich (eds.), *Social Order and Public Philosophy.* Fayetteville: University of Arkansas Press.

———. 1990. *Industrialization as an Agent of Social Change* (Edited by David R. Maines and Thomas J. Morrione). New York: Aldine De Gruyter.

Blumer, Herbert, and Philip Hauser. 1933. *Movies, Delinquency and Crime.* New York: Macmillan.

Bogardus, Emory. 1960. *The Development of Social Thought* (4th ed.). New York: McKay.

Bogdan, Robert, and Stephen J. Taylor. 1975. *Introduction to Qualitative Research Methods.* New York: Wiley.

Bolles, Richard Nelson. 1998. *The 1998 What Color is My Parachute: A Practical Manual for Job Hunters and Career Changers.* Berkeley, CA: Ten Speed.

Bowers, John Waite, and Donovan J. Ochs. 1971. *The Rhetoric of Agitation and Control*. Reading, MA: Addison-Wesley.

Boyle, Susan C. 1989. *Social Mobility in the United States: Historiography and Methods*. New York: Garland.

Broadhead, Robert S. 1980. "Qualitative Analysis In Evaluation Research: Problems and Promises of an Interactionist Approach." *Qualitative Analysis* 3(1):23–40.

Broadhead, Robert S., and Kathryn J. Fox. 1990. "Takin' It To The Streets: AIDS Outreach as Ethnography." *Journal of Contemporary Ethnography* 19(3):322–348.

Bronner, Stephen Eric. 1994. *Of Critical Theory and Its Theorists*. Cambridge, MA: Blackwell.

Brown, L. Guy. 1931. "The Sociological Implications of Drug Addiction." *Journal of Educational Sociology* 4:358–369.

Browne, Joy. 1973. *The Used-Car Game: The Sociology of the Bargain*. Lexington, MA: Lexington Press.

Bruce, Brendan. 1992. *Images of Power: How the Image Makers Shape our Leaders*. London, UK: Kegan Page.

Buechler, Steven M. 1993. "Beyond Resource Mobilization? Emerging Trends in Social Movement Theory." *The Sociological Quarterly* 34 (2):217–235.

———. 1995. "New Social Movement Theories." *The Sociological Quarterly* 36 (3):441–464.

Burns, Tom R., and Helena Flam. 1987. *The Shaping of Social Organization: Social Rule System Theory with Applications*. Newbury Park, CA: Sage.

Burnyeat, Myles. 1980. *The Theaetetus of Plato*. Indianapolis: Hackett.

Bury, R. G. 1933. *Sextus Empiricus: Outlines of Pyrrhonism*. Cambridge, MA: Harvard University Press.

Cain, Roy. 1994. "Managing Impressions of an AIDS Service Organization: Into the Mainstream or Out of the Closet?" *Qualitative Sociology* 17(1):43–61.

Callinicos, Alex. 1989. *Against Postmodernism: A Marxist Critique*. Cambridge, UK: Polity Press.

Cambridge Ancient History (The). 1970. (multivolume set; 3rd ed.) London: Cambridge University Press.

Caplan, Marc. 1983. *Ralph Nader Presents A Citizen's Guide to Lobbying*. New York: Dembner Books.

Carlson, Rae. 1984. "What's Social About Social Psychology? Where's the Person in Personality Research?" *Journal of Personality and Social Psychology* 47:1304–1309.

Carnegie, Dale. 1936. *How to Win Friends and Influence People*. New York: Simon and Schuster.

Carver, Terrell. 1983. *Marx and Engels: The Intellectual Relationship.* Norfork, UK: Harvester.

Charlton, Joy, and Rosanna Hertz. 1989. "Guarding Against Boredom: Security Specialist in the U.S. Air Force." *Journal of Contemporary Ethnography* 18(3):299–326.

Charmaz, Kathy. 1991. *Good Days, Bad Days: The Self in Chronic Illness and Time.* New Brunswick, NJ: Rutgers University Press.

———. 1995. "Between Positivism and Postmodernism: Implications for Methods." Pp. 43–72 in Norman K. Denzin (ed.), *Studies in Symbolic Interaction,* Vol. 17. Greenwich, CT: JAI.

Chayko, Mary. 1993. "What is Real in the Age of Virtual Reality? 'Reframing' Frame Analysis for a Technological World." *Symbolic Interaction* 16:171–181.

Chester, Tina Westlake. 1995. "The Processes and Problematics of Coordinating Events: Planning the Wedding Reception." Paper presented at Qualitative and Ethnographic Research Conference. McMaster University, Hamilton, Ontario.

Christie, Richard, and Florence L. Gies. 1970. *Studies in Machiavellianism.* New York: Academic.

Cicero (c. 102–43 B.C.). *De Inventione.* Trans. by H. M. Hubbell. Cambridge, MA: Harvard University Press (1949).

———. *De Oratore.* Trans. by E. W. Sutton. Cambridge, MA: Harvard University Press (1942).

———. *Rhetorica Ad Herennium.* Trans. by Harry Caplan. Cambridge, MA: Harvard University Press (1954).

Clairmont, Donald H., and Dennis William Magill. 1974. *Africville: The Life and Death of a Canadian Black Community.* Toronto: McClelland and Stewart.

Clark, Ruth Anne, and Jesse G. Delia. 1976. "The Development of Functional Persuasive Skills in Childhood and Early Adolescence." *Child Development* 47:1008–1014.

Clarke, M. L. 1996. *Rhetoric at Rome* (3rd ed.). New York: Routledge.

Clegg, Stewart R. 1989. *Frameworks of Power.* Newbury Park, CA: Sage.

Cockerham, William C. 1979. "Green Berets and the Symbolic Meaning of Heroism." *Urban Life* 8(1):94–113.

Cole, G. D. H. 1959. *A History of Socialist Thought.* London: Macmillan.

Coleman, James S. 1974. *Power and the Structure of Society.* New York: Norton.

———. 1990. *Foundations of Social Theory.* Cambridge, MA: Harvard University Press.

Collins, Randall. 1989. "Sociology: Proscience or Antiscience?" *American Sociological Review* 54:124–139.

———. 1994. *Four Sociological Traditions.* New York: Oxford University Press.

Cook, K. S., and J. M. Whitmeyer. 1992. "Two Approaches to Social Structure: Exchange Theory and Network Analysis." *Annual Review of Sociology* 18:109–127.

Cooley, Charles Horton. 1909. *Social Organization: A Study of the Larger Mind.* New York: Shocken.

Cooper, John. 1997. *Plato: The Collected Works.* Indianapolis: Hackett.

Cooper, Martha D., and William Nothstine. 1992. *Power Persuasion: Moving an Ancient Art into the Media Age.* Greenwood, IN: The Education Video Group.

Coser, Lewis A. 1967. *Continuities in the Study of Social Conflict.* New York: Free Press.

———. 1976. "Sociological Theory From the Chicago Dominance to 1965." *Annual Review of Sociology* 2:145–160.

Couch, Carl. 1968. "Collective Behavior: An Examination of Some Stereotypes." *Social Problems* 15:310–322.

———. 1979. "Anselm Strauss . . . Negotiations: Varieties, Contexts, Processes, and Social Order." *Symbolic Interaction* 2:159–163.

———. 1984. "Symbolic Interaction and Generic Sociological Principles." *Symbolic Interaction* 7:1–14.

———. 1987. *Researching Social Processes in the Laboratory.* Greenwich, CT: JAI.

———. 1989. "From Hell to Utopia and Back to Hell: Charismatic Relationships." *Symbolic Interaction* 12:265–279.

Couch, Carl J., Stanley L. Saxton, and Michael A. Katovich. 1986a. *Studies in Symbolic Interaction: The Iowa School.* Part A. Greenwich, CT: JAI.

———. 1986b. *Studies in Symbolic Interaction: The Iowa School.* Part B. Greenwich, CT: JAI.

Coulon, Alain. 1995. *Ethnomethodology* ([1987] trans. by Jacqueline Coulon and Jack Katz). Thousand Oaks, CA: Sage.

Cox, Andrew, Paul Furlong, and Edward Page. 1985. *Power in Capitalist Societies.* Sussex, UK: Wheatsheaf.

Craig, Gordon A. 1979. "On the Nature of Diplomatic History: The Relevance of Some Old Books." Pp. 21–42 in Paul G. Lauren (ed.), *Diplomacy.* New York: Free Press.

Cressey, Donald. 1953. *Other People's Money. A Study in the Social Psychology of Embezzlement.* Glencoe, IL: Free Press.

Cressey, Paul G. 1932. *The Taxi-Dance Hall.* Chicago: University of Chicago Press.

Dahrendorf, Ralph. 1959. *Class and Class Conflict in Industrial Society.* Stanford, CA: Stanford University Press.

Danesi, Marcel. 1993. *Vico, Metaphor, and the Origin of Language.* Bloomington: Indiana University Press.

Daniels, Arlene Kaplan. 1988. *Invisible Careers: Women Civic Leaders from the Volunteer World.* Chicago: University of Chicago Press.

Darrough, William D. 1984. "In the Best Interest of the Child: Negotiating Parental Cooperation for Probation Placement." *Urban Life* 13(2–3):123–153.

Davis, Fred. 1959. "The Cabdriver and His Fare: Facets of a Fleeting Relationship." *American Journal of Sociology* 65:158–165.

———. 1961. "Deviance Disavowal: The Management of Strained Interaction by the Visibly Handicapped." *Social Problems* 9(2):120–132.

———. 1963. *Passage through Crisis.* Indianapolis: Bobbs-Merrill.

Davis, Phillip W. 1983. "Restoring the Semblance of Order: Police Strategies in the Domestic Disturbance." *Symbolic Interaction* 6(2):261–278.

Davis, Phillip W., and Pamela McKenzie-Rundle. 1984. "The Social Organization of Lie-Detector Tests." *Urban Life* 13(2–3):177–205.

Dawson, Lorne. 1988. *Reason, Freedom and Religion: Closing the Gap Between the Humanistic and Scientific Study of Religion.* New York: Peter Lang.

Dawson, Lorne, and Robert Prus. 1993a. "Interactionist Ethnography and Postmodernist Discourse: Affinities and Disjunctures in Approaching Human Lived Experiences." Pp. 147–177 in Norman K. Denzin (ed.), *Studies in Symbolic Interaction,* Vol. 15. Greenwich, CT: JAI.

———. 1993b. "Human Enterprise, Intersubjectivity, and the Ethnographic Other: A Reply to Denzin and Fontana. Pp. 193–200 in Norman K. Denzin (ed.), *Studies in Symbolic Interaction,* Vol. 15. Greenwich, CT:JAI.

———. 1995. "Postmodernism and Linguistic Reality Versus Symbolic Interactionism and Obdurate Reality." Pp. 105–124 in Norman K. Denzin (ed.), *Studies in Symbolic Interaction,* Vol.17. Greenwich, CT: JAI.

De Callières, Francois. 1716. *On the Matter of Negotiating with Princes.* Trans. by A.F. Whyte. Notre Dame, IN: University of Notre Dame (1963).

Delia, Jesse G. 1987. "Communication Research: A History." Pp. 20–98 in Charles R. Berger and Steven H. Chaffee (eds.), *Handbook of Communication Science.* Newbury Park, CA: Sage.

Denzin, Norman K. 1992. *Symbolic Interaction and Cultural Studies: The Politics of Interpretation.* Cambridge, MA: Blackwell.

———. 1993. "The Postmodern Sensibility." Pp. 179–188 in Norman K. Denzin (ed.) *Studies in Symbolic Interaction,* Vol. 15. Greenwich, CT: JAI.

———. 1996. "Prophetic Pragmatism and the Postmodern: A Comment on Maines." *Symbolic Interaction* 19(4):341–355.

Denzin, Norman K., and Yvonna S. Lincoln. 1994. *Handbook of Qualitative Research.* Thousand Oaks, CA: Sage.

Derrida, Jacques. 1976. *Of Grammatology.* Translated by G. Spivak. Baltimore: John Hopkins University Press.

———. 1978. *Writing and Difference.* Trans. by A. Bass. London: Routledge and Kegan Paul.

DeVault, Marjorie L. 1996. "Talking Back to Sociology: Distinctive Contributions of Feminist Methodology." *Annual Review of Sociology* 22:29–50.

Dietz, Mary Lorenz. 1983. *Killing for Profit: The Social Organization of Felony Homicide.* Chicago: Nelson-Hall.

———. 1994. "On Your Toes: Dancing Your Way into the Ballet World." Pp. 66–84 in Mary Lorenz Dietz, Robert Prus, and William Shaffir (eds.), *Doing Everyday Life: Ethnography as Human Lived Experience.* Toronto: Copp Clark Longman.

Dietz, Mary Lorenz, and Michael Cooper. 1994. "Being Recruited: The Experiences of 'Blue Chip' High School Athletes." Pp. 109–125 in Mary Lorenz Dietz, Robert Prus, and William Shaffir (eds.), *Doing Everyday Life: Ethnography as Human Lived Experience.* Toronto: Copp Clark Longman.

Dilthey, Wilhelm. 1988. *Introduction to the Human Sciences: An Attempt to Lay a Foundation for the Study of Society and History* (Einleitung in die Geistewissenschaften, Vol. 1 of Wilhelm Dilthey, Gesammelte Schriften). Trans. by Ramon Betanzos. Detroit: Wayne State University Press.

Dingwall, Robert, and Phil M. Strong. 1985. "The Interactional Critique of Organizations: A Critique and Reformulation." *Urban Life* 14:205–231.

Dix, Dorothy. 1939. *How to Win and Hold a Husband.* Garden City, NY: Doubleday.

Duncan, Otis Dudley, David Featherman, and Beverly Duncan. 1972. *Socioeconomic Background and Achievement.* New York: Seminar.

Dunn, Robert. 1997. "Self, Identity, and Difference: Mead and the Poststructuralists." *The Sociological Quarterly* 38:687–705.

Durkheim, Emile. 1895. *The Rules of the Sociological Method.* Trans. by S.A. Solvay and E.G. Catlin. New York: Free Press (1958).

———. 1897. *Suicide.* Trans. by J. A. Spaulding and G. Simpson. New York: Free Press (1951).

———. 1933. *The Division of Labor In Society.* New York: Free Press.

———. 1961. *Moral Education: A Study in the Theory and Application of the Sociology of Education.* New York: Free Press.

Ebaugh, Helen Rose. 1988. *Becoming an Ex: The Process of Role Exit.* Chicago: University of Chicago Press.

Edgerton, Robert. 1967. *The Cloak of Competence: Stigma in the Lives of the Mentally Retarded.* Berkeley: University of California Press.

Edwards, Charles M. Jr., and Russell A. Brown. 1959. *Retail Advertising and Sales Promotion.* Englewood Cliffs, NJ: Prentice-Hall.

Eggert Max. 1992. *The Perfect Interview.* New York: Wings.

Ehrlich, Carol. 1976. *The Conditions of Feminist Research.* Baltimore, MA: Research Group One, Report 21.

Elms, Alan. 1975. "The Crises of Confidence in Social Psychology." *American Psychologist* 30:967–976.

Emerson, Richard M. 1962. "Power-Dependence Relations." *American Sociological Review* 17:31–41.

———. 1976. "Social Exchange Theory." *Annual Review of Sociology* 2:335–362.

Emerson, Robert M. 1969. *Judging Delinquents.* Chicago: Aldine.

———. 1981. "On Last Resorts." *American Journal of Sociology* 87:1–22.

———. 1983. *Contemporary Field Research.* Boston: Little, Brown.

———. 1994. "Doing Discipline: the Junior High School Scene. Pp. 260–272 in Mary Lorenz Dietz, Robert Prus, and William Shaffir (eds.), *Doing Everyday Life: Ethnography as Human Lived Experience.* Toronto: Copp Clark Longman.

Emerson, Robert M., Rachel I. Fretz, and Linda L Shaw. 1995. *Writing Ethnographic Fieldnotes.* Chicago: University of Chicago Press.

Emerson, Robert M., and Sheldon L. Messinger. 1977. "The Micro-Politics of Trouble." *Social Problems* 25:121–134.

Emerson, Robert M., E. Burke Rochford, Jr., and Linda L. Shaw. 1983. "The Micropolitics of Trouble in a Psychiatric Board and Care Facility." *Urban Life* 12(3):349–367.

Empiricus, Sextus (c. 200 A.D.). *Outlines of Pyrrhonism.* Trans. by R. G. Bury. Cambridge, MA: Harvard University Press (1933).

Enos, Richard Leo. 1993. *Greek Rhetoric Before Aristotle.* Prospect Heights, IL: Waveland.

———. 1995. *Roman Rhetoric: Revolution and the Greek Influence.* Prospect Heights, IL: Waveland.

Ericson, Richard B., Patricia M. Baranek, and Janet B.L. Chan. 1987. *Visualizing Deviance: A Study of News Organization.* Toronto: University of Toronto Press.

———. 1989. *Negotiating Control: A Study of News Sources.* Toronto: University of Toronto Press.

Ermarth, Michael. 1978. *Wilhelm Dilthey: The Critique of Historical Reason.* Chicago: University of Chicago Press.

Estes, Caroll, and Beverly Edmonds. 1981. "Symbolic Interaction and Social Policy Analysis." *Symbolic Interaction* 4:75–86.

Ettema, James S., D. Charles Whitney, and Daniel B. Wackman. 1987. "Professional Mass Communicators." Pp. 747–780 in Charles R. Berger and Steven H. Chaffee (eds.), *Handbook of Communication Science.* Newbury Park, CA: Sage.

Evans, Donald. 1994. "Socialization into Deafness." Pp. 129–142 in Mary Lorenz Dietz, Robert Prus, and William Shaffir (eds.), *Doing Everyday Life: Ethnography as Human Lived Experience.* Toronto: Copp Clark Longman.

Evans, Donald and W.W. Falk. 1986. *Learning to be Deaf.* Berlin: De Gruyter.

Falbo, Toni, and Letitia Anne Peplau. 1980. "Power Strategies in Intimate Relationships." *Journal of Personality and Social Psychology* 38(4):618–628.

Faris, Ellsworth. 1937. *The Nature of Human Nature.* New York: McGraw-Hill.

Faulkner, Robert R., and Douglas B. McGaw. 1977. "Uneasy Homecoming: Stages in the Reentry Transition of Vietnam Veterans." *Urban Life* 6:303–328.

Faupel, Charles E. 1991. *Shooting Dope: Career Patterns of Hard-Core Heroin Users.* Gainesville: University of Florida Press.

Fay, Brian. 1996. *Contemporary Philosophy of Social Science.* Cambridge, MA: Blackwell.

Fee, Elizabeth. 1983. *Women and Health: The Politics of Sex in Medicine.* Farmingdale, NY: Baywood.

Festinger, Leon, Henry Riecken, and Stanley Schacter. 1956. *When Prophecy Fails.* New York: Harper & Row.

Finley, Gordon E., and Carolyn A. Humphreys. 1974. "Naive Psychology and the Development of Persuasive Appeals in Girls." *Canadian Journal of Behavioral Science* 6(1):75–80.

Fishman, Laura T. 1990. *Women at the Wall: A Study of Prisoners' Wives Doing Time on the Outside.* Albany: State University of New York Press.

Fishman, Mark. 1980. *Manufacturing the News.* Austin: University of Texas Press.

Fiske, John. 1987. *Television Culture.* New York: Routledge.

Florez, Carl P., and George L. Kelling. 1984. "The Hired Hand and the Lone Wolf: Issues in the Use of Observers in Large-Scale Program Evaluation." *Urban Life* 12(4):423–443.

Fontana, Andrea. 1993. "Interactionist Ethnography and Postmodern Discourse Revisited." Pp. 189–192 in Norman K. Denzin (ed.), *Studies in Symbolic Interaction*, Vol. 15. Greenwich, CT: JAI.

Foucault, Michel. 1979. *Discipline and Punish: The Birth of the Prison* [1975]. New York: Vintage.

Frank, William W., and Charles L. Lapp. 1959. *How to Outsell the Born Salesman.* New York: Collier-Macmillan.

Frankel, Boris. 1983. *Beyond the State: Dominant Theories and Socialist Strategies.* London: Macmillan.

Frazer, Charles, and Leonard N. Reid. 1979. "Children's Interaction With Commercials." *Symbolic Interaction* 2:79–96.

Freeman, Kathleen. 1949. *The Pre-Socratic Philosophers* (2nd ed.). Oxford: Basil Blackwell.

French, J. R. P., and B. H. Raven. 1959. "The Social Basis of Power." Pp. 118–149 in D. Cartwright (ed.), *Studies in Social Power.* Ann Arbor, MI: Institute of Social Research.

French, Marilyn. 1992. *The War Against Women.* New York: Summit.

Gamson, William A., David Croteau, William Hoynes, and Theodore Sasson. 1992. "Media Images and the Social Construction of Reality." *Annual Review of Sociology* 18:373–393.

Gandhi, M. K. 1951. *Non-Violent Resistance (Satyagraha).* New York: Schocken.

Gans, Herbert J. 1967. *The Levittowners: Ways of Life and Politics in a New Suburban Community.* New York: Antheon.

Gardner, Carol Brooks. 1986. "Public Aid." *Urban Life* 15(1):37–69.

Garfinkel, Harold. 1956. "Conditions of Successful Degradation Ceremonies." *American Journal of Sociology* 61:420–424.

———. 1967. *Studies in Ethnomethodology.* Englewood Cliffs, NJ: Prentice-Hall.

Gergen, Kenneth. 1982. *Toward Transformation in Social Knowledge.* New York: Springer-Verlag.

———. 1985 "The Social Constructionist Movement in Modern Psychology." *American Psychologist* 40:266–275.

Giddens, Anthony. 1976. *New Rules of the Sociological Method: A Positive Critique of Interpretive Sociology.* London: Hutchinson.

———. 1984. *The Constitution of Society: Outline of the Theory of Structuration.* Cambridge, UK: Polity.

Giles, Howard, and John M. Wiemann. 1987. "Language, Social Comparison, and Power." Pp. 350–384 in Charles R. Berger and Steven H. Chaffee (eds.), *Handbook of Communication Science.* Newbury Park, CA: Sage.

Girard, Joe. 1977. *How to Sell Anything to Anybody.* New York: Warner.

Glaser, Barney, and Anselm Strauss. 1965. *Awareness of Dying.* Chicago: Aldine.

———. 1967. *The Discovery of Grounded Theory.* Chicago: Aldine.

Goffman, Erving. 1959. *The Presentation of Self in Everyday Life.* New York: Anchor.

———. 1961. *Asylums.* New York: Anchor.

———. 1963. *Stigma.* Englewood Cliffs, NJ: Spectrum.

———. 1971. *Relations in Public.* New York: Harper & Row.

———. 1972. *Frame Analysis.* New York: Harper & Row.

Gouldner, Alvin. 1954. *Wildcat Strike: A Study of an Unofficial Strike.* London: Routledge & Paul.

———. 1965. *Enter Plato: Classical Greece and the Origins of Social Theory.* New York: Basic.

Gramsci, Antonio. 1971. *Selections from the Prison Notebooks.* Q. Hoare and G. N. Smith (eds.). New York: International.

Grimes, Michael D. 1991. *Class in Twentieth-Century American Sociology: An Analysis of Theories and Measurement Strategies.* New York: Praeger.

Grills, Scott. 1989. Designating Deviance: Championing Definitions of The

Appropriate and Inappropriate Through a Christian Political Voice. Doctoral Dissertation, McMaster University, Hamilton, Ontario.

———. 1994. "Recruitment Practices of the Christian Heritage Party." Pp. 96–108 in Mary Lorenz Dietz, Robert Prus, and William Shaffir (eds.), *Doing Everyday Life: Ethnography as Human Lived Experience.* Toronto: Copp Clark Longman.

———. 1998. *Fieldwork Settings: Accomplishing Ethnographic Research.* Thousand Oaks, CA: Sage.

Gross, Alfred. 1959. *Salesmanship.* New York: Ronald.

Grossberg, Lawrence. 1986. "History, Politics and Postmodernism: Stuart Hall and Cultural Studies." *Journal of Communication Inquiry* 10(2):61–77.

Grossberg, Lawrence, Cary Nelson, and Paula A. Treichler. 1992. *Cultural Studies.* New York: Routledge.

Gulley, Bill. 1980. *Breaking Cover* (with Mary Ellen Reese). New York: Simon & Schuster.

Gulliver, P. H. 1979. *Disputes and Negotiations: A Cross-Cultural Perspective.* New York: Academic.

Gusfield, Joseph R. 1955. "Social Structure and Moral Reform: A Study of the Woman's Christian Temperance Union." *American Journal of Sociology* 61:221–232.

———. 1963. *Symbolic Crusade: Status Politics and the American Temperance Movement.* Urbana: University of Illinois Press.

———. 1981. *The Culture of Public Problems.* Chicago: University of Chicago Press.

———. 1984. "On the Side: Practical Action and Social Constructivism in Social Problems Theory." Pp. 31–51 in Joseph W. Schneider and John I. Kitsuse (eds.), *Studies in the Sociology of Social Problems.* Norwood, NJ: Ablex.

———. 1989. "Constructing the Ownership of Social Problems: Fun and Profit in the Welfare State." *Social Problems* 26:431–441.

———. 1996. *Contested Meanings: The Construction of Alcohol Problems.* Madison: University of Wisconsin Press.

Gusterson, Hugh. 1993. "Exploding Anthropology's Canon in the World of the Bomb: Ethnographic Writing on Militarism." *Journal of Contemporary Ethnography* 22(1):59–79.

Guthrie, W. K. C. 1971. *The Sophists.* New York: Cambridge University Press.

Haas, Jack. 1972. "Binging: Educational Control among High Steel Ironworkers." *American Behavioral Scientist* 16:27–34.

———. 1977. "Learning Real Feelings: A Study of High Steel Ironworkers Reactions to Fear and Danger." *Sociology of Work and Occupations* 4:147–170.

Haas, Jack, and William Shaffir. 1987. *Becoming Doctors: The Adaption of a Cloak of Competence.* Greenwich, CT: JAI.

Hall, Ian. 1983. Playing for Keeps: The Careers of Front-line Workers in Institutions for Developmentally Handicapped Persons. M.A. Thesis. University of Waterloo, Waterloo, Ontario.

Hall, Peter M. 1972. "A Symbolic Interactionist Analysis of Politics." Pp. 35–75 in Andrew Effrat (ed.), *Perspectives in Political Sociology.* Indianapolis: Bobbs-Merrill.

———. 1979. "The Presidency and Impression Management." Pp. 283–305 in Norman K. Denzin (ed.), *Studies in Symbolic Interaction,* Vol. 2. Greenwich, CT: JAI.

———. 1995. "The Consequences of Qualitative Analysis for Sociological Theory: Beyond the Microlevel." *The Sociological Quarterly* 36:397–423.

———. 1997. "Meta-Power, Social Organization, and the Shaping of Social Action." *Symbolic Interaction* 20:397–418.

Hall, Peter M., and Patrick J.W. McGinty. 1997. "Policy as the Transformation of Intentions: Producing Program from Statute." *The Sociological Quarterly* 38:439–467.

Hall, Peter M., and Dee Ann Spencer-Hall. 1982. "The Social Condition of the Negotiated Order." *Urban Life* 11(3):328–349.

Hall, Stuart. 1980. "Cultural Studies: Two Paradigms." *Media, Culture and Society* 2:57–72.

———. 1992. "Cultural Studies and its Theoretical Legacies." Pp. 277–294 in Lawrence Grossberg, Cary Nelson, and Paula A. Treichler (eds.), *Cultural Studies.* New York: Routledge.

Hannerz, Ulf. 1992. "The Global Ecumenae as a Network of Networks." Pp. 335–356 in Adam Kuper (ed.), *Conceptualizing Society.* New York: Routledge.

Hargreaves, David, Stephen Hestor, and Frank Melor. 1975. *Deviance in Classrooms.* London: Routledge and Kegan Paul.

Harmon, Robert B. 1971. *The Art and Practice of Diplomacy: A Selected and Annotated Guide.* Metuchen, NJ: Scarecrow.

Harré, Rom, and Paul Secord. 1972. *The Explanation of Social Behavior.* Oxford: Basil Blackwell.

Harrison, Deborah, and Lucie Laliberté. 1994. *No Life Like It: Military Wives in Canada.* Toronto: Lorimer.

Harrison, Michael I. 1994. *Diagnosing Organizations: Methods, Models, and Processes.* Beverly Hills, CA: Sage.

Hawkins, Keith. 1984. "Creating Cases in a Regulatory Agency." *Urban Life* 12(4):371–395.

Henslin, James. 1968. "Trust and the Cabdriver." Pp. 138–158 in Marcello

Truzzi (ed.), *Sociology and Everyday Life*. Englewood Cliffs, NJ: Prentice-Hall.

Heraclitus (Heracleitus; c. 540–480 B.C.). See Freeman, Sprague.

Herder, Johann Gottfried v. 1784. *Outlines of a Philosophy of the History of Man*. Trans. by T. Churchill [1799] and reprinted by Bergman Publishers, New York (c. 1966).

Herman, Nancy. 1993. "Return to Sender: Reintegrative Stigma-Management Strategies of Ex-Psychiatric Patients." *Journal of Contemporary Ethnography* 22(3):295–330.

Herodotus (c. 484–425 B.C.). *Herodotus*. Trans. by A. D. Godley. Cambridge, MA: Harvard University Press (1921).

Hirsch, Erich L. 1990. "Sacrifice for the Cause: Group Processes, Recruitment, and Commitment in a Student Social Movement." *American Sociological Review* 55:243–254.

Hobbes, Thomas. 1629. *Thucydides' The History of the Peloponnesian War*. (Reprinted, 1975, in Richard B. Schlatter, *Hobbes' Thucydides*). New Brunswick, NJ: Rutgers University Press.

———. 1651. *Leviathan* (edited by C. B. McPherson). Middlesex, UK: Penguin (1968).

Hoffer, Eric. 1951. *The True Believer*. New York: Harper & Row.

Hollingshead, A. B. 1949. *Elmtown's Youth*. New York: Wiley.

Holstein, James A., and Gale Miller. 1990. "Rethinking Victimization: An Interactional Approach to Victimology." *Symbolic Interaction* 13(1):103–122.

Homans, George C. 1958. "Social Behavior as Exchange." *American Journal of Sociology* 63:597–606.

———. 1961. *Social Behavior: Its Elementary Forms*. London: Routledge and Paul.

Howard, Judith A., Philip Blumstein, and Pepper Schwartz. 1986. "Sex, Power, and Influence Tactics in Intimate Relationships." *Journal of Personality and Social Psychology* 51(1):102–109.

Hrebenar, Ronald J., and Ruth K. Scott. 1982. *Interest Group Politics in America*. Englewood Cliffs, NJ: Prentice-Hall.

Hunt, Jennifer. 1985. "Police Accounts of Normal Force." *Urban Life* 13(4):315–341.

Hunt, Morton, and Bernice Hunt. 1977. *The Divorce Experience*. New York: New American Library.

Hunt, Scott A. 1991. Constructing Collective Identity in a Peace Movement. Doctoral Dissertation, University of Nebraska, Lincoln, Nebraska.

Hunt, Scott A., and Robert D. Benford. 1994. "Identity Talk in the Peace and Justice Movement." *Journal of Contemporary Ethnography* 22(4):488–517.

Hunter, Albert. 1974. *Symbolic Communities: The Persistence and Change of Chicago's Local Communities.* Chicago: University of Chicago Press.

———. 1993. "Local Knowledge and Local Power: Notes on the Ethnography of Local Community Elites." *Journal of Contemporary Ethnography* 22(1):36–58.

Hunter, Floyd. 1953. *Community Power Structure: A Study of Decision Makers.* Chapel Hill: University of North Carolina Press.

———. 1959. *Top Leadership, USA.* Chapel Hill: University of North Carolina Press.

Ilich, John. 1992. *Dealbreakers and Breakthroughs: The Ten Most Common and Costly Negotiation Mistakes and How to Overcome Them.* New York: Wiley.

Ingraham, Larry H. 1984. *The Boys in the Barracks: Observations on American Military Life.* Philadelphia: Institute for the Study of Human Issues.

Irini, Styllianoss, and Robert Prus. 1982. "Doing Security Work: Keeping Order in the Hotel Setting." *Canadian Journal of Criminology* 24(1):61–82.

Isocrates (436–338 B.C.). *Nicocles or the Cyprians* in *Isocrates* Vol. I. Trans. by George Norlin. Cambridge, MA: Harvard University Press (1928).

———. *To Demonicus* in *Isocrates* Vol. I. Trans. by George Norlin. Cambridge, MA: Harvard University Press (1928).

———. *To Nicocles* in *Isocrates* Vol. I. Trans. by George Norlin. Cambridge, MA: Harvard University Press (1928).

Jacobs, Bruce A. 1992a. "Undercover Deception: Reconsidering Presentations of Self." *Journal of Contemporary Ethnography* 21(2):200–225.

———. 1992b. "Undercover Drug-Use Evasion Tactics: Excuses and Neutralization." *Symbolic Interaction* 15:435–453.

———. 1994. "Undercover Social-distancing Techniques." *Symbolic Interaction* 17(4):395–410.

Jacobs, James B., and Harold G. Retsky. 1975. "Prison Guards." *Urban Life* 4(1):5–29.

Jacobs, Mark D. 1990. *Screwing the System and Making it Work: Juvenile Justice in the No-Fault Society.* Chicago: University of Chicago Press.

Joas, Hans. 1985. *G. H. Mead: A Contemporary Reexamination of His Thought.* Cambridge: Polity.

Johnson, Richard. 1991. "Frameworks of Culture and Power: Complexity and Politics in Cultural Studies." *Cultural Studies* 3(1):17–61.

Johnston, Hank, Enrique Larana, and Joseph R. Gusfield. 1994. "Identities, Grievances, and New Social Movements." Pp. 3–35 in Enrique Larana, Hank Johnston, and Joseph R. Gusfield (eds.), *New Social Movements: From Ideology to Identity.* Philadelphia: Temple University Press.

Johnstone, Christopher Lyle. 1996. *Theory, Text, Context: Issues in Greek Rhetoric and Oratory.* Albany: State University of New York Press.

Jones, Edward E. 1964. *Ingratiation: A Social Psychological Analysis.* New York: Appleton-Century-Crofts.

Jorgensen, Danny. 1989. *Participant Observation.* Newbury Park, CA: Sage.

Kadmon, Adam. 1995. "Letter to the Editor (re: the Frankfort School and the representation of Marxism)" *Contemporary Sociology* 24:716–717.

Kahn, George N. 1963. *The 36 Biggest Mistakes Salespeople Make and How to Correct Them.* Englewood Cliffs, NJ: Prentice-Hall.

Karsh, Bernard, Joel Seidman, and Daisy M. Lilienthal. 1953. "The Union Organizer and His Tactics: A Case Study." *American Journal of Sociology* 59:113–122.

Kauffman, Kelsey. 1988. *Prison Officers and Their World.* Cambridge, MA: Harvard University Press.

Kaufman, Harold F. 1959. "Toward an Interactional Conception of Community." *Social Forces* 38:8–17.

Keiser, R. Lincoln. 1969. *The Vice Lords: Warriors of the Streets.* New York: Holt, Rinehart and Winston.

Kellner, Douglas. 1995. *Media Culture: Cultural Studies, Identity and Politics Between the Modern and the Postmodern.* London: Routledge.

Kennedy, Gavin. 1994. *The Perfect Negotiation.* New York: Wings.

Kennedy, George. 1963. *The Art of Persuasion in Greece.* Princeton, NJ: Princeton University Press.

———. 1972. *The Art of Rhetoric in the Roman World.* Princeton, NJ: Princeton University Press.

Key, V.O., Jr. 1955. *Politics, Parties, and Pressure Groups* (3rd ed.). New York: Crowell.

Kinsey, Barry A. 1985. "Congressional Staff: The Cultivation and Maintenance of Personal Networks in an Insecure Work Environment." *Urban Life* 13(4):395–422.

Kipnis, David, Stuart M. Schmidt, and Ian Wilkinson. 1980. "Intraorganizational Influence Tactics: Explorations in Getting One's Way." *Journal of Applied Psychology* 65(4):440–452.

Kissinger, Henry. 1994. *Diplomacy.* New York: Simon & Schuster.

Klandermans, Bert. 1984. "Mobilization and Participation: Social-Psychological Expansions of Resource Mobilization Theory." *American Sociological Review* 49:583–600.

———.1997. *The Social Psychology of Protest.* Cambridge, MA: Blackwell.

Klandermans, Bert, Hanspeter Kriesi, and Sidney Tarrow. 1988. *International Social Movement Research: From Structure to Action: Comparing Social Movement Research Across Cultures.* Vol. 1. Greenwich, CT: JAI.

Klapp, Orrin. 1962. *Heroes, Villains and Fools.* San Diego, CA: Aegis.

———. 1964. *Symbolic Leaders.* Chicago: Aldine.

———. 1969. *Collective Search for Identity.* New York: Holt, Rinehart and Winston.

———. 1971. *Social Types: Process, Structure and Ethos.* San Diego, CA: Aegis.

Koch, Sigmund. 1981. "The Nature and Limits of Psychological Knowledge." *American Psychologist* 36:257–269.

Kolakowski, Leszek. 1978. *Main Currents of Marxism* (3 vols.). Oxford: Oxford University Press.

Kotter, John P. 1985. *Power and Influence.* New York: Free Press.

Kunda, Gideon. 1992. *Engineering Culture: Control and Commitment in a High-Tech Corporation.* Philadelphia: Temple University Press.

Kuhn, Manford. 1954. "Kinsey's View on Human Behavior." *Social Problems* 1:119–125.

———. 1964. "Major Trends in Symbolic Interaction over the Past Twenty-five Years." *Sociological Quarterly* 5:61–84.

Kuhn, Thomas S. 1962. *The Structure of Scientific Revolutions* (Rev. ed., 1970). Chicago: University of Chicago Press.

Lantz, Herman R. 1958. *People of Coal Town.* New York: Columbia University Press.

Larana, Enrique, Hank Johnston, and Joseph R. Gusfield. 1994. *New Social Movements: From Ideology to Identity.* Philadelphia: Temple University Press.

Lasswell, Harold D., Ralph D. Casey, and Bruce Lannes Smith. 1935. *Propaganda and Promotional Activities: An Annotated Bibliography.* Minneapolis: University of Minnesota Press. (Reprinted 1962, 1969, by University of Chicago Press, Chicago).

Laurer, Robert H., and Warren H. Handel. 1977. *The Theory and Application of Symbolic Interaction.* Boston: Houghton Mifflin.

Lawler, Edward J. 1992. "Power Process in Bargaining." *The Sociological Quarterly* 33(1):17–34.

Layder, Derek. 1985. "Power, Structure and Agency." *Journal for the Theory of Social Behaviour* 15(2):131–149.

Le Bon, Gustave. 1922. *The Crowd: A Study of the Popular Mind.* London: T. Fisher Unwin.

Lee, Alfred McClung. 1951. *New Outline of the Principles of Sociology.* New York: Barnes & Noble (Subsequent editions in 1955, 1969).

Leiter, Kenneth. 1980. *A Primer on Ethnomethodology.* New York: Oxford University Press.

Lemert, Edwin. 1951. *Social Pathology.* New York: McGraw-Hill.

———. 1953. "An Isolation and Closure Theory of Naive Check Forgery." *The Journal of Criminal Law, Criminology and Police Science* 44:296–307.

———. 1962. "Paranoia and the Dynamics of Exclusion." *Sociometry* 25:2–25.

———. 1967. *Human Deviance, Social Problems and Social Control.* Englewood Cliffs, NJ: Prentice-Hall.

Lenin, V. I. 1970. *Against Revisionism, In Defense of Marxism.* (Papers from 1899–1921; from V.I. Lenin's Collected Works). Moscow: Progress.

Lesieur, Henry. 1977. *The Chase.* New York: Anchor.

Lester, Marilyn, and Stuart C. Hadden. 1980. "Ethnomethodology and Grounded Theory Methodology." *Urban Life* 9:3–33.

Lever, Ralph. 1573. *The Art of Reason, Rightly Termed Witcraft.* Menston, UK: Scholar Press (1972).

Lewis, David V. 1981. *Power Negotiating Tactics and Techniques.* Englewood Cliffs, NJ: Prentice-Hall.

Ling, Monica. 1963. *How to Increase Sales and Put Yourself Across by Telephone.* Englewood Cliffs, NJ: Prentice-Hall.

Lipset, Seymour Martin. 1960. *Political Man: The Social Bases of Politics.* New York: Doubleday.

———. 1996. "Steady Work: An Academic Memoir." *Annual Review of Sociology* 22:1–27.

Lipset, Seymour Martin, Martin A. Trow, and James S. Coleman. 1956. *Union Democracy: The Internal Politics of the International Typographical Union.* Glencoe, IL: Free Press.

Lipsky, M. 1968. "Protest as a Political Resource." *American Political Science Review* 62:1144–1158.

Livy (Titus Livius, 59 B.C.–17 A.D.). *The History of Rome From Its Foundation.* Baltimore: Penguin (1960, 1982).

Lofland, John. 1966. *The Doomsday Cult.* Englewood Cliffs, NJ: Prentice-Hall.

———. 1970. "Interactionist Imagery and Analytic Interruptus." Pp. 35–45 in Tamotsu Shibutani (ed.), *Human Nature and Collective Behavior: Papers in Honor of Herbert Blumer.* Englewood Cliffs, NJ: Prentice-Hall.

———. 1976. *Doing Social Life.* New York: Wiley.

———. 1981. "Collective Behavior: The Elementary Forms." Pp. 411–446 in Morris Rosenberg and Ralph H. Turner (eds.), *Social Psychology: Sociological Perspectives.* New York: Basic.

———. 1993. *Polite Protesters: The American Peace Movement of the 1980's.* Syracuse: Syracuse University Press.

———. 1996. *Social Movement Organizations: Guide to Research on Insurgent Realities.* New York: Aldine de Gruyter.

Lofland, John, and Michael Fink. 1982. *Symbolic Sit-ins: Protest Occupations at the California Capitol.* Washington, DC: University Press of America.

Lofland, John, and Lyn Lofland. 1995. *Analyzing Social Settings* (3rd ed.). Belmont, CA: Wadsworth.

Long, Norton E. 1958. "The Local Community as an Ecology of Games." *American Journal of Sociology* 64:251–261.

Loseke, Donileen R. 1989. "Evaluation Research and the Practice of Social Services: A Case for Qualitative Methodology." *Journal of Contemporary Ethnography* 18(2):202–223.

Lucas, Rex A. 1971. *Minetown, Milltown, Railtown: Life in Canadian Communities of Single Industry.* Toronto: University of Toronto Press.

Luckenbill, David F. 1979. "Power: A Conceptual Framework." *Symbolic Interaction* 2:97–114.

Lukes, Stephen. 1974. *Power: A Radical View.* London: Macmillan.

Lyman, Stanford M. 1997. *Postmodernism and a Sociology of the Absurd.* Fayetteville: University of Arkansas Press.

Lyman, Stanford M., and Marvin Scott. 1989. *A Sociology of the Absurd* (2nd ed.). Dix Hills, NY: General Hall.

Lynch, Richard. 1993. *Lead!: How Public and Nonprofit Managers can Bring out the Best in Themselves and Their Organizations.* San Francisco: Jossey-Bass.

Lyotard, Jean-Francois. 1984. *The Postmodern Condition.* Trans. by Geoff Bennington and Brian Massumi. Minneapolis: University of Minnesota Press.

Machiavelli, Niccolò. 1950. *The Prince and the Discourses.* Trans. by Luigi Ricci and E. R. P. Vincent, with an introduction by Max Lerner. New York: Random House.

MacLeod, Bruce A. 1993. *Club Date Musicians: Playing the New York Party Circuit.* Urbana: University of Illinois Press.

Maines, David R. 1977. "Social Organization and Social Structure in Symbolic Interactionist Thought." *Annual Review of Sociology* 3:235–259.

———. 1988. "Myth, Text, and Interactionist Complicity in the Neglect of Blumer's Macrosociology." *Symbolic Interaction* 11(1):43–57.

———. 1989. "Repackaging Blumer: The Myth of Herbert Blumer's Astructural Bias." Pp. 383–413 in Norman K. Denzin (ed.), *Studies in Symbolic Interaction,* Vol. 10. Greenwich, CT: JAI.

———. 1996a. "On Choices and Criticism: A Reply to Denzin." *Symbolic Interaction* 19(4):357–362.

———. 1996b. "On Postmodernism, Pragmatism, and Plasters: Some Interactionist Thoughts and Queries." *Symbolic Interaction* 19(4):323–340.

Maisel, Louis Sandy. 1982. *From Obscurity to Oblivion: Running in the Congressional Primary.* Knoxville: University of Tennessee Press.

———. 1994. *The Parties Respond: Changes in American Parties and Campaigns.* San Francisco: Westview.

Mann, Michael. 1986. *The Sources of Social Power: Vol. 1, A History of Power From the Beginning to A.D. 1760.* Cambridge: Cambridge University Press.

———. 1993. *The Sources of Social Power: Vol. 2, The Rise of Classes and Nation States, 1760–1914.* New York: Cambridge University Press.

Marks, James T. 1990. Volunteering: Patterns of Interaction and the Process of Helping. M.A. Thesis. University of Waterloo, Waterloo, Ontario.

Martin, Brian. 1989. "Gene Sharp's Theory of Power." *Journal of Peace Research* 26:213–222.

Martin, Henri-Jean. 1988. *The History and Power of Writing.* Trans. by Lydia G. Cochrane. Chicago: University of Chicago Press (1994).

Martindale, Don. 1981. *The Nature and Types of Sociological Theory* (2nd ed.). Boston: Houghton Mifflin.

Marwell, G., and D. R. Schmitt. 1967. "Dimensions of Compliance-Gaining Behavior." *Sociometry* 30:350–364.

Marx, Karl. 1971. *A Contribution to the Critique of Political Economy* [1859]. (Trans. and edited by S.W. Ryazanskaya). London: Dobb, Lawrence & Wishart.

Marx, Karl, and Friedrich Engels. 1964. *The German Ideology* [1846] (Trans. and edited by S. Ryazanskaya). Moscow: Progress.

———. 1968. *The Communist Manifesto* [Manifesto of the Communist Party-1848]. Peking: Foreign Language Press.

Marx, Karl, Friedrich Engels, and V. I. Lenin. nd. *On Scientific Communism.* Moscow: Progress.

Matza, David. 1964. *Delinquency and Drift.* New York: Wiley.

Mayer, Tom. 1994. *Analytical Marxism.* Thousand Oaks, CA: Sage.

McCarthy, John D., and Mayer N. Zald. 1977. "Resource Mobilization and Social Movements: A Partial Theory." *American Journal of Sociology* 82(6):1212–1241.

McGinniss, Joe. 1969. *The Selling of the President 1968.* New York: Pocket Books.

McKirahan, Richard D., Jr. 1994. *Philosophy Before Socrates.* Indianapolis: Hackett.

McLeod, Jack M., and Jay G. Blumler. 1987. "The Macrosocial Level of Communication Science." Pp. 271–322 in Charles R. Berger and Steven H. Chaffee (eds.), *Handbook of Communication Science.* Newbury Park, CA: Sage.

McMahon, Martha. 1995. *Engendering Motherhood: Identity and Self Transformation in Women's Lives.* New York: Guilford.

McNulty, Elizabeth W. 1994. "Generating Common Sense Knowledge Among Police Officers." *Symbolic Interaction* 17(3):281–294.

McPhail, Clark. 1991. *The Myth of The Madding Crowd.* New York: Aldine de Gruyter.

———. 1994. "The Dark Side of Purpose: Individual and Collective Violence in Riots." *The Sociological Quarterly* 35(1):1–32.

———. 1997. "Stereotypes of Crowds and Collective Behavior: Looking Backward, Looking Forward." Pp. 35–58 in D. E. Miller, M. Katovich, and S. Saxton (eds.), *Constructing Complexity.* Supplement 3 of *Studies in Symbolic Interaction.* Greenwich, CT: JAI.

McPhail, Clark, and Ronald T. Wohlstein. 1986. "Collective Locomotion as Collective Behavior." *American Sociological Review* 51:447–463.

McQuail, Denis. 1983. *Mass Communication Theory: An Introduction.* Beverly Hills, CA: Sage.

McRobbie, Angela. 1992. "Post-Marxism and Cultural Studies: A Postscript." Pp. 719–730 in Lawrence Grossberg, Cary Nelson, and Paula A. Treichler (eds.), *Cultural Studies.* New York: Routledge.

Mead, George H. 1934. *Mind, Self and Society* (edited by Charles W. Morris). Chicago: University of Chicago Press.

———. 1938. *The Philosophy of the Act.* Chicago: University of Chicago Press.

Meehan, Albert J. 1986. "Record-Keeping Practices in the Policing of Juveniles." *Urban Life* 15(1):70–102.

———. 1992. "'I Don't Prevent Crime, I Prevent Calls': Policing as a Negotiated Order." *Symbolic Interaction* 15:455–480.

Mehan, Hugh B., and H. Lawrence Wood. 1975. *The Reality of Ethnomethodology.* New York: John Wiley.

Meltzer, Bernard, and John Petras. 1972. "The Chicago and Iowa Schools of Symbolic Interactionism." Pp. 43–57 in Jerome G. Manis and Bernard N. Meltzer (eds.), *Symbolic Interactionism.* Boston: Allyn and Bacon.

Meltzer, Bernard, John W. Petras and Larry T. Reynolds. 1975. *Symbolic Interactionism: Genesis, Varieties and Criticism.* London: Routledge and Kegan Paul.

Merton, Robert K. 1957. *Social Theory and Social Structure.* New York: Free Press.

Meyer, David S., and Nancy Whittier. 1994. "Social Movement Spillover." *Social Problems* 41 (2):277–298.

Michels, Robert. 1962. *Political Parties* [1915]. New York: Free Press.

Michener, H. Andrew, and Robert W. Suchner. 1972. "The Tactical Use of Social Power." Pp. 239–289 in James T. Tedeschi (ed.), *The Social Influence Process.* New York: Aldine-Atherton.

Milbrath, Lester W. 1963. *The Washington Lobbyists.* Chicago: Rand-McNally.

Miller, Arthur G. 1986. *The Obedience Experiments: A Case Study of Controversy in Social Science.* New York: Praeger.

Millot, Benoit. 1988. "Symbol, Desire and Power." *Theory, Culture and Society* 5:675–694.

Mills, C. Wright. 1956. *The Power Elite.* New York: Oxford University Press.

———. 1962. *The Marxists.* New York: Brandt and Brandt.

Mintzberg, Henry. 1973. *The Nature of Organizational Work.* New York: Harper & Row.

Mizruchi, Mark S. 1996. "What Do Interlocks Do?: An Analysis, Critique, and Assessment of Research on Interlocking Directorates." *Annual Review of Sociology* 22:271–298.

Morrill, Calvin. 1995. *The Executive Way: Conflict Management in Corporations.* Chicago: University of Chicago Press.

Morris, Aldon D., and Carol McClung Mueller. 1992. *Frontiers in Social Movement Theory.* New Haven, CT: Yale University Press.

Mosca, Gaetano. 1939. *The Ruling Class* [1896] (edited and revised by Arthur Livingston). New York: McGraw-Hill.

Moskos, Charles C., Jr. 1976. "The Military." *Annual Review of Sociology* 2:55–77.

Nelson, Cary, Paula A. Treichler, and Lawrence Rosenberg. 1992. "Cultural Studies: An Introduction." Pp. 1–22 in Lawrence Rosenberg, Cary Nelson, and Paula A. Treichler (eds.), *Cultural Studies.* New York: Routledge.

Nesbit, Robert. 1966. *The Sociological Tradition.* New York: Basic.

Ng, Sik Hung. 1980. *The Social Psychology of Power.* New York: Academic Press.

Nierenberg, Gerald. 1968. *The Art of Negotiating: Psychological Strategies for Gaining Advantageous Bargains.* New York: Cornerstone.

Nietzsche, Friedrich. 1986. *Human, All too Human* [1878, 1886] (Trans. by R. J. Hollingdale). Cambridge: Cambridge University Press.

Nimmo, Dan, and James E. Combs. 1983. *Mediated Political Realities.* New York: Longman.

Norris, James S. 1982. *Selling-The How and Why.* Englewood Cliffs, NJ: Prentice-Hall.

Odegard, Peter H. 1967. "Introduction" to Arthur F. Bentley, *The Process of Government.* Cambridge, MA: Harvard University Press.

Olesen, Virginia. 1994. "Feminisms and Models of Qualitative Research." Pp. 158–174 in Norman K. Denzin and Yvonna S. Lincoln (eds.), *Handbook of Qualitative Research.* Thousand Oaks, CA: Sage.

Olsen, Marvin E., and Martin N. Marger. 1993. *Power in Modern Societies.* San Francisco: Westview.

Olson, Lynn M. 1995. "Record Keeping Practices: Consequences of Accounting Demands in a Public Clinic." *Qualitative Sociology* 18(1):45–70.

Olson, Mancur. 1965. *The Logic of Collective Action: Public Goods and the Theory of Groups.* Cambridge, MA: Harvard University Press.

Ornstein, Norman J., and Shirley Elder. 1978. *Interest Groups, Lobbying and Policymaking.* Washington, DC: Congressional Quarterly Press.

Paizis, Suzanne. 1977. *Getting Her Elected: A Political Woman's Handbook.* Sacramento, CA: Creative Editions.

Pareto, Wilfredo. 1966. *Wilfredo Pareto: Sociological Writings* (Trans. by Derick Mirfin). New York: Praeger.

Park, Robert E. 1939. *An Outline of the Principles of Sociology.* New York: Barnes & Noble.

———. 1972. *The Crowd and the Public and Other Essays* (Henry Elsner, ed.; trans. by Charlotte Elsner). Chicago: University of Chicago Press.

Park, Robert E., and Ernest W. Burgess. 1921. *Introduction to the Science of Sociology.* Chicago: University of Chicago Press.

Parnas, Raymond. 1967. "The Police Response to Domestic Disturbances." *Wisconsin Law Review:* 914–960.

Parsons, Talcott. 1963. "On the Concept of Influence." *Public Opinion Quarterly* 27:37–62.

Patai, Daphne, and Noretta Koertge. 1995. *Professing Feminism: Cautionary Tales from the Strange World of Women's Studies.* New York: Basic.

Peele, Norman Vincent. 1952. *The Power of Positive Thinking.* Englewood Cliffs, NJ: Prentice-Hall.

———. 1990. *The Power of Positive Living.* Garden City, NY: Doubleday.

Peyrot, Mark. 1985. "Coerced Voluntarism: The Micropolitics of Drug Treatment." *Urban Life* 13(4):343–365.

Pfeffer, Jeffery. 1981. *Power in Organizations.* Marshfield, MA: Pitman.

———. 1992. *Managing with Power: Politics and Influence in Organizations.* Boston: Harvard Business School Press.

———. 1997. *New Directions of Organization Theory.* New York: Oxford University Press.

Pfohl, Stephen J. 1978. *Predicting Dangerousness: The Social Construction of Psychiatric Reality.* Lexington, MA: D. C. Heath.

Platinga, Theodore. 1980. *Historical Understanding in the Thought of Wilhelm Dilthey.* Toronto: University of Toronto Press.

Plato (427–347 B.C.). *Cratylus.* Trans. by Benjamin Jowett. In Edith Hamilton and Huntington Cairns (eds.), *The Collected Dialogues of Plato.* Princeton, NJ: Princeton University Press (1961).

———. *Gorgias.* Trans. by Robin Waterfield. New York: Oxford University Press (1994).

———. *Plato: The Collected Works.* John M. Cooper (ed.). Indianapolis: Hackett (1997).

———. *Republic.* Trans. by Paul Shorey. In Edith Hamilton and Huntington Cairns (eds.), *The Collected Dialogues of Plato.* Princeton, NJ: Princeton University Press (1961).

———. *The Collected Dialogues of Plato.* Edith Hamilton and Huntington Cairns (eds.). Princeton, NJ: Princeton University Press (1961).

———. *The Laws.* Trans. by A.E. Taylor. New York: Dutton (1969).

———. *Theaetetus.* Trans. by Francis Macdonald Cornfield. In Edith Hamilton and Huntington Cairns (eds.), *The Collected Dialogues of Plato.* Princeton, NJ: Princeton University Press (1961).

Platt, Gerald M., and Chad Gordon. 1994. *Self, Collective Behavior and Society: Essays Honoring the Contributions of Ralph H. Turner.* Greenwich, CT: JAI.

Podolefsky, Aaron. 1990. "Mediator Roles in Simbu Conflict Management." *Ethnology* 29:67–81.

Polybius (208–120 B.C.). *Polybius: The Histories.* Trans. by W.R. Paton. Cambridge, MA: Harvard University Press (1922).

Polychroniou, Chronis. 1993. *Socialism: Crisis and Renewal.* Westport, CT: Praeger.

Popper, K. R. 1957. *The Open Society and Its Enemies (2 vols.).* London: Routledge and Kegan Paul.

Porter, John. 1965. *The Vertical Mosaic.* Toronto: University of Toronto Press.

Porter, Sam. 1996. "Contra-Foucault: Soldiers, Nurses and Power." *Sociology* 30(1):59–78.

Post, Emily. 1922. *Etiquette: In Society, in Business, in Politics, and at Home.* New York: Funk and Wagnell.

Poulakos, John. 1995. *Sophistical Rhetoric in Classical Greece.* Columbia: University of South Carolina Press.

Powell, Walter. 1985. *Getting into Print: The Decision-Making Process in Scholarly Publishing.* Chicago: University of Chicago Press.

Pozzolini, A. 1970. *Antonio Gramsci: An Introduction to His Thought* (Trans. by Anne Showstack). London: Pluto.

Price, Stephen S. 1959. *How to Speak with Power.* New York: McGraw Hill.

Price, Vincent, and Donald F. Roberts. 1987. "Public Opinion Process." Pp. 781–816 in Charles R. Berger and Steven H. Chaffee (eds.), *Handbook of Communication Science.* Newbury Park, CA: Sage.

Prus, Robert. 1973. Revocation Related Decision-Making by the Parole Agent: A Labeling Approach. Ph.D. Dissertation. University of Iowa, Iowa City, IA.

———. 1975a. "Labeling Theory: A Reconceptualization and a Propositional Statement on Typing." *Sociological Focus* 8:79–96.

———. 1975b. "Resisting Designations: An Extension of Attribution Theory into a Negotiated Context." *Sociological Inquiry* 45:3–14.

———. 1976. "Religious Recruitment and the Management of Dissonance: A Sociological Perspective." *Sociological Inquiry* 46:127–134.

———. 1978. From Barrooms to Bedrooms: Towards a Theory of Interpersonal Violence." Pp. 51–73 in M. A. B. Gammon (ed.), *Violence in Canada.* Toronto: Methuen.

———. 1983. "Drinking as Activity: An Interactionist Analysis." *Journal of Studies on Alcohol* 44(3):460–475.

———. 1987. "Generic Social Processes: Maximizing Conceptual Development in Ethnographic Research." *Journal of Contemporary Ethnography* 16(3):250–291.

———. 1989a. *Making Sales: Influence as Interpersonal Accomplishment.* Newbury Park, CA: Sage.

———. 1989b. *Pursuing Customers: An Ethnography of Marketing Activities.* Newbury Park, CA: Sage.

———. 1991. "Attributing Trust and Invoking Skepticism: Shoppers' Encounters with Uncertainty and Risk." Qualitative Analysis Conference, Carleton University, Ottawa, Ontario.

———. 1992a. "Influence Work in Human Service Settings: Lessons from the Marketplace." Pp. 41–56 in Gale Miller (ed.), *Current Research on Occupations and Professions*, Vol. 7. Greenwich, CT: JAI.

———. 1992b. "Producing Social Science: Knowledge as a Social Problem in Academia." Pp. 57–78 in Gale Miller and James Holstein (eds.), *Perspectives in Social Problems*, Vol. 3. Greenwich, CT: JAI.

———. 1992c. "Tenuous Relationships: Loyal, Fickle, and Default Patronage." Paper presented at Qualitative Analysis Conference, Carleton University, Ottawa, Ontario.

———. 1993a. "Encountering the Mass Media: Consumers as Targets and Tacticians." Paper presented at Studying Human Lived Experience: Symbolic Interaction and Ethnographic Research '93, University of Waterloo, Waterloo, Ontario.

———. 1993b. "Shopping With Companions: Images, Influences and Interpersonal Dilemmas." *Qualitative Sociology* 16:87–109.

———. 1994a. "Consumers as Targets: Autonomy, Accountability, and Anticipation of the Influence Process. *Qualitative Sociology* 17:243–262.

———. 1994b. "Generic Social Processes: Intersubjectivity and Transcontextuality in the Social Sciences." Pp. 393–412 in Mary Lorenz Dietz, Robert Prus, and William Shaffir (eds.), *Doing Everyday Life: Ethnography as Human Lived Experience*. Toronto: Copp Clark Longman.

———. 1996a. "Adolescent Life-Worlds and Deviant Involvements: A Research Agenda for Studying Adolescence as Lived Experience." Pp. 7–69 in Gary O'Berick (ed.) *Not a Kid Anymore: Canadian Youth, Crime, and Subcultures*. Toronto: Nelson Canada.

———. 1996b. *Symbolic Interaction and Ethnographic Research: Intersubjectivity and the Study of Human Lived Experience*. Albany: State University of New York Press.

———. 1997a. "Shoppers as Elusive Targets." Pp. 221–246 in D. E. Miller, M. Katovich, and S. Saxton (eds.), *Constructing Complexity*. Supplement 3 of *Studies in Symbolic Interaction*. Greenwich, CT: JAI.

———. 1997b. *Subcultural Mosaics and Intersubjective Realities: An Ethnographic Research Agenda for Pragmatizing the Social Sciences*. Albany: State University of New York Press.

Prus, Robert, and Lorne Dawson. 1991. "Shop 'til You Drop: Shopping as Recreational and Laborious Activity." *Canadian Journal of Sociology* 16:145–164.

———. 1996. "Obdurate Reality and the Intersubjective Other: The Problematics of Representation and the Privilege of Presence." Pp. 245–

257 in Robert Prus, *Symbolic Interaction and Ethnographic Research*. Albany: State University of New York Press.

Prus, Robert, Mary Lorenz Dietz, and William Shaffir. 1997a. "Doing Ethnographic Research: Fieldwork as Practical Accomplishment." Pp. 191–249 in Robert Prus, *Subcultural Mosaics and Intersubjective Realities: An Ethnographic Research Agenda for Pragmatizing the Social Sciences*. Albany: State University of New York Press.

———. 1997b. "Writing Ethnographic Research Reports: Some Practical Considerations for Students." Pp. 251—285 in Robert Prus, *Subcultural Mosaics and Intersubjective Realities: An Ethnographic Research Agenda for Pragmatizing the Social Sciences*. Albany: State University of New York Press.

Prus, Robert, and Augie Fleras. 1996. "'Pitching' Images of the Community to the Generalized Other: Promotional Strategies of Economic Development Officers." Pp. 99–128 in Helena Znaniecki Lopata (ed.), *Current Research on Occupations and Professions: Getting Down to Business*. Vol. 9. Greenwich, CT: JAI.

Prus, Robert, and Wendy Frisby. 1990. "Persuasion as Practical Accomplishment: Tactical Manoeuverings at Home Party Plans." Pp. 133–162 in Helena Znaniecki Lopata (ed.), *Current Research on Occupations and Professions: Societal Influences*. Vol. 5. Greenwich, CT: JAI.

Prus, Robert, and Styllianoss Irini. 1980. *Hookers, Rounders, and Desk Clerks: The Social Organization of the Hotel Community*. Salem, WI: Sheffield (1988).

Prus, Robert, and C.R.D. Sharper. 1977. *Road Hustler: The Career Contingencies of Professional Card and Dice Hustlers*. Lexington, MA: Lexington Books

———. 1991. *Road Hustler: Hustlers, Magic and the Thief Subculture*. New York: Kaufman and Greenberg.

Prus, Robert, and John R. Stratton. 1976. "Parole Revocation Decision-Making: Private Typings and Official Designations." *Federal Probation* 40(1):48–53.

Quintilian (Quintilianus, Marcus Fabius) (c. 35–100 A.D.). *The Institutio Oratoria of Quintilian*. Trans. by H.E. Butler. Cambridge, MA: Harvard University Press (1920).

Ray, Marsh. 1961. "The Cycle of Abstinence and Relapse among Heroin Addicts." *Social Problems* 9:132–140.

Reardon, Kathleen K. 1991. *Persuasion in Practice*. Newbury Park, CA: Sage.

Reinharz, Shulamit. 1992. *Feminist Methods in Social Research*. New York: Oxford University Press.

Richman, Joel. 1983. *Traffic Wardens: An Ethnography of Street Administration*. Manchester, UK: University of Manchester Press.

Rickman, H. P. 1976. *W. Dilthey: Selected Writings*. New York: Cambridge University Press.

―――. 1988. *Dilthey Today: A Critical Appraisal of the Contemporary Relevance of His Work*. Westport, CT: Greenwood.

Ritzer, George. 1996. *Sociological Theory*. New York: McGraw-Hill.

Robinson, Daniel R. 1989. *Aristotle's Psychology*. New York: Columbia University Press.

Rochford, E. Burke. 1982. "Recruitment Strategies, Ideology, and Organization in the Hare Krishna Movement." *Social Problems* 24:399–410.

―――. 1986. *Hare Krishna In America*. New Brunswick, NJ: Rutgers University Press.

Roebuck, Julian B., and Wolfgang Frese. 1976. *The Rendezvous: A Case Study of an After-Hours Club*. New York: Free Press.

Rogers, Everett M., and J. Douglas Storey. 1987. "Communication Campaigns." Pp. 817–846 in Charles R. Berger and Steven H. Chaffee (eds.), *Handbook of Communication Science*. Newbury Park, CA: Sage.

Rogers, Mary F. 1974. "Instrumental and Infra-Resources: The Bases of Power." *American Journal of Sociology* 79(6):1418–1433.

―――. 1977. "Goffman on Power." *The American Sociologist* 12:88–95.

Rose, Arnold. 1967. *The Power Structure: Political Process in American Society*. New York: Oxford University Press.

Rosenfield, Lawrence. 1971. "An Autopsy of the Rhetorical Tradition." Pp. 64–77 in Lloyd F. Ritzer and Edwin Black (eds.), *The Prospect of Rhetoric*. Englewood Cliffs, NJ: Prentice-Hall.

Rosnow, Ralph L., and Gary Alan Fine. 1976. *Rumor and Gossip: The Social Psychology of Hearsay*. New York: Elsevier.

Ross, H. Lawrence. 1980. *Settled Out of Court: The Social Process of Insurance Claims Adjustment* (2nd ed.). Chicago: Aldine.

Rossides, Daniel. 1990. *Social Stratification*. Englewood Cliffs, NJ: Prentice-Hall.

Roth, Julius. 1962. "The Treatment of Tuberculosis as a Bargaining Process." Pp. 575–588 in Arnold Rose (ed.), *Human Behavior and Social Process*. Boston: Houghton-Mifflin.

Rousseau, Jean-Jacques. 1966. *On the Origin of Language*. Trans. by John H. Moran and Alexander Gode. New York: Frederick Ungar.

Roy, Donald. 1968. "The Union Organizing Campaign as a Problem of Social Distance: Three Crucial Dimensions of Affiliation-Disaffiliation." Pp. 49–66 in Howard S. Becker, Blanche Geer, David Reisman, and Robert Weiss (eds.), *Institutions and the Person: Papers Presented to Everett C. Hughes*. Chicago: Aldine.

Roznaczuk, Ronald. 1998. Selling Oneself: The Social Construction of Real Estate Agent-Client/Customer Relationships. Ph.D. Dissertation. University of Waterloo, Waterloo, Ontario.

Rubin, Herbert J. 1987. "Rule Making, Exceptioning, and County Land Use Decisions." *Urban Life* 15(3–4):299–330.

Rubin, Jeffrey, and Bert R. Brown. 1975. *The Social Psychology of Bargaining and Negotiation.* New York: Academic.

Rubington, Earl. 1968. "Variations in Bottle-Gang Controls." Pp. 308–316 in Earl Rubington and Martin Weinberg (eds.), *Deviance: The Interactionist Perspective.* New York: Macmillan.

Rubinstein, Jonathan. 1973. *City Police.* New York: Ballantine.

Rule, Brendan Gail, Gay L. Bisanz, and Melinda Kohn. 1985. "Anatomy of a Persuasion Schema: Targets, Goals, and Strategies." *Journal of Personality and Social Psychology* 48(5):1127–1140.

Sanders, Clinton. 1974. "Psyching Out the Crowd: Folk Performers and Their Audiences." *Urban Life and Culture* 3(3):264–282.

———. 1989. *Customizing the Body: The Art and Culture of Tattooing.* Philadelphia: Temple University Press.

———. 1994. "Annoying Owners: Routine Interactions with Problematic Clients in a General Vetinary Practice." *Qualitative Sociology* 17:159–170.

———. 1995. "Stranger than Fiction: Insights and Pitfalls in Post-modern Ethnography." Pp. 89–104 in Norman K. Denzin (ed.), *Studies in Symbolic Interaction,* Vol. 17. Greenwich, CT: JAI.

Sandys, John Edward. 1920. *A History of Classical Scholarship.* New York: Hafner (1964).

Schein, Edgar H., Inge Schneier, and Curtis H. Barker. 1961. *Coercive Persuasion: A Socio-psychological Analysis of the "Brainwashing" of American Civilian Prisoners by the Chinese Communists.* New York: Norton.

Schiller, F. C. S. 1908. *Plato or Protagoras?* Oxford: Blackwell.

Schirer, William. 1959. *The Rise and Fall of the Third Reich: A History of Nazi Germany.* Greenwich, CT: Fawcett Crest.

Schlatter, Richard Bulger. 1975. *Hobbes' Thucydides.* New Brunswick, NJ: Rutgers University Press.

Schmid, Thomas, and Richard S. Jones. 1991. "Suspended Identity: Identity Transformation in a Maximum Security Prison." *Symbolic Interaction* 14(4):415–432.

———. 1993. "Ambivalent Actions: Prison Adaption Strategies of First-Time, Short-Term Inmates." *Journal of Contemporary Ethnography* 21(4):439–463.

Schneck, Stephen Frederick. 1987. "Michel Foucault on Power/Discourse, Theory and Practice." *Human Studies* 10:15–33.

Schottenloher, Karl. 1989. *Books and the Western World.* Trans. by W. D. Boyd and I. H. Wolfe. Jefferson, NC: McFarland.

Schramm, Wilbur, and Donald R. Roberts. 1971. *The Process and Effects of Mass Communication.* Urbana: University of Illinois Press.

Schutz, Alfred. 1943. "The Problem of Rationality in the Social World." *Economica* 10:130–149.

———. 1962. *Collected Papers I: The Problem of Social Reality.* The Hague: Martinus Nijhoff.

———. 1964. *Collected Papers II: Studies in Social Theory.* The Hague: Martinus Nijhoff.

———. 1967. *The Phenomenology of the Social World.* ([1932] trans. by George Walsh and Frederick Lehnert). Evanston, IL: Northwestern University Press.

Schwalbe, Michael. 1995. "The Responsibilities of Sociological Poets." *Qualitative Sociology* 18:393–413.

Schwartzman, Edward. 1989. *Political Campaign Craftsmanship: A Professional's Guide to Campaigning for Public Office.* New Brunswick, NJ: Transaction.

Scott, Lois. 1981. Being Somebody: The Negotiation of Identities in a Community Context. M.A. Thesis (Kinesiology). University of Waterloo, Waterloo, Ontario.

Seibold, David R., James G. Cantrill, and Renee A. Meyers. 1985. "Communication and Interpersonal Influence." Pp. 551–611 in Mark L. Knapp and Gerald R. Miller (eds.), *Handbook of Interpersonal Communication.* Beverly Hills, CA: Sage.

Selznick, Philip. 1966. *TVA and the Grass Roots.* New York: Harper and Row.

Sen, B. 1988. *A Diplomat's Handbook of International Law and Practice* (3rd ed.). Boston: Martinus Nijhoff.

Severin, Werner J., and James W. Tankard, Jr. 1988. *Communication Theories: Origins, Methods, Uses* (2nd. ed.). New York: Longman.

Sextus Empiricus (c. 200 A.D.). *Outlines of Pyrrhonism.* Trans. by R. G. Bury. Cambridge, MA: Harvard University Press (1933).

Shadegg, Stephen C. 1964. *How to Win an Election: The Art of Political Victory.* New York: Taplinger.

Shaffir, William. 1974. *Life In A Religious Community: The Lubavitcher Chassidim in Montreal.* Toronto: Holt, Rinehart and Winston.

———. 1993. "Jewish Messianism Lubavitch Style: An Interim Report." *The Jewish Journal of Sociology* 35:115–128.

———. 1995. "When Prophecy is Not Validated: Explaining the Unexpected in a Messianic Campaign." *The Jewish Journal of Sociology* 37:119–136.

Shaffir, William, and Robert Stebbins. 1991. *Experiencing Fieldwork.* Newbury Park, CA: Sage.

Sharman, David. 1994. *The Perfect Meeting.* New York: Wings.

Sharp, Gene. 1973. *The Politics of Nonviolent Action.* Boston: Porter Sargent.

Shaw, Clifford. 1930. *The Jack-Roller: A Delinquent Boy's Own Story.* Chicago: University of Chicago Press.

Sheperd, Gordon. 1987. The Social Construction of a Religious Prophecy. *Sociological Inquiry* 5:394–414.

Shibutani, Tamotsu. 1966. *Improvised News: A Sociological Study of Rumor.* Indianapolis: Bobbs-Merrill.

Simmel, Georg. 1950. *The Sociology of Georg Simmel.* Trans. and edited by Kurt H. Wolff. New York: Free Press.

———. 1955. *Conflict and the Web of Group-Affiliations.* Trans. by Kurt Wolff and Reinhard Bendix. New York: Free Press.

———. 1978. *The Philosophy of Money* (1907). Trans. by Tom Bottomore and David Frisby. Boston: Routledge and Kegan Paul.

Simon, Rita J. 1995. *Neither Victim Nor Enemy: Women's Freedom Network Looks at Gender in America.* Lanham, MD: University Press of America.

Simpson, Dick. 1981. *Winning Elections: A Handbook in Participatory Politics.* Athens: Ohio University Press.

Skvoretz, J., and D. Willer. 1993. "Exclusion and Power: A Test of 4 Theories in Power." *American Sociological Review* 58:801–818.

Smelser, Neil J. 1962. *The Theory of Collective Behavior.* New York: Free Press.

———. 1994. "Preface." Pp. xiii–xxii in Gerald M. Platt and Chad Gordon (eds.), *Self, Collective Behavior and Society: Essays Honoring the Contributions of Ralph H. Turner.* Greenwich, CT: JAI.

Smith, Dorothy E. 1990. *The Conceptual Practices of Power: A Feminist Sociology of Knowledge.* Toronto: University of Toronto Press.

Smith, Charles W. 1989. *Auctions: The Social Construction of Value.* Berkeley: University of California Press.

Smith, John. 1657. *Mystery of Rhetoric Unveil'd.* Menston, UK: Scholarly Press (1969).

Smith, Kenneth J. and Linda Liska Belgrave. 1995. "The Reconstruction of Everyday Life: Experiencing Hurricane Andrew." *Journal of Contemporary Ethnography* 24:244–269.

Snow, David A. 1979. "A Dramaturgical Analysis of Movement Accommodation: Building Idiosyncrasy Credit as a Movement Mobilization Strategy." *Symbolic Interaction* 2:23–44.

———. 1986. "Organization, Ideology and Mobilization: The Case of the Niciren Shoshu of America." In David G. Bromley and Philip E. Hammond (eds.), *The Future of New Religious Movements.* Macon, GA: Mercer University Press.

Snow, David A., and Robert D. Benford. 1988. "Ideology, Frame Resonance, and Participant Mobilization." *International Social Movement Research* 1:197–217.

———. 1992. "Master Frames and Cycles of Protest." Pp. 133–155 in Aldon D. Morris and Carol McClung Mueller (eds.), *Frontiers in Social Movement Theory.* New Haven, CT: Yale University Press.

Snow, David A., and Phillip W. Davis. 1994. "Turner's Contributions to the Study of Collective Behavior: An Elaboration and Critical Assessment." Pp 97–115 in Gerald M. Platt and Chad Gordon (eds.), *Self,*

Collective Behavior and Society: Essays Honoring the Contributions of Ralph H. Turner. Greenwich, CT: JAI.

Snow, David A., E. Burke Rochford, Jr., Steven K. Worden, and Robert Benford. 1986. "Frame Alignment Processes, Micromobilization, and Movement Participation." *American Sociological Review* 51:464–481.

Snow, Robert. 1983. *Creating Media Culture.* Beverly Hills, CA: Sage.

Snyder, Eldon E. 1994. "Getting Involved in the Shuffleboard World." Pp. 85–95 in Mary Lorenz Dietz, Robert Prus, and William Shaffir (eds.), *Doing Everyday Life: Ethnography as Human Lived Experience.* Toronto: Copp Clark Longman.

Sommers, Christina Hoff. 1994. *Who Stole Feminism?: How Women have Betrayed Women.* New York: Simon & Schuster.

———. 1995. "Who Stole Feminism?" Pp. 231–246 in Simon, Rita J. (ed.), *Neither Victim nor Enemy: Women's Freedom Network Looks at Gender In America.* Lanham, MD: University Press of America.

Sprague, Rosamond Kent. 1972. *The Older Sophists: A Complete Translation by Several Hands of the Fragments in Die Fragmente der Vorsokratiker* (edited by Diels-Kranz). Columbia: University of South Carolina Press.

Stanley, Liz, and Sue Wise. 1983. *Breaking Out: Feminist Ontology and Epistemology.* New York: Routledge.

———. 1993. *Breaking Out Again: Feminist Ontology and Epistemology.* New York: Routledge.

Stebbins, Robert. 1984. *The Magician.* Toronto: Clarke Irwin.

———. 1990. *The Laugh Makers: Stand-up Comedy as Art, Business, and Life-Style.* Kingston, Ontario: McGill-Queen's University Press.

Steffensmeier, Darrell. 1986. *The Fence: In the Shadow of Two Worlds.* Totawa, NJ: Rowman and Littlefield.

Stoecker, Randy. 1995. "Community, Movement, Organization: The Problem of Identity Convergence in Collective Action." *Sociological Quarterly* 36(1):111–130.

Strauss, Anselm. 1970. "Discovering New Theory From Previous Theory." Pp. 46–53 in T. Shibutani (ed.), *Human Nature and Collective Behavior: Papers in Honor of Herbert Blumer.* Englewood Cliffs, NJ: Prentice-Hall.

———. 1971. *The Contexts of Social Mobility.* Chicago: Aldine.

———. 1978a. "A Social World Perspective." Pp. 119–128 in Norman Denzin (ed.), *Studies in Symbolic Interaction,* Vol. 1. Greenwich, CT:JAI.

———. 1978b. *Negotiations: Varieties, Contexts, Processes, and Social Order.* San Francisco: Jossey-Bass.

———. 1982. "Interorganizational Negotiation." *Urban Life* 11(3):350–367.

———. 1984. "Social Worlds and their Segmentation Processes." Pp. 123–139 in Norman K. Denzin (ed.), *Studies in Symbolic Interaction,* Vol. 5. Greenwich, CT: JAI.

———. 1991. *Creating Sociological Awareness: Collective Images and Symbolic Representations*. New Brunswick, NJ: Transaction.

———. 1993. *Continual Permutations of Action*. Hawthorne, NY: Aldine de Gruyter.

Strauss, Leo, and Joseph Cropsey. 1987. *History of Political Philosophy* (3rd ed.). Chicago: University of Chicago Press.

Stryker, Sheldon. 1980. *Symbolic Interactionism: A Social Structural Version*. Menlo Park, CA: Benjamin/Cummings.

Sutherland, Edwin. 1937. *The Professional Thief*. Chicago: University of Chicago Press.

———. 1950. "The Diffusion of Sexual Psychopath Laws." *American Journal of Sociology* 56:142–148.

Suttles, Gerald D. 1968. *The Social Order of the Slum: Ethnicity and Territory in the Inner City*. Chicago: University of Chicago Press.

———. 1976. "Urban Ethnography: Situational and Normative Accounts." *Annual Review of Sociology* 2:1–17.

———. 1990. *The Man-Made City: The Land-Use Confidence Game in Chicago*. Chicago: University of Chicago Press.

Tannenbaum, Frank. 1938. *Crime and the Community*. New York: Columbia University Press.

Tarrow, Sidney. 1994. *Power in Movement: Social Movements Collective Action and Politics*. New York: Cambridge University Press.

Tedeschi, James T. 1972. *The Social Influence Process*. Chicago: Aldine.

Tedeschi, James T., and Thomas V. Bonoma. 1972. "Power and Influence: An Introduction." Pp. 1–49 in James T. Tedeschi (ed.), *The Social Influence Process*. Chicago: Aldine.

Tedeschi, James T., and Paul Rosenfeld. 1980. "Communication in Bargaining and Negotiation." Pp. 225–248 in Michael C. Roloff and Gerald Miller (eds.), *Persuasion: New Directions in Theory and Research*. Beverly Hills, CA: Sage.

Thibault, John, and Harold H. Kelly. 1959. *The Social Psychology of Groups*. New York: Wiley.

Thucydides (c. 460–400 B.C.). *The History of the Peloponnesian War*. Trans. by Thomas Hobbes (1629). Reprinted in Richard B. Schlatter (1975), *Hobbes' Thucydides*. New Brunswick, NJ: Rutgers University Press.

Tilly, Charles. 1978. *From Mobilization to Revolution*. Reading, MA: Addison-Wesley.

Tilly, Charles, Louise Tilly, and Richard H. Tilly. 1975. *The Rebellious Century: 1830–1930*. Cambridge, MA: Harvard University Press.

Trounstine Philip J., and Terry Christensen. 1982. *Movers and Shakers: The Study of Community Power*. New York: St. Martin's Press.

Truman, David B. 1951. *The Governmental Process: Political Interests and Public Opinion*. New York: Knopf.

Tsu, Sun (c. 500 B.C.). *The Art of War.* Trans. by Lionel Giles. Pp. 13–63 in Thomas R. Phillips (ed.), *Roots of Strategy.* Harrisburg, PA: Stackpole (1985).

Tuchman, Gaye. 1978. *Making News: A Study in the Construction of Reality.* New York: Free Press.

Turner, Jonathan. 1978. *The Structure of Sociological Theory.* Homewood, IL: Dorsey.

Turner, Ralph H. 1969. "The Public Perception of Protest." *American Sociological Review* 34:815–831.

———. 1994. "Epilogue." Pp. 379–387 in Gerald M. Platt and Chad Gordon (eds.), *Self, Collective Behavior and Society: Essays Honoring the Contributions of Ralph H. Turner.* Greenwich, CT: JAI.

Turner, Ralph H., and Lewis M. Killian. 1972. *Collective Behavior.* Englewood Cliffs, NJ: Prentice-Hall.

Ulmer, Jeffery T. 1994. "Trial Judges in a Rural Court Community: Contexts, Organizational Relations, and Interaction Strategies." *Journal of Contemporary Ethnography* 23(1):79–108.

Useem, Bert, Camille Graham Camp, and George M. Camp. 1996. *Resolution of Prison Riots: Strategies and Policies.* New York: Oxford University Press.

Van Maanen, John. 1984. "Making Rank: Becoming an American Police Sergeant." *Urban Life* 13(2–3):155–176.

Van Zandt, David E. 1991. *Living in the Children of God.* Princeton, NJ: Princeton University Press.

Vegetius, Renatus Flavius (c. 390 A.D.). *The Military Institutions of the Romans.* Trans. by John Clarke. Pp. 65–175 in Thomas R. Phillips (ed.), *Roots of Strategy.* Harrisburg, PA: Stackpole (1985).

Vico, Giambattista. 1744. *New Science.* Trans. by T. G. Bergin and M. H. Fisch. Ithaca, NY: Cornell University Press (1948).

Vidich, Arthur J., and Joseph Bensman. 1958. *Small Town in Mass Society: Class, Power and Religion in a Rural Community.* Princeton, NJ: Princeton University Press (1968).

Volosinov, V. N. 1930. *Marxism and the Philosophy of Language.* Trans. by Ladislav Matejka and I.R. Titunik. New York: Seminar Press (1973).

Walker, Jack L., Jr. 1991. *Mobilizing Interest Groups in America: Patrons, Professions, and Social Movements.* Ann Arbor: University of Michigan Press.

Waller, Willard. 1930. *The Old Love and the New.* Carbondale: Southern Illinois University Press (1967).

———. 1932. *The Sociology of Teaching.* New York: Russel and Russel (1961).

Warner, F. Lloyd and Paul S. Lunt. 1941. *The Social Life of a Modern Community* (Yankee City Series, 1). New Haven, CN: Yale University Press.

Warren, Carol A. B. 1983. "The Politics of Trouble in an Adolescent Psychiatric Hospital." *Urban Life* 12(3):327–348.

Wartenburg, Thomas E. 1990. *The Forms of Power: From Domination to Transformation.* Philadelphia: Temple University Press.

Weber, Max. 1960. *Max Weber: An Intellectual Portrait.* Edited by Rhinehard Bendix. New York: Doubleday-Anchor.

———. 1968. *Economy and Society: An Outline of Interpretive Sociology.* Guenther Roth and Claus Wittich (eds.). New York: Bedminster.

Wharton, Carol S. 1989. "Splintered Visions: Staff/Client Disjunctions and Their Consequences for Human Service Organizations." *Journal of Contemporary Ethnography* 18(1):50–71.

Whitmeyer, J. M. 1994. "Social-Structure and the Actor: The Case of Power in Exchange Networks." *Social Psychology Quarterly* 57:177–89.

———. 1997. "Mann's Theory of Power: A (Sympathetic) Critique." *British Journal of Sociology* 48:210–225.

Whittier, Nancy. 1995. *Feminist Generations: The Persistence of the Radical Women's Movement.* Philadelphia: Temple University Press.

Whyte, William Foote. 1943. *Street Corner Society: The Social Structure of an Italian Slum.* Chicago: University of Chicago Press.

Wilkinson, Harry. 1993. *Influencing People in Organizations: Concepts and Cases.* Fort Worth, TX: Dryden.

Williams, Raymond. 1977. *Marxism and Literature.* New York: Oxford University Press.

Williams, Robin M., Jr. 1984. "Field Observations and Surveys in Combat Zones." *Social Psychology Quarterly* 47(2):186–192.

Winter, David. 1973. *The Power Motive.* New York: Free Press.

Wipper, Audrey. 1977. *Rural Rebels: A Study of Two Protest Movements in Kenya.* New York: Oxford University Press.

Wiseman, Jacqueline. 1970. *Stations of the Lost: The Treatment of Skid Row Alcoholics.* Englewood Cliffs, NJ: Prentice-Hall.

———. 1983. "Towards a Theory of Policy Intervention in Social Problems." *Social Problems* 27:3–18.

Wolf, Charlotte. 1994. "Conversion into Feminism." Pp. 143–157 in Mary Lorenz Dietz, Robert Prus, and William Shaffir (eds.), *Doing Everyday Life: Ethnography as Human Lived Experience.* Toronto: Copp Clark Longman.

Wolf, Daniel. 1991. *The Rebels: A Brotherhood of Outlaw Bikers.* Toronto: University of Toronto Press.

Wolff, Kurt H. 1950. *The Sociology of Georg Simmel.* New York: Free Press.

Wolpe, Bruce C. 1990. *Lobbying Congress: How the System Works.* Washington, D.C.: Congressional Quarterly.

Wolpe, Joseph M. D. 1958. *Psychotherapy by Reciprocal Inhibition.* Stanford, CA: Stanford University Press.

———. 1990. *The Practice of Behavior Therapy* (4th ed.). New York: Pergamon.

Wood, James R., Eugene A. Weinstein, and Ronald Parker. 1967. "Children's Interpersonal Tactics." *Sociological Inquiry* 37:129–138.

Wood, Julia T. 1994. *Gendered Lives: Communication, Gender and Culture.* Belmont, CA: Wadsworth.

Wright, C. W. 1948. *Better Speeches For All Occasions.* Toronto: Ambassador.

Wrighter, Carl P. 1972. *I Can Sell You Anything.* New York: Ballantine.

Wrong, Dennis H. 1988. *Power: Its Forms, Bases, and Abuses* (1979). Chicago: University of Chicago Press.

Zald, Meyer N., and Roberta Ash. 1966. "Social Movement Organizations: Growth, Decay, and Change." *Social Forces* 44:327–340.

Zald, Mayer N., and John D. McCarthy. 1979. *The Dynamics of Social Movements: Resource Mobilization, Social Control, and Tactics.* Cambridge, MA: Winthrop.

Zeitlin, Irving. 1973. *Rethinking Sociology.* New York: Appleton-Century-Crofts.

Zimmerman, Don H. 1978. "Ethnomethodology." *The American Sociologist* 13:6–15.

Zurcher, Louis A., Jr. 1965. "The Sailor Aboard Ship: A Study of Role Behavior in a Total Institution." *Social Forces* 43:389–400.

———. 1982. "The Staging of Emotion: A Dramaturgical Analysis." *Symbolic Interaction* 5(1):1–22.

Zurcher, Louis, A. Jr., R. George Kirkpatrick, Robert G. Kushing, and Charles K. Bowman. 1971. "The Anti-Pornography Campaign: A Symbolic Crusade." *Social Problems* 19:217–237.

Zurcher, Louis A. Jr., and David A. Snow. 1981. "Collective Behavior: Social Movements." Pp 467–482 in Morris Rosenberg and Ralph H. Turner (eds.), *Social Psychology: Sociological Perspectives.* New York: Basic.

Index of Names

A

Adler, Patricia, 151, 202n, 244n,
Adorno, T. W., 59n
Agger, Ben, 33
Alexander, Jeffrey C., 128
Alexander the Great, 101, 102, 104
Alinksy, Saul D., 73, 109
Altheide, David L., 81, 87n, 162, 230, 246n
Anderson, Nels, 151
Apollo, 91
Argyris, Chris, 118n
Aristotle, xvi, 11, 12, 54n, 55n, 56n, 57n, 67,
    87n, 89, 90, 91, 93, 94, 95, 96, 97, 98, 100,
    101, 102, 104, 110, 111, 112n, 113n, 114n,
    115n, 116n, 117n, 204n, 209, 243n, 246n,
    268n
Aristophanes, 99, 116n
Aronson, Ronald, 32, 33
Ash, Roberta, 85n
Athens, Lonnie, 165n, 166n
Atkinson, Max, 118n
Atkinson, Michael, 151, 244n, 248n
Augustine, 104
Avineri, Shlomo, 58n

B

Bagdikian, Ben H., 79
Barnes, Harry Elmer, 54n, 91, 92, 112n
Barton, Roger, 118n
Baudrillard, Jean, 34, 79
Becker, Howard P., 54n, 91, 92, 112n
Becker, Howard S., 32, 61n, 151, 160n,
    162n, 204n, 220, 234, 244n, 248n, 267n
Bell, Colin, 88n
Bell, Daniel, 51
Bellah, Robert, 51
Bendix, Rhinehard, 165n
Benford, Robert D., 75, 76, 146, 149, 150,
    151, 163n, 234, 247n, 248n, 268n

Benhabib, Seyla, 45
Bennett, W. Lance, 79
Bensman, Joseph, 83, 151, 205n, 267n
Bentley, Arthur F., xi, 65, 77, 78, 86n
Berger, Charles R., 53n, 54n, 66
Berger, Peter, xvi, 13, 43, 67, 92, 95, 115n,
    161n, 197, 244n
Berry, D. H., 93
Best, Joel, 58n, 244n
Biernacki, Patrick, 151
Bigus, Odis E., 141, 203n, 204n
Billig, Michael, 67, 84n, 103, 105, 112n,
    117n, 247n
Bittner, Egon, 151, 205n, 243n, 267n
Blalock, Hubert M., Jr., 56n
Blau, Peter, 28, 53n, 56n, 62n, 205n
Blount, Thomas, 117n
Blumberg, Abraham, 151, 176, 207n, 243n
Blumer, Herbert, xi, xiv, 4, 6, 8, 9, 14, 41,
    59n, 67, 69, 70, 71, 72, 81, 84n, 85n, 86n,
    92, 98, 103, 110, 111, 123, 124, 125, 128,
    131, 133, 134, 139, 140, 141, 146, 149,
    160n, 161n, 221, 229, 230, 234, 244n,
    246n, 248n, 266n
Bogardus, Emory, 54n, 112n
Bogdan, Robert, 160n, 162n
Bolles, Richard Nelson, 119n
Bonoma, Thomas V., 66, 201n
Boyle, Susan C., 56n
Brown, L. Guy, 151, 241, 249n
Brown, Russell A., 118n
Browne, Joy, 204n
Buechler, Steven M., 86n
Burgess, Ernest W., 69
Burns, Tom R., 25, 26, 27
Burnyeat, Myles, 115n
Bury, R. G., 114n

C

Ceasar, Julius, 93

Callinicos, Alex, 32, 33
Campbell, Robert A., 161n
Caplan, Marc, 86n, 118n,
Carlson, Rae, 84n
Carnegie, Dale, 119n
Carver, Terrell, 57n, 58n
Charlton, Joy, 248n
Charmaz, Kathy, 58n, 151
Chayko, Mary, 202n
Christensen, Terry, 88n
Cicero, 90, 93, 103, 117n
Clairmont, Donald H., 83
Clark, Ruth Anne, 66, 202n
Clarke, M. L., 94
Clegg, Stewart R., 20, 31, 47, 49, 53, 54n,
    57n, 59n
Cockerham, William C., 248n
Cole, G. D. H., 57n
Coleman, James S., 28, 51
Collins, Randall, 128
Combs James E., 87n
Comte, Auguste, 20, 77, 104, 133
Cook, K. S., 88n
Cooley, Charles Horton, 125, 133, 134
Cooper, John, 115n
Cooper, Martha D., 67, 103, 105
Cooper, Michael 266n, 268n, 269n
Cornfield, Francis Macdonald, 95
Coser, Lewis A., 50, 51, 84n, 128
Couch, Carl, 69, 70, 75, 85n, 141, 146, 149,
    165n, 203n, 206n, 207n, 268n
Coulon, Alain, 14, 45
Craig, Gordon A., 118n
Cratylus, 96, 114n
Cressey, Paul G., 151, 269n, 234n, 268n

D

Dahrendorf, Ralph, 47, 48, 49, 77
Davis, Fred, 151, 203n, 266n
Davis, Kingsley, 51
Dawson, Lorne, 33, 37, 55n, 59n, 60n, 62n,
    140, 152, 160n, 161n, 266n, 267n
De Callières, François, 105, 107, 108, 118n,
    202n, 207n, 241n, 248n
Delia, Jesse G., 66, 87n, 202n
Denzin, Norman K., 41, 60n
Derrida, Jacques, 34, 40, 44
Descartes, René, 104
DeVault, Marjorie L., 42, 43
Dewey, John, xi, 12, 77, 105, 111, 125

Dietz, Mary Lorenz, 165n, 166n, 266n,
    268n, 269n
Dilthey, Wilhelm, 7, 12, 91, 98, 105, 125,
    128, 132, 133, 134, 161n
Dix, Dorothy, 119n
Duncan, Otis Dudley, 56n
Dunn, Robert, 59n
Durkheim, Emile, 11, 12, 18, 20, 21, 23, 24,
    54n, 83, 104, 105, 128, 133

E

Ebaugh, Helen Rose, 151, 241
Edgerton, Robert, 173, 176, 266n
Edmonds, Beverly, 85n, 147, 221
Edwards, Charles M. Jr., 118n
Eggert, Max, 119n
Ehrlich, Carol, 60n
Elder, Shirley, 77, 78
Elms, Alan, 84n
Emerson, Richard M., 28, 163n
Emerson, Robert M., 154, 162, 163n, 190,
    205n, 207n, 209, 211, 243n, 266n
Engels, Friedrich, 30, 32, 40, 57n, 58n, 59n
Enos, Richard Leo, 91, 103, 112n, 246n
Ericson, Richard B., 81, 246n
Ermarth, Michael, 92, 128, 132, 161n
Estes, Caroll, 85n, 147, 221

F

Falbo, Toni, 202n
Faris, Ellsworth, 125
Faulkner, Robert R., 248n
Faupel, Charles E., 151
Fay, Brian, 103
Fee, Elizabeth, 42
Ferguson, Adam, 20
Fine, Gary Alan, 86n
Finley, Gordon E., 66, 202n
Fishman, Laura T., 249n
Fishman, Mark, 81, 246n
Fiske, John, 81
Flam, Helena, 25, 26, 27
Fleras, Augie, 152, 179, 244, 246n, 267n,
    269n
Forster, E. S., 89
Foucault, Michel, 12, 26, 34, 35, 36, 37, 39,
    41, 44, 49, 59n, 62n, 118n
Frank, William W., 118n

Frankel, Boris, 32
Frazer, Charles, 230
Freeman, Kathleen, 112n, 113n, 246n
French, J. R. P., 25, 163n
French, Marilyn, 61n
Freud, Sigmund, 34, 59n
Friedson, Eliot, 26
Frisby, Wendy, 183, 204n, 244n, 266n, 267n, 269n

G

Gamson, William A., 78
Gandhi, M. K., 109
Gans, Herbert J., 83
Garfinkel, Harold, 13, 44, 45, 62n, 163n, 204n, 243n, 244n
Gergen, Kenneth, 84n
Gerver, Israel, 151, 205n, 267n
Giddens, Anthony, 21, 25, 26, 55n, 56n, 163n
Giles, Howard, 87n
Girard, Joe, 188n
Glaser, Barney G., 141, 151
Glazer, Nathan, 51
Gordon, Chad, 75
Goffman, Erving, xi, 66, 67, 76, 110, 141, 146, 147, 149, 150, 151, 163n, 173, 176, 179, 181, 189, 202n, 203n, 204n, 211, 243n, 245n, 249n, 266n, 268n
Gorgias, 3, 117n
Gouldner, Alvin, 54n, 57n, 91, 92
Gramsci, Antonio, 40, 49, 79, 80, 81
Grimes, Michael D., 56n
Grills, Scott, 151, 179, 204n, 234, 244n, 245n, 248n, 266n, 267n, 269n, 270n
Gross, Alfred, 118n
Grossberg, Lawrence, 33, 38
Gumplowicz, Ludwig, 77
Gusfield, Joseph R., 73, 85n, 234, 244n
Guthrie, W. K. C., 112

H

Haas, Jack, 151, 175, 176, 179, 208n, 267n, 269n
Hadden, S. C., 141
Hall, Peter M., 146, 147, 148, 163n, 206n, 207n, 221, 234n
Hall, Stuart, 33, 38, 39, 40, 59, 60, 62n

Handel, Warren H., 160n
Hannerz, Ulf, 162n
Harmon, Robert B., 118n
Harré, Rom, 84n
Harrison, Deborah, 45
Harrison, Michael I., 118n
Hauser, Philip, 81, 229, 230, 246n, 266n
Hegel, Georg, 104, 105
Heidegger, Martin, 34
Henslin, James, 204n
Heraclitus, 96, 115n
Hercules, 91
Herder, Johann Gottfried v., 91
Herman, Nancy, 248n
Herodotus, 93
Hertz, Rosanna, 248n
Hobbes, Thomas, 12, 18, 20, 54n, 105, 117n
Hoffer, Eric, 85n
Hollingshead, A. B., 56n, 83
Holstein, James A., 251, 266n, 268n
Homans, George C., 12, 28, 56n, 62n, 66, 205n
Horkheimer, Max, 59n
Howard, Judith A., 66, 202n
Hrebenar, Ronald J., 86n
Hubbell, H. M., 90
Hughes, Everett, 72
Hume, David, 20
Humphreys, Carolyn A., 66, 202n
Hunt, Bernice, 164n
Hunt, Morton, 164n
Hunt, Scott A., 75, 76n, 146, 149, 150, 151, 163n, 234, 247n, 248n
Hunter, Floyd, 62n, 88n
Husserl, Edmund, 103

I

Ilich, John, 118n
Ingraham, Larry H., 248n.
Irini, Styllianoss, 152, 165n, 166n, 179, 183, 243n, 267n, 268n
Isocrates, xvi, 11, 55n, 94, 98, 101, 102, 104, 117n, 177

J

Jacobs, Bruce A., 202n, 204n
James, William, 111, 160n
Johnson, John M., 162n, 246n

Johnson, Richard, 38
Johnston, Hank, 73, 85n
Johnstone, Christopher Lyle, 112n
Jones, Edward E., 66, 201n, 203n
Jones, Richard S., 249n
Jorgensen, Danny, 160n, 162n
Jowett, Benjamin, 209

K

Kahn, George N., 118n
Kant, Immanuel, 104
Karsh, Bernard, 151, 165n, 202n, 204n, 234, 244n, 245n, 268n
Katovich, Michael A., 207n
Keiser, R. Lincoln, 166n, 183, 208n, 244n, 245n, 248n
Kelly, Harold H., 66
Kennedy, Gavin, 118n
Kennedy, George, 91, 103, 112n, 116n, 246n
Key, V. O., Jr., 86n
Killian, Lewis, 70, 72, 75
Kinsey, Barry A., 150, 234, 248n
Kipnis, David, 66, 202
Kissinger, Henry, 118n, 248n
Klandermans, Bert, 74, 86n
Klapp, Orrin, 67, 69, 72, 85n, 147, 163n, 165n, 171, 173, 179, 181, 187, 203n, 204n, 234, 244n, 245n, 248n, 268n
Koch, Sigmund, 84n
Kolakowski, Leszek, 30, 31, 32, 51, 57n, 59n, 62n
Korsch, Karl, 59n
Kotter, John P., 118n
Kunda, Gideon, 267n, 269n, 270n
Kuhn, Manford, 60n, 75, 86n, 130
Kuhn, Thomas, 162n

L

Laliberté, Lucie, 45
Lantz, Herman R., 83
Lapp, Charles L., 118n
Larana, Enrique, 73
Lasswell, Harold D., 87n
Laurer, Robert H., 160n
Lawler, Edward J., 56n, 163n
Layder, Derek
Lazarsfeld, Paul, 50, 51
Le Bon, Gustave, 69

Lee, Alfred McClung, 70
Leiter, Kenneth, 14n, 45
Lemert, Edwin, 151, 154, 163n, 164n, 171, 200, 267n, 268n
Lenin, V. I., 32, 73
Lesieur, Henry, 151, 208n, 241, 248n, 267n
Lester, Marilyn, 141
Lever, Ralph, 117n
Lewis, David V., 118n
Ling, Monica, 118n
Lipset, Seymour Martin, 50, 51, 58n
Lipsky, M., 85n
Livy, 93, 117n
Lofland, John, 61n, 74, 75, 85n, 86n, 160n, 162n, 204n, 141, 151, 171, 179, 183, 203n, 245n, 266n, 267n
Lofland, Lyn, 61n, 160n, 162n, 204n
Lucas, Rex, 83
Lucetius, 93
Luckenbill, David F., 162n, 163n
Luckmann, Thomas, xvi, 13, 43, 67, 92, 95, 115n, 161n, 197, 244n
Lukács, Gygorgy, 59n
Lukes, Stephen, 47, 48, 49, 53n
Lyman, Stanford M., 59n, 204n
Lynch, Richard, 118n
Lyotard, Jean-Francois, 34, 35, 37, 39, 59n, 62n

M

Machiavelli, Niccoló, 11, 12, 18, 49, 50, 54n, 102, 104, 105–107, 165n
MacLeod, Bruce A., 151, 175, 179, 203n, 244n, 267n, 270n
Madison, James, 77
Magill, Dennis William, 83
Maines, David R., 59n, 160n, 163n
Maisel, Louis Sandy, 86n
Mann, Michael, 54n
Mao Tse Tung, 73
Marcuse, Herbert, 59n
Marger, Martin N, 53n
Marks, James T., 243n
Martin, Brian, 118n
Martin, Henri-Jean, 105, 112n, 117n
Martindale, Don, 54n
Marwell, G., 66, 201n
Marx, Karl, 11, 12, 18, 30, 31, 32, 40, 41, 44, 49, 54n, 57n, 58n, 59n, 77, 104, 105, 118n, 128

Mayer, Tom, 33
McCarthy, John D., 69, 73, 85n
McGaw, Douglas B., 248n
McGinniss, Joe, 163n
McGinty, Patrick J. W., 146, 147, 221
McKirahan, Richard D., Jr., 112n
McMahon, Martha, 46
McPhail, Clark, 70, 75, 85n
McQuail, Denis, 81, 87n
McRobbie, Angela, 38, 39
Mead, George H., xi, xiv, 4, 8, 14, 41, 43, 67,
   70, 84n, 92, 98, 103, 105, 111, 116n, 123,
   125, 126, 131, 133, 135, 141, 149, 160n,
   173, 202n, 204n
Meehan, Albert J., 205n, 207n, 243n, 267n
Mehan, Hugh B., 14, 45, 25
Meltzer, Bernard, 86n, 130
Mercury, 91
Merton, Robert K., 21, 24, 25, 50
Messinger, Sheldon L., 163n, 209, 211, 243n
Meyer, David S., 85n
Michels, Robert, 18, 30, 49, 50, 58n
Milbrath, Lester W., 78, 234, 248n
Mill, J. S., 19, 20, 104, 133
Miller, Gale, 251, 266n, 268n
Mills, C. Wright, 25, 26, 47, 48, 49, 62n,
Mizruchi, Mark S., 88n
Moore, Wilbert, 51
Morris, Aldon D., 73
Mueller, Carol McClung, 73

N

Nader, Ralph, 109
Nelson, Cary, 38, 39
Nesbit, Robert, 53n, 58n
Newby, Howard, 88n
Ng, Sik Hung, 53n, 54n, 56n
Nierenberg, Gerald, 118n
Nietzsche, Friedrich, 19, 59n, 105
Nimmo, Dan, 87n
Norlin, George, 99, 102
Norris, James S., 118n
Nothstine, William, 67, 103, 105

O

Odegard, Peter H., 77, 78, 86n
Olesen, Virginia, 43
Olsen, Marvin E., 53n

Olson, Mancur, 85n
Ornstein, Norman J., 77, 78

P

Paizis, Suzanne, 86n, 118n
Pareto, Wilfredo, 18
Park, Robert E., 68, 69, 70, 71, 72, 84n, 125
Parsons, Talcott, 12, 21, 24, 25, 26, 50
Peele, Norman Vincent, 119n
Peirce, Charles Sanders, 105, 111, 160n
Peplau Letitia Anne, 202n
Petras, John, 86n, 13
Peyrot, Mark, 249n
Pfeffer, Jeffery, 25, 27
Plato, xvi, 3, 12, 54n, 57n, 67, 87n, 91, 93,
   94, 95, 96, 97, 98, 102, 103, 104, 112n,
   113n, 114n, 115n, 116n, 187, 232, 233,
   245n
Platt, Gerald M., 75
Polybius, 93
Popper, K. R., 54n, 57n, 91, 92
Porter, John, 56n
Post, Emily, 119n
Poulakos, John, 112n
Powell, Walter, 81
Protagoras, 67, 94, 95, 113n, 115n, 116n
Prus, Robert, 6, 14, 33, 55n, 62n, 125, 134,
   136, 141, 142, 144, 152, 154, 160n, 161n,
   162n, 163n, 177, 179, 182, 204n, 205n,
   216, 217, 229, 243n, 244n, 246n, 248n,
   249n, 267n, 269n, 270n, 277n

Q

Quintilian (Quintilianus, Marcus Fabius),
   103, 116n, 117n

R

Raven, B. H., 25, 163n
Ray, Marsh, 151, 241, 248n
Reid, Leonard N., 230
Reinharz, Shulamit, 43
Reynolds, Larry T., 130,
Ritzer, George, 128
Robinson, Daniel R., 116n
Rochford, E. Burke, 75, 86n, 151, 245n
Rogers, Mary F., 55n

Rose, Arnold, 53n, 62n, 88n
Rosenfeld, Paul, 53n
Rosenfield, Lawrence, 93, 99, 103, 104, 105
Rosnow, Ralph L., 86n
Ross, H. Lawrence, 151, 207n, 243n
Ross, W. D., 96, 98, 116
Rossi, Peter, 51
Rossides, Daniel, 56n
Roth, Julius, 151, 205n, 241, 266n
Rousseau, Jean-Jacques, 12, 105
Roznaczuk, Ronald, 204n
Rubington, Earl, 151, 244n
Rule, Brendan Gail, 66, 202n

S

Sanders, Clinton, 59n, 175, 179, 204n, 266
Sandys, John Edward, 112n
Saunders, Trevor J., 94
Saxton, Stanley L., 207n
Schiller, F. C. S., 115n
Schirer, William, 165n
Schlatter, Richard Bulger, 117n
Schmid, Thomas, 249n
Schmitt, D. R., 66, 201n
Schottenloher, Karl, 105, 112n, 117n
Schutz, Alfred, 13, 55n, 67, 98, 115n, 125, 161n, 197, 244n
Schwartzman, Edward, 86n, 118n
Scott, Lois, 269n
Scott, Marvin, xi, 204n
Scott, Ruth K., 86n
Secord, Paul, 84n
Seibold, David R., 53, 54n, 66
Selznick, Philip, 50, 51
Sextus Empiricus, 95, 114n
Shadegg, Stephen C., 86n, 118n
Shaffir, William, 151, 161n, 175, 176, 179, 244n, 245n, 267n, 269n
Sharman, David, 118n
Sharp, Gene, 109, 118n
Sharper, C. R. D., 152, 167m 173m 177, 179n, 202n, 203n, 244n, 268n, 269n
Shaw, Clifford, 151
Shibutani, Tamotsu, 86n
Shorey, Paul, 232
Simmel, Georg, 7, 12, 18, 56n, 68, 69, 72, 77, 83, 84n, 85n, 105, 125, 141, 160n, 206n, 207n, 209, 243n
Simon, Rita J., 43, 45, 60n
Simpson, Dick, 86n, 118n

Skvoretz, J., 56n
Smelser, Neil J., 51, 69, 71, 85n
Smith, Charles W., 269n
Smith, Dorothy E., 44
Smith, John, 117n
Snow, David A., 75, 76, 86n, 163n
Snow, Robert P., 246n
Snyder, Eldon E., 269n
Socrates, 3, 87n, 94, 95, 96, 98, 112n, 113n, 114n, 117n, 187
Sommers, Christina Hoff, 44
Spencer-Hall, Dee Ann, 206n
Sprague, Rosamond Kent, 114n
Stanley, Liz, 42, 43, 44, 45, 46, 60n, 61n
Stebbins, Robert, 151, 161n, 176
Steffensmeier, Darrell, 151
Stoecker, Randy, 86n
Strauss, Anselm, 6, 7, 14, 125, 140, 141, 146, 148, 149, 151, 160n, 162n, 206, 207n
Stryker, Sheldon, 130
Sutherland, Edwin, 151, 176, 204n, 234, 244n
Suttles, Gerald D., 83

T

Tarde, Gabriel, 69
Tarrow, Sidney, 86n
Taylor, A. E., 253
Taylor, Stephen J., 160n, 162n
Tedeschi, James T., 53n, 66, 201n
Thibault, John, 66
Thomas, W. I., 125
Thucydides, 93, 117n
Tilly, Charles, 85n
Trounstine Philip J., 88n
Truman, David B., 77, 78
Tuchman, Gaye, 81, 246n
Turner, Jonathan, 128
Turner, Ralph H., 70, 71, 72, 75, 76n, 85n, 86n
Tzu, Sun, 117n, 118n

U

Useem, Bert, 118n

V

Van Zandt, David E., 151, 179, 183, 204n, 243n, 245n

Vegetius, Renatus Flavius, 118n
Vidich, Arthur J., 83

W

Walker, Jack L., Jr., 78
Waller, Willard, 17, 151
Warner, W. Lloyd, 83
Waterfield, Robin, 3
Weber, Max, 11, 12, 18, 20, 21, 22, 24, 25,
    27, 54n, 55n, 83, 85n, 104, 105, 118n,
    128, 163n, 165n, 203n
Whitmeyer, J. M., 54n, 56n, 88n
Whittier, Nancy, 46, 85n
Whyte, William Foote, 83
Wiemann, John M., 87n
Wilkinson, Harry, 118n
Willer, D., 56n
Williams, Raymond, 29, 33, 38, 59, 60, 62n
Williams, Robin M., Jr., 51, 236n
Windelband, Wilhelm, 69
Wipper, Audrey, 85n
Wirth, Louis, 72
Wise, Sue, 42, 43, 44, 45, 46, 60n, 61n

Wiseman, Jacqueline, 85n, 151, 241, 244n,
    248n, 266n
Wittgenstein, Ludwig, 34
Wohlstein, Ronald T., 75
Wolf, Charlotte, 46, 151, 183, 204n, 268n
Wolf, Daniel, 151, 165n, 166n, 175, 202n,
    204n, 208n, 234, 243n, 244n, 245n, 248n,
    266n, 267n, 268n, 269n, 270n
Wolpe Bruce C., 118n
Wolpe, Joseph M. D., 119n
Wood, H. Lawrence, 14, 45
Wood, James R., 66, 201n
Wood, Julia, 43, 44, 61n
Worden, Steven K., 75, 86n
Wrighter, Carl P., 118n
Wrong, Dennis H., 25, 26, 53n, 163n
Wundt, Wilhelm, 19, 20, 104, 133

Z

Zald, Meyer N., 69, 73, 85n
Zeitlin, Irving, 128
Zimmerman, Don H., 14, 45
Zurcher, Louis A., Jr., 75, 85n, 86n, 144n,
    248n

A

Accomplish (accomplishing, accomplishment). *See* activity, intersubjectivity, power, symbolic interaction, tacticians, tactics, targets
Accountability, 198–199, 258, 264. *See also* autonomizing tactics, targets
Activity (act, acting, action, interaction). *See also* agency, associations, collective events, generic social processes, intersubjectivity, language, objects, reality, subcultures, symbolic interaction, tacticians, tactics, targets, treatments
and empirical world (Herbert Blumer), 7, 9
engaging in tactical enterprise, 12, 167–208
experiencing target roles, 12, 251–270
extending the theater of operations, 12, 209–249
influence work, 167–270
language as enabling, 3, 8, 9, 10, 22, 24, 37, 45, 59n, 60n, 62n, 90, 92, 98, 99, 100, 102, 103, 126, 128, 129, 135, 143, 226
postmodernist neglect of, 33–37
as premise of group life, 8, 126–127
separating theory and action, 104, 273
structuralist neglect of, 52–53, 104, 110
subcultural mosaics and intersubjective realities, 134–139
and symbolic interaction, 3–10, 123–277
Adversary (adversarial). *See* bargaining, competitors, conflict, influence, military, political agendas, rhetoric, tacticians, tactics, targets
Affiliational networks. *See* associations, subcultures
Agency (human), 3–10, 18, 25, 26, 37, 52–53, 56n, 74, 94–98, 110, 113n, 123–277. *See also* activity, deliberation, ethnography, intersubjectivity, language, symbolic interaction, tacticians, tactics, targets
disregarding agency, 52–53, 104, 110, 150, 273
and early Greeks, 89–105
usurping agency, 188–192
Agents. *See also* agency, diplomacy, tacticians, tactics, treatments
control agents, 238–241
third-party agents (representatives), 211–212
undercover agents, 202n
Ahistorical myth (and symbolic interaction), 132
Alliances. *See* associations, activity, collective events, theater of operations
Alignments. *See* associations, activity, collective events, theater of operations
Antiscience myth (and symbolic interaction), 133–134
Assertiveness training, 109, 119n
Assisting (assistance). *See also* tacticians, tactics, targets
claiming target status, 258–259
and cultivating relationships, 180–181, 203n
involving third parties, 199, 210–214
seeking help from others, 98, 196–198, 209–249, 258–259
volunteer associations, 243n–244n
Associations (forming and coordinating), 131, 136, 137, 144–145, 167–270. *See also* collective events, government, subcultures, tacticians, tactics, targets
as generic social processes, 144–145, 214–218
encountering outsiders, 217–218
establishing associations, 215–216
extending the theater of operations, 89, 209–249
objectifying associations, 216–217

totalizing associations, 225–227
Assumptions (and the human sciences). *See also* structuralism, symbolic interaction
of ethnographic research (interactionist), 7–9, 123–127, 139–141
of symbolic interactionism, 3–10, 123–127
Astructuralist myth (and symbolic interaction), 130–131
Atheoretical myth (and symbolic interaction), 132–133
Authority, 21, 23, 24, 26, 48, 58n, 167. *Also see* objectification, power, tacticians, tactics
Autonomizing practices (by tacticians), 198–199. *See also* influence, tactics, target roles

B

Bargaining, 66, 193–196, 207n. *See also* collective events, competition, exchange, leveraging tactics, tactics
Bureaucracy, 22, 24, 27, 49, 50

C

Careers (career contingencies; involvement processes), 142–143, 171–172, 202n, 212, 236, 238, 240. *See also* generic social processes, process, tacticians
and control agency work, 240
and military, 238
of power relations (Herbert Blumer), 146
and political involvement, 236
and tactician roles, 154, 163n–164n, 167–172, 201, 221–225
Celebrity (celebrities), 69, 72, 147. *See also* charisma, identity, rhetoric
Charisma (charismatic), 21, 22, 55n, 75, 149, 165n, 179–180. *See also* identity, rhetoric
pursuing positional control, 221–225
tactician mystique, 179–180
Chicago-school (of symbolic interactionism), xiv, 14n, 72, 86n, 123, 131, 141, 242, 271. *See also* symbolic interaction
Coalitions. *See* associations, collective events, theater of operations
Collective behavior, 7, 9, 17, 68–76, 85n, 139, 147, 214–218, 221, 261–265, 269n–

271. *See also* associations, collective events, theater of operations
social problems as collective behavior (Herbert Blumer), 70–71, 162n–163n
Collective events (participating in), 214–218, 261–265, 269n–270n. *See also* activity, associations, collective ventures, military agendas, political forums, tactics, theater of operations
Collectivist approaches (to power), 17, 23, 26, 30, 68–76, 89, 123, 162n–163n, 209–249, 261–265. *See also* associations, collective behavior, collective events, interest groups, tacticians, tactics, targets
Collective resistance. *See also* collective events, collectivist approaches, tacticians, tactics, targets, theater of operations
and marxist nexus, 29–52
and political agendas, 231–265
and target roles, 109, 119n, 257–259
Collective ventures (extending the theater), 214–218, 261–265
Columbia socialism (and Robert Michels), 49–51
Communication. *See* intersubjectivity, language, media, symbolic interaction
Community. *See also* activity, collective events, intersubjectivity, language, power, subcultural mosaics, symbolic interaction
community ties and assistance, 197–198
community studies of power, 68, 82–84
extending the theater of operations, 209–249
myth of simple human community, 134–139, 162n
priority over individual, 8, 94, 98, 126, 128–129
as subcultural mosaics, 134–139
Compete (competition, competitive, competitors), 9, 68, 82, 90, 126, 147, 149, 164n, 186, 218, 223, 259–261, 268n–269n. *See also* media, military, political forums, power, tacticians, tactics, targets
assuming competitive stances, 223, 259–261
bargaining, 193–196
Compliance. *See also* tacticians, tactics, targets, treatments
complying with others' desires (cultivating relationships), 181–182
literature in psychology, 65–67

Conflict (as social process), 9, 17, 19, 23, 25, 26, 27, 29, 39, 48, 50, 56n, 68, 69, 77, 83, 84n, 90, 106, 123, 124, 126, 130, 135, 149, 218, 237, 248n, 273. *See also* collective events, compete, military, morality, political forums, symbolic interaction
  and marxist nexus, 29–52
Consume (consumers, consuming). *See* activity, media, tacticians, tactics, targets
Constructionist (social constructionism) viewpoint, xvi, xvii, 4, 13–14, 39, 43, 52, 54n, 60n, 67, 72, 73, 81, 92–96, 115n, 123, 126, 138, 177, 236, 276n. *See also* intersubjectivity, symbolic interaction
Content analysis, 14n, 40, 73, 247n
Control agencies (and agents), 238–241, 243n, 247n, 248n. *See also* associations, political forums, subcultures, tactics, targets, totalizing associations, treatments,
Conversational analysis (and ethnomethodology), 14
Cooperation (as social process). *See* activity, collective events, collective ventures, symbolic interaction, tactics, targets
  and ethnographic research, 139–141, 275–277
Crowds, 69, 75. *See* collective behavior, collective events
Cultivating networks of supporters (pursuing positional control), 222–223
Cultivating relationships, 177–184, 203n, 222. *See also* associations, positional control, tacticians, tactics
  acknowledging tactical mystique, 179–180
  complying with others' desires, 181–182
  encouraging trust, 182
  expressing empathy, 180
  fostering loyalty, 182–183
  getting noticed, 178–179
  helping others, 180–181
  spending time with others, 180
Cultural studies, xiv, 29, 38–42. *See also* culture, marxist nexus, postmodernism
Culture. *See also* activity, intersubjectivity, language, symbolic interaction
  cultural problematic, 62n, 134–139
  as subcultural mosaic, 134–139
Cynicism
  and impossibility of knowing (Plato), 96
  and postmodernism, 33–37

D

Debasing (and neutralizing) tactics, 100, 101, 186–187. *See also* power, rhetoric, tactics
Deception, 31, 80, 83, 107, 117n, 118n, 174–177, 202n. *See also* images, intersubjectivity, magic, objectification, tactics, trust
  and diplomacy (François De Callières), 107–110
  and marxist agenda, 31–32
  and power (Niccoló Machiavelli), 106–107
  theory of, 174–177
Degradation ceremonies (Harold Garfinkel), 243n. *See also* rhetoric, tactics
Deliberation (speech and agency), 3, 8, 89, 96, 97, 98, 99, 112n, 113n, 116n. *See also* activity, agency, reflectivity, symbolic interaction, tacticians, tactics, targets
Deviance. *See* control agencies, labeling, morality, tactics, targets, treatments
Diplomacy (diplomats), 107–110, 118n, 202n, 207n, 237, 242n, 248n. *See also* deception, government, tactics
Distancing. *See* autonomizing practices, debasing tactics, tactics, targets
Dominate (domination), 3, 10, 17, 18, 21, 36, 47, 48, 49, 50, 69, 81, 87n, 123, 152, 156, 181, 271. *See also* government, power, tacticians, tactics, targets
  and Michel Foucault, 35–37
  and Robert Michels, 49–51
  and Georg Simmel, 69
Doing activity. *See* activity, intersubjectivity, symbolic interaction, tactics
Dramaturgical approach (Erving Goffman). *See* impression management

E

Education. *See* knowledge
Elusive self (as target), 256. *See also* autonomizing practices, targets
Empathy (cultivating relationships), 180
Empirical (social world), xiv, 7, 9, 128, 140. *See also* methodology, ethnography, symbolic interaction
Empower (empowering, empowerment), xi, 3, 31, 108–110, 271. *See also* power, tactics

Enacted. *See* activity, agency, power, symbolic interaction, tactics

Encapsulation (Henry Lesieur), 208n

Enhancing practices, 172–184. *See also* deception, impression management, media, tactics
- attending to target circumstances, 173–174
- cultivating relationships, 177–184
- formulating plans and making preparations, 173
- shaping images of reality, 174–177

Enterprise (human). *See* activity, symbolic interaction, tacticians, tactics, targets

Ethnography (ethnographers, ethnographic research), xvi, 4, 9, 76, 78, 81, 82, 103, 139–141, 162n, 275–276. *See also* activity, generic social processes, intersubjectivity, methodology, symbolic interaction
- additional source materials on methodology, 162n
- disregarding the ethnographic other, 32, 52–53, 56n, 74, 82, 103, 128
- as essential for the study of human condition, 7–9, 123, 139–141, 149, 160n, 275–276
- interactionist assumptions, 6–10, 124–127
- and intersubjectivity, 7–9, 134–141
- and generic social processes, 141–145
- methodological practices (observation, participant-observation, interviewing), 8–9, 139–141, 162n, 275–276

Ethnomethodology (Harold Garfinkel), 13n–14n, 44–45

Everything is in flux (Heraclitus, Protagoras), 94–96

Exchange, 195–196. *See also* bargaining, tactics
- exchange theory (also equity theory), 28–29, 56n, 62n, 66, 88n, 205n

Exercising persistence, 199–201. *See also* tacticians, tactics

Extending the theater of operations, 209–249. *See* theater of operations

F

Factors (variables) in the social sciences, 4, 19, 20–63, 66, 71, 72, 73, 79, 103, 104, 112n, 127, 130, 131, 133, 150, 190, 202n, 273. *See also* methods, structuralism

Feminism, 42–47, 151, 183, 245n. *See also* methods, theory
- multiple theoretical and methodological viewpoints, 42–45
- affinities with symbolic interaction, 43–47

Focusing practices, 184–186. *See also* tacticians, tactics
- indicating lines of action, 184
- promoting target interests, 184–186

Foreign (policy, relations), 107, 108, 118n, 235, 248n. *See also* diplomacy, government, military, outsiders

Forms, 22, 91, 101, 102, 104. *See also* associations, generic social processes, objects, objectification, reality
- and early Greeks (Plato, Aristotle), 91, 96, 101, 102, 104
- forms of association (Georg Simmel), 18, 56n, 68–69, 76, 125, 141
- symbolic interaction and full range of association, 9, 36, 111, 123–124, 130

Forming and coordinating associations. *See* associations

Framing (and collective behavior; Robert Benford), 76, 150

Functionalism (as rational order structuralism), xiii, xiv, 21–29, 51, 71–72, 81, 84n, 92. *See also* factors, methodology, structuralism

G

Generic social processes (GSPs), 68, 83, 123, 141–145, 233. *See also* activity, careers, processes, subcultures, symbolic interaction
- engaging subcultural life-worlds, 143–144
- experiencing power relations (as GSP), 145, 167–270
- forming and coordinating associations, 144–145, 214–218
- participating in situations (careers), 142–143

Government (governmental agendas, forums, interchange), 50, 77–78, 86n, 87n, 90, 91, 101, 102, 104, 106, 107, 148, 209, 231–241. *See also* collective events, policy, political forums, power
- advantage of stronger (Plato), 231–232
- and control agencies, 238–241
- implementing governmental forums, 233–236

Government (*continued*)
and military, 236–238
multiplicity of groups, 77, 233
as social process, 231–241
Groups. *See* associations, collective events,
insiders, subcultures, theater of
operations
Greeks (early Greek classics, civilization,
scholarship; Hellenes, Ionians). xvi, 11,
17, 18, 55n, 67, 89–105, 110, 273. *See
also* rhetoric
and history, 90–93
multiple and mixed (social science) viewpoints, 92–93
and language, 90, 92, 94, 97–104
and pragmatism/interactionism, 92–105,
110
sociology of knowledge, 92–96
and structuralism, 18, 91–93
GSP(s). *See* generic social processes

H

Hellenes (Hellenistic). *See* Greeks.
Help (helping). *See* assisting
History (historical, historians), 10, 11, 17,
19, 22, 30, 36, 39, 46, 54n, 59n, 70, 71,
73, 80, 89, 90, 91, 93, 103, 104, 106, 107,
108, 110, 111, 117n, 118n, 131, 136, 157,
237, 261, 274. *See also* generic social processes, process,
theory
ahistorical myth (and symbolic interaction), 132
and early Greeks, 90–93
history of social thought, 54n, 90–93,
112
natural history of social problems
(Blumer), 70–71, 162n–163n
Human advantages (Plato), 3
Human agency. *See* agency
Human condition. *See also* activity, intersubjectivity, language, symbolic interaction
assumptions regarding, 3–10, 124–127
early Greek images of, 89–105
and subcultural mosaics, 134–139
Human enterprise. *See* activity, generic social processes, power, symbolic interaction, tactics
Human sciences. *See* social sciences, symbolic interaction

I

Identity (Identities), 72, 73, 137, 182, 203n,
226. *See also* associations, charisma, images, impression management, rhetoric,
subculture, symbolic interaction, tacticians, targets
claiming target status, 258–259
collective search for identity (Orrin
Klapp), 72–73
defining self as competitor, 223, 259–261
defining self as tactician, 163n–164n,
167–172
defining self as target, 163n, 251–270
Illusion. *See* deception, images, impression
management, magic, reality
Images (image work), 7, 8, 21, 31, 54n,
55n, 72, 79, 80–81, 93, 100, 101, 102,
114n, 115n, 116n, 119n, 127, 129, 146,
147, 148, 174–177, 179, 182, 198, 223,
238. *See also* charisma, deception, enhancing practices, impression management, intersubjectivity, reality, rhetoric,
tactics
shaping images of reality, 174–177
Impression management (Erving Goffman),
146, 147, 149–150, 174, 176, 181, 202n,
211. *See also* agency, symbolic interaction
Inducements (and other treatments) 192–
193, 205n. *See also* bargaining, control
agencies, tacticians, tactics, targets
Influence (and resistance). *See also* control
agencies, government, media, military,
politics, power, resistance, rhetoric, tacticians, tactics, targets
attending to human interchange, 3–10,
123–277
and early Greeks, 90, 101
engaging in tactical enterprise, 167–208
experiencing target roles, 251–270
extending the theater of operations, 209–
249
interactionist literature on, 145–152
tactical (political, practical) advisors, 101–
110
Ingratiation, 66, 203n. *See also* impression
management, tactics
Insiders (and outsiders; ingroups and out-
groups), 9, 61n, 137, 156, 207n, 216–
217, 220, 233, 258, 268n. *See also* associations, neutralizing strategies, outsiders,
positional control

Interaction (interactionist). *See* symbolic interaction. *See also* activity, associations, generic social processes, power, subcultures

Interest groups, 47–49, 68, 71, 77–78, 86n, 146, 214–218, 231–242
and political science (Arthur Bentley), 77–78
and interactionism (Herbert Blumer), 86n
and marxism 29–52 (especially Ralph Dahrendorf, 47–48)

Intergroup relations. *See* associations, collective events, competitors, government, insiders, military, political agendas, tacticians, tactics, targets

Intersubjective (intersubjectivist, intersubjectivity), xvi, xvii, 3–10, 123–166. *See also* activity, language, objectification, symbolic interaction
achieving intersubjectivity, 3–13, 123–127
critique of structuralist social science, 52–53
and ethnographic research, 7–9, 139–141, 275–276
intersubjective realities (and subcultural mosaics), 134–139
power as intersubjective accomplishment, 3–13, 123–277
as premise of symbolic interaction, 8, 126
respecting the intersubjective (community-based) other, xvi, 6–10, 133, 139–141, 160n
versus subjectivity, 128–129

Intimate familiarity (Herbert Blumer) and social science, 8, 70, 134. *See also* ethnography, intersubjectivity, symbolic interaction

Involvement processes. *See* associations, career contingencies, generic social processes, collective events, tacticians, tactics, targets

Iron law of oligarchy (Robert Michels), 18, 49–50

Iowa school of symbolic interaction, 86n

K

Knowledge (knowing), 33, 34, 58n, 59n, 71, 79, 91, 92, 94–96, 114n, 115n, 116n, 135, 139, 143, 229. *See also* intersubjectivity, objects, reality, social science, symbolic interaction, theory
and early Greeks, 89–105 (especially 94–96)
impossibility of knowing (Socrates, Plato), 96, 112n, 115n
irresistible argument about truth (Aristotle), 116n
skeptic tradition (Sextus Empiricus), 114

L

Labeling process, 163n. *See also* identity, rhetoric, symbolic interaction

Language. *See also* activity, intersubjectivity, media, reality, rhetoric, speech, symbolic interaction, writing
and early Greeks, 89–105 (especially 90, 92, 94, 97–104), 112
as enabling device, 3, 8, 9, 10, 22, 24, 37, 45, 59n, 60n, 62n, 90, 92, 98, 99, 100, 102, 103, 126, 128, 129, 135, 143, 226
generating and encountering (media) messages, 228–231
and postmodernist fictions, 33–37

Leadership. *See* charisma, power, tactician, tactics
pursuing positional control, 221–225

Legislation. *See* control agencies, deviance, government, morality, policy, political forums, tactics

Leveraging tactics, 188–198. *See also* tacticians, tactics, targets
appealing to existing relationships, 196–198
bargaining with targets, 193–196
establishing consensus, 188
using inducements and other treatments, 192–193
usurping agency, 188–192

Life-worlds (also social worlds). *See* subcultures, subcultural mosaic

Linguistic. *See* language

Literature on power (general references to, reviews of), xiv–xvi, 3–5, 12–13, 17–119 (20, 27, 53n–54n, 56n, 57n, 65, 79, 84n, 87n, 88n, 109, 119n), 145–152, 251. *See also* power, social science, tacticians, tactics, targets, theory

Loyalty. *See also* associations, tactics, trust
appealing to existing relationships, 196–
198
fostering loyalty, 182–183

M

Macro (and micro) analysis, xiv, xv, 4–5,
9, 12, 52–53, 76, 107, 129–130, 231–
241
Magic, 167, 174–177, 201n. *See also* deception, images, tactics
Man is the measure (Protagoras), 94–96.
See also (early) Greeks, reality, relativism, symbolic interaction
impossibility of knowing (Socrates, Plato),
96
irresistible argument about truth (Aristotle), 116n
Manage (managing, management). *See*
charisma, identity, positional control,
power, tacticians, tactics, theater of
operations
Marketing (marketplace). *See* bargaining,
objects, tactics
Marxist nexus (marxism, marxist oppression
thesis), xiii, xiv, 29–52, 68, 77, 92, 107.
See also structuralism
Columbia socialism, 49–51
critical theory, 38, 57n, 59n–60n
cultural studies, 38–42
effective as ideology, 62n
end of marxism, 32–33
Frankfurt school, 38, 59n–60n
fundamentalist orientations, 30–33
futility (as social science) of, 29, 32–33,
51–52, 57n
marxist-feminism, 40, 42–47
nexus, 29–30
oppression thesis, 29
and Plato (*Republic, The Laws*), 57n
pluralist offshoots, 47–49
postmodernism, 33–37, 40, 41, 44, 49,
57n, 58n–59n, 67, 247n
Marxist-feminism, 42–47. *See also* marxist
nexus
Mass communication. *See* media
Mass media. *See* media
Media, 78–82, 87n, 118n, 119n, 190, 228–
231, 232, 242, 247n. *See also* intersubjectivity, language, tactics, targets

as social, enacted phenomenon, 82, 228–
231
experiencing the media, 229–231
literature on, 78–82
mystique, 80–81, 230
using the media to influence, 228–231
Methods (methodology, methodological), 4,
5, 6, 8, 9, 24, 27, 28, 31, 37, 38, 40, 45,
48, 51, 56n, 57n, 60n, 61n, 65, 67, 68,
74, 78, 83, 89, 104, 110, 113n, 127, 130,
134, 139–141, 142, 160n, 162n, 272, 274,
275, 276. *See also* ethnography, structuralism, symbolic interaction
and cultural studies, 38–42
and feminism, 43–47
and fundamentalist marxism, 57n
and postmodernism, 33–37
and symbolic interactionism, 4–10, 124–
141, 275–276
Micro (and macro) analysis, xi, 4–5, 129–
130. *See also* macro, structure, symbolic
interaction, theory
micro myth (and symbolic interaction),
129–130
Military (operations), 58n, 89, 93, 106,
117n, 118n, 165n, 226, 236–238, 248n.
See also associations, collective events,
government, policy, political forums
Mind (minded, mindedness). *See* activity,
agency, deliberation, intersubjectivity,
knowing, language, reality, symbolic
interaction
Money, 3, 24, 206n–207n, 220. *See also* bargaining, objects, tactics
Moral entrepreneurs (Howard Becker), 32,
220. *See also* morality
Morality (moral, moralist), xiii, 6, 11, 13, 18,
30, 34, 37, 51, 53, 54n, 60n, 61n, 90, 92,
93, 94, 95, 97, 100, 104, 105, 106, 114n,
116n, 140, 182, 187, 200, 220, 226, 237,
239, 259, 271, 272, 273, 275, 276. *See also*
associations, collective events, control
agencies, (early) Greeks, social problems, social science, subcultures, totalizing agencies
Mosaic. *See* subcultural mosaic
Mystique. *See also* power, tactics
of collective events, 265
media mystique, 80–81, 230
power mystique, xi, 3, 10, 84, 179–180,
271, 273, 276–277n
tactician mystique, 179–180

N

Names (naming) of things. *See also* labeling, language, rhetoric, symbolic interaction
and Plato, 114n–115n
Negotiable (negotiating, negotiation), 4, 8, 48, 71, 76, 87n, 107, 109, 110, 118n, 126, 148, 151, 154, 162n, 163n, 193, 207n, 256. *See also* bargaining, government, money, tactics
as premise of symbolic interaction, 126
Network analysis, 87n–88n
Neutralizing (and debasing) strategies, 117n, 186–187, 223. *See also* images, rhetoric, tactics
New social movements (theory), 72–73. *See also* collective behavior
Nonviolent resistance (as ideology), 109. *See also* tacticians, tactics, targets

O

Obdurate reality (Herbert Blumer), 37, 59n. *See also* activity, reality, symbolic interaction
empirical social reality, 7–9
Objectify (objectification), 10, 14n, 36, 66, 126, 129, 161n, 192, 197, 206n, 216, 236, 272, 273, 275. *See also* intersubjectivity, reality, relativity, symbolic interaction
Objects [objects], 8, 14n, 60n, 79, 94, 96, 98, 114n, 124, 126, 127, 128, 129, 131, 136, 146, 156, 159, 161n, 186, 187, 189, 194, 205n, 207n, 229, 244n, 267n, 274, 277n. *See also,* activity, bargaining, intersubjectivity, objectify, symbolic interaction
definition of, 14n
Office holders. *See also* tacticians, tactics
pursuing positional control, 221–225
tactical advice to, 86n, 101–108, 109, 118n
Oligarchy. *See also* government
and government turnover (Aristotle), 209
iron law of oligarchy (Robert Michels), 49–50
Oppression thesis (and marxist nexus), 29–52
Order theorists (rational order structuralism), 20–29. *Also see* structuralism, power
Organizations (organizational). *See* associations, collective events, office holders,
tacticians, tactics, targets, theater of operations
Outsiders (and insiders), 9, 61n, 137, 144, 156, 157, 207n, 217–218, 238, 241, 258, 259, 268n. *See also* associations, collective events, power
encountering outsiders, 217–218

P

Paramount reality (and subcultural life-worlds), 137. *See also* intersubjectivity, reality, symbolic interaction
Participant viewpoints, xiii, 3–10, 22, 37, 45, 75, 76, 124–127, 167–172, 273. *See also* agency, ethnography, intersubjectivity, symbolic interaction
neglect of, 52–53, 104, 110, 150, 273
Participant-observation. *See* ethnography
Peace (and war), 85n, 89, 90, 236, 247n, 248n. *See also* military, political forums, tactics
use of rhetoric to promote (Aristotle), 89
Persistence (exercising), 199–201. *See also* tacticians, tactics
Perspective (perspectival, multiperspectival), 8, 48, 70, 72, 94, 115, 126, 136, 176–177. *See also* intersubjectivity, knowledge, reality, subcultural mosaic, subculture, symbolic interaction
as premise of symbolic interaction, 8, 126
privileging viewpoints, 37
Persuasion. *See* rhetoric, tacticians, tactics, targets
Phenomenological sociology, 13n–14n. *See also* ethnomethodology, intersubjectivity, constructionist, symbolic interaction
Philosophy (philosophical). *See also* (early) Greeks, knowing, reality, relativism, theory
disregarding human lived experience, 103, 104
Physical (vs. human/social) sciences. *See* methodology, intersubjectivity, language, symbolic interaction
Policy (policies), 30, 70, 85n, 147, 148, 218–221, 225, 227, 231–241, 248n, 276n. *See also* collective events, military, power, social problems
developing political agendas, 231–242
generating and enforcing policy, 218–221

Policy (*continued*)
implementing governmental forums, 233–236
Political advice, 86n, 101–108, 117n, 118n. *See also* political forums, power, tacticians
to diplomats (François De Callières), 107–108
to princes (Aristotle), 101, 104
to princes (Isocrates), 102, 104
to princes (Niccolò Machiavelli), 102, 104, 105–107
Political (governmental) forums and engagements, 18, 231–241, 245n. *See also* associations, collective events, policy, power, tacticians, tactics, targets
Political power, 3, 147. *See also* political forums
Political science (scientists), 20, 65, 77–78, 91, 101, 103, 104, 108. *See also* political forums, social science, structuralism and Aristotle, 101–102
Positional control (pursuing), 221–225. *See also* associations, tacticians, tactics
assuming strategic assignments, 223
attending to leadership images, 223
becoming absorbed in power motifs, 225
becoming entrenched in the organization, 224–225
cultivating networks of supporters, 222–223
cultivating relationships with insiders, 177–184, 222
extending nodes of influence, 223–224
neutralizing competitors, 223
Positivism. *See* factors, methods, structuralism, theory
Postmodernism (poststructuralism), xi, xiv, 29, 33–37, 40, 41, 44, 49, 57n, 58n–59n, 67, 79, 80, 134, 247n. *See also* knowing, marxist nexus, reality, relativism
and cultural studies, 38–42
affinities/disjunctures with symbolic interaction, 33, 36–37
Power. *See also* activity, language, symbolic interaction, tacticians, tactics, targets
agenda for volume, xiii, 3–10, 271–272
collectivist approaches to, 17, 23, 26, 30, 68–76, 89, 123, 162n–163n, 209–249, 261–265
community studies of, 82–84
compliance and influence literature (psychology), 65–67

conceptual themes (major variants, flow) in this volume, 19
conflictual (primarily; marxist nexus), 29–52
control agencies, 238–241
criterion for defining relevant literature, 5, 65, 84, 272
cultural studies, 38–42
deception, 106–110, 174–177
definition (interactionist) of, 9–10, 152–154
definitional essences, 3–10, 152–154
demystifying, 3–10
disregarding agency (analysts), 52–53, 104, 110, 150, 273
empowering, xi, 3, 31, 108–110, 271
enacted/enterprise, xiii, xvi, 3–10, 17, 22, 23, 24, 25, 26, 27, 30, 31, 36, 45, 49, 52–53, 66, 69, 72, 78, 89, 92, 98–102, 104, 107, 123–277
enduring concern (early Greeks), 89–105
exchange (and equity) theory, 28–29
extending the theater of operation, 12, 209–249
and full range of association, 9, 36, 111, 123–124, 130
as generic social process, 145, 167–270
functionalism (rational order structuralism), 20–29
interactionist approach to, xiii, xiv, 6–10, 123–166, 167–277
interactionist literature on, 145–152
interchangeability of participant viewpoints, 12, 153, 155, 164n, 252, 275
interest group dynamics, 47–49, 68, 71, 77–78, 86n, 146, 214–218, 231–242
as intersubjective accomplishment, 3–12, 123–277
marxist nexus, 29–52
media, 78–82, 229–231
motif, 4, 12, 15–119
mystique, xi, xiv, 3, 10, 84, 158, 179–180, 271, 276–277n
network analysis, 87n–88n
not key to understanding society, 84, 123, 145, 272
not remedial, 5, 111
overwhelming area of study, xiii, 18
as positional (structuralist), 17–63, 65–88
positional control (pursuing), 221–225
postmodernism, 33–37, 41, 44, 49, 58n–59n, 67, 80, 247n

power players (barons), 157–158, 221–225
power sites (Foucault), 26, 35–36, 49
as processual, 3–10, 22, 23, 24, 25, 27, 28, 44, 52–53, 56n–57n, 67, 70, 72, 73, 75, 76, 78, 80, 81, 82, 86n, 94–96, 123–277
rational order structuralism, 20–29
research agenda for power as enacted, 3–13, 167–277
rhetoric (and the early Greeks), 89–105 (especially 89, 92, 99–104), 117n
stratificationists, 28, 83
structuralist approaches, 17–119
structuralist limitations, 52–53
structuration (Giddens), 25, 55n–56n
symbolic interactionism, 3–10, 123–277
synthetic order theorists, 25–28
tactician roles and practices, 101–110, 152–154, 167–249
target roles and practices, 109–110, 153, 251–270
totalizing associations, 225–227
unbounded, 157–158
unilateral, 155–157
and violence, 158–159
Pragmatic (pragmatism, pragmatists), xi, xiv, xvi, 7, 20, 77, 78, 87n, 93, 95, 97, 98, 111, 112n, 116n, 125, 140, 141, 160n. *See also* activity, intersubjectivity, knowledge, objects, reality, symbolic interaction
Primary tacticians. *See* theater of operations, positional control, tacticians
Process, 3–10, 22, 23, 24, 25, 27, 28, 44, 52–53, 56n–57n, 67, 70, 72, 73, 75, 76, 78, 80, 81, 82, 86n, 94–96, 100, 103, 109, 110, 123–277. *See also* activity, generic social processes, process, symbolic interaction
everything is in flux (Heraclitus, Protagoras), 94–96
as premise of symbolic interaction, 8, 126–127
Propaganda. *See* media
Psychology (psychological), 8, 19, 20, 28, 54n, 65–67, 84n, 103, 116n, 119, 133, 136, 166n, 270n, 274. *See also* factors, methods, structuralism, social science, theory
and Aristotle, 116n
approaches to power, 19
compliance (and influence) literature, 65–67
psychological manipulation, 19
and rhetoric, 103–104

Q

Quantitative analysis (research), 50–51. *See also* factors, methods, structuralism

R

Rational (rationalities, rationality), xv, 7, 13, 18, 20–29, 45, 55n, 68, 70, 75, 83, 87n, 88n, 97, 109, 112n, 113n, 116n, 117n, 127, 132, 133, 134–139, 148, 185, 273. *See also* intersubjectivity, reality, structuralism, theory
interactionist notions of, 3–10, 124–127, 134–139
rational-economic orientation, 18, 28, 56n, 73
rational order structuralism, 20–29, 107
subcultural mosaics and intersubjectivity, 134–139
Reality (real, realism, realities), xi, xvi, 10, 13n, 59n, 75, 80, 87n, 92, 94, 95, 97, 103, 112n, 116n, 126, 129, 149, 150, 167, 174–177, 192, 201, 274, 275. *See also* activity, constructionist, intersubjectivity, language, objects, objectification, subcultures, symbolic interaction
being tested, 129
empirical social world, xiv, 7–9, 128, 140
as intersubjectively constituted, enacted, 126, 134–139
paramount reality (and ethnographic inquiry), 137
and symbolic interactionism, 3–10, 123–166
Receptive self, 253–254. *See also* targets
Referrals (third-party), 212. *See also* tactics
Reflectivity (self), 8, 65, 76, 85n, 92, 107, 108, 110, 115, 129. *See also* activity, agency, deliberation, intersubjectivity, language, rationality, symbolic interaction, tacticians, tactics, targets
as enacted in the study of power, 123–277
as premise of symbolic interaction, 8, 126
Regulating deviance. *See* control agencies, policy, tactics, treatment
Relational. *See also* associations, intersubjectivity, tacticians, tactics, targets
as a premise of symbolic interaction, 8, 126

Relationships. *See* associations, collective events, cultivating relationships, generic social processes, power, tacticians, tactics, targets, theater of operations

Relativism (relative, relativistic). *See also* objectification, pragmatism, reality, symbolic interaction
and early Greeks, 89–105 (especially, 94–99), 110, 112n, 114n–116n
and postmodernism, 33–37, 41
and symbolic interactionism, 3–10, 123–127, 134–139
and Weber, Merton, 24

Religion (religions, religious), 18, 57n, 58n, 79, 83, 91, 95, 97, 105, 106, 113n, 151, 152, 226, 228, 229, 234, 241. *See also* associations, morality, objects, collective events, subcultures, totalizing associations
and early Greeks, 89–105 (especially, 91, 95, 96, 97, 105), 113n

Representatives (third-party). *See* third party agents

Reputations. *See* identity, impression management, labeling, rhetoric

Research. *See* ethnography, factors, methods, structuralism, symbolic interaction, theory

Resistance (and influence). *See also* collective events, collectivist approaches, military, negotiation, political forums, tactics, targets
targets as tacticians, 256–259 (and 167–249)

Resources (and power), 20, 24, 26, 29, 55n, 56n, 65, 69, 73–75, 79, 81, 85n, 86n, 89, 101, 185, 198, 223, 237
resource mobilization theory, 69, 73–75, 85n, 86n

Restrained self (as target), 253. *See also* targets

Revolution. *See also* government, power, tacticians, tactics, targets
and Aristotle, 101–102, 209
and marxists, 30, 32

Rhetoric, 67, 87n, 89, 90, 92, 97, 98, 99–104, 110, 112n, 113n, 114n, 116n, 117n, 187, 204n, 243n, 246n. *See also* (early) Greeks, language, symbolic interaction, tactics
and Aristotle, 67, 89, 90, 100–101
and peace and war, 89
and psychology, 104

S

Sanctions. *See* activity, agency, bargaining, objects, tactics, treatments

Science (scientific inquiry), 57n, 59n, 60n, 91, 112n, 133–134, 141, 161n, 274. *See also* knowledge, language, methodology, reality, social science, structuralism
antiscience myth (and symbolic interaction), 133–134
and early Greeks, 91, 112
and human subject matter, 3–10, 123–166

Self. *See* activity, agency, deliberation, identity, intersubjectivity, language, reflectivity, subculture, symbolic interaction, tacticians, tactics, targets

Selling (and buying). *See* bargaining

Skepticism. *See* knowing, reality

Social construction of reality, xvi, 13–14. *See also* constructionism, intersubjectivity, language, objectification, reality, symbolic interaction
and early Greeks, 89–105 (especially 92–96)

Social movements, 57n, 67, 72–75, 76, 86n, 147, 149–150, 165n. *See also* associations, collective behavior, collective events, theater of operations
social movement spillover (Meyer and Whittier), 85n–86n

Social problems. *See also* control agencies, morality, policy
as collective behavior (Herbert Blumer), 70–71, 162n–163n

Social process. *See* action, generic social processes, intersubjectivity, process, symbolic interaction

Social science (scientists), xiii, xiv, xvi, 6, 7, 8, 11, 17, 20, 29, 41, 46, 47, 76, 81, 82, 83, 84, 89, 90, 91, 92, 94, 98, 104, 107, 108, 110, 111, 112n, 123, 127, 130, 132, 133, 134, 135, 138, 148, 159n, 162n, 172, 177, 190, 191, 195, 240, 272, 274, 275, 276, 277. *See also* intersubjectivity, methodology, social theory, symbolic interaction
and early Greeks, 89–105

Social theory (theorists). *See* theory

Sociology of knowledge, xvi. *See also* constructionism, knowing, reality, symbolic interaction and early Greeks, 89–105 (especially 92–96)

Sophists, 67, 94, 99, 100, 103, 113n–114n, 117n. *See also* (early) Greeks, rhetoric

protection from (Plato, Aristotle)

Speech (spoken word), 3, 94, 98, 99, 100, 101, 104, 113n, 115. *See also* intersubjectivity, language, rhetoric, symbolic interaction

Spending time with others (cultivating relationships), 180. *See also* tactics

Stigma (Erving Goffman), 147, 203n. *See also* impression management

Strategies. *See* tactics

Strategic assignments (pursuing positional control), 223. *See also* tactics

Stratification (stratificationists), 28, 83

Structuration theory (Anthony Giddens), 25, 55n–56n

Structure (structuralism, structuralists), xv, 4, 6 17–119, 130, 131, 132, 150, 160n, 185, 261, 273, 274. *See also* factors, methodology, theory

astructural myth (and symbolic interaction), 130–132

insider (disciplinary) critiques of, 84

and limitations for study of power, 52–53, 62n, 130–132

and marxist nexus, 29–52

and postmodernists, 33–37

rational order structuralism, 20–29

structural conduciveness and collective behavior (Neil Smelser), 71–72

synthetic order theorists, 25–29

Subculture (subcultures). *See also* associations, generic social processes, intersubjectivity, subcultural mosaics, symbolic interaction

generic dimensions of, 141–145

interactionist research on, 150–152

subcultural mosaics and intersubjective realities, 134–139

Subcultural mosaics, 7, 45, 53, 62n, 134–139. *See also* activity, intersubjectivity, subculture, symbolic interaction

Subjective myth (and symbolic interactionism), 128–129

Symbolic interaction (interactionism, interactionist), xiii, xiv, 3–14, 123–277. *See also* activity, ethnography, generic social processes, intersubjectivity, language, subculture, tacticians, tactics, targets

assumptions (premises), 6–10, 124–127

and cultural studies, 41–42

and early Greek concepts, 92–105, 110

and ethnographic research, 7–9, 139–141, 275–277

and feminism, 45–47

and full range of association, 9, 36, 111, 123–124, 130

generic social processes, 141–145

interactionist literature on power, 145–152

misconceptions of, 127–134

more extended statements on, 125

neglecting power, xiv, 6, 123

and sexuality, 60n

and study of power (as enacted), 3–12, 123–277

and subcultural mosaics, 134–139

Symbolic interchange. *See* activity, intersubjectivity, language, symbolic interaction,

Symbolic leaders (Orrin Klapp), 147, 203n

Symbolic reality. *See* reality

Sympathetic introspection (Charles Horton Cooley), 134. *See also* ethnography

Synthetic order theorists, 25–28. *See also* power, structuralism, theory

T

Tactical advice (see political advice, tacticians, tactics), xiii, 11, 68, 86n, 89, 100, 102, 105–111, 117n–118n. *See also* tacticians, tactics, targets

Tacticians. *See also* deception, power, rhetoric, tactics, targets

absorbed in power motifs, 225

agent intentions vs. typology of tactics, 167–171

competitors as tacticians, 223, 259–261

control agents as tacticians, 238–241

diplomats as tacticians, 107–110, 118n, 207n

engaging in tactical enterprise, 163n–164n, 167–249, 256–265

ethnographers as tacticians, 139–141, 275–277

extending the theater of operations, 209–249

involving third parties, 210–214

magicians as tacticians, 167, 174–177

media users as tacticians, 228–231

marxists as tacticians, 29–52

Tacticians (*continued*)
  military personnel as tacticians, 236–238
  mystique (attributed to tacticians), 179–
    180
  politicians (and princes) as tacticians,
    165n, 101–108, 231–241
  positional control (pursuing), 221–225
  religious leaders as tacticians, 183, 204n
  salespeople as tacticians, 182, 183, 202n,
    203n, 204n, 268n
  as targets, 153, 251–270
  targets as tacticians, 109–110, 152–154,
    256–265 (also 167–249)
  unbounded power, 157–158, 166n
  unilateral endeavors, 155–157
  union organizers as tacticians, 165n, 202n,
    204n, 268n
  usurping agency, 188–192
Tactics (and means of invoking tactician
    roles). *See also* collective events, collecti-
    vist approaches, government, power,
    rhetoric, tacticians, targets
  acknowledging tactician mystique, 179–
    180
  assuming competitive stances, 223, 259–
    261
  assuming privileged relationships, 196–
    197
  assuming tactical orientations, 162n–
    163n, 167–249, 256–265
  attending to leadership images, 223
  attending to target circumstances, 173–
    174
  autonomizing tactics, 198–199
  bargaining, 193–196
  becoming entrenched in organizations,
    224–225
  coding tactics as problematic, 169–171
  complying with others' desires, 181–182
  consulting with third parties, 211
  cultivating relationships (and networks),
    177–184, 222–223
  developing collective ventures (associa-
    tions), 214–218
  developing political agendas, 231–242
  emphasizing community ties, 197–198
  encountering outsiders, 217–218, 235–238
  encountering practical limitations, 183–
    184
  encouraging trust, 182
  enhancing practices, 172–184
  establishing associations, 215–216

establishing consensus, 188
establishing control agencies, 238–241
exercising persistence, 199–201
expressing empathy, 180
extending nodes of influence, 223
extending the theater of operations, 209–
  249
focusing practices, 184–186
fostering loyalty, 182–183
generating and enforcing policy, 218–221
getting noticed, 178–179
helping others, 180–181
implementing governmental forums, 233–
  236
indicating lines of action, 184
ingratiation, 68
intentions vs. typology, 167–171
interchangeability of viewpoints, 12, 153,
  155, 164n, 252, 275
invoking deception, 174–177
invoking military operations, 236–
  238
last resorts, 154, 190
leveraging tactics, 188–198
making third-party referrals, 212
neutralizing and debasing strategies, 186–
  187
obtaining representatives, 211–212
objectifying associations, 216–217
promoting target interests, 184–186
promoting totalizing associations, 225–227
psychological literature on, 65–67
pursuing adjudication, 213–214
pursuing cooperation in ethnographic research, 139–141, 275–277
pursuing positional control, 221–225
pursuing strategic assignments, 223
rhetoric as tactical endeavor, 3, 62n, 89,
  99–104, 204n
shaping images of reality, 174–177
secrecy (and undercover), 202n, 210
spending time with others, 180
tactical advisors, 86n, 89, 105–111, 118n–
  119
tactical openness, 201
targets as tacticians, 109–110, 153, 256–
  265
totalizing associations, 225–227
unevenness of applications, 167–172, 199
using inducements and other treatments,
  192–193, 205n
using the media, 78–82, 228–231

usurping agency, 188–192, 204n–205n, 267n

working with third-party agents, 210–214

and violence, 158–159

Target(s). *See also* associations, government, media, military, tacticians, tactics

agency usurped by tacticians, 188–192, 204n–205n

assuming target roles, 153, 163n, 251–270

claiming target status, 258–259

collective involvements, 261–265

competitive involvements, 223, 259–261

and control agencies, 240–241

elusive self, 256, 267n–268n

enduring cautions, 178

ethnographers as targets, 275–277

experiencing treatments (and inducements), 192–193

interchangeability of viewpoints, 12, 153, 155, 164n, 252, 275

and media, 82, 228–231

neglect of target activities, 251

perceptions of (French and Raven), 25

receptive self, 253–254

retailers as targets, 266n–267n

restrained self, 253

as self-defined, 152–154, 156, 163n, 164n

subject to influence, 253–256

as tacticians, 109–110, 256–259 (also 167–249)

volunteers, 243n–244n

vulnerable self, 79, 204n–205n, 254–255

Technology, 17, 30, 58n, 79, 80, 82, 90, 91, 134, 162n, 202n, 230, 237, 271. *See also* activity, knowledge, language, science

Theater of operations (extending the), 12, 170, 209–249, 258, 271

assuming competitive stances, 223

cultivating relationships (and networks), 177–184, 222–223

developing collective ventures, 214–218

developing political agendas, 231–241

establishing control agencies, 238–241

generating and enforcing policy, 218–221

implementing governmental forums, 233–236

invoking military operations, 236–238

promoting totalizing associations, 225–227

pursuing positional control, 221–225

targets as tacticians, 256–265

using the media, 228–231

working with third-party agents, 212–214

Theory (theorists, social theory, social theorists), xi, xv, xvi, 5, 6, 11, 12, 13, 17, 18, 19, 24, 27, 52–54, 56, 65, 67, 68, 73, 74, 85n, 88n, 90, 91, 97, 98, 104, 105, 106, 107, 108, 110, 127–134, 162n, 201, 274. *See also* (early) Greeks, intersubjectivity, literature on power, power, social science, structuralism, symbolic interaction

atheoretical myth (and symbolic interaction), 132–133

collectivist approaches to power, 17, 23, 26, 30, 68–76, 89, 123, 162n–163n, 209–249, 261–265

and community studies, 82–84

compliance and influence literature, 65–67

of deception, 174–177

disassociated from action, 52–54, 84, 104, 110, 273

interest group dynamics, 47–49, 68, 71, 77–78, 86n, 146, 214–218, 231–242

marxist nexus, 29–52

mass media, 78–82, 229–231

misconceptions of symbolic interaction, 127–134

paratheory, 161n

rational order structuralism, 20–29

symbolic interaction, 3–13, 123–277

Things. *See* intersubjectivity, objects, objectification, reality, symbolic interaction

Third-party agents, 194, 195, 199, 209–214, 242n, 243n, 254, 259–261. *See also* diplomats, tacticians, tactics, targets, theater of operations

analysts as third parties, 153, 156

multiple roles (Georg Simmel), 209

Total institutions (Erving Goffman), 147, 245n–246n. *See also* control agencies

Totalizing associations (TAs), 225–227, 245n. *See also* associations, control agencies, subcultures, total institutions

Tradition. *See also* intersubjectivity, objectification, rational order structuralism,

Treatment(s) and inducements, 165n, 192–193, 205n, 219, 241, 249n. *See also* bargaining, control agencies, leveraging tactics, tacticians, tactics, targets

Typologies, 24, 25, 26, 46, 69, 70, 71, 84n, 85n, 150

and collective behavior, 69, 70, 71, 72, 74, 84

Typologies (*continued*)
  ideal types (Max Weber), 21–23, 85n
  of tactics vs. agent intentions, 167–171
Trust, 182. *See also* deception, impression
  management, loyalty, tactics

U

Unbounded power, 157–158, 166n
Undercover work, 202n. *See also* deception,
  diplomacy
Unilateral dimensions of power (tacticians,
  targets, third parties), 155–157
  secretive endeavors, 210
Unions, 165n, 202n, 204n, 229. *See also* associations, collective events, power, tacticians, tactics
Usurping agency, 188–192, 204n–205n, 267n

V

Value-added approach (to collective
  behavior-Neil Smelser), 69, 71–72

Variables. *See* factors, methodology,
  structuralism
Verstehen, 27, 55n, 125. *See also* intersubjectivity, symbolic interaction
Victims (victim-status), 29, 89, 251, 258–
  259, 266n. *See also* tacticians, tactics,
  targets
Violence (and human relations), 30, 31, 32,
  48, 109, 158–159, 165n–166n. *See also*
  control agencies, military, tacticians, tactics, treatments
  as definitional essences, 158–159
Volunteer (volunteering), 243n–244n. *See
  also* assistance
Vulnerable self (as target), 204n–205n,
  254–255, 260. *See also* tactics, targets

W

Western civilization (western thought), 90–
  92, 111
Writing (written language), 18, 91, 99, 104–
  105, 108, 112. *See also* intersubjectivity,
  language, media, symbolic interaction